Knowledge Management

Knowledge Management
Classic and Contemporary Works

Edited by
Daryl Morey
Mark Maybury
Bhavani Thuraisingham

The MIT Press
Cambridge, Massachusetts
London, England

First MIT Press paperback edition, 2002

This book was set in Sabon by Mary Reilly Graphics.

Printed and bound in the United States of America.

Library of Congress Cataloging-in-Publication Data

Knowledge management : classic and contemporary works / edited by Daryl Morey, Mark Maybury, Bhavani Thuraisingham.
    p. cm.
  Includes bibliographical references and index.
  ISBN 0-262-13384-9 (hc : alk. paper), 0-262-63261-6 (pb)
   1. Knowledge management. I. Morey, Daryl. II. Maybury, Mark T. III. Thuraisingham, Bhavani M.

  HD30.2 .K63686 2001
  658.4'038—dc21   00-046042

10 9 8 7 6 5 4 3

For their generous support, this collection
is dedicated to our spouses
Ellen, Michelle, and Thevendra

Contents

Preface

This collection is a valuable resource for leaders in government, industry, or academia who are interested in starting or evaluating a knowledge management program, are currently implementing a knowledge management program, or are simply interested in expanding their knowledge.

The discipline of knowledge management has become a hot topic in business because of its prospects for dramatic improvement in organizational effectiveness. This book is intended to serve as a logical entry point for leaders who are interested in knowledge management and want to become grounded in the seminal concepts and contemporary thinking from multiple perspectives. Readers in government, industry, or academia who are interested in starting a knowledge management program, are currently implementing a knowledge management program, or are simply interested in expanding their knowledge, will find this book useful. The chapters can be read sequentially, or they can be read individually when the reader is faced with an issue that a chapter addresses.

The book is organized by three topics critical to the success and understanding of knowledge management: strategy, process, and metrics. Each section begins with a seminal work from a leader in the field. The Strategy section is concerned with the motivation and vision for knowledge management, along with how to structure a knowledge management program to achieve desired outcomes. Peter Senge's "A Leader's New Work: Building Learning Organizations" underlines the importance of increasing growing the knowledge in your organization through organizational learning. The Process section is concerned using knowledge management to make existing practices more effective, speeding up organizational learning, and implementing knowledge management. The excerpt from Hirotaka Takeuchi and Ikujiro Nonaka's *The Knowledge*

Creating Company, provides a foundational theory on how the knowledge creating process works. Finally, the Metrics section focuses on measurements for improving the understanding of what impact knowledge management is having on an organization and how to measure the effectiveness of a knowledge management program. The excerpt from Robert Kaplan and David Norton's *The Balanced Scorecard* provides an outline and example metrics on how to measure the growth of knowledge through learning in an organization.

Within each section, previously unpublished chapters of contemporary efforts elucidate and further develop some of the foundational concepts and ideas on strategy, process, and metrics. Each chapter has gone through a peer review and selection process focusing on originality, significance, and correctness. The seminal works were chosen from a list of highly referenced pieces by an editorial review board of experts. These classic works are followed by a reflection by the original authors, providing their contemporary perspective on their landmark contribution.

All books, even collected works, are influenced by the bias of the editors. In particular, there is a strong bias toward a learning centric view of knowledge management in this collection as opposed to an information centric view. The learning centric view emphasizes that knowledge is the "capability to act effectively" and is derived from learning. Knowledge management in this view is a management function that accelerates learning. The information centric approach is best understood by looking at the definition of knowledge management from the Gartner Group:

Knowledge Management is a discipline that promotes an integrated approach to identifying, managing and sharing all of an enterprise's information assets, including database, documents, policies and procedures as well as unarticulated expertise and experience resident in individual workers.

The editors' bias toward the learning-centric view stems from the observation that it does not matter how well you manage your information if it cannot be understood and turned into actionable knowledge—the ability to do. In many cases, the differences between the two views are subtle because managing your information flows is often the most effective way to accelerate learning. However, the learning centric view opens up the possibility of exploring different avenues to accelerating learning.

The following steps outline how this collection could be used to help start a knowledge management program in your organization.

1. Read Peter Senge's "A Leader's New Work" and his reflection on that original work to understand why your organization's long-term competitive advantage depends on your ability to learn faster than your competition.

2. In the strategy section, several frameworks for creating a knowledge management program are proposed by Skyrme; Seemann, De Long, Stucky, and Guthrie; and Ives, Torrey, and Gordon. The editors suggest that you use your understanding of your business and these frameworks to develop a program tailored to your organization and business environment. A knowledge-management framework is vital for a successful program as it guides decision making throughout the implementation.

3. Read the excerpt from Nonaka and Takeuchi's *The Knowledge Creating Company* and their reflection on that original work. This will give you a theoretical underpinning of one view of how knowledge is transferred and what processes will most likely benefit from a formal knowledge management program.

4. Reinhardt gives an overview of the organizational learning process. Integrate the processes in your organization with the organizational learning process to get an understanding of the strongest lever points to achieve improvement.

5. If targeting your knowledge management process to specific elements within your organization is crucial, Ruggles and Little provide a different lens on what processes to select for improvement from the new field of Complex Adaptive Systems. Grundstein provides an approach, called GAMETH, that will help you locate crucial knowledge in your company and the critical process that should be improved to positively affect the bottom line.

6. If your organization has a new product development process that is central to its competitiveness, Dorothy Leonard's overview shows how knowledge management and an understanding of tacit knowledge can improve that process.

7. Knowledge sharing improvement is central to almost any knowledge management program. Lawton provides lessons learned from her experience in implementing a knowledge-sharing improvement program at Buckman Labs.

8. Finally, Carol Willett provides a case study of the implementation of a knowledge management program at StorageTek.

9. The last step of any improvement program is to determine how you will measure its success. Read the excerpt from Kaplan and Norton's *The*

Balanced ScoreCard. Use this important tool, or the complimentary framework proposed by Sveiby, as the foundation for creating metrics for your knowledge management program.

10. Use the contribution by Bassi and Van Buren to provide metrics ideas and to determine what metrics will help you effectively evaluate your knowledge management program. Use Bontis's overview of the intellectual capital metrics literature to provide further guidance on what metrics will work in your organization.

11. Finally, Lock Lee provides an innovative approach to determining knowledge sharing performance, which is an area of particular importance to most knowledge management programs.

Our experience designing and employing knowledge management strategies and processes within a corporate setting as well as learning through others has yielded the beginning of some principles to remember and an associated set of (*italicized*) actions to take when implementing knowledge management:

• People, and the cultures that influence their behaviors, are the most critical resources for successful knowledge creation, dissemination, and application. *Understand and influence them.*

• Cognitive, social, and organizational learning processes are essential to the success of a knowledge management strategy. *Focus your strategy on enhancing these processes.*

• Measurement, benchmarking, and incentives are essential to accelerate the learning process and to drive cultural change. *Create a tailored balanced scorecard to target what you want to improve.*

• Knowledge management programs can yield impressive benefits to individuals and organizations if they are purposeful, concrete, and action oriented. *Make yours so.*

We encourage you to find your own truth in these pages and share your experiences. As you read the collection, you are encouraged to contact the authors and editors with your thoughts. To facilitate this, we have put together a Contact the Authors section at the back of the book. Create your own network of learning partners.

Acknowledgments

This collection was necessarily a collaborative venture and we are indebted to the many people who helped make it a reality. We express particular gratitude to the following individuals for their unique contributions:

• The Knowledge Management Consortium <http://www.km.org> and BRINT <http://www.brint.com>, for use of their mailing list to announce the book's call for papers.

• Knowledge Inc. <http://www.knowledgeinc.com/> and Leverage <http://www.pegasuscom.com/leverage.html> for announcing the call for papers in their newsletter.

• Marie Spadano, for her administrative support throughout the process.

• The many contributors, for their reviews of the chapters in the book.

• The Editorial Review board—Bipin Junnarkar <BipinJ@aol.com>, Gordon Petrash <gordon.petrash@us.pwcglobal.com>, Michael Kran <michael.kran@kran.com>, and Stephen Buckley <sbuckley@sol-ne.org>

Introduction

Can Knowledge Management Succeed Where Other Efforts Have Failed?

Margaret Wheatley

We all know we need to be much more skilled at the organizational survival skills that parade under the banner of Knowledge Management. Organizations need to be smarter, faster, more innovative, and more agile. The complexity of the twenty-first century world has speeded up the pace of evolution, and those who cannot learn, adapt, and change simply will not survive.

We all know this. Learning is what saves us. Knowledge Management should be something eagerly accepted by leaders, it should be an incredibly easy sell. Yet KM appears at a time when most organizations are battered and bruised by decades of fads, by investments in too many organizational change efforts that have not delivered what they promised. These experiences have exhausted us, made many cynical, and left at least some of us worried that we'll never learn how to create organizations that can thrive in the 21st century.

We need KM to succeed. But to achieve success when so much else has failed, we need to understand organizations differently. We need to notice what we have learned from all those failures. I am suggesting that we take the time to reflect on those experiences and harvest our own knowledge lest we proceed blindly down the same familiar path that leads to disappointment. As we walk into the future, beckoned by this emerging field of Knowledge Management, we need time to reflect on and share what we have learned. Fortunately, this book helps us do just that.

Plato defined knowledge as "justified, true belief." In Western management, we have a set of beliefs that are particular to our culture. Most often, we cannot see these beliefs, even though they become visible in behavior and the choices we make. For several years now I have been trying to bring these beliefs into focus, in order to understand why change efforts succeed or fail. Here are several of our "justified" beliefs that I think seriously impede us from creating the organizations we need:

• Organizations are machines. We create separate parts—tasks, roles, functions—and engineer (and reengineer) them to achieve predetermined performance levels. It is the role of managers to recombine the parts to achieve those outcomes. Strangely, we also seem to believe that people can be treated as machines.
• Only material things are real. We work hard to try and make invisible "things" (like knowledge) assume material form. We accomplish this by assigning numbers to them. This practice combines with the next belief;
• Only numbers are real. (This belief is ancient, dating back to the sixth century BC.) These two beliefs lead to;
• You can only manage what you can measure. And this need for measurement has created a new deity to worship, which is;
• Technology saves.

These beliefs are clearly evident in how many organizations have approached Knowledge Management. I think they explain why we are having problems. In Takeuchi and Nonaka's article, they contrast Western and Japanese approaches to KM. Their critique of our practice in the West exposes these underlying beliefs with great clarity. They comment that we have focused on explicit knowledge—knowledge one can see and document—instead of dealing with the rich but intangible realm of "tacit" knowledge. They also say that we have focused our efforts on developing measures for and assigning values to knowledge. And continuing with a tradition that began with Frederick Taylor, we have called it "Knowledge Management," and treated it as a responsibility that can be assigned to a few of the elite.

Their assessment of Western approaches to KM makes our beliefs visible. As long as we think of knowledge as a substance to be engineered, as a material "thing" to be produced, measured, catalogued, warehoused, traded, and shipped, we will not succeed. The language of KM is littered with this "thing" thinking. We want to "capture" knowledge; to inventory it; to push it into or pull it out from people. David Skyrme, from the UK, writes that in both Britain and the U.S., a common image of KM is of "decanting the human capital into the structural capital of an organization." I do not know how this imagery affects you, but I personally do not want to have my head opened, my cork popped, to be emptied of what I know by having it poured into an organizational vat.

This prospect is not what motivates me to notice what I know, or to share it.

These language choices have serious implications. They reveal that we think knowledge is an entity, something that exists independent of person or context, capable of being moved about and manipulated for organizational advantage. We need to step away from this language and, more importantly, the beliefs that engendered it. We need to think of knowledge differently so we can step off our well-trodden road to implementation failure.

Many authors in this volume challenge us with different beliefs and experiences. They have gone into these bold experiments ahead of us and returned with reports of the thickets and snares that prevent successful KM implementation, and provide clear insights about the processes and attitudes that make it work. As you read their different models, techniques, and technologies, I urge you to listen for a unified voice that resounds in their chronicles. As a chorus, they warn that we will seriously stumble if we do not attend in profound new ways to what we always want to ignore: the human dimension.

Think, for a moment, about what you know about knowledge, not from an organizational perspective, but from your life experience. In myself, I notice that knowledge is something I create because I am in relationship to another person, event, or idea. I engage with something outside myself, think about what it might mean, and develop interpretations that make sense to me. Knowledge is something I create through my engagement with the world. This may be why Plato called it "justified, true belief." It feels true for me, justified, because it works in my life.

From Biology, it is evident that all life engages in knowledge creation. We humans are no different. When asked to do a task, most of us feel the need to change it in some way. We fine-tune it, we adapt it to our unique context, and we add our own improvements to how the task is done. We are developing new knowledge all the time. A few months ago, I sat on an airport commuter bus and listened in amazement as the driver trained a newly hired employee. For thirty minutes I eavesdropped as she energetically revealed the secrets and efficiencies she had discovered for how to get to the airport in spite of severe traffic or bad weather. It was a nonstop, virtuoso performance of knowledge sharing, and I am sure her supervisor had no idea that this was going on. People develop better ways of doing their work all the time, and we like to brag about it. In many surveys (a 1998 U.S. one is quoted in an article here), workers report that most of what they learn about their job, they learn from informal conversations. They also report that they frequently have ideas for improving work but do not tell their bosses.

If knowledge creation is natural, and if wanting to share what you know is so humanly satisfying, then what is the problem? In organizations, what sends these behaviors underground? Why do workers go dumb? Fortunately, the answers to these questions are found in many of the experiences relayed in this book. Here are a few lessons I have gleaned.

1   Knowledge is created by human beings   (One article title says this better, "Knowledge Sharing Is a Human Behavior.") If we want to work with knowledge, we must attend to human needs and dynamics. (Perhaps we should rename it "Human Knowledge" to remind ourselves of what it is.) This learning is filled with implications for our practice. It refocuses our attention on each other and what we need, rather than trying to "decant" us. It can help us notice that when we focus on such things as "assets," that it is not knowledge that is the asset. People are.

2   Human needs and motivation lead us naturally to create knowledge. Study after study confirms that people want their work to provide growth, recognition, meaning, and good relationships. We want our lives to mean something, we want to contribute to others, we want to learn, we want to be together. And we must be involved in decisions that affect us. If we believed these studies, it would make working together far more productive and enjoyable. We would recognize that there are many positive energies available. We could trust and respect one another; we could rely on one another. As a species, we are actually very good to work with.

3   Everybody is a knowledge worker   This truth was stated by one of my clients as an operating principle. If everybody is assumed to be creating knowledge, then the organization has a responsibility to provide open access to information to everyone. And we could assume that knowledge will be found everywhere in the organization, not just in a few functions or some special people. This is a clear learning from the Japanese experience with KM, and also from my bus ride.

4 People choose to share their knowledge This learning reverberates in several articles. "A common problem in most KM programs," writes David Skyrme, "is that individuals do not share their knowledge." But we willingly share what we know if we think it is important to the work, if we feel encouraged to learn, if we want to support a colleague. The discovery in every organization of self-organized Communities of Practice is evidence of this willingness. Some of the conditions that make people willing to learn and share their learnings are: people understand and support the work objective or strategy; people understand how their work adds value to the common objective; people know and care about each other; people feel personally connected to their leaders; people feel respected and trusted.

5 Knowledge management is not about technology This would seem obvious from the preceding learnings, but it feels important to stress because, in the West, we are dazzled by technical solutions. If people are not communicating, we just create an intranet; if we don't know what we know, we just create an inventory data base; if we are geographically dispersed, we just put videocams on people's desks. But these technical solutions do not solve a thing if other aspects of the culture—the human dimension—are ignored. BP did succeed in connecting their offshore rigs using desktop videocams. But they were also working simultaneously to create a culture that recognized individual contribution, and to rally employees behind a bold new vision. And other organizations provide evidence that in the absence of face-to-face meetings, people have a hard time sharing knowledge. I think it is important to remember that technology does not connect us. Our relationships connect us, and then we eagerly use the technology. We share knowledge because we are in relationship, not because we have broader bandwidth.

6 Knowledge is born in chaotic processes that take time The irony of this learning is that it demands from us two things we do not have: a tolerance for messy, nonlinear processes, and time. But creativity is only available when we relax into confusion, open our minds to not knowing, and wait for insight to surprise us. New knowledge is born in messy processes that take time. Insights and innovations are the result of nurturing; they cannot be commanded to appear instantly, no matter how desperately we need them. In the UK, Arthur Andersen now lists self-awareness and reflection as critical leadership skills. Many authors here refer to companies that have created architectural spaces to encourage informal conversations, mental spaces to encourage reflection, and learning spaces to encourage journal writing and other reflective thought processes. These many examples are quite provocative because they run counter to prevailing tendencies for instant answers and breathless decision-making. They also illuminate the fact that until we attend to reflection, until we make space for thinking, we will not be able to generate knowledge, or to know what knowledge we already possess. We cannot argue with the clear demands of knowledge—it requires time to grow. It grows inside human relationships. Relationships and creativity are always messy.

One last reflection. Takeuchi and Nonaka remind us that knowledge, unlike information, is about, "commitment and beliefs; it is a function of a particular stance, perspective or intention. In this respect, the creation of new knowledge is as much about ideals as it is about ideas." We really need to contemplate this wisdom. It can help us see more clearly the work that we name as Knowledge Management. We need to understand that we are working with "ideals," the strong energies that power human work. People want to learn and grow. We want to work for purposes we believe in. Working for an organization that is intent on creating knowledge is a wonderful motivator, not because the organization will be more profitable, but because our lives will feel more worthwhile. Of the many learnings available from our colleagues, I find this the most promising.

SECTION I

Introduction: Strategy

Strategy: Compelling Word, Complex Concept

Gordon Petrash

Strategy—Webster's definition

A: a careful plan or method: a clever stratagem. B: the art of devising or employing plans or stratagems toward a goal.

The way the word "strategy" is defined and understood within an organization is critical before any meaningful discussion about "Strategy" (with a capital S) can take place. This is somewhat evident in the chapters that make up the knowledge management strategy section. Each of the authors advances the notion of strategy with a slightly different definition and in varying contexts. All of their uses of the word and concept are valid. The imperative is that the author defines the term and that the reader understands the context.

I am continually perplexed with discussions regarding mega-terms and concepts like Strategy, Learning Organization, Leadership, Intellectual Capital, and Knowledge Management because of the shear challenge of bringing the participants to a common understanding of the definition of terms being referenced. It doesn't matter that there may not be a common agreement on these terms as long as I understand your meaning and you mine.

Therefore, for the sake of this discussion, my use of the word *Strategy* is defined and elaborated as follows—a plan and a process that accomplishes the enterprise's desired outcome. It is a plan for action with clear and measurable goals linked to these outcomes. It is many times dynamic, having the ability to adapt to new information or situations. In the end it is the enterprise's best knowledge and collective experience focused on the accomplishment of its goals.

The Enterprise Strategy is the road map of how to get to the desired destination. It is not the primary purpose of the strategy to determine whether the destination is correct. That is left to the "vision and purpose" of the enterprise. The strategy may reveal things about the vision and purpose and certainly can impact them. But all too often within organizations, the strategy and the vision get intertwined and begin to cause each to lose focus and discipline.

Peter Senge addresses the importance of the definition of terms in context. His paper "Reflection on 'A Leader's New Work: Building Learning Organizations,'" characterizes part of the problem with the advancement of the concept with the "sloppy use of the word leader." How the word is used in organizations is different from how it is used within the literature. He points out that leader is often meant to mean executive, which in many cases preempts leadership from occurring elsewhere in the organization.

Peter has adopted the definition for leadership by organizations as the following: In the abstract—"leadership is the capacity of a human community to create its future." In operation—"leadership is the ability in an organization to initiate and to sustain significant change, to work effectively with the forces that shape change." I find these definitions of leadership very palatable.

Peter also defines "knowledge" "as the capacity for effective action, clearly distinguishing it from data and information." Knowledge and Knowledge Management are words and terms that are being bantered around quite a bit today. Peter makes an observation that these are terms that have become fads. He makes the point that Knowledge Management is just another term in the ongoing continuum of business management evolution.

Leaders enable transformation. Creating a learning organization is one of the vehicles for accomplishing this. Peter's paper is thought provoking and challenging regarding these often used terms and concepts.

David Skyrme's paper, "Developing a Knowledge Strategy: From Management to Leadership," supports the premise that knowledge management has flirted with becoming a fad but in fact, has move beyond fad to take its place as part of the ongoing business management improvement evolution. The management of knowledge has firmly taken its place as one of the fundamental elements required for developing strategy. David attributes knowledge management's attainment of this stature in the past few years through the following sequence of events.

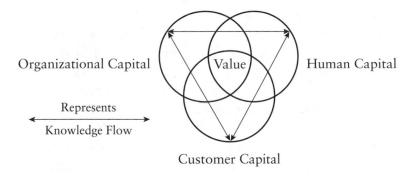

Organizational Capital

Human Capital

Represents

Knowledge Flow

Customer Capital

Figure I.1
Intellectual capital growth from knowledge flows

1. Recognition that knowledge and other Intellectual Capital have value by underpinning value creation and future value, both of which impact share price
2. Demonstration of clear business examples where management of knowledge has given companies competitive advantage
3. Availability of improved collaboration technology
4. The realization that business processes are a continuous evolution and knowledge management was the logical next step

The integration of knowledge management processes and principals into business strategy has significant measurable benefits that are outlined in his paper "The Knowledge Advantage." David certainly helps to make the case for knowledge management as a real part of the business management process and strategic thinking. He breaks the knowledge contribution to strategy into two "Thrusts."

1. Making knowledge that is already known easily accessible.
2. Innovation, the creation of new knowledge that has value.

David advances the value of knowledge management by referencing very clear and measurable "Levers." Knowledge management in practice is not linear; it laces the management of explicit knowledge and tacit knowledge together with the value proposition cited in the strategy. Managing knowledge is not an easy task. He describes the management of tacit knowledge as an "oxymoron."

Because it is difficult and messy doesn't mean it cannot be done. David presents very real approaches to managing knowledge more effectively and as an element of the business strategy. I particularly subscribe to his prediction that future business success will be determined through "Knowledge Leadership" rather than "Knowledge Management." The enabling of the knowledge movement and innovation rather than the hard processes of disciplined management would seem to be more palatable to creative people, thus encouraging better performance and more successes.

"Knowledge Sharing Is a Human Behavior," by William Ives, Ben Torry, and Cindy Gordon, really focuses on people as the key element of successful knowledge management. "Sharing insights and best practices is a human behavior that is critical to the success of any knowledge management system yet it is counter to the culture found in most organizations." This is a fact that we all know and experience day in and day out in our work and personal lives. Andersen Consulting has developed a human performance model that specifies what a person needs to optimally perform any business task, as well as what leadership must be provided in order to align performance with business strategies.

They have identified the following principal factors:

• Understanding the business context.
• Organizational performance factors—structure and roles, processes, culture, and physical environment.
• Individual performance factors—direction, measurement, means, ability, motivation.

These factors must work in concert in order for human performance to be optimized. Each is necessary but by itself, not sufficient.

Knowledge management is personal. It is difficult and uncomfortable to put performance perimeters around humans. But it can be done and is being done every day in every organization. In many cases it is not formalized or explicit. The authors have put together a compelling argument that for organizations to be successful, they need to share knowledge. Their paper effectively shows the key factors that must be managed in order for this to effectively happen and ultimately impact organizational performance.

I think this chapter will stir some controversy among those that feel we are coming ever closer to managing and measuring people by some overriding business management process. And in doing so, we may start to lose the individual's face in the attempt to more effectively manage human capital to enhance organizational performance. I conceptually buy into the Andersen Consulting "Human Performance Model." How it is implemented and presented by leadership, as in so many cases of implementing business models, is critical to its success.

"Building Intangible Assets: A Strategic Framework for Investing in Intellectual Capital" by Patricia Seemann, David De Long, Susan Stuckey, and Edward Guthrie, addresses intellectual capital, its definition, and how better managing the raw material "knowledge," builds more of it.

The authors describe Intellectual Capital as being composed of Human, Social, and Structural Capital. All three are further defined in the paper. I particularly like their definition of knowledge management—"the deliberate design of processes, tools, structures, etc., with the intent to increase, renew, share, or improve the use of knowledge represented in any of the three elements of intellectual capital."

I have used Figure I.1 to define Intellectual Capital and show the impact the management of knowledge has on it. The knowledge flows grow each of the types of capital and at the same time, brings them into a more coincident position. In both dynamics, the area in the center, "Value," increases in size. This is the conceptual high ground, high value that is targeted by Intellectual Capital Management, Knowledge management, and Learning Organization concepts. This paper fits nicely into my own philosophy of Intellectual Capital.

Each of the papers has different definitions and approaches to key elements that are critical to strategy. These differences in no way should distract the reader from seeing the underlining similarities in the analysis and themes of all four of these papers. I have gleaned the following from them:

• The definition, and the context of the terms must be understood before dialogue and action take place
• Knowledge management is but another step in a continuum of the ever evolving business management process
• Intellectual Capital, Knowledge Management, and Learning Organization are terms rooted in action and the creation of value
• An integrated approach that blends into existing business practices is the most effect way to cause sustainable positive change
• Measures are critical for successful implementation
• An enabling leadership approach is the preferred approach

• Cultural change is needed for sustainable benefit

• It all starts with the individual and ends with the individual. Models and processes do not create new knowledge or value only people do

• A winning business strategy must have the management and leveraging of knowledge as one of its cornerstones

• Strategy is the implementation of knowledge toward measurable objectives that accomplish the enterprises vision and purpose

To quote Charles Savage, a leading thinker and mentor in the area of Strategy Development, Intellectual Capital Management, and Knowledge Management, "we are on a long journey and the trip has just begun." These papers will catalyze readers to focus their thinking on a critical aspect of business management and possibly advance their own and our journey toward an ever evolving business model that enables the creation of "value."

1

Classic Work: The Leader's New Work: Building Learning Organizations

Peter Senge

Over the past two years, business academics and senior managers have begun talking about the notion of the learning organization. Ray Stata of Analog Devices put the idea succinctly in these pages last spring: "The rate at which organizations learn may become the only sustainable source of competitive advantage." And in late May of this year, at an MIT-sponsored conference entitled "Transforming Organizations," two questions arose again and again: How can we build organizations in which continuous learning occurs? and, What kind of person can best lead the learning organization? This chapter, based on Senge's recently published book, *The Fifth Discipline: The Art and Practice of the Learning Organization*, begins to chart this new territory, describing new roles, skills, and tools for leaders who wish to develop learning organizations.

Building Learning Organizations

Human beings are designed for learning. No one has to teach an infant to work, or talk, or master the spatial relationships needed to stack eight building blocks that don't topple. Children come fully equipped with an insatiable drive to explore and experiment. Unfortunately, the primary institutions of our society are oriented predominantly toward controlling rather than learning, rewarding individuals for performing for others rather than for cultivating their natural curiosity and impulse to learn. The young child entering school discovers quickly that the name of the game is getting the right answer and avoiding mistakes—a mandate no less compelling to the aspiring manager.

Reprinted from *Sloan Management Review* 32, no.1 (Fall 1990) by permission of the publisher. © 1990 by Sloan Management Review Association. All rights reserved.

"Our prevailing system of management has destroyed our people," writes W. Edwards Deming, leader in the quality movement.[1] "People are born with intrinsic motivation, self-esteem, dignity, curiosity to learn, joy in learning. The forces of destruction begin with toddlers—a prize for the best Halloween costume, grades in school, gold stars, and on up through the university. On the job, people, teams, divisions are ranked—reward for the one at the top, punishment at the bottom. MBO, quotas, incentive pay, business plans, put together separately, division by division, cause further loss, unknown and unknowable."

Ironically, by focusing on performing for someone else's approval, corporations create the very conditions that predestine them to mediocre performance. Over the long run, superior performance depends on superior learning. A Shell study showed that, according to former planning director Arie de Geus, "a full one-third of the Fortune "500" industrials listed in 1970 had vanished by 1983.[2]" Today, the average lifetime of the largest industrial enterprises is probably less than half the average lifetime of a person in an industrial society. On the other hand, de Geus and his colleagues at Shell also found a small number of companies that survived for seventy-five years or longer. Interestingly, the key to their survival was the ability to run "experiments in the margin," to continually explore new businesses and organizational opportunities that create potential new sources of growth.

If anything, the need for understanding how organizations learn and accelerating that learning is greater today than ever before. The old days when a Henry Ford, Alfred Sloan, or Tom Watson learned for the organization are gone. In an increasingly dynamic, interdependent, and unpredictable world, it is simply no longer possible for anyone to "figure it all out at the top." The old model, "the top thinks and the local acts," must now give way to integrating thinking and acting at all levels. While the challenge is great, so is the potential payoff. "The person who figures out how to harness the collective genius of the people in his or her organization," according to former Citibank CEO Walter Wriston, "is going to blow the competition away."

Adaptive Learning and Generative Learning

The prevailing view of learning organizations emphasizes increased adaptability. Given the accelerating pace of change, or so the standard view goes, "the most successful corporation of the 1990s," according to *Fortune* magazine, "will be something called a learning organization, a consummately adaptive enterprise.[3]" As the Shell study shows, examples of traditional authoritarian bureaucracies that responded too slowly to survive in changing business environments are legion.

But increasing adaptiveness is only the first stage in moving toward learning organizations. The impulse to learn in children goes deeper than desires to respond and adapt more effectively to environmental change. The impulse to learn, at its heart, is an impulse to be generative, to expand our capability. This is why leading corporations are focusing on *generative* learning, which is about creating, as well as *adaptive* learning, which is about coping.[4]

The total quality movement in Japan illustrates the evolution from adaptive to generative learning. With its emphasis on continuous experimentation and feedback, the total quality movement has been the first wave in building learning organizations. But Japanese firms' view of serving the customer has evolved. In the early years of total quality, the focus was on "fitness to standard," making a product reliably so that it would do what its designers intended it to do and what the firm told its customers it would do. Then came a focus on "fitness to need," understanding better what the customer wanted and then providing products that reliably met those needs. Today, leading edge firms seek to understand and meet the "latent need" of the customer—what customers might truly value but have never experienced or would never think to ask for. As one Detroit executive commented recently, "You could never produce the Mazda Miata solely from market research. It required a leap of imagination to see what the customer *might* want.[5]"

Generative learning, unlike adaptive learning, requires new ways of looking at the world, whether in understanding customers or in understanding how to better manage a business. For years, U.S. manufacturers sought competitive advantage in aggressive controls on inventories, incentives against overproduction, and rigid adherence to production forecasts. Despite these incentives, their performance was eventually eclipsed by Japanese firms who saw the challenges of manufacturing differently. They realized that eliminating delays in the production process was the key to reducing instability and improving cost, productivity, and service. They worked to build networks of relationships with trusted suppliers and to redesign physical production processes so as to reduce delays in materials procurement, production set up, and in-process inventory—a much higher-leverage approach to improving both cost and customer loyalty.

As Boston Consulting Group's George Stalk has observed, the Japanese saw the significance of delays because they saw the process of order entry, production scheduling, materials procurement, production, and distribution *as an integrated system*. "What distorts the system so badly is time," observed Stalk—the multiple delays between events and responses. "These distortions reverberate throughout the system, producing disruptions, waste, and inefficiency".[6] Generative learning requires seeing the systems that control events. When we fail to grasp the systemic source of problems, we are left to "push on" symptom rather than eliminate underlying causes. The best we can ever do is adaptive learning.

The Leader's New Work

"I talk with people all over the country about learning organizations, and the response is always very positive," says William O'Brien, CEO of the Hanover Insurance companies. "If this type of organization is so widely preferred, why don't people create such organizations? I think the answer is leadership. People have no real comprehension of the type of commitment it requires to build such an organization".[7]

Our traditional view of leaders—as special people who set the direction, make the key decisions, and energize the troops—is deeply rooted in an individualistic and nonsystemic worldview. Especially in the West, leaders and heroes—great men (and occasionally women) who rise to the fore in times of crisis. So long as such myths prevail, they reinforce a focus on short-term events and charismatic heroes rather than on systemic forces and collective learning.

Leadership in learning organizations centers on subtler and ultimately more important work. In a learning organization, leaders' roles differ dramatically from that of the charismatic decision maker. Leaders are designers, teachers, and stewards. These roles require new skills: the ability to build shared vision, to bring to the surface and challenge prevailing mental models, and to foster more systemic patterns of thinking. In short, leaders in learning organizations are responsible for building organizations where people are continually expanding their capabilities to shape their future—that is, leaders are responsible for learning.

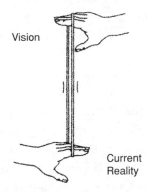

Vision

Current
Reality

Figure 1.1
The principle of creative tension

Creative Tension: The Integrating Principle

Leadership in a learning organization starts with the principle of creative tension.[8] Creative tension comes from seeing clearly where we want to be, our "vision," and telling the truth about where we are, our "current reality." The gap between the two generates a natural tension (see figure 1.1).

Creative tension can be resolved in two basic ways: by raising current reality toward the vision, or by lowering the vision toward current reality. Individuals, groups, and organizations who learn how to work with creative tension learn how to use the energy it generates to move reality more reliably toward their visions.

The principle of creative tension has long been recognized by leaders. Martin Luther King, Jr., once said, "Just as Socrates felt that it was necessary to create a tension in the mind, so that individuals could rise from the bondage of myths and half truths...so must we...create the kind of tension in society that will help men rise from the dark depths of prejudice and racism".[9]

Without vision there is no creative tension. Creative tension cannot be generated from current reality alone. All the analysis in the world will never generate a vision. Many who are otherwise qualified to lead fail to do so because they try to substitute analysis for vision. They believe that, if only people understood current reality, they would surely feel the motivation to change. They are then disappointed to discover that people "resist" the personal and organizational changes that must be made to alter reality. What they never grasp is that the natural energy for changing reality comes from holding a picture of what might be that is more important to people than what is.

But creative tension cannot be generated from vision alone; it demands an accurate picture of current reality as well. Just as King had a dream, so too did he continually strive to "dramatize the shameful conditions" of racism and prejudice so that they could no longer be ignored. Vision without an understanding of current reality will more likely foster cynicism than creativity. The principle of creative tension teaches that an accurate picture of current reality is just as important as a compelling picture of a desired future.

Leading through creating tension is different than solving problems. In problem solving, the energy for change comes from attempting to get away from an aspect of current reality that is undesirable. With creative tension, the energy for change comes from the vision, from what we want to create, juxtaposed with current reality. While the distinction may seem small, the consequences are not. Many people and organizations find themselves motivated to change only when their problems are bad enough to cause them to change. This works for a while, but the change process runs out of steam as soon as the problems driving the change become less pressing. With problem solving, the motivation for change is extrinsic. With creative tension, the motivation is intrinsic. This distinction mirrors the distinction between adaptive and generative learning.

New Roles

The traditional authoritarian image of the leader as "the boss calling the shots" has been recognized as oversimplified and inadequate for some time. According to Edgar Schein, "Leadership is inter-twined with culture formation." Building an organization's culture and shaping its evolution is the "unique and essential function" of leadership.[10] In a learning organization, the critical roles of leadership—designer, teacher, and steward—have antecedents in the ways leaders have contributed to building organizations in the past. But each role takes on new meaning in the learning organization and, as will be seen in the following sections, demands new skills and tools.

Leader as Designer

Imagine that your organization is an ocean liner and that you are "the leader." What is your role?

I have asked this question of groups of managers many times. The most common answer, not surprisingly, is "the captain." Others say, "The navigator, setting the direction." Still others say, "The helmsman, actually controlling the direction," or, "The engineer down there stoking the fire, providing energy," or, "The social director, making sure everybody's enrolled, involved, and communicating." While these are legitimate leadership roles, there is another which, in many ways, eclipses them all in importance. Yet rarely does anyone mention it.

The neglected leadership role is the *designer* of the ship. No one has a more sweeping influence than the designer. What good does it do for the captain to say, "Turn starboard 30 degrees," when the designer has built a rudder that will only turn to port, or which takes six hours to turn to starboard? It's fruitless to be the leader in an organization that is poorly designed.

The functions of design, or what some have called "social architecture," are rarely visible; they take place behind the scenes. The consequences that appear today are the result of work done long in the past, and work today will show its benefits far in the future. Those who aspire to lead out of a desire to control, or gain fame, or simply to be at the center of the action, will find little to attract them to the quiet design work of leadership.

But what, specifically, is involved in organizational design? "Organization design is widely misconstrued as moving around boxes and lines," says Hanover's O'Brien. "The first task of organization design concerns designing the governing ideas of purpose, vision, and core values by which people will live." Few acts of leadership have a more enduring impact on an organization than building a foundation of purpose and core values.

In 1982, Johnson and Johnson found itself facing a corporate nightmare when bottles of its best-selling Tylenol were tampered with, resulting in several deaths. The corporation's immediate response was to pull all Tylenol off the shelves of retail outlets. Thirty one million capsules were destroyed, even though they were tested and found safe. Although the immediate cost was significant, no other action was possible given the firm's credo. Authored almost forty years earlier by president Robert Wood Johnson, Johnson and Johnson's credo states that permanent success is possible only when modern industry realizes that:

• service to its customers comes first;
• service to its employees and management comes second;
• service to the community comes third; and
• service to its stockholders, last.

Such statements might seem like motherhood and apple pie to those who have not seen the way a clear sense of purpose and values can affect key business decisions. Johnson and Johnson's crisis management in this case was based on that credo. It was simple, it was right, and it worked.

If governing ideas constitute the first design task of leadership, the second design task involves the policies, strategies, and structures that translate guiding ideas into business decisions. Leadership theorist Philip Selznick calls policy and structure the "institutional embodiment of purpose".[11] "Policy making (the rules that guide decisions) ought to be separated from decision making," says Jay Forrester.[12] "Otherwise, short-term pressures will usurp time from policy creation."

Traditionally, writers like Selznick and Forrester have tended to see policy making and implementation as the work of a small number of senior managers. But that view is changing. Both the dynamic business environment and the mandate of the learning organization to engage people at all levels now make it clear that this second design task is more subtle. Henry Mintzberg has argued that strategy is less a rational plan arrived at in the abstract and implemented throughout the organization than an "emergent phenomenon." Successful organizations "craft strategy" according to Mintzberg, as they continually learn about shifting business conditions and balance what is desired and what is possible.[13] The key is not getting the right strategy but fostering strategic thinking. "The choice of individual action is only part of...the policymaker's need," according to Mason and Mitroff.[14] "More important is the need to achieve insight into the nature of the complexity and to formulate concepts and world views for coping with it."

Behind appropriate policies, strategies, and structures are effective learning processes; their creation is the third key design responsibility in learning organizations. This does not absolve senior managers of their strategic responsibilities. Actually, it deepens and extends those responsibilities. Now, they are not only responsible for ensuring that an organization have well-developed strategies and policies, but also for ensuring that processes exist whereby these are continually improved.

In the early 1970s, Shell was the weakest of the big seven oil companies. Today, Shell and Exxon are arguably the strongest, both in size and financial health. Shell's ascendancy began with frustration. Around 1971 members of Shell's "Group Planning" in London began to foresee dramatic change and unpredictability in world oil markets. However, it proved impossible to persuade managers that the stable world of steady growth in oil demand and supply they had known for twenty years was about to change. Despite brilliant analysis and artful presentation, Shell's planners realized, in the words of Pierre Wack, that they "had failed to change behavior in much of the Shell organization".[15] Progress would probably have ended there, had the frustration not given way to a radically new view of corporate planning.

As they pondered this failure, the planners' view of their basic task shifted: "We no longer saw our task as producing a documented view of the future business environment five or ten years ahead. Our real target was the microcosm (the 'mental model') of our decision makers." Only when the planners reconceptualized their basic task as fostering learning rather than devising plans did their insights begin to have an impact. The initial tool used was "scenario analysis," through which planners encouraged operating managers to think through how they would manage in the future under different possible scenarios. It mattered not that the managers believed the planners' scenarios absolutely, only that they became engaged in ferreting out the implications. In this way, Shell's planners conditioned managers to be mentally prepared for a shift from low prices to high prices and from stability to instability. The results were significant. When OPEC became a reality, Shell quickly responded by increasing local operating company control (to enhance maneuverability in the new political environment), building buffer stocks, and accelerating development of non-OPEC sources—actions that its competitors took much more slowly or not at all.

Somewhat inadvertently, Shell planners had discovered the leverage of designing institutional learning processes, whereby, in the words of former planning director de Geus, "Management teams change their shared mental models of their company, their markets, and their competitors."[16] Since then, "planning as learning" has become a byword at Shell, and Group Planning has continually sought out new learning tools that can be integrated into the planning process. Some of these are described below.

Leader as Teacher

"The first responsibility of a leader," writes retired Herman Miller CEO Max de Pree, "is to define reality".[17] Much of the leverage leaders can actually exert lies in helping people achieve more accurate, more insightful, and more empowering views of reality.

Leader as teacher does not mean leader as authoritarian expert whose job it is to teach people the "correct" view of reality. Rather, it is about helping everyone in the organization, oneself included, to gain more insightful views of current reality. This is in line with a popular emerging view of leaders as coaches, guides, or facilitators.[18] In learning organizations, this teaching role is developed further by virtue of explicit attention to people's mental models and by the influence of the systems perspective.

The role of leader as teacher starts with bringing to the surface people's mental models of important issues. No one carries an organization, a market, or a state of technology in his or her head. What we carry in our heads are assumptions. These mental pictures of how the world works have a significant influence on how we perceive problems and opportunities, identify courses of action, and make choices.

One reason that mental models are so deeply entrenched is that they are largely tacit. Ian Mitroff, in his study of General Motors, argues that an assumption that prevailed for years was that, in the United States, "Cars are status symbols. Styling is therefore more important than quality".[19] The Detroit automakers didn't say, "We have a mental model that all people care about is styling." Few actual managers would even say publicly that all people care about is styling. So long as the view remained unexpressed, there was little possibility of challenging its validity or forming more accurate assumptions.

But working with mental models goes beyond revealing hidden assumptions. "Reality," as perceived by most people in most organizations, means pressures that must be borne, crises that must be reacted to, and limitations that must be accepted. Leaders as teachers help people restructure their views of reality to see beyond the superficial conditions and events into the underlying causes of problems—and therefore to see new possibilities for shaping the future.

Specifically, leaders can influence people to view reality at three distinct levels: events, patterns of behavior, and systemic structure.

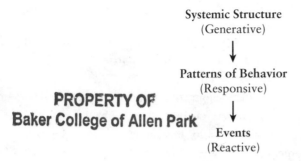

Systemic Structure
(Generative)

↓

Patterns of Behavior
(Responsive)

↓

Events
(Reactive)

The key question becomes where do leaders predominantly focus their own and their organization's attention?

Contemporary society focuses predominantly on events. The media reinforces this perspective, with almost exclusive attention to short-term, dramatic events. This focus leads naturally to explaining what happens in terms of those events: "The Dow Jones average went up sixteen points because high fourth-quarter profits were announced yesterday."

Pattern-of-behavior explanations are rarer, in contemporary culture, than event explanations, but they do occur. "Trend analysis" is an example of seeing patterns of behavior. A good editorial that interprets a set of current events in the context of long-term historical changes is another example. Systemic, structural explanations go even further by addressing the question. "What causes the patterns of behavior?"

In some sense, all three levels of explanation are equally true. But their usefulness is quite different. Event explanations—who did what to whom —doom their holders to a reactive stance toward change. Pattern-of-behavior explanations focus on identifying long-term trends and assessing their implications. They at least suggest how, over time, we can respond to shifting conditions. Structural explanations are the most powerful. Only they address the underlying causes of behavior at a level such that patterns of behavior can be changed.

By and large, leaders of our current institutions focus their attention on events and patterns of behavior, and, under their influence, their organizations do likewise. That is why contemporary organizations are predominantly reactive, or at best responsive—rarely generative. On the other hand, leaders in learning organizations pay attention to all three levels, but focus especially on systemic structure; largely by example, they teach people throughout the organization to do likewise.

Leader as Steward

This is the subtlest role of leadership. Unlike the roles of designer and teacher, it is almost solely a matter of attitude. It is an attitude critical to learning organizations.

While stewardship has long been recognized as an aspect of leadership, its source is still not widely understood. I believe Robert Greenleaf came closest to explaining real stewardship, in his seminal book *Servant Leadership*.[20] There, Greenleaf argues that "The servant leader is servant first.... It begins with the natural feeling that one wants to serve, to serve *first*. This conscious choice brings one to aspire to lead. That person is sharply different from one who is leader first, perhaps because of the need to assuage an unusual power drive or to acquire material possessions."

Leaders' sense of stewardship operates on two levels: stewardship for the people they lead and stewardship for the larger purpose or mission that underlies the enterprise. The first type arises from a keen appreciation of the impact one's leadership can have on others. People can suffer economically, emotionally, and spiritually under inept leadership. If anything, people in a learning organization are more vulnerable because of their commitment and sense of shared ownership. Appreciating this naturally instills a sense of responsibility in leaders. The second type of stewardship arises from a leader's sense of personal purpose and commitment to the organization's larger mission. People's natural impulse to learn is unleashed when they are engaged in an endeavor they consider worthy of their fullest commitment. Or, as Lawrence Miller puts it, "Achieving return on equity does not, as a goal, mobilize the most noble forces of our soul".[21]

Leaders engaged in building learning organizations naturally feel part of a larger purpose that goes beyond their organization. They are part of changing the way businesses operate, not from a vague philanthropic urge, but from a conviction that their efforts will produce more productive organizations, capable of achieving higher levels of organizational success and personal satisfaction than more traditional organizations. Their sense of stewardship was succinctly captured by George Bernard Shaw when he said,

This is the true joy in life, the being used for a purpose you consider a mighty one, the being a force of nature rather than a feverish, selfish clod of ailments and grievances complaining that the world will not devote itself to making you happy.

New Skills

New leadership roles require new leadership skills. These skills can only be developed, in my judgment, through a lifelong commitment. It is not enough for one or two individuals to develop these skills. They must be distributed widely throughout the organization. This is one reason that understanding the *disciplines* of a learning organization is so important. These disciplines embody the principles and practices that can widely foster leadership development.

Three critical areas of skills (disciplines) are building shared vision, surfacing and challenging mental models, and engaging in systems thinking.[22]

Building Shared Vision

How do individual visions come together to create shared visions? A useful metaphor is the hologram, the three-dimensional image created by interacting light sources.

If you cut a photograph in half, each half shows only part of the whole image. But if you divide a hologram, each part, no matter how small, shows the whole image intact. Likewise, when a group of people come to share a vision for an organization, each person sees an individual picture of the organization at its best. Each shares responsibility for the whole, not just for one piece. But the component pieces of the hologram are not identical. Each represents the whole image from a different point of view. It's something like poking holes in a window shade; each hole offers a unique angle for viewing the whole image. So, too, is each individual's vision unique.

When you add up the pieces of a hologram, something interesting happens. The image becomes more intense, more lifelike. When more people come to share a vision, the vision becomes more real in the sense of a mental reality that people can truly imagine achieving. They now have partners, cocreators; the vision no longer rests on their shoulders alone. Early on, when they are nurturing an individual vision, people may say it is "my vision." But, as the shared vision develops, it becomes both "my vision" and "our vision."

Encouraging Personal Vision   Shared visions emerge from personal visions. It is not that people only care about their own self-interest—in fact, people's values usually include dimensions that concern family, organization, community, and even the world. Rather, it is that people's capacity for caring is *personal*.

Communicating and Asking for Support   Leaders must be willing to continually share their own vision, rather than being the official representative of the corporate vision. They also must be prepared to ask, "Is this vision worthy of your commitment?" This can be difficult for a person used to setting goals and presuming compliance.

Visioning as an Ongoing Process   Building shared vision is a never-ending process. At any one point there will be a particular image of the future that is predominant, but that image will evolve. Today, too many managers want to dispense with the "vision business" by going off and writing the Official Vision Statement. Such statements almost always lack the vitality, freshness, and excitement of a genuine vision that comes from people asking, "What do we really want to achieve?"

Blending Extrinsic and Intrinsic Visions   Many energizing visions are extrinsic—that is, they focus on achieving something relative to an outsider, such as a competitor. But a goal that is limited to defeating an opponent can, once the vision is achieved, easily become a defensive posture. In contrast, intrinsic goals like creating a new type of product, taking an established product to a new level, or setting a new standard for customer satisfaction can call forth a new level of creativity and innovation. Intrinsic and extrinsic visions need to coexist; a vision solely predicated on defeating an adversary will eventually weaken an organization.

Distinguishing Positive from Negative Visions   Many organizations only truly pull together when their survival is threatened. Similarly, most social movements aim at eliminating what people don't want: for example, antidrugs, antismoking, or antinuclear arms movements. Negative visions carry a subtle message of powerlessness: people will only pull together when there is sufficient threat. Negative visions also tend to be short term. Two fundamental sources of energy can motivate organizations: fear and aspiration. Fear, the energy source behind negative visions, can produce extraordinary changes in short periods, but aspiration endures as a continuing source of learning and growth.

Surfacing and Testing Mental Models

Many of the best ideas in organizations never get put into practice. One reason is that new insights and initiatives often conflict with established mental models. The leadership task of challenging assumptions without invoking defensiveness requires reflection and inquiry skills possessed by few leaders in traditional controlling organizations.[23]

Seeing Leaps of Abstraction   Our minds literally move at lightning speed. Ironically, this often slows our learning, because we leap to generalizations so quickly that we never think to test them. We then confuse our generalizations with the observable data upon which they are based, treating the generalizations *as if they were data*. The frustrated sales rep reports to the home office that "customers don't really care about quality, price is what matters," when that actually happened was that three consecutive large customers refused to place an order unless a larger discount was offered. The sales rep treats her generalization, "customers care only about price," as if it were absolute fact rather than an assumption (very likely an assumption reflecting her own views of customers and the market).

Balancing Inquiry and Advocacy   Most managers are skilled at articulating their views and presenting them persuasively. While important, advocacy skills can become counterproductive as managers rise in responsibility and confront increasingly complex issues that require collaborative learning among different, equally knowledgeable people. Leaders in learning organizations need to have both inquiry and advocacy skills.[24]

Specifically, when advocating a view, they need to be able to:

- explain the reasoning and data that led to their view;
- encourage others to test their view (e.g., Do you see gaps in my reasoning? Do you disagree with the data upon which my view is based?); and
- Do you have either different data, different conclusions, or both?). When inquiring into another's views, they need to:
- actively seek to understand the other's view, rather than simply restating their own view and how it differs from the other's view, and
- make their attributions about the other and the other's view explicit (e.g., Based on your statement that . . . ; I am assuming that you believe . . . ; Am I representing your views fairly?).

If they reach an impasse (others no longer appear open to inquiry), they need to:

- ask what data or logic might unfreeze the impasse, or if an experiment (or some other inquiry) might be designed to provide new information.

Distinguishing Espoused Theory from the Theory in Use　We all like to think that we hold certain views, but often our actions reveal deeper views. For example, I may proclaim that people are trustworthy, but never lend friends money and jealously guard my possessions. Obviously, my deeper mental model (my theory in use), differs from my espoused theory. Recognizing gaps between espoused views and theories in use (which often requires the help of others) can be pivoted to deeper learning.

Recognizing and Defusing Defensive Routines　As one CEO in our research program puts it, "Nobody ever talks about an issue at the 8:00 business meeting exactly the same way they talk about it at home that evening or over drinks at the end of the day." The reason is what Chris Argyris calls "defensive routines," entrenched habits used to protect ourselves from the embarrassment and threat that comes with exposing our thinking. For most of us, such defenses began to build early in life in response to pressures to have the right answers in school or at home. Organizations add new levels of performance anxiety and thereby amplify and exacerbate this defensiveness. Ironically, this makes it even more difficult to expose hidden mental models, and thereby lessens learning.

The first challenge is to recognize defensive routines, then to inquire into their operation. Those who are best at revealing and defusing defensive routines operate with a high degree of self-disclosure regarding their own defensiveness (e.g., I notice that I am feeling uneasy about how this conversation is going. Perhaps I don't understand it or it is threatening to me in ways I don't yet see. Can you help me see this better?).

Systems Thinking

We all know that leaders should help people see the big picture. But the actual skills whereby leaders are supposed to achieve this are not well understood. In my experience, successful leaders often are "systems thinkers" to a considerable extent. They focus less on day-today events and more on underlying trends and forces of change. But they do this almost completely intuitively. The consequence is that they are often unable to explain their intuitions to others and feel frustrated that others can not see the world the way we do.

One of the most significant developments in management science today is the gradual coalescence of managerial systems thinking as a field of study and practice. This field suggests some key skills for future leaders.

Seeing Interrelationships, Not Things, and Processes, Not Snapshots

Most of us have been conditioned throughout our lives to focus on things and to see the world in static images. This leads us to linear explanations of systemic phenomenon. For instance, in an arms race each party is convinced that the other is *the cause* of problems. They react to each new move as an isolated event, not as part of a process. So long as they fail to see the interrelationships of these actions, they are trapped.

Moving beyond Blame We tend to blame each other or outside circumstances for our problems. But it is poorly designed systems, not incompetent or unmotivated individuals, that cause most organizational problems. Systems thinking shows us that there is no outside—that you and the cause of your problems are part of a single system.

Distinguishing Detail Complexity from Dynamic Complexity Some types of complexity are more important strategically than others. Detail complexity arises when cause and effect are distant in time and space, and when the consequences over time of interventions are subtle and not obvious to many participants in the system. The leverage in most management situations lies in understanding dynamic complexity, not detail complexity.

Focusing on Areas of High Leverage   Some have called systems thinking the "new dismal science" because it teaches that most obvious solutions don't work—at best, they improve matters in the short run, only to make things worse in the long run. But there is another side to the story. Systems thinking also shows that small, well-focused actions can produce significant, enduring improvements, if they are in the right place. Systems thinkers refer to this idea as the principle of "leverage." Tackling a difficult problem is often a matter of seeing where the high leverage lies, where a change—with a minimum of effort—would lead to lasting, significant improvement.

Avoiding Symptomatic Solutions   The pressures to intervene in management systems that are going awry can be overwhelming. Unfortunately, given the linear thinking that predominates in most organizations, interventions usually focus on symptomatic fixes, not underlying causes. This results in only temporary relief, and it tends to create still more pressures later on for further, low-leverage intervention. If leaders acquiesce to these pressures, they can be sucked into an endless spiral of in-creasing intervention. Sometimes the most difficult leadership act are to refrain from intervening through popular through popular quick fixes and to keep the pressure on everyone to identify more enduring solutions.

While leaders who can articulate systemic explanations are rare, those who *can* will leave their stamp on an organization. One person who had this gift was Bill Gore, the founder and long-time CEO of W. L. Gore and Associates (makers of Gore-Tex and other synthetic fiber products). Bill Gore was adept at telling stories that showed how the organization's core values of freedom and individual responsibility required particular operating policies. He was proud of his egalitarian organization, in which there were (and still are) no "employees," only "associates," all of whom own shares in the company and participate in its management. At one talk, he explained the company's policy of controlled growth: "Our limitation is not financial resources. Our limitation is the rate at which we can bring in new associates. Our experience has been that if we try to bring in more than a 25 percent per year increase, we begin to bog down. Twenty-five percent per year growth is a real limitation; you can do much better than that with an authoritarian organization." As Gore tells the story, one of the associates, Esther Baum, went home after this talk and reported the limitation to her husband. As it happened, he was an astronomer and mathematician at Lowell Observatory. He said, "That's a very interesting figure." He took out a pencil and paper and calculated and said, "Do you realize that in only fifty-seven and a half years, everyone in the world will be working for Gore?"

Through this story, Gore explains the systemic rationale behind a key policy, limited growth rate—a policy that undoubtedly caused a lot of stress in the organization. He suggests that, at larger rates of growth, the adverse effects of attempting to integrate too many new people too rapidly would begin to dominate. (This is the "limits to growth" systems archetype explained below.) The story also reaffirms the organization's commitment to creating a unique environment for its associates and illustrates the types of sacrifices that the firm is prepared to make in order to remain true to its vision. The last part of the story shows that, despite the self-impose limit, the company is still very much a growth company.

The consequences of leaders who lack systems thinking sills can be devastating. Many charismatic leaders manage almost exclusively at the level of events. They deal in visions and in crises, and little in between. Under their leadership, an organization hurtles from crisis to crises. Eventually, the worldview of people in the organization becomes dominated by events and reactiveness. Many, especially those who are deeply committed, become burned out. Eventually, cynicism comes to pervade the organization. People have no control over their time, let alone their destiny.

Similar problems arise with the "visionary strategist," the leader with vision who sees both patterns of change and events. This leader is better prepared to manage change. He or she can explain strategies in terms of emerging trends, and thereby foster a climate that is less reactive. But such leaders still impart a responsive orientation rather than a generative one.

Many talented leaders have rich, highly systemic intuitions but cannot explain those intuitions to others. Ironically, they often end up being authoritarian leaders, even if they don't want to, because only they see the decisions that need to be made. They are unable to conceptualize their strategic insights so that these can become public knowledge, open to challenge and further improvement.

New Tools

Developing the skills described above requires new tools—tools that will enhance leaders' conceptual abilities and foster communication and collaborative inquiry. What follows is a sampling of tools starting to find use in learning organizations.

Systems Archetypes

One of the insights of the budding, managerial systems-thinking field is that certain types of systemic structures recur again and again. Countless systems grow for a period, then encounter problems and cease to grow (or even collapse) well before they have reached intrinsic limits to growth. Many other systems get locked in runaway vicious spirals where every actor has to run faster and faster to stay in the same place. Still others lure individual actors into doing what seems right locally, yet which eventually causes suffering for all.[25]

Some of the system archetypes that have the broadest relevance include:

Balancing Process with Delay   In this archetype, decision makers fail to appreciate the time delays involved as they move toward a goal. As a result, they overshoot the goal and may even produce recurring cycles. Classic example: Real estate developers who keep starting new projects until the market has gone soft, by which time an eventual glut is guaranteed by the properties still under construction.

Limits to Growth   A reinforcing cycle of growth grinds to a halt, and may even reverse itself, as limits are approached. The limits can be resource constraints, or external or internal responses to growth. Classic examples: Product life cycles that peak prematurely owing to poor quality or service, the growth and decline of communication in a management ream, and the spread of a new movement.

Shifting the Burden   A short-term "solution" is used to correct a problem, with seemingly happy immediate results. As this correction is used more and more, fundamental long-term corrective measures are used less. Over time, the mechanisms of the fundamental solution may atrophy or become disabled, leading to even greater reliance on the symptomatic solution. Classic example: Using corporate human resource staff to solve local personnel problems, thereby keeping managers from developing their own interpersonal skills.

Eroding Goals   When all else fails, lower your standards. This is like "shifting the burden," except that the short-term solution involves letting a fundamental goal, such as quality standards or employee morale standards, atrophy. Classic example: A company that responds to delivery problems by continually upping its quoted delivery times.

Escalation   Two people or two organizations, who each see their welfare as depending on a relative advantage over the other, continually react to the other's advances. Whenever one side gets ahead, the other is threatened, leading it to act more aggressively to reestablish its advantage, which threatens the first, and so on. Classic examples: Arms, race, gang warfare, price wars.

Tragedy of the Commons[25]   Individuals keep intensifying their use of a commonly available but limited resource until all individuals start to experience severely diminishing returns. Classic examples: Sheepherders who keep increasing their flocks until they overgraze the common pasture; divisions in a firm that share a common sales force and compete for the use of sales reps by upping their sales targets, until the sales force burns out from over extension.

Growth and Underinvestment   Rapid growth approaches a limit that could be eliminated or pushed into the future, but only by aggressive investment in physical and human capability. Eroding goals or standards cause investment that is too weak, or too slow, and customers get increasingly unhappy, slowing demand growth and thereby making the needed investment (apparently) unnecessary or impossible. Classic example: Countless once-successful growth firms that allowed product or service quality to erode, and were unable to generate enough revenues to invest in remedies.

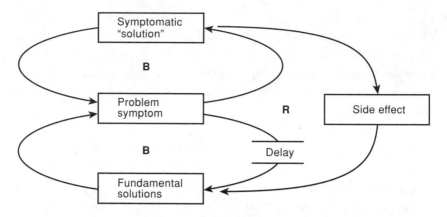

Figure 1.2
"Shifting the burden" archetype template. In the "shifting the burden" template, two balancing processes (B) compete for control of a problem symptom. Both solutions affect the symptom, but only the fundamental solution treats the cause. The symptomatic "solution" creates the additional side effect (R) of deferring the fundamental solution, making it harder and harder to achieve.

The Archetype template is a specific tool that is helping managers identify archetypes operating in their own strategic areas (see figure 1.2).[27] The template shows the basic structural form of the archetype but lets managers fill in the variables of their own situation. For example, the shifting the burden template involves two balancing process ("B") that compete for control of a problem symptom. The upper, symptomatic solution provides a short-term fix that will make the problem symptom go away for a while. The lower, fundamental solution provides a more enduring solution. The side effect feedback ("R") around the outside of the diagram identifies unintended exacerbating effects of the symptomatic solution, which, over time, make it more and more difficult to invoke the fundamental solution.

Several years ago, a team of managers from a leading consumer goods producer used the shifting the burden archetype in a revealing way. The problem they focused on was financial stress, which could be dealt with in two different ways: by running marketing promotions (the symptomatic solution) or by product innovation (the fundamental solution). Marketing promotions were fast. The company was expert in their design and implementation. The results were highly predictable. Product innovation was slow and much less predictable, and the company had a history over the past ten years of product-innovation mismanagement. Yet only through innovation could they retain a leadership position in their industry, which had slid over the past ten to twenty years. What the managers saw clearly was that the more skillful they became at promotions, the more they shifted the burden away from product innovation. But what really struck home was when one member identified the unintended side effect: the last three CEOs had all come from advertising function, which had become the politically dominant function the corporation, thereby institutionalizing the symptomatic solution. Unless the political values shifted back toward product and process innovation, the managers realized, the firm's decline would accelerate—which is just the shift that has happened over the past several years.

Charting Strategic Dilemmas

Management teams typically come unglued when confronted with core dilemmas. A classic example was the way U.S. manufacturers faced the low cost-high quality choice. For years, most assumed that it was necessary to choose between the two. Not surprisingly, given the short-term pressures perceived by most managements, the prevailing choice was low cost. Firms that chose high quality usually perceived themselves as aiming exclusively for a high quality, high price market niche. The consequence of this perceived either-or choice have been disastrous, even fatal, as U.S. manufacturers have encountered increasing international competition from firms that have chosen to consistently improve quality *and* care.

In a recent book, Charles Hampden-Turner presented a variety of tools for helping management teams confront strategic dilemmas creatively.[28] He summarizes the process in seven steps:

Eliciting the Dilemmas   Identifying the opposed values that form the "horns" of the dilemma, for example, cost as opposed to quality, or local initiative as opposed to central coordination and control. Hampden-Turner suggests that humor can be a distinct asset in this process since "the admission that dilemmas even exist tends to be difficult for some companies."

Mapping   Locating the opposing values as two axes and helping managers identify where they see themselves, or their organization, along the axes.

Processing   Getting rid of nouns to describe the axes of the dilemma. Present participles formed by adding "ing" convert rigid nouns into processes that imply movement. For example, central control versus local control becomes "strengthening national office" and "growing local initiatives." This loosens the bond of implied opposition between the two values. For example, it becomes possible to think of "strengthening national services from which local branches can benefit."

Framing/Contextualizing   Further softening the adversarial structure among different values by letting "each side in turn be the frame or context for the other." This shifting of the "figure-ground" relationship undermines any implicit attempts to hold one value as intrinsically superior to the other, and thereby to become mentally closed to creative strategies for continuous improvement of both.

Sequencing   Breaking the hold of static thinking. Very often, values like low cost and high quality appear to be in opposition because we think in terms of a point in time, not in terms of an on-going process. For example, a strategy of investing I new process technology and developing a new production-floor culture of worker responsibility may take time and money in the near term, yet reap significant long-term financial rewards.

Waving/Cycling   Sometimes the strategic path toward improving both values involves cycles where both values will get "worse" for a time. Yet, at a deeper level, learning is occurring that will cause the next cycle to be at a higher plateau for both values.

Synergizing   Achieving synergy where significant improvement is occurring along all axes of all relevant dilemmas. (This is the ultimate goal, of course.) Synergy, as Hampden-Turner points out, is a uniquely systemic notion, coming from the Greek *syn-ergo* or "work together."

"The Left-Hand Column ": Surfacing Mental Models

The idea that mental models can dominate business decisions and that these models are often tacit and even contradictory to what people espouse can be very threatening to managers who pride themselves on rationality and judicious decision making. It is important to have tools to help managers discover for themselves how their mental models operate to undermine their own intentions.

One tool that has worked consistently to help managers see their own mental models in action is the "left-hand column" exercise developed by Chris Argyris and his colleagues. This tool is especially helpful in showing how we leap from data to generalizations.

When working with managers, I start this exercise by selecting a specific situation I which I am interacting with other people in a way that is not working, that is not producing the learning that is needed. I write out a sample of the exchange, with the script on the right-hand side of the page. On the left-hand side, I write what I am thinking but not saying at each stage in the exchange (see sidebar).

The left-hand column exercise not only brings hidden assumptions to the surface, it shows how they influence behavior. In the example, I make two key assumptions about Bill: He lacks confidence and he lacks initiative. Neither may be literally true, but both are evident in my internal dialogue, and both influence the way I handle the situation. Believing that he lacks confidence, I skirt the fact that I've heard the presentation was a bomb. I'm afraid that if I say it directly, he will lose what little confidence he has, or he will see me as unsupportive. So I bring up the subject of the presentation obliquely. When I ask Bill what we should do next, he gives no specific course of action. Believing he lacks initiative, I take this as evidence of his laziness; he is content to do nothing when action is definitely required. I conclude that I will have to manufacture some form of pressure to motivate him, or else I will have to take matters into my own hands.

The Left-Hand Column: An Exercise

Imagine my exchange with a colleague, Bill, after he made a big presentation to our boss on a project we are doing together. I had to miss the presentation, but I've heard that it was poorly received.

Me: How did the presentation go?

Bill: Well, I don't know. It's really too early to say. Besides, we're breaking new ground here.

Me: Well, what do you think we should do? I believe that the issues you were raising are important.

Bill: I'm not sure. Let's just wait and see what happens.

Me: You may be right, but I think we need to do more than just wait.

What I'm Thinking

Everyone says the presentation was a bomb.

Does he really not know how bad it was? Or is he not willing to face up to it?

He really is afraid to see the truth. If he only had more confidence, he could probably learn from a situation like this.

I can't believe he doesn't realize how disastrous that presentation was to our moving ahead.

I've got to find some way to light a fire under the guy.

Me: How did the presentation go?

Bill: Well, I don't know. It's too early to say. Besides, we're breaking new ground here.

Me: Well, what do you think we should do? I believe that the issues you are raising are important.

Bill: I'm not so sure. Let's just wait and see what happens.

Me: You may be right, but I think we may need to do more than just wait.

The exercise reveals the elaborate webs of assumptions we weave, within which we become our own victims. Rather than dealing directly with my assumptions about Bill and the situation, we talk around the subject. The reasons for my avoidance are self-evident: I assume that if I raised my doubts, I would provoke a defensive reaction that would only make matters worse. But the price of avoiding the issue is high. Instead of determining how to move forward to resolve our problems, we end our exchange with no clear course of action. My assumptions about Bill's limitations have been reinforced. I resort to a manipulative strategy to move things forward.

The exercise not only reveals the need for skills in surfacing assumptions, but that we are the ones most in need of help. There is no one right way to handle difficult situations like my exchange with Bill, but any productive strategy revolves around a high level of self-disclosure and willingness to have my views challenged. I need to recognize my own leaps of abstraction regarding Bill, share the events and reasoning that are leading to my concern over the project, and be open to Bill's views on both. The skills to carry on such conversations without invoking defensiveness take time to develop. But if both parties in a learning impasse start by doing their own left-hand column exercise and sharing them with each other, it is remarkable how quickly everyone recognizes their contribution to the impasse and progress starts to be made.

Learning at Hanover Insurance

Hanover Insurance has gone from the bottom of the property and liability industry to a position among the top 25 percent of U.S. insurance companies over the past twenty years, largely through the efforts of CEO William O'Brien and his predecessor, Jack Adams. The following comments are excerpted from a series of interviews Senge conducted with O'Brien as background for his book:

Senge: Why do you think there is so much change occurring in management and organizations today? Is it primarily because of increased competitive pressures?

O'Brien: That's a factor, but not the most significant factor. The ferment in management will continue until we find models that are more congruent with human nature.

One of the great insights of modern psychology is the hierarchy of human needs. As Maslow expressed this idea, the most basic needs are food and shelter. Then comes belonging. Once these three basic needs are satisfied, people begin to aspire toward self-respect and esteem, and toward self-actualization—the fourth- and fifth-order needs.

Our traditional hierarchical organizations are designed to provide for the first three levels, but not the fourth and fifth. These first three levels are now widely available to members of industrial society, but our organizations do not offer people sufficient opportunities for growth.

Senge: How would you assess Hanover's progress to date?

O'Brien: We have been on a long journey away from a traditional hierarchical culture. The journey began with everyone understanding some guiding ideas about purpose, vision, and values as a basis for participative management. This is a better way to begin building a participative culture than by simply "letting people in on decision making." Before there can be meaningful participation, people must share certain values and pictures about where we are trying to do, We discovered that people have a real need to feel that they're part of an ennobling mission. But developing shared visions and values is not the end, only the beginning.

Next we had to get beyond mechanical, linear thinking. The essence of our jobs as managers is to deal with "divergent" problems—problems that have no simple answer. "Convergent" problems—problems that have a "right" answer—should be solved locally. Yet we are deeply conditioned to see the world in terms of convergent problems. Most managers try to force-fit simplistic solutions and undermine the potential for learning when divergent problems arise. Since everyone handles the linear issues fairly well, companies that learn how to handle divergent issues will have a great advantage.

The next basic stage in our progression was coming to understand inquiry and advocacy. We learned that real openness is rooted in people's ability to continually inquire into their own thinking. This requires exposing yourself to being wrong—not something that most managers are rewarded for. But learning is very difficult if you cannot look for errors or incompleteness in your own ideas.

What all this builds to is the capability throughout an organization to manage mental models. In a locally controlled organization, you have the fundamental challenge of learning how to help people make good decisions without coercing them into making particular decisions. By managing mental models, we create "self-concluding" decisions—decisions that people come to themselves—which will result in deeper conviction, better implementation, and the ability to make better adjustments when the situation changes.

Senge: What concrete steps can top managers take to begin moving toward learning organizations?

O'Brien: Look at the signals you send through the organization. For example, one critical signal is how you spend your time. It's hard to build a learning organization if people are unable to take the time to think through important matters. I rarely set up an appointment for less than one hour. If the subject is not worth an hour, it shouldn't be on my calendar.

Senge: Why is this so hard for so many managers?

O'Brien: It comes back to what you believe about the nature of your work. The authoritarian manager has a "chain gang" mental model: "The speed of the boss is the speed of the gang. I've got to keep things moving fast, because I've got to keep people working." In a learning organization, the manager shoulders an almost sacred responsibility: to create conditions that enable people to have happy and productive lives. If you understand the effects the ideas we are discussion can have on the lives of people in your organization, you will take the time.

Learning Laboratories: Practice Fields for Management Teams
One of the most promising new tools is the learning laboratory or "microworld ": constructed microcosms of real-life settings in which management teams can learn how to learn together.

The rationale behind learning laboratories can best be explained by analogy. Although most management tams have great difficulty learning (enhancing their collective intelligence and capacity to create), in other domains team learning is the norm rather than the exception—team sports and the performing arts, for example. Great basketball teams do not start off great. They learn. But the process by which these teams learn is, by and large, absent from modern organizations. The process is a continual movement between practice and performance.

The vision guiding current research in management learning is to design and construct effective practice fields for management teams. Much remains to be done, but the broad outlines are emerging.

First, since team learning in organizations is an individual-to-individual and individual-to-system, phenomenon, learning laboratories must combine meaningful business issues with meaningful interpersonal dynamics. Either alone is incomplete.

Second, the factors that thwart learning about complex business issues must be eliminated in the learning lab. Chief among these is the inability to experience the long-term, systemic consequences of key strategic decisions. We all learn best from experience, but we are unable to experience the consequences of many important organizational decisions. Learning laboratories remove this constraint through system dynamics simulation games that compress time and space.

Third, new learning skills must be developed. One constraint on learning is the inability of managers to reflect insightfully on their assumptions, and to inquire effectively into each other's assumptions. Both skills can be enhanced in a learning laboratory, where people can practice surfacing assumptions in a low-risk setting. A note of caution: It is far easier to design an entertaining learning laboratory than it is to have an impact on real management practices and firm traditions outside the learning lab. Research on management simulations has shown that they often have greater entertainment value than educational value. One of the reasons appears to be that many simulations do not offer deep insights into systemic structures causing business problems. Another reason is that they do not foster new learning skills. Also, there is no connection between experiments in the learning lab and real life experiments. These are significant problems that research on learning laboratory design is now addressing.

Developing Leaders and Learning Organizations

In a recently published retrospective on organization development in the 1980s, Marshall Sashkin and N. Warner Burke observe the return of an emphasis on developing leaders who can develop organizations.[29] They also note Schein's critique that most top executives are not qualified for the task of developing culture.[30] Learning organizations represent a potentially significant evolution of organizational culture. So it should come as no surprise that such organizations will remain a distant vision until the leadership capabilities they demand are developed. "The 1990s may be the period," suggested Sashkin and Burke, "during which organization development and (a new sort of) management development are reconnected."

I believe that this new sort of management development will focus on the roles, skills, and tools for leadership in learning organizations. Undoubtedly, the ideas offered above are only a rough approximation of this new territory. The sooner we begin seriously exploring the territory, the sooner the initial map can be improved—and the sooner we will realize an age-old vision of leadership:

The wicked leader is he who the people desire.

The good leader is he who the people revere.

The great leader is he who the people say, "We did it ourselves."

—Lao Tsu

References

1. P. Senge, *The Fifth Discipline: The Art and Practice of the Learning Organization* (New York: Doubleday/Currency, 1990).

2. A.P. de Geus, "Planning as Learning," *Harvard Business Review*, March–April 1998, pp. 70–84.

3. B. Dodmain, *Fortune*, 3 July 1989, pp. 48–62.

4. The distinction between adaptive and generative learning has its roots in the distinction between what Argyris and Schon have called their "single-loop" learning, in which individuals or groups adjust their behavior relative to fixed goals, norms, and assumptions, and "double-loop" learning, in which goals, norms, and assumptions, as well as behavior, are open to change (e.g., see C. Argyris and D. Schon, *Organizational Learning: A Theory-in-Action Perspective* (Reading, Mass.: Addison-Wesley, 1978).

5. All unattributed quotes are from personal communications with the author.

6. G. Stalk, Jr., "Time: The Next Source of Competitive Advantage," *Harvard Business Review*, July–August 1988, pp. 41–51.

7. Senge (1990).

8. The principle of creative tension comes from Robert Fritz' work on creativity. See R. Fritz *The Path of Least Resistance* (New York: Ballantine, 1989) and *Creating* (New York: Ballantine, 1990).

9. M. L. King, Jr., "Letter from Birmingham Jail," *American Visions*, January–February 1986, pp. 52–59.

10. E. Schein, *Organizational Culture and Leadership* (San Francisco: Jossey-Bass, 1985). Similar views have been expressed by many leadership theorists. For example, see: P. Selznick, *Leadership in Administration* (New York: Harper & Row 1957); W. Bennis and B. Nanus, *Leaders* (New York: Harper & Row, 1985) and N. M. Tichy and M. A. Devanna, *The Transformational Leader* (New York: John Wiley & Sons, 1986).

11. Selznick (1957).

12. J.W. Forrester, "A New Corporate Design," *Sloan Management Review* (formerly *Industrial Management Review*), Fall 1965, pp. 5–17.

13. See, for example, H. Mintzberg, "Crafting Strategy," *Harvard Business Review*, July-August 1987, pp. 66–85.

14. R. Mason and I. Mitroff, *Challenging Strategic Planning Assumptions* (New York: John Wiley & Sons, 1981), p. 16.

15. P. Wack, "Scenarios: Uncharted Waters Ahead," *Harvard Business Review*, September-October 1985, pp. 73–89.

16. de Geus (1988).

17. M. de Pree, Leadership Is an Art (New York: Doubleday, 1989), p. 9.

18. For example, see T. Peters and N. Austin, *A Passion for Excellence* (New York: Random House, 1985) and J. M. Kouzes and B. Z. Posner, *The Leadership Challenge* (San Francisco: Jossey-Bass, 1987).

19. I. Mitroff, *Break-Away Thinking* (New York: John Wiley & Sons, 1988), pp. 66–67

20. R.K. Greenleaf, *Servant Leadership: A Journey into the Nature of Legitimate Power and Greatness* (New York: Paulist Press, 1977).

21. L. Miller, *American Spirit: Visions of a New Corporate Culture* (New York: William Morrow, 1984), p. 15.

22. These points are condensed from the practices of the five disciplines examined in Senge (1990).

23. The ideas below are based to a considerable extent on the work of Chris Argyris, Donald Schon, and their Action Science colleagues. C. Argyris and D. Schon, *Organizational Learning: A Theory-in-Action Perspective* (Reading, Mass.: Addison-Wesley, 1978); C. Aragyris, R. Putnam, and D. Smith, Action Science (San Francisco: Jossey-Bass, 1985); C. Argyris, *Strategy, Change, and Defensive Routines* (Boston: Ptiman, 1985); and C. Argyris, *Overcoming Organizational Defenses* (Englewood Cliffs, N.J.: Prentice-Hall, 1990).

24. I am indebted to Diana Smith for the summary points below.

25. The system archetypes are one of several systems diagramming and communication tool. See D.H. Kim, "Toward Learning Organizations: Integrating Total Quality Control and Systems Thinking" (Cambridge, Massachusetts: MIT Sloan School of Management, Working Paper No. 3037–89-BPS, June 1989).

26. This archetype is closely associated with the work of ecologist Garrett Hardin, who coined its label. G. Hardin, "The Tragedy of the Commons," *Science*, 13 December 1968.

27. These templates were originally developed by Jennifer Kemeny, Charles Kiefer, and Michael Goodman of Innovation Associates, Inc., Framingham, Mass.

28. C. Hampden-Turner, *Charting the Corporate Mind* (New York: The Free Press, 1990).

29. M. Sashkin and W.W. Burke, "Organization Development in the 1980s" and "An End-of-the-Eighties Retrospective," in *Advances in Organization Development*, ed. F. Masarik (Norwood, N.J.: Ablex, 1990).

40. E. Schein (1985).

2

Reflection on "A Leader's New Work: Building Learning Organizations"

Peter Senge

The basic ideas laid out in *The Leader's New Work* have stood up pretty well over the past decade. Most of the leaders with whom we have worked through the SoL (Society for Organizational Learning) consortium have in fact served as teachers, stewards, and designers. Many have succeeded in contributing to significant change, viewed both from the standpoint of creating more meaningful and more productive work environments. Yet, significant change remains elusive for most companies because there persists deep confusion about who are the leaders, confusion that the paper did not contribute toward clarifying.

Without realizing it, I got trapped in this confusion through sloppy use of the word "leader." I was not sensitive enough to how the word is used, both within organizations and within the literature. The tendency is to use the word leader as a synonym for executive or top manager. This is one of the single biggest problems we have today in the United States and in other cultures.

The problem when we use leader to mean executive is twofold. First, it implies that there are not any other leaders in the organization. It tends to reinforce a deep-seeded habit in an awful lot of companies for people to point up and say, "We can't really do anything until the leaders are on board." The idea that leaders "drive change" is nonsense, but it is a view you hear again and again in companies. The incessant search for the hero CEO to revitalize change-resistant enterprises may be the primary reason such institutions remain change resistant. Our experiences have shown repeatedly that there is no substitute for diverse communities of leaders at many levels.

Second, using leader as a synonym for top manager means that we have no real definition of leadership. We do not need two words to describe the same thing. To put it bluntly, when we talk about leadership, we do not have a clue of what we are talking about. Everybody talks about leadership and everybody thinks it is critical to strategy, critical to how organizations evolve, critical to developing learning cultures. Yet we have no agreed upon definition. This does not mean that there is a lack of definitions. There are various definitions that are very useful in the literature. Robert Greenleaf has written beautifully about "the leader as servant," serving those led and serving a higher purpose. Edgar Schein says that leaders are people who build cultures. Yet, people often read such definitions to mean that the leader is the CEO who builds the culture. Moreover, I think most writers in the business and academic press either tacitly or explicitly accept this view as well because the "hero CEO" is such a deeply embedded cultural icon.

To counter these problems, we have adopted a definition of leadership in our work that is very simple yet radically different from the mainstream notions. There is an abstract version and a more operational version. The abstract version states that, "leadership is the capacity of a human community to create its future." The operational definition states that, "leadership is the ability of people in an organization to initiate and to sustain significant change, to work effectively with the forces that shape change." In this sense, leadership and change are inseparable. The important point about this definition is the emphasis on collective capacity, not on individual hero leaders.

For example, one type of leadership that has been absolutely essential in every single successful change effort within the SoL community has been active, talented, and imaginative local line leaders. We have actually found, effective local line leadership, not executive leadership, to be the essential ingredient in making significant change real, in moving from concept to capability, from idea to action. The reason for this is really very simple. Any innovation that is worthwhile to how an enterprise operates is worthwhile only because it improves the capacity of the enterprise to create value—value for customers, value for shareholders, value for students, etc.... The managers closest to the action where value is being created are the local line managers—not executives. The executives are more responsible for the environment, the overall organizational climate, and the overall direction, than for specific goals and work practices. Specific goals have to be worked out by the people who have managerial accountability for achieving results. New work practices have to be supported by local line managers. Local "bosses" have more impact on the quality of commitment, enthusiasm, and people's willingness to risk than do executives. If you are trying to test whether something new and promising really adds value, you have to go where the value is being generated.

A scenario I see over and over is when the executives work hard for a year to hammer out a brilliant new strategy with their consultants. Then, everybody moans and groans for the next five years because nobody has implemented the new strategy. Or, alternatively, executives work out a new organization design. But the reorganization proves disappointing—it never results in significant new products, new customer relationships, or new work practices. But, why are these problems surprising? Implementation is the work of hundreds, maybe thousands of people throughout the organization. If they are not on board, translating new ideas into new practices never happens. Alternatively, we have seen many examples where local line leaders have initiated significant changes, which have taken root in their own operations, and gradually spread widely—with no executive involvement at all. The importance of local line leaders for creating change may be the single most important insight in the past nine years of our work at the Society for Organizational Learning (SoL).

Similarly, we have found another type of crucial leadership that is still more unappreciated. These are the "internal networkers," the people who spread new ideas, who connect innovative line leaders with one another, who work quietly and behind the scenes to support important new initiatives. These people may be internal HR staff or internal consultants, engineers, salespeople, or production workers. Their formal role is less important than their informal role as "seed carriers," thinking partners, and coaches

So, by talking about "leaders" without recognizing these different types of leaders, I implicitly reinforced the notion that leaders were executives. In fact, the generic roles of teacher, steward, and designer are relevant to all types of leaders. But, I fear what I had to say was interpreted as only pertaining to executives. I think that was a real shortcoming, at least when viewed retrospectively.

Similarly, looking back, there was probably no way to foresee how the call for building learning organizations set out in *A Leader's New Work* would eventually be rearticulated through "knowledge management."

There are two aspects to knowledge management, the fad and the substance. The substance is not going to go away because understanding the nature of organizational knowledge, the processes whereby knowledge is generated, and the processes whereby knowledge diffuses are deep issues that I expect committed leaders to be wrestling with for the next 10 to 20 years. It is a critical set of issues.

The fad of knowledge management is just that. And most business people are starting to see through it. What has happened is that many consulting firms have repackaged their old IT products and resold them as "knowledge management." This fad will pass. People in business are not stupid. They will see through that pretty quickly. Two years ago, a colleague in a SoL member company who is responsible for the IT business in a big part of the company said, "15 years ago, I was an EDP expert, then I became a MIS expert, then I became an IT expert, now I am a knowledge management expert. But, all this time I have been doing pretty much the same thing." One way that fads operate is by putting new labels on old stuff.

To separate the practitioners from the charlatans, the first step is to ask whoever is talking about knowledge management to stop and define knowledge. Nine times out of ten, they have no definition, or their definition is a bunch of gobbledygook that you cannot figure out what the hell they are saying. One definition of knowledge from the philosophy of language is that "knowledge is the capacity for effective action." This is a useful definition, in part because it means that knowledge cannot be confused with information.

It is also useful because this is the only knowledge that organizations care about. No organization, no manager in her or his right mind cares about abstract, theoretical knowledge, unless it supports more effective action. Learning is the process whereby human beings build knowledge, enhance their capacity for effective action. Organizational learning is the process whereby organizations enhance their capacity for effective action. Personally, I find that knowledge management is an awkward term, because I think the idea that knowledge is something you manage makes it like a thing. Capacity for effective action is not a thing. Further, you cannot transfer it—one person cannot get it and give it to another. It is not physical. If you know how to walk and I do not, can you "give walking" to me? You cannot give somebody capacity. The essence of all learning strategies is to create environments where human beings enhance their capacity. The art of teaching is the art of creating an environment where one person's knowledge or capacity allows that person to design an environment that enables somebody else to learn. The teacher does not give the student knowledge.

This is why the interest in knowledge and information is so illuminating. You can give information, but you cannot give knowledge. You can only create an environment where the other person can gain knowledge if they choose to do so. This really shifts the whole focus of attention. The real questions in knowledge management do not concern capture, storage, and retrieval. These are questions about information. They are often relevant to how knowledge diffuses insofar as new information can be part of creating new knowledge. But it is not equivalent to creating new knowledge. The real questions around knowledge are:

What do we know how to do now—What is our current capacity for effective action, especially knowledge that is crucial for generating value (core competencies)?

What are we trying to learn—and what will enable us to learn faster and deeper?

How do you take the knowledge in one area and use it as the foundation for building knowledge in other areas?

Such questions about knowledge are really core issues, and they are the same set of issues that we have always been concerned with in organizational learning for many years. Organizational learning is the process by which organizations generate and diffuse knowledge.

I agree very strongly with Nonaka and Takeuchi's view that all learning involves explicit knowledge and tacit knowledge. A very simple way to say that is that all learning involves thinking and acting. This view that learning involves thinking and acting goes back, in the west, to John Dewey, one hundred years ago. If there is no acting, there is no learning. If there is no thinking, there is no learning. That is part of the problem with behaviorism. It is just focused on acting. It does not deal with the conceptualizing or sense making that is also essential for learning. I really like Nonaka and Takeuchi's framework. I think the reason these are good ideas is that they are foundational. It is foundational to talk about learning as a process that involves thinking and acting, explicit knowledge and tacit knowledge.

The process whereby human beings go from tacit to explicit knowledge is quite complex and leads to crucial issues and questions that are often missed, These issues, in my mind, lie at the heart of knowledge management.

Some people occasionally talk about converting tacit knowledge to explicit knowledge. I do not like that word "convert." Talking about converting makes it sound like a simple process of one-thing goes in and something else comes out. At a recent MIT seminar, a researcher said she had visited a company that was busy "capturing" their tacit knowledge. She said, "I hope they have a big bag." Tacit knowledge and explicit knowledge are different logical types. One does not convert to the other. You don't pour one into the other.

An alternative view is that human beings reflect and conceptualize. We invent conceptualizations, just like we invent stories to make sense about our experiences. That is a creative process, not a conversion process. It is a creation process and in any creative process the key is discipline. People who are not schooled in the creative arts think that artists just go out and make things up. Well, they do at one level, but they do it after years and years of discipline and training and rigor in their thinking. The movement from the tacit to the explicit can be called the conceptualizing process. And, it requires a set of disciplines that most people in organizations lack. It is the meat and potatoes of system dynamics, the approach to understanding complex human systems that has been developing for forty years at MIT and elsewhere. It is how you go from the tacit knowledge of the people in a system to a meaningful conceptualization of how that system is currently working. It involves metaphors. It involves story telling. But primarily it involves theory creation.

Daniel Kim has said, "I wonder if 20 years from now, we will be able to talk about managers as researchers." When people start to recognize that moving from tacit knowledge to explicit knowledge involves theory building, it opens up a whole new territory called managerial theory building. Managers cannot off-load that on somebody else. I think consultants and academic researchers can help, but I think it is something that will prove to be an essential task for management. Theory building means enabling reflection and conceptualization on the part of people living in a complex human system. This theory may be about particular processes like product development or distribution, or it may be what more overarching matters, like what Drucker has called "the theory of the business." But the important point is that the theory is grounded in people's experience and that it is continually being tested against that experience. For me, Nonaka and Takeuchi's framework opens up these sorts of issues; these are issues I had not thought about when the original article "The Leader's New Work" was written.

Last, there are a host of practical concerns about what it means to lead in developing a learning organization omitted from the article. For example, a valid criticism that has been leveled against organizational learning is that is difficult to track one's progress in becoming a learning organization. One of the things that a lot of people like to create these days are instruments. There are lots of instruments for assessing your abilities as a learning organization. Every week, I bump into somebody with a new instrument. I think they might be useful, but I am very skeptical. We have a major research initiative that we created last year called "the assessment initiative." The question we are tackling is "How do we assess learning?" That is another way of saying "How do we really learn about learning?" Assessment is an inherent part of the learning process. No one can learn anything, anywhere, at anytime if they cannot see how they are progressing. How can a child learn to walk if they cannot turn 3 steps into 9 steps? Obviously, assessing is an integral and absolutely inseparable from learning. Assessing involves interpreting where we are now, judging what is working and not working, and conceiving of ways to improve. Assessing for learning is critical, and it might turn out to be a key leverage point in accelerating learning processes. That is why it is a major SoL research initiative.

However, there is a different way the word assessment is used that is very problematic. It is also used in the sense of assessing for evaluation. Outsiders looking at the assessment instruments say, "How do we know they're getting anything done?" That is a different set of questions. There is no aim at learning; the aim is to evaluate. I am not saying evaluation is bad. It is a perfectly understandable, very honest, and very appropriate question. However, it is real important to distinguish the two aims, assessing for learning versus assessing for evaluating. The problem is, everyone is busy assessing for evaluating and very few are assessing for learning. Because of this, most of the instruments are only marginally useful. Some of them are helpful for assessing learning. But most are just about evaluating; they are not actually accelerating the learning process. Yet, assessing is crucial; if you are not assessing for learning, you are not learning.

But, these important omissions not withstanding, I feel that there were some important core ideas in *The Leaders New Work*. In particular, for leaders of all sorts to attend to the challenges of design and stewarding seems as important to me today as it was ten years ago—especially for executive leaders caught up in the pressures to attend to short-term performance and neglect long-term health. This has been illustrated powerfully by the experiences of Shell Oil, a SoL member for many years. Starting around 1994, Shell's executives, with the leadership of CEO Phil Carroll, began fundamental rethinking of the firm's purpose and governance philosophy. This resulted in shifting from a traditional, centrally controlled, hierarchical, bureaucratic corporation to four highly autonomous profit and loss businesses corresponding to exploration and production; marketing, distribution, and sales; chemicals; and services. Starting in 1995, each business has its own internal board and full financial statement. In the early 1990s the company was under financial stress; by 1997 it had record profits and an exciting new array of business opportunities brought about by a network of over 30 strategic alliances. During this time, Phil and many of the other top managers became role models. Phil never slammed his fist on the table and said, "you have to change." He just kept saying, "we have to change." He focused on stewardship with his own team and their credibility, and his own behavior. Shortly before he retired, he reflected "You have to start, in the first place, with yourself. Every process of transformation is a series of individual learnings and decisions by people. It has to start with personal change. The abstraction of corporate change is a result, not a method."

3

Developing a Knowledge Strategy: From Management to Leadership

David J. Skyrme

Knowledge management has moved rapidly beyond the stage of a fad. This chapter reviews why this is so, and shows how knowledge can be used as a lever of business strategy. Knowledge-enhanced business strategies are built on two broad thrusts—managing what you already know and innovation, the creation and commercialization of new knowledge. Seven strategic knowledge levers are used to achieve business benefits. They include exploiting knowledge in people, products and processes. Critical success factors for knowledge initiatives are outlined. A crucial one of these is the need to shift from a management (custodial) view of knowledge to one that is dynamic and innovative. Thus, our sights should be on knowledge leadership rather than merely knowledge management.

Fad or Fundamental?

Knowledge management has established itself as a key part of many organization's knowledge strategy. From being considered something of a fad in 1995–1996, it impinged on the consciousness of many business leaders in 1997–1998. Numerous books have appeared since the seminal book by Nonaka and Takeuchi, *The Knowledge Creating Company*, published in 1995.[1] Some of the more recently published and popular titles are Tom Stewart's *Intellectual Capital*,[2] Debra Amidon's *The Ken Awakening*,[3] and Karl Erik Sveiby's *The New Organizational Wealth*.[4] Butterworth-Heinemann has also launched a series—Resources for the Knowledge-based Economy.[5] The general management press has regular features on knowledge management and there are several business conferences each month, some now focusing on specific industries or professions. Clearly, knowledge is a "hot topic." But will it be a temporary fad, or is it something more fundamental?

Management interest in knowledge is not new. Peter Drucker is credited with coining the phrase knowledge worker in the 1960s, and has written about it extensively in his various books over the succeeding decades.[6] Sveiby, Nonaka, Stata, and Seely Brown, among others, were articulating the role of knowledge in creating strategic advantage during the late 1980s and early 1990s. At the time, though, few senior executives in the West took their work seriously. Perhaps they were too busy downsizing and unwittingly losing some crucial knowledge to take notice! Among the reasons that interest has heightened in the last few years are the following:

• The growing recognition that knowledge and other forms of "intellectual capital" are the hidden assets in a company. They do not appear on the balance sheet in annual reports, yet they underpin value creation and future earnings potential. Knowledge intensive companies, like Microsoft and Glaxo Wellcome, have market values at least 10 times the value of their physical assets.

• A growing number of cases where better understanding and management of knowledge has brought demonstrable bottom line benefits. For example, Texas Instruments has saved the cost of a new semiconductor plant by sharing best practice, while BP has reduced the time to bring a new oil well on stream through sharing learning across oil fields.

• Improved collaborative technologies that enhance person-to-person communications, thus helping the development of knowledge across organizational and geographies boundaries. Groupware such as Lotus Notes and the widespread adoption of intranets have helped this process.

• The realization that initiatives such as Business Process Reengineering only go so far; the search for the Holy Grail of management success continues, and knowledge was next in line, boosted by the active encouragement of the large major consultancy firms.

Alongside these developments, the knowledge movement exhibits many characteristics of a fad. New magazines and journals devoted to knowledge have been launched.[7] Vendors of various tools, especially information retrieval and document management software, have been rebadged and promoted as knowledge management tools, even if there has been no significant change in the product. Conferences that previously went under the banner of information management have now become knowledge management conferences. This hype has raised the profile of knowledge and attracted management attention.

Beneath the fad, however, are fundamental approaches to better management of organizational resources, of which knowledge is arguably the most important. It is human knowledge that develops new products, comes up with creative marketing campaigns, discerns customers wants and develops special relationships with suppliers and business partners. If you delve beneath the fad, you will find good examples of organizational learning, business transformation, better innovation processes, accounting for intangible assets, information management and knowledge-based computer systems. All are different roots of today's knowledge management. Virtually every organization has good examples of knowledge management practice, even if they are called something different. What a focus on knowledge offers is a unifying perspective that helps people from different branches of knowledge management connect, explore their common roots and develop a common language for sharing their experiences.

The Knowledge Advantage

The chairmen and chief executives of many organizations refer to "people as our greatest asset" in their annual report. Certainly, the salary bill in many organizations is a relatively high proportion of fixed costs, although the way that many companies actually treat their employees reveals the shallowness of such statements. However, ask any senior executive what the key success factors are for their organization's future prosperity and you will find that knowledge and people feature in many of them—knowledge of customers, knowledge of markets, people who can strike venture alliance deals, experts in specific technologies, etc.

By exploiting this knowledge, organizations can achieve a range of benefits:

• Avoidance of costly mistakes—The experience of organizations losing knowledge as they have downsized or restructured has made them more aware of the costs of "reinventing the wheel," General Motors uses debriefing sessions to share lessons more widely through the company.
• Sharing of best practices—Companies like Amoco save millions of dollars a year by taking the knowledge from their best performers and applying it in similar situations elsewhere.
• Faster problem solving—By using videoconferencing at offshore oil platforms, BP can tap into expertise elsewhere in the company and minimize production downtime when problems occur.

• Faster development times—By developing learning networks and learning from similar past situations, companies like Schlumberger improve their rate of innovation.

• Better customer solutions—By feeding customer problems into their computer network, sales and support staff at Buckman Laboratories gain access to expertise throughout their organization in developing innovative customer solutions.

• Gaining new business—Consultants at ICL can access and combine the best available knowledge quickly and bid on proposals that would otherwise be too costly or slow to assemble.

• Improved customer service—By putting solutions to customer problems in a shareable knowledge base, companies such as Sun improved the level of customer service. Customers can also download software patches over the Internet.

These examples demonstrate the benefits that can be achieved by integrating the knowledge dimension into business strategies and core processes.

What strategies are companies adopting to create future wealth and maximize the returns on these knowledge assets? Our research finds that strategies are based on two broad thrusts and seven specific levers.

Two Thrusts of Strategy

This thrust focuses on making known and accessible knowledge that already exists, for example, by sharing best practices. This thrust is best paraphrased as, "if only we knew what we knew." Too frequently, people in one part of an organization reinvent the wheel or fail to solve customer problems because the knowledge they need is elsewhere in the company but not known or accessible to them. Has your organization ever purchased expensive research for knowledge it already had? In one case, a department of AT&T spent $79,449 to glean information that could be found in a publicly available Bell Corporation Technical Information Document, priced $13![8] Has your customer service department spent long hours figuring out how to deal with a problem, when another department has the solution at its fingertips? The list of underutilized knowledge in most organizations is endless. Hence, the first knowledge management initiative of many companies (between a third and a half according to surveys) is that of installing or improving an intranet. Some of the early content created on these intranets are "expert directories," databases of best practice and catalogues of various information resources.

Best practice knowledge sharing often emanates from quality programs. It is not unusual to find in globally dispersed organizations factors of three to one difference in performance between the performance between the best and worse performers for a specific business or industrial process. By sharing the knowledge of the best performers with other parts of the business, the overall performance can be improved. Texas Instruments TI-BEST program was the result of a quality initiative, in which excellence was defined for each main process. A combination of expert facilitators, best practice databases and an office of best practice, helped plant managers and staff scattered around TI's world-wide manufacturing plants connect with each other, swap experiences and visit exemplars of best practice. As a result, this sharing of existing knowledge saved TI from having to invest in a further semiconductor fabrication plant to cope with increased demand. The net result was an initial saving of a $500 million outlay.[9]

The second major thrust of knowledge focused strategies is that of innovation, the creation of new knowledge and commercializing it as valuable products and services. This is sometimes referred to as knowledge innovation.[3] Many managers mistakenly believe this is about R&D and creativity. Our research has generally found no shortage of creativity in organizations. The real challenge is to convert ideas into products and services or improved business processes, doing it faster and better than competitors. Unfortunately, many organizations operate regimes that create despair and frustration among creative people. For example, a frequent comment by our interviewees is, "the system stifles me; after hitting your head against a brick wall several times, you don't bother to make suggestions."

In contrast, 3M is a company renowned for its innovativeness. A corporate goal of deriving 40 per cent of revenues from products less than five years old helps create the right motivation. It backs "people more than projects" and gives them 15 percent of their time to experiment on their own ideas. It tolerates a certain amount of mistakes, since these can give valuable insights and provide opportunities for learning. 3M provides a climate where innovation can thrive.

However, an organization's innovation processes must not lose potentially good ideas. What happens to the 90 percent or so that is filtered out in a typical development process as unsuitable, unworkable, or otherwise inappropriate? Schlumberger addresses this potential knowledge loss by capturing them in an idea bank. Alongside is a database of client needs and problems. These two pools of knowledge are constantly updated and compared. Today's ideas that are not commercially viable may prove to be just the ticket a few years later when new customer needs and technologies emerge.

This second thrust of knowledge strategy is the most difficult, yet ultimately has the best potential for improved company performance. We are not talking here of incremental improvements of 5 to 10 per cent year on year, which is typical of the level that might result from sharing best practice. With this thrust, companies can achieve breakthroughs in product or process performance of factors of 10 or more. Innovation has made knowledge-based companies like Amazon.com and Formula One racing worth millions of dollars in just a few years.

Seven Strategic Levers

There are seven levers that organizations commonly use to exploit knowledge (table 3.1). The main ones are knowledge in people, products and processes.

• Customer Knowledge. In virtually every survey, customer knowledge tops the list as an organization's most vital knowledge. Customers can provide valuable insight into the use of products and can help a supplier clarify unmet needs. Many organizations do not integrate their various sources of customer knowledge. Information received about problems on customer support lines is not fed back to developers. Sales representatives do not systematically capture customer feedback that is of no immediate relevance to the sale in hand. In contrast, Steelcase opens customer knowledge channels by talking to customer's customers, the ultimate end-users of their office furniture. It uses video ethnography to understand how their products are used and can be redesigned to improve the effectiveness of knowledge work. As a result it has created award winning office modules, that although premium priced (in excess of $10,000 per work setting) quickly recoups its investment through much higher knowledge worker productivity.

• Knowledge in People. Knowledge in people's heads is often more valuable than that encapsulated in databases. The skills and experience of employees need to be continually tapped. "Learning Organization" pro-grams are one way of nurturing and applying under-utilized talent. At Anglian Water, executives reaching retirement share their experience with colleagues and deposit some of their knowledge before they leave through videotaped interviews and contributions to knowledge bases. Other companies use learning networks and knowledge share fairs, as a better way to diffuse personal knowledge throughout an organization.

• Knowledge in Products. "Intelligent" or "smart" products can com-mand premium prices and be more beneficial to users, as is information that surrounds products. One example is the "intelligent" oil drill that bends and weaves its way to extract more oil than ever from the pockets of oil in underground formations. Another is the integration of various information and knowledge sources—the state of crop growth from satellite photographs, the effect of chemicals, near-term weather condi-tions—to determine the precise doses of agrochemical to apply to fields of crops. The same result can be achieved with 40 per cent less fertilizer than is normal. Campbell's "Intelligent Quisine" is an example of how knowledge of the customer, in this case an individual, can provide cus-tomized products that can command premium prices.

• Knowledge in Processes. Business processes in many companies hinder customer service. They often represent an idealized way of doing busi-ness at a historic point in time. Applying processes to meet current needs often involve "work arounds" and seeking advice from business experts. CIGNA, when it reengineered its business processes for underwriting insurance risk, captured the knowledge of its best experts and embedded it as hints and help files in the computer workflow program. In addition, contact details of experts allow users to access their latest thinking.

• Organizational Memory. This lever helps the process of identifying "knowing what we know." Computer databases on intranets are a com-mon form of organizational memory, but many suffer though lack of organization or ease of navigation. In addition, much organizational memory is embedded in procedures, business systems and (not surpris-ingly) people's heads. Sifting, indexing and cataloguing are all useful means of making this lever work. Organizations like PriceWaterhouse-Coopers have found that a thesaurus—a structured catalogue of knowl-edge—helps to link knowledge from different parts of the business that may be expressed in different terminology. Knowledge centers also act as hubs for knowledge flows, connecting those seeking knowledge to those databases or people best equipped to provide it.

• Knowledge in Relationships. Frequently overlooked is the depth of personal knowledge in relationships. Two people who have worked together for a long time instinctively know the another's approach and

Table 3.1
Seven Knowledge Levers

Lever	Key activities	Example
Customer knowledge	Developing deep knowledge sharing relationships. Understanding the needs of your customers' customers. Articulating unmet needs. Identifying new opportunities.	Steelcase, an office product manufacturer, has totally redefined its market into knowledge worker productivity through opening a customer knowledge channel from its product end-users into its R&D.
Knowledge in people	Knowledge sharing fairs. Innovation workshops. Expert and learning networks. Communities of Practice.	Alongside various knowledge initiatives, Anglian Water has a Learning Organization program and corporate university. It encourages individuals and teams to develop their knowledge continually, through formal development programs.
Knowledge in products and services	Knowledge embedded in products. Surround products with knowledge, e.g., in user guides, and enhanced knowledge-intensive services.	Campbell Soup's "Intelligent Quisine" (IQ) delivers weekly packages of nutritionally designed, portion controlled meals to those suffering hypertension or high cholesterol.
Knowledge in processes	Embedding knowledge into business processes and management decision making.	CIGNA makes its best underwriting knowledge available as guidance screens in computerized underwriting processes. This helped turn a loss into a profit.

Table 3.1
(continued)

Lever	Key activities	Example
Organizational memory	Knowledge sharing. Best practice databases. Directories of expertise. Online documents, procedures and discussion forums. Intranets.	PriceWaterhouseCoopers is typical of several consultancies that have knowledge databases to allow sharing of knowledge. It also has knowledge centers, hubs where human analysts and navigators link consultants to knowledge. This helps them deliver better advice to their clients.
Knowledge in Relationships	Improving knowledge flows between suppliers, employees, shareholders, community, etc.—using this knowledge to inform key strategies.	Toshiba collects comparative data on suppliers ranking 200 quantitative and qualitative factors. It has an active suppliers network and association where knowledge is shared and suppliers are integrated into future strategies.
Knowledge assets	Identifying intellectual and knowledge assets. Measuring and monitoring their development.	Dow Chemical Intellectual Assets Management team takes an active role in managing patents and other intellectual assets in order to develop their value. It has generated over $125 million in additional revenues from this activity.

what needs to be expressed and what can be taken for granted. With frequent restructuring, this knowledge is easily lost. With the growing need for collaboration with customers, suppliers, and many other business partners, companies need to capture some of this knowledge and provide forums where these relationships can be strengthened. Toshiba has both formal and informal approaches. Databases hold key information on suppliers and their performance, but much more comes out of its active supplier networks where future plans and strategies are discussed and other knowledge shared.

• Knowledge Assets. The growing discrepancy between market and book value in many knowledge-intensive companies means that traditional financial accounting methods are failing to capture details of these assets. Applying the principle "what get measured get managed," many companies are instituting more formal systems to capture information about their intangible assets or intellectual capital—commonly divided into human assets (skills, knowledge and experience), organizational capital (systems, process, databases), customer assets (number, quality and depth of relationship) and intellectual property (patents, copyright, trademarks, etc.). Dow Chemical's intellectual asset management program initially focused on patents. It created an inventory of them and analyzed how well they were being exploited. Through licensing, sale or simply not paying retention fees, over $125 million in additional revenues has been generated. Other companies look at their internally held information bases and see how they can be sold as information products in the open market. Skandia is at the forefront of reporting its intellectual capital measures publicly. It produces twice yearly intellectual capital supplements to its company reports and accounts.[10]

These are not the only ways that companies are creating strategic advantage through knowledge but gives an idea of how effort can be focused to good effect. The levers are not mutually exclusive. In practice, many knowledge programs concentrate on just two or three.

Knowledge Management in Practice

A consistent thread through the levers of strategy is that different types of knowledge are involved. Many writers and academics give elaborate definitions of the differences between data, information, and knowledge alongside even higher order concepts like intelligence and wisdom. Other categorizations distinguish declarative or procedural knowledge, and factual or systemic knowledge. In business practice, such distinctions, while intellectually interesting, are peripheral. The most relevant distinction is that between explicit and tacit knowledge. Explicit knowledge is that which is codified, written down, held as a computer record or expressed in some other tangible form. This can also be construed as its embodiment in information. Implicit knowledge, according to a widely recognized definition by Nonaka and Takeuchi, is that which "is highly personal and hard to formalize. Subjective insights, intuitions and hunches fall into this category of knowledge...."[1]

Explicit knowledge has the advantage that it is easily reproducible and therefore easily disseminated around the organization. However, it then has to be internalized by individuals and applied in specific contexts. Tacit knowledge is less diffusable and either needs converting as far as possible into explicit knowledge or transferring through mechanisms like observation, personal communications, on-the-job learning and so on. Its very intangibility makes its management a challenge.

The knowledge management challenge is two fold, depending on the type of knowledge involved. For explicit knowledge, it involves a systematic approach to organizing information, making it available and disseminating it. Information Resources Management (IRM), which is outlined later, is an effective way to do this. The approach is systematic, lends itself to computerization and appeals to technologists. The trickier challenge is how to manage tacit knowledge. Knowledge management in this sense could be considered an oxymoron, since you cannot really manage personal knowledge as organizational knowledge. This knowledge is in people's heads and "people walk," leave the organization and take their knowledge with them. The two complementary knowledge management approaches to deal with tacit knowledge are:

1. Converting it to a more explicit form—in documents, processes, databases, etc. This is often referred to as "decanting the human capital into the structural capital of an organization." This is the main emphasis of many European and US knowledge programs.

2. Enhancing tacit knowledge flow through better human interaction, such that knowledge is diffused around the organization and not held in the heads of a few. In Japan, various "socialization" activities support this kind of knowledge flow that by its very nature also sparks the generation of new ideas and knowledge. Add some basic elements of good human resource management, including a stimulating environment, personal development plans, motivation and suitable reward and recognition systems (such as knowledge sharing awards and stock options), then there is less chance of your best knowledge workers wanting to leave.

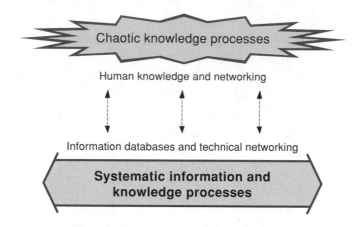

Figure 3.1
Different knowledge management challenges

It is the handling of this second area by which most knowledge management programs will succeed or fail. Many tacit knowledge activities are serendipitous in nature—the winning business idea that was drawn up on the back of a napkin during conversation over dinner, or the casual encounter at the coffee machine that sparked off a new fruitful line of enquiry. Organizations must therefore create conditions in which such tacit knowledge activities can more easily occur. They need to understand better what motivates their knowledge workers, and pay attention to developing the most suitable organizational settings and mechanisms.

Most traditional office buildings significantly hamper knowledge sharing—enclosed manager's offices, a stifling ambience, few opportunities to interact informally. In contrast, places like Skandia's Future Centre in Vaxholm, or British Airways new office complex at Waterside near Heathrow (also designed by a Scandinavian Architect) are designed to create environments where knowledge sharing is more natural.[11]

So far in this chapter, I have avoided defining the term knowledge management. Rather like culture, knowledge management has many definitions, depending on the perspective of the writer. Here is one that was derived following research into knowledge management best practice for Creating the Knowledge-based Business:[10] "Knowledge Management is the explicit and systematic management of vital knowledge—and its associated processes of creation, organization, diffusion, use and exploitation."

• Explicit: knowledge is explicitly recognized as a corporate asset and reflected in its language, documents, business strategies and plans;
• Systematic: its management is too important to be left to chance or ad-hoc opportunities
• Vital: there's lots of knowledge around; organizations only have time to focus on that which is most important;
• Content and process perspective (nouns and verbs): there are organizational processes that can enhance the value of knowledge by making it more easily accessible and making it available at the right place in the right format at the right time.

More important than definitions is what organizations are actually doing to maximize the potential of their knowledge resources. Typical projects found within organizational knowledge initiatives include:

• Creation of knowledge databases—best practices, expert directories, market intelligence, etc.
• Active process management—of knowledge gathering, classifying, storing, etc.
• Development of knowledge centers—focal points for knowledge skills and facilitating knowledge flow.
• Nurturing of Communities of Practice—these are networks of individuals with common interests who informally share knowledge; such knowledge webs often transcend organizational boundaries and draw in external experts.
• Introduction of collaborative technologies—intranets or groupware for rapid information access
• The appointment of a Chief Knowledge Officer, or somebody at senior level, with specific responsibility to initiate new knowledge practices within the organization and to develop knowledge sharing and innovation infrastructures.

Today there are many examples of such initiatives, but many, like BPR and introduction of IT systems before them, are heading for failure. At the heart of success is the integration of both "hard" (technological) and "soft" (human and organizational) knowledge infrastructures.

Technology Enhanced Knowledge Infrastructure
One of the practical problems of developing knowledge strategies or adding a knowledge dimension to other strategies is the complex nature of knowledge. As we now know from many disappointing artificial intelligence initiatives of the 1970s, you cannot easily package knowledge

into a black box and have it perform miracles. A potentially worrying trend about today's knowledge management movement is that IT managers, information professionals and software suppliers are jumping on the bandwagon and merely substituting the word "knowledge" for "information." That is not to say that information is unimportant, since a good IT infrastructure, good information resources management (as practiced by librarians) and effective information solutions, such as data mining, decision support tools, document management and groupware, are essential foundations. Three aspects of "hard" infrastructure worthy of specific attention are information resources management, knowledge bases and collaborative technologies.

Information Resources Management (IRM)

This element of hard infrastructure puts the focus on the I in IT—information. There is a well-developed discipline of information resources management (IRM), but in practice it is woefully used in many companies. IRM deals with processes for nurturing information as an asset:[12]

• Identification. Information and knowledge needed in key business and decision processes are identified. Key internal and external sources are validated.
• Gathering. Based on needs, a proactive approach is used to collect vital information, rather than relying on simply collecting that which is easier to obtain.
• Classifying. This is a traditional librarian skill. Few search engines can access information as efficiently as an information specialist using well-organized database.
• Dissemination. These are processes to make information readily available, either by "pull" from online databases or by "push" (e.g., via electronic mail) to those whose interest profiles suggest it will be useful.
• Verification and Quality. An effective information resource is one where information is validated and qualified. Feedback from users on relevance is used to maintain information quality. Outdated information is archived.

Some of the most effective knowledge programs have a knowledge center that combines business experts with information specialists. These centers act as a focal point for knowledge flow and for the application of IRM.

Creating Knowledge Bases

As noted earlier, the encapsulation of knowledge into databases, is effectively putting it into information format. This leads to another oxymoron: a "knowledge base," which is really a database about knowledge. Database formats have the obvious advantages of transmittability, ease of access, and speed of dissemination. However, they filter out some of the key ingredients that distinguish knowledge from information—contextual richness, the human cognitive dimension and tacit knowledge. Effective knowledge sharing therefore needs something beyond databases.

There are several ways in which conventional databases can be made more useful through addition of more "knowledge base" ingredients:

• Adding contextual information to individual entries. Where was this information used? What factors need to be considered when using it?

• Validating the quality of the information. Once information has been used, commentary should be added by users on its relevance, accuracy and helpfulness.

• Using standard templates and formats. Familiarity with layout, and knowing where exactly to seek specific information speeds up access.

• Providing clear navigation aids. At any time users should have a good feel of where they are in knowledge space, and be able to navigate quickly to areas of interest.

• Using a thesaurus of terms, such that retrieval queries made using one term automatically embrace other terms.

• User oriented information provision. Too frequently information on intranets is organized from the provider's perspective, such as by department or responsibility. A user-centric view would organize information by situation or problem. For example, Siemens has an engineering problem database, which the user accesses via a hierarchical problem tree.

• Giving details of originator. Users can contact contributors directly, e.g., via email hypertext links or "click for conversation" icons that automatically dial the contributor's telephone.

• Offering an experts database with pointers to people and information on the location of experts and expertise, rather than the expertise itself.

• Addition of multimedia material, e.g., a visual demonstration of an entry, such as a team at work. BP uses video clips to illustrate oilrig practice and for interviews with experts.

The best "knowledge bases" add a human element, usually in the form of a database helper, such as an information adviser at a knowledge center. These advisers are the personal interface between the user and the database. They dialogue with their clients in a consultancy and advisory mode. A good knowledge center adviser will understand the context of the enquiry: the nature of the business, the work of the client, and their evolving needs and personal styles. They will also have a good knowledge of source, and of their quality and relevance. Their own personal networks means that they can act as pivotal links between people with queries and others who might have the solution. Such individuals are often the key links in an organization's vital "web of knowledge."

Collaborative Technologies

Our ongoing research into a wide range of knowledge tools and technologies continues to show that it is collaborative technologies that have the most impact on developing a successful organizational knowledge program.[13] These technologies connect people to information, but more importantly people to people, on a global basis. The commonly used technologies in this category are:

Internet/intranet   Installing an intranet is often the first activity of knowledge program. It makes it easy for users to access "any information, any where, at any time." Booz Allen and Hamilton's Knowledge Online is an intranet that provides a wealth of information (e.g., best practice, industry trends, database of experts) to their consultants worldwide. Through active information management by knowledge editors (subject experts and librarians) the information remains well structured and relevant. Remember too, that the Internet today is more than simply Web information pages. It includes email discussion lists, multimedia presentations and Web conferencing (like a bulletin board), all-important tools for knowledge development and exchange.

Groupware/Lotus Notes   Groupware products like Lotus Notes offer several features over and above intranets, although the two are converging. They provide discussion databases, different levels of security (especially useful for remote access by mobile workers). Users such as Thomas Miller & Co., a London-based manager of insurance mutual companies, access their "organizational memory" as well as current news feeds in areas of interest, through one of Lotus Notes's key features, its multiple "views." Thus, they can view information by geographic area, name of client, industry, type of risk, topic, etc., according to the task in hand.

Videoconferencing   The development of desk-top videoconferencing makes it practicable for dispersed knowledge workers to have a face-to-face conversation over a telecommunications link, while at the same time viewing and even manipulating computer held information. At BP, desk-top videoconferencing has helped achieve better communication and higher levels of trust. Many problems at off-shore oil fields can now be solved without resorting to jumping into the next available helicopter as was formerly the case.

The benefits of these technologies are well known, for example, asynchronous as well as synchronous communications, access to the most current information, recording of information, access to expertise, even when the existence of the expert is not previously known, etc. The value of such mechanisms increases if there is a continual process of knowledge editing and refining. Elements of transient conversation are reviewed for ongoing relevance, synthesized, and sometimes rewritten, for example, into more formal thought pieces or best practice databases. This can be done either by subject matter experts, as part of their knowledge-sharing role, or by abstractors especially skilled at doing this. Although stored messages and discussion might remain anyway as part of organizational memory, the editing process makes the knowledge available in a more understandable format, without all the iterations that occurred during its development.

Despite ever increasing functionally in collaborative technologies, organizations frequently do not get the benefits they anticipate from collaborative technologies. They fail to give due attention to people and organizational processes—the elements of "soft infrastructure."

The Human Dimension
A common problem in most knowledge management programs is that individuals do not share their knowledge, a problem that is compounded when people work virtually over a globally distributed network. Most organizations need a change of culture. There is no quick fix. They need

to apply levers of organizational change over a period of time, including:

• Leadership by example. Bob Buckman, when CEO of Buckman Laboratories, actively participated in computer forums to help sales people on the front-line, and he expected his managers to do the same!

• Knowledge sharing events. These bring people together in exhibition and workshop settings, so that they can share their expertise. Often face-to-face contact is an important prerequisite to effective computer knowledge networking.

• Embedding learning into every day processes. This includes building in reflection time at meetings and writing down feelings and experiences in learning diaries. Larger projects will have post-project reviews where lessons are drawn from a semi-structured process involving a wide range of participants. This learning is codified and becomes part of the organization's formal "lessons learned" knowledge base.

• Active moderation of online discussions. Many discussion databases are limited in usefulness because they do not have critical mass or because certain contributors, sometimes unwittingly, discourage dialogue. Active moderators will post items gained elsewhere, and work behind the scenes to encourage contributions and to moderate online behavior.

• Reward systems. Many companies do not reward people for sharing information. Management consultancies now include people's contribution to their knowledge bases as part of their performance and salary review.

A complementary approach is to draw people together in "communities of practice." Electronic communities are well known on the Internet, in the form of newsgroups, discussion lists, etc. In the organizational context, such communities have a sharper purpose and more is at stake. Their purpose may be mutual learning of new techniques, sharing best practice or a shared goal on a project or corporate program. Companies like Shell actively nurture these communities, and blend online activities with embedding learning methods into regular work practice.

Creating Successful Knowledge Strategies

A comparison of leaders and laggards in exploiting knowledge strategies reveals some interesting contrasts.[14] From these, and further discussions with and observations of leaders, seven recurring success factors have been derived. These are listed below, along with some pertinent questions to gauge to what extent your organization is addressing them.

1   There are clear and explicit links to business strategy.   This does not mean that investment justification has been made in financial terms of return on investment. In fact, many leading companies invest in knowledge management before they fully understand the business benefits. What it does mean is that they can articulate the contribution of knowledge to their business objectives. When considering your business strategy ask these questions. Is the knowledge strategy something separate or is it simply another layer or view of existing business strategy? How does knowledge or know-how add value to your business strategy? Conversely, what exploitable knowledge products, processes or expertise emanate from your business strategy?

2   Be knowledgeable about knowledge.   There is a real understanding of the knowledge advantage and of the concepts of knowledge (e.g., tacit and explicit), its organizational processes, of how other organizations are tackling knowledge management. How much is knowledge discussed in your organization? How well is it understood? Where are the experts on knowledge management? Is the knowledge dimension a key element of every product plan, marketing plan, strategic initiative, annual budget, and personal development plan?

3   A compelling vision and architecture drives the knowledge agenda. Often this simple visual framework is easily understood and communicated. It portrays the role of knowledge in an organization's success and it depicts the key activities and responsibilities for its management. Is the knowledge facet of your business well articulated? Is there a coherent framework that guides management decisions? Would an investor give you millions of dollars to exploit your intangible ideas?

4   Information and knowledge processes are both systematic and chaotic. Information is managed as a resource, using the discipline of information resources management (IRM). On the other hand, the environments and organization processes are in place to encourage knowledge sharing. Do you have systematic processes for capturing knowledge (both external and internal), organizing it, and sharing it throughout your organization? Do you have processes that enhance knowledge creation and innovation? Do you run share fairs that bring users and providers of knowledge together in informal ways? Is time left at the end of meetings for reflection and review, such that learning is gathered? Does your office environment have more than 75% shared space—open areas, meeting rooms, etc? Do you have policies and procedures to protect your knowledge assets?

5   A well-developed technological infrastructure ('hard').   The technological infrastructure provides a wide range of information and person-to-person collaboration facilities such as computer conferencing, videoconferencing and document management. It also provides effective information retrieval tools as well as opportunities to experiment with emergent technologies such as intelligent agents, text summarizers and knowledge mapping tools. Are people and information readily accessible through your computer and communications networks anywhere in the world, 24-hours a day, 365 days a year? Do these networks extend outside the organization—to customers, suppliers, and world-class experts? Can you find what or who you want quickly and efficiently?

6   A knowledge enriching culture.   This is one that encourages knowledge sharing, learning, experimentation and innovation. Time is allowed, even encouraged, for individuals and teams to step back from day-to-day frenetic activity to reflect and think. Are mistakes viewed as learning opportunities or harshly punished? Are your organization structures flexible and adaptive? Are your personnel systems geared to recognizing and rewarding individual and team knowledge contributions?

7   Knowledge leadership and champions.   There are knowledge leaders throughout the organization. Top management is supportive of, or even better actively promotes, the knowledge agenda. There are individuals, such as CKOs (Chief Knowledge Officers), who have specific responsibility for enhancing corporate strategy through better application and management of knowledge. Is knowledge enthusiastically talked about throughout your business? Is there an obvious network of knowledge practitioner—a community of knowledge practice? Does your CEO visibly reiterate the importance of your organizational knowledge to your business success?

One factor, not yet at the critical stage, but whose importance is increasing is that of intellectual capital measurement. As noted earlier, many existing financial and other performance measures do not help an organization understand its knowledge contribution or focus on its management. Forward-looking organizations are recognizing the need to measure more systematically the contribution of knowledge. Intangible assets are categorized and monitored. Knowledge flows are mapped. As well as the balanced business scorecard, that adds nonfinancial measures alongside financial ones, there are a number of new measurement systems specifically focused on knowledge and intellectual capital measurement. These include Skandia's Navigator, Karl Erik Sveiby's Intangible Assets Monitor, Philip M'Pherson's Inclusive Valuation Methodology (IVMTM), and Intellectual Capital Services IC IndexTM.[15]

From Management to Leadership

It was questioned earlier whether knowledge management was a fad. Although the hype and relabeling of other activities has many elements of a passing fad, the discussion in this chapter suggests that the underlying disciplines and methods represent sound management practice for intangibles like knowledge on which the future prosperity of an organization largely depends. However, the term knowledge management is something of an oxymoron, especially when knowledge in people's heads is concerned. The word *management* suggests custodianship, even control, and a concentration on managing resources that already exist. A better term is knowledge leadership. In contrast to management, "leadership" is about constant development and innovation—of information resources, of individual skills (an important part of the knowledge resource) and of knowledge and learning networks. It embraces both the sharing of what is known, and innovation—the two thrusts of a knowledge-enhanced strategy.

Conclusion

This chapter has discussed the crucial role of knowledge as an element of business strategy. Seven specific levers of strategy have been identified, and illustrated with examples of good practice. Effective knowledge management requires attention to both explicit and tacit knowledge, to both hard (technology) and soft (people and processes) infrastructures. A common pitfall is to fall into the trap of viewing knowledge management as primarily a technological solution with a focus on information.

Organizations must take a wider perspective of the role of knowledge. They need to manage information as an important resource, something that few are doing well. However, an organization's most valuable knowledge is human expertise and the processes by which it is shared and enhanced. This is at the heart of creating value through new products and services and enhanced business processes. It needs a knowledge sharing culture that encourages the free flow of knowledge, open dialogue across organizational boundaries, and the nurturing of knowledge networks. It is the integration of "hard" and "soft" that sets apart those organizations who have truly embraced knowledge as a key dimension of business strategy.

An even more important characteristic for future success will be a shift from knowledge management to knowledge leadership, where innovation and development takes precedence over sharing what you already know. Knowledge leadership provides a metaphor for the future that goes well beyond the immediate fad of knowledge management.

References

1. Nonaka, Ikujiro, and Takeuchi, Hirotaka, *The Knowledge Creating Company*, Oxford University Press (1995).

2. Stewart, Thomas A., *Intellectual Capital: The New Wealth of Organizations*, Doubleday (1997).

3. Amidon, Debra M., *Innovations Strategy for the Knowledge Economy: The Ken Awakening*, Butterworth-Heinemann (1997)

4. Sveiby, Karl-Erik, *The New Organizational Wealth: Managing and Measuring Intangible Assets*, Berrett Koehler (1997).

5. Books in the series include *Knowledge Management and Organizational Design*, ed. Paul S. Myers (1996); *Knowledge in Organizations*, ed. Laurence Prusak (19970; *Knowledge Management Tools*, ed. Rudy L. Ruggles III (1997); *The Strategic Management of Intellectual Capital*, ed. David A. Klein (1998).

6. Drucker, Peter F., *The Post Capitalist Society*, Butterworth-Heinemann (1993).

7. Examples include *Knowledge Inc., Knowledge Management, Knowledge Management review, KM World, Journal of Knowledge Management.*

8. Oppenheim, Charles, "Tangling with Intangibles," *Information World Review*

4 (December 1995), 54.

9. Johnson, Cindy, "Leveraging Knowledge for Organizational Excellence," *Journal of Knowledge Management* 1, no. 1 (September 1997): 50–56.

10. Full descriptions of many of the case examples cited can be found in David J. Skyrme and Debra M. Amidon, *Creating the Knowledge-based Business* (Business Intelligence, 1997).

11. "The Workplace Revolution," Special Supplement, *The Times*, 20 July 1998.

12. Willard, Nick, "Information Resources Management," *Aslib Information* 21, no. 5 (May 1993).

13. Wyllie, Jan, "Making Sense of Mind Tools," I3 UPDATE No. 17 at http://www.skyrme.com/updates/ (March 1998).

14. Skyrme, David and Amidon, Debra, "The Knowledge Agenda," *Journal of Knowledge Management* 1, no. 1 (September 1997): 27–37.

15. The various methods are described respectively in Leif Edvinsson and Michael Malone, *Intellectual Capital* (HarperBusiness, 1997); Karl Erik Sveiby, *The New Organizational Wealth: Managing and Measuring Intangible Assets* (Berrett Koehler, 1997); P. K. M'Pherson, "Accounting for the Value of Information," *Aslib Proceedings* 46, no. 9 (September 1994): 203–215; Johan Roos, Göran Roos, Leif Edvinsson, and Nicola Dragonetti, *Intellectual Capital: Navigating in the New Business Landscape*, (Macmillan, 1997). Comparisons, case studies and management guidelines will be found in David J. Skyrme, *Measuring the Value of Knowledge* (Business Intelligence, 1998).

4

Building Intangible Assets: A Strategic Framework for Investing in Intellectual Capital

Patricia Seemann, David De Long, Susan Stucky, and Edward Guthrie

An almost paralyzing conceptual confusion around the terms intellectual capital, knowledge management, and organizational learning threatens many strategic initiatives designed to build an organization's intangible assets. The purpose of this chapter is to put some structure around the enormous space now inhabited by the notion of managing intellectual capital. Drawing on nearly a decade of experience in the field, we will: (1) provide a practical model that defines and links the concepts of intellectual capital, knowledge management, and organizational learning; (2) present a strategic framework for deciding where and how to invest in intellectual capital; and (3) provide an overview of the principles for effectively implementing strategic knowledge initiatives.

The Executive's Challenge

There is growing recognition among executives today that intellectual capital, that is, the sum total of a firm's skills, knowledge and experience is critical to sustaining competitiveness, performance, and shareholder value. With equity market valuations of many companies today exceeding the book value of their assets many times over, investors and analysts are looking for more evidence of what firms are doing to secure and improve the performance of their "intangibles." Much of this market value derives from the knowledge assets, or intellectual capital, that underlie a firm's performance.

But many early attempts at developing and managing knowledge assets have been plagued by confusion and sometimes failure because of uncertainty about what intellectual capital and knowledge management are, and what approach must be used to effectively develop intangible assets.

For example, the CEO of an international pharmaceutical company declared three years ago that his firm needed to become a "learning organization." But he issued the directive without explaining how it related to the company's business strategy, what he expected the outcomes to be, or who would be responsible for leading the effort. A series of "cool" knowledge-related initiatives quickly sprung up, but they had no links to the business or common understanding of what was to be achieved. As a result, they quickly fizzled. Within a year, the concept of "knowledge management" had lost credibility and was being ridiculed throughout the company.

This is an example of the challenge that confronts executives today, who must not only grasp conceptually what constitutes their firm's intellectual capital, but also apply the leadership skills needed to innovate effectively in this area.

Elements of Intellectual Capital

To integrate the concept of intellectual capital into an organization's business strategy, executives need a definition of the concept that is clear, actionable, and comprehensive. We suggest that there are three elements of intellectual capital.[1]

Human capital is the knowledge, skills, and experiences possessed by individual employees. It comprises both explicit conceptual knowledge, such as how to create a budget, use an e-mail system, or execute a stock trade, as well as more tacit knowledge, such as how to negotiate a sale, write an advertisement, or interpret marketing data.

The purpose of managing human capital is to ensure that the business has the right mix of talent at the right time to implement the firm's corporate strategy. Human capital raises questions about the company's current level of individual skills compared to the competition. Where will the talent for the firm's five-year plan come from? How will management attract, retain, and develop these individuals?

"Structural capital" is basically everything that remains in a firm after it's employees go home. It includes the explicit, rule-based knowledge embedded in the organization's work processes and systems, or encoded in written policies, training documentation, or shared data bases of "best practices." It also includes intellectual property, recognized by patents and copyrights.

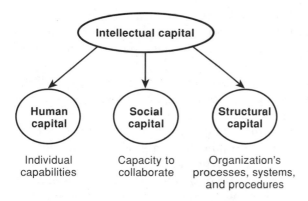

Figure 4.1
Key components of intellectual capital

Definitions of intellectual capital, however, have usually failed to account for a third critical resource. "*Social capital*" is reflected in the ability of groups to collaborate and work together and is a function of trust*. Effective networks of relationships characterized by high levels of trust are a valuable and often overlooked resource in the creation and use of knowledge.

Social capital is critical for three reasons.

1. *Reduces transaction costs.* Trust makes networks and work communities effective because in an environment of professional trust, decisions are reached more quickly and their execution is more readily relied upon. In other words, this element of intellectual capital increases the efficiency of action—within teams, as well as across hierarchical and organizational boundaries—and, thus, reduces transaction costs.[2] Trust is critical in facilitating the sharing and use of new knowledge. Thus, the importance of leadership is one factor that cannot be overemphasized in the successful management of intellectual capital because trust must start at the top with senior executives serving as role models.

2. *Produces higher quality knowledge.* People are more likely to rigorously debate and hone ideas when they trust each other than when they have doubts about each other.

In a U.S. pharmaceutical company, for example, low levels of social capital in drug development teams often kept groups from confronting problems in their research data. Instead, critical discussions took place "off-line" in the corridors, cafeteria, or by one-on-one emails. This meant these ideas never entered the mainstream work of the group, and, as a result, the work tended to succumb to political considerations rather than scientific ones. The lack of trust and inability to confront the state of their collective knowledge collaboratively resulted in serious project delays and embarrassing and very costly questions from regulatory authorities years later.

3. *A source of inimitable competitive advantage.* Social capital is the way people work together, negotiate meaning, and design the myriad of decisions and transactions they make together every day. This is highly contextual and specific to the groups performing the work. It is extremely difficult to imitate and replicate high levels of trust and collaboration. This is reflected by the growing tendency of competitors to try to hire away not just individuals but entire teams, in fields such as investment management. This results in the simultaneous acquisition of both human and social capital.

What Is "Knowledge Management"?

We believe that intellectual capital and knowledge management are not interchangeable concepts. "Knowledge management" is more operational in nature and follows strategic decisions about which elements of intellectual capital to invest in. The three types of knowledge assets described above comprise an organization's intellectual capital. Knowledge management describes management's efforts to ensure that these assets are continually in motion, being enhanced, shared, sold, or used,

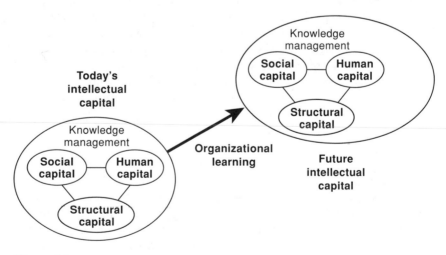

Figure 4.2
Intellectual capital grows with use

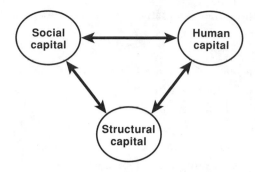

Figure 4.3
Elements of intellectual capital are interdependent

and that they generate superior business results (see figure 4.2). An essential characteristic of knowledge is that it only generates value for the firm when it is used effectively in practice. Unlike financial capital, keeping knowledge in reserve rarely creates economic value.

Knowledge management can be thought of as the deliberate design of processes, tools, structures, etc., with the intent to increase, renew, share, or improve the use of knowledge represented in any of the three elements of intellectual capital. Unfortunately, among many firms and technology vendors the concept of knowledge management has taken on a very narrow definition, so that it now implies only the implementation of information technology to develop "structural capital." A common example of this is the misguided assumption that merely implementing shared databases or document repositories will enhance knowledge creation and use. While managing each element of intellectual capital is essential, it is seldom sufficient. Managing the integration of human, structural, and social capital is the key to effectively building intellectual assets.

Integrating Three Types of Knowledge

One of the most overlooked aspects of building intellectual capital is the fact that different types of knowledge are interdependent and impact each other's value and performance in an organization (see figure 4.3). Just as executives are careful about choosing in what markets and products they will invest financial resources, so too should they be careful in choosing where and how to invest in different types of intellectual capital. Investment choices must take into account the interdependencies of different knowledge assets and how they interact. There are three points to keep in mind.

1   Avoid focusing on only one element of intellectual capital.   The European division of a major U.S. manufacturer, for example, tried to get its service reps to share tips with the field by designing a knowledge repository, or database, that comfortably fit the work. Although individual reps were entering tips from the field, it took a group of analysts months to validate the tips and, as a result, the system was used little. It turned out that the employees' management had assigned to validate the field lessons were not respected by the service reps for their experience and knowledge of the business. Thus, by only focusing on the knowledge base (structural capital) and failing to consider the levels of trust in the validators (social capital), this investment was a disappointment.

Except in unusual cases, developing one element of intellectual capital will be inadequate because, ultimately, the interaction of structural, human, and social capital determines the value of management's investment. Since investments in one kind of knowledge will often pay off only if the levels of the other two are adequate, any strategy to build intellectual capital must develop mutually reinforcing types of knowledge.

Managers often assume that trust must be built before knowledge will be exchanged. But building trust first is an uncertain and time-consuming approach. In practice, we have found the development of trust actually will be accelerated when people work jointly on an important business problem, which forces them to have a detailed exchange of knowledge to understand each other's perspectives. In other words, bringing two distinct types of human capital together, e.g., investment and insurance managers, to jointly address a concrete business problem in a project team is a more powerful way of building social capital, while at the same time creating new knowledge about the business. But this approach will work only if management allows time for the two sides to explain their experiences and perspectives to each other. In this case, the interaction of human and social capital are what produce the payoff.

2   Anticipate changes in the relationships between elements of intellectual capital.   For example, introducing a new financial control system may require bringing in a host of expensive financial and information technology experts. But, as the new system is developed and better understood, its transactions can be routinized and embedded in standardized processes and systems. Thus, over time, management needs to shift its emphasis from attracting and retaining specialized human capital to building structural capital with processes and technology.

The interaction between the three elements is a dynamic process, which means their levels of interdependency are continually shifting. Executives must view knowledge management as a dynamic process where priorities will change in response to the demands of the competitive environment and to the organization's evolving mix of knowledge assets.

3 Look for indirect investments. Launching a business in Asia, a multinational oil company needed to build social capital among its local workforce, which was plagued by a poor communication infrastructure in the developing country. To address the problem, management actually invested in structural capital by building a knowledge center, which was staffed by an experienced businessperson that served as a full time knowledge coordinator, facilitating access to the center's resources. Senior management's investment in the structural capital visible in the center demonstrated a commitment to the value of capturing and sharing knowledge. But, more importantly, the conveniently located physical space encouraged informal gatherings and enhanced the development of relationships among employees. Do not assume that knowledge capabilities are always best enhanced by direct investment. The interdependencies of intellectual capital elements mean that building resources often requires investing indirectly by developing another type of knowledge.

What Is a "Learning Organization"?
Learning—both individual and organizational—is the process by which knowledge assets are increased over time. Every organization learns. But, to be successful, leaders must seek to align both individual and collective learning with the strategic intent of the firm. This means that as executives design their business strategies, they need to determine what, specifically—and when—their firms need to learn, and create mechanisms to do so.

For example, if an insurance firm is trying to make inroads into the investment management business, it's executives will have to make sure that their firm learns the new business while continuing to advance its knowledge of the insurance business. A knowledge management strategy, therefore, may include hiring new talent, designing joint projects, implementing job rotations, and altering organizational structures to facilitate the flow of the new knowledge between existing and new businesses.

In other words, effective organizational learning is the result of explicit management efforts to build intellectual capital in support of the firm's strategy. Learning must be aligned with the current business strategy to ensure that knowledge being acquired supports future needs, instead of simply building on historical practices and strengths.

Deciding Where and How to Invest

Firms are increasingly investing in intellectual capital, but the process of deciding where and how to invest remains relatively undisciplined, resulting in disappointing returns and wasted resources. For example, our research has shown that executives often invest in information technology hoping that by creating structural capital people will share knowledge. But the only result is many databases that no one uses. In other instances, management imports new talent only to find that it does not "stick" in the existing culture. To avoid these mistakes, there are several principles that should define the approach taken to deciding where to invest in knowledge management.

1   Understand core business processes and define key business drivers. For example, executives in a European pharmaceutical company decided to focus on their drug development process, specifically improving the quality of new drugs and reducing the time to market. Management recognized that product quality and development time were key long term profit drivers, so they concentrated knowledge management efforts in this area. Defining core processes and business drivers are a prerequisite for identifying where the greatest payoffs can come from leveraging knowledge.

2   Focus on knowledge that will support critical formal and informal decision-making. In the case of the pharmaceutical company above, the knowledge management team recognized that the documentation used by government regulators to evaluate new drugs was the critical output in the drug development process. Thus, they focused on the decisions made throughout the process of creating the documentation and identified the types of knowledge needed to improve decision making along the way. Decisions determine business outcomes, so understanding the key types of decisions and the role knowledge can play is essential.

3 Complexity of decisions will determine focus of intellectual capital investments. Many decisions are made autonomously and require only coordination with others and some degree of alignment with the firm's strategic intent. In cases where decisions are being made independently of each other, the primary focus should be on developing structural capital, such as communication systems or knowledge repositories, although individual level skills may also be very important.

Other decisions will be effective only if they are taken and implemented jointly, requiring mutual commitment along with an integrated and shared understanding of the problem, solution design, and implementation process. Decisions requiring more integration should have social and human capital as their investment focus with investments in structural capital being a lower priority.

Overlooking investments in building social capital is a common and costly mistake where integration is the business goal. For example, we have found that when drug development teams do not trust each other, critical data can be overlooked and go unchallenged because the strongest people in the group will push their ideas on others, even when their thinking should be questioned and later proves costly.

The degree of integration required in decision making is not consistent throughout a firm, so knowledge management needs should be assessed for different levels and units of the organization. For example, functional areas within a division may require more integration because of the unit's ongoing need to develop new products or services. In the same global corporation, geographically organized businesses may be autonomous and require a different set of coordination mechanisms to create and share knowledge. The degree of integration or differentiation required is a major factor that determines the development priorities of knowledge management initiatives. And each situation calls for a mix of different techniques and approaches.

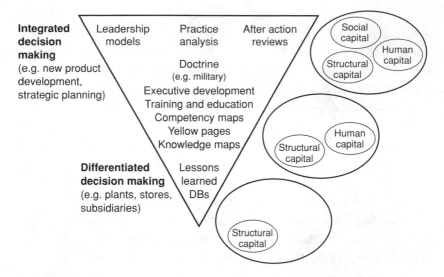

Figure 4.4
Investment guide

4   Types of decisions will also determine knowledge management tools and techniques needed.   If enhanced integration is central to improving business performance, then the mechanisms, tools, and projects needed must support the development of all three types of intellectual capital (see figure 4.4). In particular, creating opportunities to collaborate and build trust is an important step in building social capital and increasing the quality of group level knowledge.

If, however, the business needs to increase intellectual capital across entities that will remain differentiated (e.g., stores, manufacturing plants, foreign subsidiaries), more resources should be put into developing structural capital through mechanisms such as knowledge maps, knowledge bases, and lessons learned systems.

How to Get Started

How does building intellectual capital actually add value to the business? Knowledge, whether in individuals, groups, or embedded in organizational processes and products, is not inherently valuable. Knowledge only becomes valuable in practice. Practice is human, social, and structural capital in action *together*. Practice is where knowledge is created and used to shape decision-making and activities related to business goals. The effective development of intellectual capital requires an understanding of this dynamic.

Practice is different from process. Process is the map of how things are supposed to happen. Practice is the way things are *actually* done in a particular part of the organization. Practice is the actual traveling, using the map initially to figure out how to get from point A to point B, but then setting it aside and working around all the uncharted road blocks. Practice develops over time and reflects the way people and groups actually create and use explicit and tacit knowledge to produce, sell, and deliver products and services.

Practice is the source of a firm's competitive advantage because it cannot be easily replicated. For example, an office furniture manufacturer that derives competitive advantage from its reputation for high quality products combines all three elements of intellectual capital to create highly effective work practices. The plant has well-designed processes and procedures, and well-trained, experienced employees, whose strong relationships—particularly between engineers and those on the manufacturing line—enable them to quickly diagnose and fix sources of quality problems.

Thus, most initiatives to build intellectual capital and enhance organizational learning should focus on the development of new practices in an organization, particularly when integrated decision making is central to effective outcomes. For example, to create new leadership practices, the furniture company's CEO championed the development of a media-rich workspace in which the senior management team could bring together many different kinds of information to support decision making. At the same time, the executive group had to develop news levels of trust that encouraged the open exchange of ideas to produce meetings that are more effective. In this case, the interaction of increased levels of social and structural capital enabled new leadership practices to emerge.

Focusing Initial Efforts

Intellectual capital initiatives will be no different from other broad, all-encompassing change initiatives. If they are too grand, they will usually fail. Effective management of intellectual capital may be a critical component of a larger business transformation, or it may be tied to narrower strategic objectives. Regardless, the initial effort should be highly focused, and it must be linked to business outcomes.

One way to pursue this approach to building intellectual capital is with a small prototype designed to test a future business concept and develop an understanding of the work practices involved. When the U.S. Army wanted to test the viability of a computerized battle force, for example, they linked a 3,000-man brigade, complete with tanks, artillery, and helicopters with a digital network. This computerized brigade engaged in a two-week exercise against a very talented opposing force that used traditional communications gear. The prototype was designed to maximize the Army's learning about the future of the digital battlefield, and provided critical inputs for strategic decisions about computerizing the entire fighting force. The key in this type of initiative is to build in roles, structures, and systems, to ensure that the organization learns as much as possible from the experience.

These knowledge management projects must meet several criteria to be effective:

• They must be strategically relevant, and provide insights about building work practices that apply knowledge in new ways. In addition, the benefits should be reasonably, or at least indirectly measurable. For example, knowledge management initiatives in new product development may be tied to reduced time to market.

• Save basic research for R&D. Components of the knowledge management prototype need to be reasonably well understood and observable in practice elsewhere. An international financial services company launching a new type of service in Europe can draw on similar well-understood practices in the U.S., for example. What is uncertain is how the European market will react and what knowledge is needed to set up and operate in European countries and cultures.

• An executive respected by both peers and superiors must lead the project. He or she must take risks and be comfortable with the uncertainty and ambiguity inherent in such a project.

• The prototype must have logical hooks into other projects, so that the results naturally feed into follow-on projects. They should not be one-offs that will not be repeated in the near future. The financial services firm trying to create a new type of customer relationship in Europe will design and develop a call center in one country. Simultaneously, the firm will design and implement a learning strategy, define and develop the required capabilities, and determine a strategy for spreading this new competence throughout Europe.

When the U.S. Army ran its simulation of the digital battlefield, senior officers learned that the power of shared context could be exponentially increased when knowledge transfer was done digitally—computer to computer. Not only did soldiers have the shared understanding of the battlefield that came from extensive training based on Army doctrine, but they also shared a common view of the battle as it developed. From foxhole to general headquarters and back at ISDN speeds, knowledge could be shared, decisions made, and actions taken.

When a knowledge prototype project is completed, senior management should have the insights needed to make critical strategic decisions. Does the firm really understand the emerging market? Do they have the intellectual capital to make it happen? Can the necessary competencies be developed or transferred from within the firm? More important, management will have glimpsed the future and how different types of knowledge must be combined in practice to create competitive advantage.

Once senior management has an idea of what future operations could be like—in practice—and the types of knowledge needed, their focus shifts to helping other parts of the organization adopt and adapt the new practice to local cultures and contexts. A common mistake in knowledge management is assuming successful projects can simply be rolled out to the rest of the organization.

For example, in launching new financial services in Europe, the company mentioned earlier realized that in the U.S. the job of interacting with clients had evolved into a functional role of client relationship manager. But managing client interactions in a European context might not be done effectively by recreating the same role. Nevertheless, understanding what the client relationship manager actually did in practice enabled those launching the European business to develop options and solutions that fit the context of the new market, without necessarily recreating the old role structure. Because much knowledge is local and embedded in social context, it must be adapted into local practice to make certain it is applied effectively.

Conclusion

If, as Harvard Business School's Shoshana Zuboff says, "Learning is the new form of labor," then knowledge is both the raw material and product of that labor. Effectively managing knowledge to build a firm's intellectual capital will increasingly become a yardstick by which executive performance is measured—both by the equity markets and by the firm's board of directors.

Part of senior management's job is to separate the hype about intellectual capital from the essential principles that underlie the emergence of the knowledge-based economy. Making the right strategic investments to build a firm's intangible assets means taking a comprehensive approach to the problem by understanding the relationships between structural, human, and social capital. It also means recognizing which types of knowledge are needed to support different business objectives. Finally, effective knowledge management means understanding that knowledge is inextricably linked to practice, and that creating value for the firm means improving how knowledge is actually used—not just captured and stored—in activities critical to the business.

Notes

* By "trust" in this context we mean professional, studied, and rational trust, which is based on a shared context (i.e., a common understanding of a business) and provides a sense of anticipated reciprocity, predictability and reliability within a group.

References

1. Recent definitions of intellectual capital have primarily emphasized two types of knowledge—human and structural capital. See, for example, Thomas A. Stewart, *Intellectual Capital: The New Wealth of Organizations* (New York: Doubleday/Currency, 1997); Leif Edvinsson and Michael S. Malone, *Intellectual Capital*, (New York: HarperBusiness, 1997).

2. For a detailed review of "social capital" theory see "Social Capital, Intellectual Capital and the Organizational Advantage," by J. Nahapiet and S. Ghoshal, *Academy of Management Review* 23, no. 2 (1998): 242–266.

5

Knowledge Sharing Is a Human Behavior

William Ives, Ben Torrey, and Cindy Gordon

Knowledge sharing is a critical human behavior that organizations need to carefully cultivate and harvest to be competitively positioned in our new knowledge based economy. As individuals join organizations, they bring with them learned behaviors from experiences that either promote or inhibit effective knowledge sharing. Knowledge leaders need to take a holistic and integrated human performance approach to changing their organizations to perform effectively in this new knowledge intensive world. This chapter explores a number of strategies to create a high performing knowledge organization including areas such as: organizational structure and roles, organizational processes, culture, physical environment, leadership and direction, measurement, means, ability and motivation. Without carefully addressing these areas, organizations will not achieve deep systemic change in their journey to become knowledge competent. We have found that when any of these factors are overlooked, the knowledge management effort suffers accordingly. At the root of knowledge management is the increased recognition that knowledge sharing is a human behavior and cannot be fostered without genuine trust and care. Treating people as strategic assets and partners must be more than verbal rhetoric; rather only through genuine leadership behavior can organizations be socialized to become knowledge sharing competent.

Sharing insights and best practices is a human behavior that is critical to the success of any knowledge management system, yet it is counter to the culture found in most organizations. This cultural issue is seen by many experts[2] as the main obstacle to implementing knowledge management since, for most firms, facilitating the capture of useful business knowledge represents a major change in employee behavior. In a 1997 survey of Fortune 1000 executives, 97 percent of respondents said there were critical business processes that would benefit from more employees having the knowledge that was currently within a few people, and 87 percent said costly mistakes are occurring because employees lack the right knowledge when it is needed[4]. Just searching for the right information can be costly. Novell, the network provider, estimates that UK businesses alone waste over $17.5 billion searching for internal information.[5] The cost of mistakes made by not finding it is probably higher. While knowledge is one of the few resources that can increase in value as it is shared, the intercompetitive environment in many organizations fosters knowledge hoarding; in these firms unique possession of knowledge is seen as power and job security. As with any major transition in employee behavior, this change from a knowledge protective to a knowledge sharing environment needs to be consistently supported in multiple and interrelated ways. To achieve success, knowledge sharing and knowledge management need to be viewed as human performance issues. This article presents a multidimensional framework developed to support change in human performance and applies it to supporting knowledge sharing behavior.

The Framework: A Human Performance Model

Human performance is complex activity influenced by many factors. It involves the performance of clearly designed business processes, as well as the capabilities and motivations within people that give rise to performance. It also involves the management actions that influence employee capability and motivation and it includes the organizational structure and environment in which performance occurs. Together these components form an interactive system where each component influences the other. The human performance model below was developed by Steve Lindauer, Craig Mindrum, and other members of our Performance Design & Development Competency Leadership team based on the work of several human performance experts.[26] This model looks at both organizational and individual factors that affect performance, and focuses on obtaining measurable outcomes that benefit the individual and the organization. It specifies what a person needs to perform optimally in any business task, as well as what management must provide in order to align performance with business strategies.

The principal factors are as follows:

- Business Context: What is the business mission and strategy? Is it understood? Are tasks aligned with it?
- Organizational Performance factors
- Structure and Roles: How are people organized to support performance?
- Processes: What are they supposed to do?
- Culture: What social and political factors affect performance?
- Physical Environment: Where do people perform?
- Individual Performance Factors
- Direction: What guidance do people receive?
- Measurement: How are they measured?
- Means: Do they have the tools to enable performance?
- Ability: Do they have the skills and knowledge to perform?
- Motivation: Will they perform?

These ten factors must be working in concert for human performance to be optimized. None of these factors, taken individually, can ensure success, as they achieve minimal effectiveness when operating in isolation. Each is necessary but, by itself, not sufficient. Each will now be addressed in terms of its contribution to knowledge sharing. Because of their interrelated nature, there is natural overlap among factors, and a number of the points could be made under several factors. Some will receive more attention than others, but all are important.

Business Context

Sveiby[29] defines knowledge as "the capacity to act," and Davenport, DeLong, and Beers[9] add that knowledge "is a high value form of information that is ready to apply to decisions and actions." This capacity or readiness to act only achieves value if it is aligned with the strategic direction of the organization to increase the desired business performance. It cannot be implemented as simply "a good idea" if one hopes for it to succeed. In a recent study of knowledge management projects, the successful ones were linked to the organization's economic performance.[9] Employees are more likely to share knowledge if it is linked with the common goals of the organization and achieves clear economic value. To do this, they need to understand and share these goals. Finerty[14] argues that knowledge sharing cannot be promoted by rewards; the only way to generate real knowledge sharing is to "build meaning into the workplace." If people really care about what they do, then they will want to share the knowledge they create. It is not enough to make sure the knowledge management system is simply aligned with the business strategy for knowledge sharing to occur. It is essential that the business strategy is communicated to employees, and that a consensus of support is created so they both understand and concur with the business context in which they operate.

In ideal cases, the business context drives the creation of the knowledge management system. At Texas Instruments, certain key customers threatened to take business elsewhere if TI could not improve its delivery dates and cycle time[24] Faced with this threat, TI launched a best practices sharing initiative that led to $1.5 billion in additional wafer fabrication capacity. They also discovered that many of the industry best practices were taking place in their own plants. If the business context drives the creation of knowledge sharing, the chances for successful implementation and significant financial impact are dramatically increased. In another case, British Petroleum Group Chief Executive, John Browne, launched the organization's Virtual teamwork Project to encourage knowledge sharing and innovation. This collection of global knowledge sharing initiatives has generally returned the investment costs within a few months and has provided a five-to-one return within the first six months.[5] One of the lessons learned was that these initiatives need to be managed as business projects, not simply as IT projects.

The knowledge management system itself can be one way to communicate the business strategy, and the act of knowledge sharing—if successful—can actually make employees feel a greater connection to the organization, which increases their likelihood to contribute knowledge in the future. If the knowledge management system is relied on as the only means for sharing the business context, however, it will not be sufficient. Employees need more personal connections with management if they are to become aligned with the business strategy. Management also has to continuously communicate and reinforce the strategy. For example, Ken Dorr, chairman and CEO of Chevron has linked knowledge sharing to organizational strategy and has been an untiring supporter as he said, "Every day that a better idea gets unused is a lost opportunity. We have to share more, and we have to share faster".[24] Chevron has realized over $650 million in benefits because of this dedication to knowledge sharing.

Organizational Structure and Roles

Knowledge sharing is best supported by a two-part organizational structure with professional dedicated knowledge management staff who own the knowledge processes, templates and technologies, and knowledge sponsors, integrators, and developers from the business units who own the knowledge content. This two-part structure and roles can help knowledge sharing in several ways. The professional knowledge management staff can guide and support employees through the act of knowledge sharing. This could include "help desk" support, structured debriefings, newsletters, recognition programs, and other means. The business units ensure the content meets business needs, is accurate and timely, and their participation helps to instill ownership in the users. Specific techniques for guidance will be covered later in the Direction section.

Within our firm, designated knowledge champions are part of the professional knowledge management staff, and whose major responsibility is to encourage and enable knowledge capture and knowledge use. The two functions are sometimes referred to by our internal staff as "value and velocity." Value relates to the capture of high quality knowledge and velocity relates to ensuring that this knowledge is used where it can provide the most business impact. There are different skills sets around promoting the capture of knowledge and designing ways to make it accessible and utilized. Both are necessary. The individuals in our internal professional staff serve an important function as change agents, especially during the early phases of knowledge management system implementation. They set and maintain a standard for personal knowledge sharing while encouraging, exhorting, and even cajoling members of the user community to engage in knowledge sharing. They also serve as the "human interface" to the knowledge management system by taking issues from the field and passing them along to the appropriate people, assuring users that they have been heard. As part of this role, they also train and support those responsible for supporting knowledge management in the business units. Since the professional knowledge management staff combines both human resource and training skills with information technology skills, it could initially be either part of HR or IT. It should be integrated, however, not split between the organizations, and both sets of skills need to be present. Wherever it is in the organization, it should have direct access and visibility to the highest levels of the organization.

Many organizations have created a new position to lead their knowledge efforts with chief knowledge officers (CKOs) as the most common name. Davenport and Prusak[10] list the three most critical tasks of a CKO as building a knowledge culture, creating the proper infrastructure, and realizing economic benefits. They add that the primary skills are deep expertise in aspects of the knowledge management process, familiarity with the appropriate technologies, understanding of the organization's business processes, as well as the general skills of a senior executive. CKOs also need to be strong advocates who can gain and sustain the support of their fellow senior executives. They need to manage both their own organization, as well as those outside of their organization who provide the necessary support within the business units they serve.

In the business units, there are several levels of roles that can both encourage and enable knowledge sharing. Knowledge sponsors are senior executives who are responsible for encouraging and recognizing the knowledge-sharing behavior of their business unit. They are held accountable and rewarded for the knowledge sharing activities of the employees in their business unit. Knowledge developers are designated content experts who create new content for the system as a dedicated, short-term assignment. Knowledge integrators operate at the functional unit or project level, and serve as the central focal point for knowledge use and knowledge sharing. This may be a part-time or dedicated rotational role, depending on the workload. To be effective, this role needs to be seen as a "career enhancing" one for the most capable. Knowledge integrators play a critical role in encouraging knowledge sharing, since they understand the issues within the business unit as well as the needs of the knowledge system. After receiving training from the knowledge management staff, they, in turn, train employees on knowledge sharing, help determine what knowledge is appropriate to share, ensure that all key knowledge is placed within the knowledge management system, ensure the quality of knowledge by dealing with such factors as accuracy, timeliness, redundancy, clarity, and other issues, and address issues of confidentiality and intellectual property rights. Similar to knowledge champions, they act as liaisons between the employees and the knowledge management staff. Knowledge sponsors have overall accountability for knowledge sharing; knowledge integrators have day-to-day responsibility to ensure it occurs. We have recently implemented a similar knowledge integration function in our European practice, with great success. One interesting observation is that a high percentage of these knowledge integrators, referred to as engagement knowledge champions, are subsequently promoted. This suggests that high performers are chosen for this role, that it is one that provides visibility, and that its tasks are valued by the firm—all of which are conditions that support increased knowledge sharing and legitimize it as a cultural value.

An important organizational unit that should not be overlooked is the traditional corporate library with its secondary research personnel. These knowledge retrieval specialists perform an important function in supporting the business units. Although it may seem that, with the advent of automated knowledge management systems, there is less need for such specialists, we are finding that this is not the case. Serving several important functions, organizational information services are coming back into their own. Within our firm, we are in the process of establishing a global knowledge center network into which the old enterprise libraries, librarians and other research people are being integrated. While the old redundant paper libraries, repeated in all locations, have gone away, the local librarians are taking on a new life as sophisticated knowledge specialists. As our internal knowledge management system, with its knowledge resources and databases, grows at an increasing rate, it becomes more difficult for line people to navigate through the increasing complexity. Knowledge center personnel have access to specialized search tools and the expertise to use them, providing information to business unit personnel more efficiently than they would be able to find it themselves. The existence of the ubiquitous system makes it very easy to provide instantaneously the research results to those who need them, often simply by providing electronic pointers or links to units of knowledge. In addition to this search function, the specialists are able to evaluate external resources, especially from the Internet, for accuracy, objectivity, completeness, etc., in a way that the ultimate user of the knowledge may not be able to. These specialists can also help in identifying knowledge gaps in the resources available. This information can than be passed onto knowledge integrators, champions, and others who are in a position to solicit new knowledge capital from project teams or subject matter experts to fill those gaps.

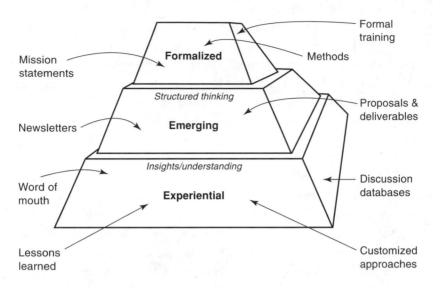

Figure 5.1
The knowledge spectrum

Organizational Processes

To foster an atmosphere in which knowledge sharing is likely to occur, it needs to be built into the daily work process. If it is a normal and expected part of the job, then it is likely to be done. If it is something done after hours on an employee's own time, it will be an uphill battle to collect knowledge contributions, regardless of how many extra incentives are offered. The U.S. Army has installed knowledge sharing as a standard part of its work in both training and real duty in the form of "after-action reviews".[25] In this approach, no effort is considered complete until it has been reviewed and its lessons obtained. As knowledge is useful only insofar as it guides action, a key success factor has been a rigorous program of applying the new insights gained through the reviews. This application demonstrates the value and encourages further contributions. During the U.S. military efforts in Bosnia, the lessons learned were distributed on a frequent basis. Because such observations as, "avoid snow-covered roads with no vehicle tracks, as they are probably mined" were credited with saving lives, members of other cooperating armies frequently requested a copy of the latest "lessons learned."

The second important process issue is the need for well-defined knowledge capture processes. Everyone should know where and how to contribute new knowledge and what happens to it after their contribution is made. There should be different processes and channels, depending on the level or type of knowledge that is shared. Expanding on the tacit-explicit distinction of Nonaka and Takeuchi,[23] Hiding and Catterall[16] recognize three levels of knowledge that range from experiential to emerging to formal as diagramed in figure 5.1 (modified from[16]).

Experiential knowledge is often tacit; it relates to specific events, and has not been generalized. It has high momentary value, often enabling a worker to solve a critical problem. This may occur through material already on the system or in consultation with a knowledge expert (often asynchronously, using a discussion database or electronic bulletin board). Formal knowledge is refined and generalized across many situations and is explicit. Emerging knowledge is both tacit and explicit; it is formal but not generalized. Examples include high-value deliverables from specific projects or successful sales proposals. While they are examples of explicit knowledge, they are designed to meet the needs of a specific situation. They can be frequently reused after varying degrees of modification, but they are not generalized knowledge. Formal knowledge is generalized and structured to educate; it reflects the synthesized and refined intelligence of the organization often through generalizing emerging knowledge.

These three types of knowledge have been likened to "unrefined data" (bits of momentarily critical information in discussions), "refined information" (highly specific formalized knowledge—deliverables, etc.), and "synthesized knowledge" (formalized knowledge that has also been generalized). This three level hierarchy illustrates the transformation that occurs as tacit knowledge becomes explicit, then fully socialized within an organization.

All three levels of knowledge provide value and need to be captured and managed within an organization, but different processes should be adopted for each. For experiential knowledge, open forums with "threaded discussions" are useful for individuals who wish to share informal insights based on specific events. After filling in an automated response form, individuals can see their item posted, follow responses to it, react to these responses, and continue the dialogue in an open manner that is accessible to all levels of the organization. Experiential knowledge can also be collected in more formal means through team debriefings (as discussed in the Direction section of this section). For emerging knowledge in project deliverables, sales proposals, or department reports, one team member (such as the engagement knowledge champion described in the previous section), should integrate the collective knowledge contributions from the group and serve as the single contact with the knowledge management system. Formal knowledge (such as integrated collections of best practices or official methods) should be made by dedicated resources from the business units who are given time away from their normal tasks to focus on quality deliverables. Everyone contributes to experiential knowledge, and dedicated team members are tasked with collecting and integrating emerging knowledge, drawing upon the group's collective efforts and insights. Specialists and subject matter experts should create formal knowledge, which is then used and refined by everyone. These three levels are addressed within our firm's knowledge management system through forums or discussion databases for experiential knowledge that are open to anyone, libraries of project deliverables and other forms of emerging knowledge that are maintained and monitored by professional staff, and methodologies of formal knowledge that are created by dedicated field staff and then tested and revised through client work.

Organizational Culture

The importance of organizational culture is one area of knowledge management with which most industry analysts seem to agree. In a 1998 survey of 650 information technology professionals by Delphi Consulting Group, 58 percent said corporate culture is the largest impediment to knowledge management.[7] Immaturity of technology was cited by 20 percent, immaturity of the knowledge management industry by 15 percent, cost by nine percent, and lack of need by three percent. Another study of knowledge management projects found that a culture that supported knowledge sharing was highly correlated with project success[8] and a 1997 survey of our firm's knowledge management engagement participants also found that culture issues are seen as the biggest challenge to implementation success. The Gartner Group suggests that lack of attention to cultural issues, rather than technical obstacles, will be the principal reason that knowledge management efforts fail.

Enterprises with cultures that systematically limit or inhibit capability, autonomy, and responsibility, as well as those in which sharing of knowledge is actively discouraged either by official or unofficial policy, will find that investment in KM technology provides (relatively) minor operational efficiencies at best.[2]

In hierarchical organizations, where employees are competing for a decreasing number of positions, knowledge sharing is less likely to occur. In relatively flat organizations that center around functional or project teams, sharing is more likely to occur because personal knowledge advantage may be seen as critical to promotion. In our own firm—as with most of the major consulting firms—a culture of sharing knowledge was in place prior to the implementation of our knowledge management system. The technology provided a better means to facilitate one of the existing core cultural values.

The Gartner Group[2] describes three types of cultures and their relative support for knowledge sharing. There are "balkanized" organizations with multiple "warlords" competing against each other in an atmosphere of mutual suspicion and information hoarding. The potential for knowledge sharing is naturally low here. There are "monarchies" with top-down authoritarian rule, and officially approved and disapproved subjects whose approval status may quickly change. The potential for knowledge sharing here is better than in the "Balkans," but is still limited. Then there are "federations" with local autonomy, a global framework, and civilized dispute resolution. Cooperation is based on enlightened self-interest, and the potential for knowledge sharing is high.

How do you develop the right culture for knowledge sharing? The solution is not one-dimensional and needs to consider the current organizational environment, the general business climate of the geographic location, and the indigenous culture. The first step is to identify knowledge sharing as a priority and then provide strong leadership, investment support, and modeling by senior executives such as that provided at Texas Instruments and Chevron discussed earlier. Trust and integrity on the part of leaders will help to unlock employee resistance to share; these traits have been rated as key success factors for business success in a knowledge-based economy.[15] Once trust is established, knowledge sharing needs to be part of everything in the organization's culture. All project reviews should include questions on knowledge sharing and reuse of knowledge. All individual performance reviews should consider knowledge sharing performance. All newsletters and communications should provide links, where appropriate, to the knowledge management system for more details. All IT applications should have knowledge bases to share and collect appropriate best practices around their use. All training courses should require use of the knowledge management system to model and encourage its use. In response to an inquiry as to how a culture of safety had been so successfully adopted at one of our chemical industry clients, the answer was that it is part of everything we do. The same applies to knowledge management. When dealing with a social culture that is resistant to knowledge sharing, it may be necessary to incorporate special activities designed to bring the group to a level of greater openness. Again, all of the human performance factors described in this chapter need to be operating in concert. The knowledge management system, itself, can be an important conveyor of the proper cultural messages by conveying stories of successful knowledge sharing.

One important cultural attribute of knowledge sharing is the need to achieve a common understanding so accurate and complete communication can occur. In the process of knowledge creation or sharing, individuals perform many communication behaviors. They will test words, use symbols, metaphors, tell stories, experiment with ideas—all with the goal of increasing shared communication, which will enable more effective knowledge sharing. The richer the communication experience, the more effective the knowledge sharing. People need freedom to spend quality time together in order to deeply communicate with one another, and achieve deeper shared learning. Too often we see organizations focus too much of their design efforts on codifying explicit knowledge and not balancing this with cultural change interventions where the following behaviors can occur:

1. "dialogue," sustained collective inquiry into every day experience, that we take for granted, creating a setting where people can become more aware of the context around their experience, and of the processes of thought and feeling that created that experience.[27]

2. "reflection & renewal," being sensitive to the surrounding world and willingness and desire to seek out opportunities to change, not falling into a comfort zone and taking the stable or changing environment for granted.

3. "communities of practice," self organizing groups who communicate with one another, because they share common work practices, interests; these groups can be formal or informal but they are defined by their behavior, not their status.

All the processes of knowledge sharing must recognize that group members are people with real human concerns, and reactions. Developing balanced cultural change strategies that support both explicit and tacit knowledge sharing strategies will be more successful.

Because knowledge sharing carries with it strong implications related to personal status and relations with others, openness to sharing will also be affected by the social or national culture within which the individual grew up, lives, and works. Certain cultures are quite reticent about sharing private thoughts or appearing to promote oneself through claiming expertise, while other cultures place a high value on demonstrating such expertise; in some cultures, asking for help from someone else is seen as a weakness. Hence, as organizations develop global knowledge management strategies, being very attentive to how different cultures define sharing, view sharing, and behaviorally share will be an important design requirement. To offer an example, there are underlying differences between Western and Eastern ways of perceiving knowledge and human existence. Nonaka contrasts the philosophies of Descartes and Nishida.[23] To the Western Cartesian, "I think, therefore I am, Nishida counters, "I love therefore I am." Descartes conceives of the individual as outside the environment, an observer standing apart from and evaluating his surroundings. Camus, Kafka, and others took this separation to the extreme of alienation from the world. In contrast, Nishida views the individual as inside the environment, an inseparable part of it. Another aspect of this difference is the strong sense of community prevalent in the East as opposed to Western individualism. This communal sense sees expression in a variety of ways such as the Japanese corporate culture with its traditional emphasis on loyalty and life-time employment, the Chinese expectation that an employer will provide cradle-to-grave benefits (including a company hospital, nursery, etc.), or the strong life-long bonds that Koreans form with school class-mates and school classes with teachers. Compare this to the high level of mobility among Western (especially North American) workers—both white collar and blue collar, and low level of company loyalty. Understanding the cultural differences is critical in answering the fundamental question of how people can be motivated to create and share knowledge, when they often have different shared meaning, and values.

What we increasingly have seen, based on our experiences in implementing knowledge management solutions, is when individuals are connected, for some logical reason, committed, trusted, respected, and loved, then the socialization processes for knowledge sharing and exploration of ideas to create new ideas is more likely to occur. These types of tendencies where emphasis is on the emotional, and even spiritual, runs counter to the more objective, and formal Western style of business discourse. It is also consistent with the increasing focus on business ethics and values in many firms. Becoming more respectful in our dealings with people will only encourage them to share one of their precious assets, their personal knowledge, something most people guard carefully.

Charles Handy, the economist, points out that in the knowledge economy, workers need to be treated very differently than in the industrial age where bosses owned the means of production. Knowledge workers now carry the means of production with them in their minds and they have a market value. They cannot be bossed around in the same way because they will leave and take their value with them. This fact is driving changes in the way organizations approach employees. The more supportive work environments of the knowledge age will not only support employee retention, they will increase knowledge sharing.

Physical Environment
The physical requirements may be taken for granted, but individuals need a quiet space where they may reflect and input contributions. This can be difficult in the middle of a busy call center or warehouse floor. One organization provided a quiet telephone area and a toll-free number for its mechanics to use to provide their insights to trained "debriefers" who knew what to look for and how to obtain useful information. Much knowledge sharing occurs outside of technology. Some of it is not by design—the sharing of best practices can occur in the coffee room or by the copy machine; however, many firms are employing team workspaces and scheduled team knowledge sharing meetings to allow for these exchanges. Many of the communities of practice within our firm hold regularly scheduled meetings—either in person or by phone—devoted to sharing insights and experience. A number of organizations such as Texas Instruments and 3M have regularly scheduled knowledge fairs where knowledge "sellers" and "buyers" can meet in a trade show environ-

ment. Andersen Consulting's Global Consulting Seminar, the firm's annual meeting, has a "village of solutions" where new ideas generated from client work are exhibited to those who can bring them to other clients.

A U.S. study cited in 1998 found that most employees thought they gained most of their work related knowledge from informal conversations around the water cooler or over meals, not from procedures manuals or formal training.[32] While this study dealt with perceptions and should not be used to eliminate formal training, it does speak to the perceived value of informal communication. A number of organizations are creating spaces specifically designed to foster this more informal exchange of knowledge. For example, the London Business School recently created an attractive space between two major departments to increase sharing between these formerly siloed departments. Reuters News Service, known for its excellent internal knowledge sharing, has installed kitchens on each floor to encourage interactions and knowledge sharing.[11] ICL, an IT services company, created a traveling space called Café VIK (Valuing ICL Knowledge) complete with tables, chairs, coffee, croissants, and information exhibits to promote the importance of knowledge sharing.[5] Our firm has created several sites—such as the Financial Ideas Exchange in New York and the Smart Store in Chicago—designed to promote innovation and knowledge sharing. Many Japanese firms have established "talk rooms" where researchers are expected to spend time sharing tea and ideas.[10] Skandia has set up a "futurizing house" that provides an environment for knowledge sharing that is enhanced by sights and even smells like fresh baked bread in order to encourage openness and innovation.[12] At the Bramalea office location of Northern Telecom in Canada, office workers can stroll inside in a park like setting, sit at the internet café and informally converse. Dupont has designed a unique office space with reclining lounge chairs, where employees sit under large canopied mechanical trees, where laptops are conveniently plugged in. In addition, office boardrooms at Dupont are colorful with zebra design chairs, all helping to create a more relaxed physical work environment where employees can connect and reconnect.

Technology can enhance the utility of these spaces. For example, network connections in these rooms can facilitate access to the knowledge management system and the increased ability to immediately input insights gained from these discussions so others can have access to them. Efforts to embellish such spaces with technology have led to the development of "meetingware" such as Ventana Group Systems (http://www.ventana.com), Meeting Works (http://www.entsol.com), and others. In addition, a new group of interior design firms are specializing in optimizing workspaces to increase performance; opportunities and developments in this area cannot be overlooked.

In a similar vein, Tom Stewart[28] commented at a 1998 conference that the best hardware device for transferring knowledge is a coffeepot. But, as Tom said, "Coffee pots don't scale." His comment highlights the challenge of getting people together in ways that encourage them to share knowledge openly, in a relaxed manner with as few structural or technological barriers as possible. The challenge is to use scaleable technologies to enhance direct human communication and interaction over distance and among large groups.

Direction

Providing proper guidance for knowledge sharing is particularly important since it is a new behavior for many. The culture may transform itself to promote knowledge sharing, but individuals must also learn how to share in useful ways. Clear purpose and clear terminology are key predictors of knowledge management success (Davenport et al. 1998). The U.S. Army has learned that the more hectic the operation, the greater the imperative for an organized system for collecting lessons learned.[25] Otherwise, the debriefing is unfocused and provides limited value. This need for guidance also applies to individuals. Our firm has developed a series of guidelines for knowledge sharing for all levels of the organization. In order to achieve real value, guidance needs to be focused on achieving improvement and innovation. When conducting event debriefings, it is important to take the experiential and emerging knowledge, as described by Hidding and Catterall,[16] and attempt to translate it into formal knowledge that can be generalized to other events; do not simply recall events, but move toward conclusions and action steps. Clear direction and guidance toward this goal can help unlock our tacit understandings and produce explicit learning. It is often said that to truly understand something, one should teach it. This is because we take our experiential knowledge and translate it into formal learning to impart to others. This process also helps to clarify one's own thinking, which often leads to new syntheses.

Argyris[1] argues that case studies and other forms of debriefings do not lead to real innovation because of our individual and organizational defensiveness. We tend to look at others' behavior, rather than focus upon inconsistencies and root causes of actions. We tend to answer the questions of our supervisors in ways that make us look good, but never question whether these are even the right questions. This is particularly true for balkanized or monarchical organizations (to use the Gartner Groups terms[2]), and partially explains why they will have more difficulties with knowledge sharing. If we focus on the recommendations for actions, it helps us to probe for root causes and positive corrective steps, rather than dwell on the experience itself and what went wrong or right. It allows us to make a positive contribution—the recommended action—which we can feel good about, rather than simply being left with past inadequacies. This guidance can occur in structured group sessions that should be held throughout the project and refined as the work progresses. If the debrief is left to the end, much will be forgotten, and the events are more likely to suffer from defensive reinterpretation.[1]

MIT's Center for Organizational Learning has developed a comprehensive approach to what they call "learning histories" that involves the collaboration of trained learning historians and those involved in the event.[19] The employees supply the events and the historians help interpret these events. This approach has provided very useful results for large companies trying to make sense of major events; however, this type of intervention cannot be applied in all cases. Useful guidance can also be as simple as a series of structured questions on a contribution form: what occurred? Why did it occur? What are the implications? How can it be improved? A tool for providing direction is the use of forced choices for categorizing information that provides a contributor with a framework that is aligned with the organization's desired categories. While category lists are extremely important for efficient information retrieval, it is possible that they become too constricting, even to the point of inhibiting knowledge sharing. Again, as with all the other factors, this approach, by itself, will not work without the proper organizational culture and all the other factors working in concert. Leaders need to model this behavior; a recent Andersen Consulting study of the qualities for the CEO of the future rates self-awareness and reflection as key attributes. This reflection and self-awareness that are necessary for knowledge generation best occurs in a culture of trust and integrity.[15] Without trust and the other human performance factors in place, employees may learn, but they will not share their learning.

Measurement

In a manufacturing economy, performance is relatively easy to measure, as production output can be counted and assessed against benchmarks and past performance; in a knowledge-based economy, however, output is harder to measure. This human performance measurement is increasingly important today, as an organization's greatest assets are within its people. These metrics for knowledge workers need to fit the job and the corporate culture, start to put a value on ideas, look at knowledge distribution as well as creation, and require input from a variety of sources.[31] To recognize that knowledge reuse and distribution is also important, Texas Instruments recently created an annual "not invented here, but I did it anyway" NIHBIDIA award.[10]

An interesting framework for measuring knowledge sharing behavior has been devised at MITRE, a US government funded research organization.[21] The Knowledge Transfer Event (KTE) serves as the measurement unit. A Knowledge Transfer Event includes: subject, description, quality, viscosity, date, teacher, and receiver. The viscosity is the complexity of the message and the quality is the utility or value to the receiver. Persons need to be on both the teaching and receiving ends of KTEs as they need to continuously learn and transfer their own knowledge. The recording of KTEs is a formal extension of the thank-you process people normally provide to teachers. The public posting of KTEs provides recognition; including them in performance measures provides rewards. By rewarding KTEs, knowledge sharing becomes a measurable part of everyone's job; it is seen as real work because it is recognized and rewarded.

In our firm, knowledge sharing behavior is evaluated at the individual and engagement, or client team, level. Like all other core skills, there is a developmental model of knowledge sharing proficiencies, and each career level in the organization is assigned an expected proficiency level. These range from knowledge use and participation in discussion databases at the initial levels, through contribution of formal knowledge capital as you gain more experience, to sponsoring knowledge creation and developing new approaches to knowledge management as you reach the higher levels. It is important that these are expectations—not role definitions that might limit behavior. No one is prohibited from exceeding expectations; on the contrary, they are rewarded for it. Each of these expectations can be translated into actions that can be documented in a review. They are readily available so that expectations are known in advance. There are also other means to assess contributions. For example, all knowledge databases can be sorted by author, which provides a public record of each person's input volume. These contributions are also easily accessible by anyone in the firm, so quality can be readily determined. Also, the number of requests for particular documents can be tracked. In addition to individual measures, there are certain expectations on engagement teams to contribute knowledge capital from their efforts, and these contributions are monitored. Congratulatory messages are sent from executive leaders when expectations are met. These individual and team measurements provide definition to knowledge sharing behavior and communicate that the organization places a value on it. When our European practice initiated congratulatory messages from senior executives to the team, the number of engagement contributions increased.

In addition to measuring knowledge sharing behavior, documenting the business impact of this behavior is critical for ongoing senior leadership support. Communicating these benefits can increase support at all levels of the organization. Skandia, the Swedish insurance firm, has pioneered measures of the value of intellectual capital that can serve as useful means to document the increased value of the knowledge capital generated by the knowledge sharing behavior.[13] It provides measures in five areas of performance: financial, customer, human, process, and renewal and development and includes them in its annual report. This work is an extremely valuable guide to how we can change our measures of corporate wealth to reflect the new knowledge-based economy. The Balanced Scorecard offers a similar approach.[18] Each can be used to set the strategic direction for knowledge sharing and then determine its impact. See the chapter in this book by Karl-Erik Sveiby for a more detailed discussion of these measures.

Not all firms are prepared to immediately change their accounting measures nor is it necessary for them to make this change as knowledge management benefits can also be measured by traditional cost benefit analysis and standard accounting means. Sample quantifiable benefits include:

- increased idea generation and reduced idea "cycle time"
- avoidance of duplicate efforts and repeating past mistakes
- decreased time to achieve employee proficiency and implement major business changes
- reduced time to market for new and innovative products and services
- increased efficiency through accessibility and continuous improvement of best practices

All knowledge management efforts should develop a measurable business case even if it is not an immediate requirement for funding as the business case will support ongoing efforts and reduce the risk of its funding being cut when budgets become tight. Examples of large benefits are available including the $1.5 billion dollar benefits of Texas Instrument and the $650 million obtained by Chevron mentioned earlier in the Business Context section. Dow Chemical also saved over $40 million in patent maintenance fees and plans to generate over $100 million in additional patent revenue as a result of its knowledge management efforts. In some cases knowledge management initiatives are part of a larger effort rather than a separate initiative. In these cases, it is important to show how knowledge management supports the overall business case.

An important part of the definition of knowledge capital is "providing value." Without linkage to strategic initiatives, reflected through some form of measurement or recording of value whether it is simply anecdotal or more quantifiable, knowledge management could become one more new solution in search of a problem. On the other hand, creating measures such as those described above can lead to unlocking the value within knowledge capital. Charles Handy, a fellow at the London Business School, and foresighted author of *The Age of Unreason*, estimates that the intellectual assets of a corporation are usually worth three or four times the tangible book value. No executive would leave his cash or factory space idle, yet if CEOs are asked how much of the knowledge in their companies is used, they typically say, "about 20%." This is also consistent with the observations of Betty Zucker who studies knowledge management at the Gottlieb Duttwiler Foundation, a Swedish think tank. Imagine the implications for a company if it could get that number just up to 30%.

Means

One of the reasons for the current rise of knowledge management is the increased use of network computing, groupware, intranets, and other technologies that make large-scale knowledge management possible. These technologies are a driving force toward the ubiquitous availability of information, and, therefore, a key driver of knowledge management. A 1997 survey of large organizations found that 91% used e-mail, 78% used the internet, and 66% used groupware.[6] Many organizations are upgrading their e-mail to IBM's Lotus Notes, Microsoft Exchange, or web technology. Where this technical infrastructure is in place, building an elementary but efficient means to support knowledge sharing becomes less of an obstacle. In an increasing number of these instances, knowledge management can be positioned as a way to better leverage existing technical investments. These existing tools can then be extended to automate and simplify the knowledge sharing process. Contribution buttons that launch preformatted e-mail messages destined for knowledge integrators or other editors can provide one means of making the knowledge capture process more accessible. Push technologies can provide user-defined structure to both knowledge access and sharing. Users can rate and categorize the knowledge they are sharing to ensure that it targets the right audience. They can also define and prioritize the type of knowledge they want to receive.

New technologies are also making knowledge capture less dependent on direct contribution by employees as the only means to acquire new knowledge. Data mining allows for knowledge identification by analyzing past performance. Content extraction may further automate the collection of experiential and emerging knowledge by selecting the meaningful aspects of documents. Electronic access to external sources of knowledge (both formal subscription information services and the "wide open" Internet), if properly integrated into the knowledge management system, provides an extremely rich resource for direct access and for recombination to create new knowledge. In addition, as previously discussed, videoconferencing, application sharing, and electronic meeting support—or "meetingware"—are useful knowledge sharing enablers. Regardless of the technologies employed, a key investment to support knowledge sharing is the creation of a taxonomy or semantic model that provides a map of the organization's understanding of knowledge and

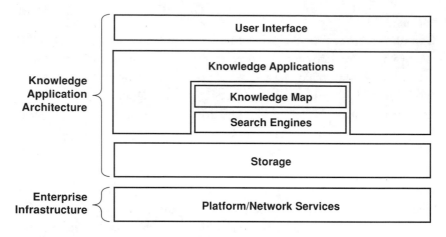

Figure 5.2
Knowledge management

helps to structure category lists for contribution classification. This provides a framework for knowledge contribution by individuals and automated knowledge capture and retrieval by the newer technologies. The knowledge map can fit into an overall knowledge management architecture composed of incremental and dependent layers as shown in figure 5.2 (Brie 1998).

This architecture represents at a high level the essential technical components of a knowledge management system. These components can be fulfilled by a variety of technologies and their description is beyond the scope of this chapter. The bottom layer pertaining to "Platform and Network Services" is usually described as the infrastructure on top of which Knowledge Management systems are developed and deployed. This layer includes all the network technology (i.e., network/communication protocol, external connectivity, modems, gateway server, etc.) as well as the different computing capabilities (i.e., operating systems, presentation services, security service, etc.) available within an organization.

The Application Architecture rests on the "Storage" layer that represents the database(s) in which the information is indexed and stored. The "Knowledge Applications" and "Search Engines" layer represents the core applications that enable users to actually perform Knowledge Management activities such as knowledge capture, knowledge retrieval through search or browse, e-mail, share information with others. At the heart of these Knowledge Applications is the enterprise knowledge architecture described above (i.e., knowledge map), that defines the user's conceptual perspective(s) of the enterprise knowledge assets (e.g., in the form of semantic models, taxonomies). Finally, the "User Interface" layer deals with all the user navigation aspects including human conceptual views of the knowledge assets.

When designing knowledge sharing technologies, users should be consulted in the functional and interface design. Knowledge sharing technologies also should be selected to meet the specific needs of particular user groups. For example, the replication capabilities in Notes currently make it very useful for those who work remotely with laptops.

While technology provides the essential means to allow for knowledge sharing in large organizations, it often dominates the other factors in this chapter, in part because it can be the most tangible. Davenport and Prusak[10] offer a useful check on the over emphasis on technology when they suggest that any major initiative, such as knowledge management, is in serious trouble if it spends more than 30% on technology because the other success factors are being over looked. In other words, if you build it there is no guarantee they will use it.

Ability

Despite the fact that individuals are taught to share at an early age, sharing in a corporate environment is a relatively new skill that requires training and ongoing support. When Glaxo Welcome made a commitment to becoming a learning organization in 1995, a small team developed an action plan to support knowledge sharing behavior.[5] An outcome of this was the Senior Executive Program to support this goal. It identified and promoted a new skill set for executives:

• network and relationship building
• managing beyond boundaries
• enabling employees to create their own "life support" systems
• developing leaders who can release the full potential of employees

Knowledge sharing skills can be taught at all levels of the organization. For example, a major health insurance provider is in the process of changing its way of doing business by establishing direct links with its providers through the Internet. This transformation results in new systems, new process and new behaviors for its employees, including a new

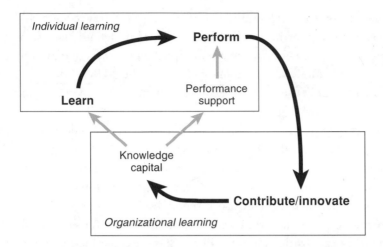

Figure 5.3
Performance improvement cycle

emphasis on knowledge sharing to improve the new processes continuously. Training sessions simulate the new work environment and introduce employees to the performance support and knowledge management tools they will use in the actual work setting. During these learning sessions employees are trained in several knowledge capture tools, including an improvement opportunity log, and allowed to use these tools as they progress through the simulated business activities. Using these knowledge capture tools during training also allows the business simulation exercises to support organizational learning around the new business processes even before employees reach their new roles. The participants can record their reactions to the new and evolving processes and provide insights for improvement while still in the learning exercises.

Knowledge management systems, such as the one just described, can be used to support both individual and organizational learning, and it is important that they are coordinated with all other individual learning initiatives and systems—training and performance support—to obtain maximum leverage from the investment in each.[17] To be more specific, learning initiatives, performance support, and knowledge management need to be designed and implemented as one consistent and continuous "closed-loop" system to increase human performance around measurable business objectives. They also need to be integrated into the work processes and the applications that support these processes. The "performance improvement cycle" diagrammed in figure 5.3 illustrates this concept.

Knowledge workers need to acquire the prerequisite skills through training prior to job performance, they need to have proper knowledge support as they perform their tasks, and then they need to be able to reflect on "lessons learned" during performance to improve their own individual learning as well as contribute innovations into organizational learning. This newly acquired individual and organizational learning—or knowledge capital—is then applied as they and their fellow knowledge workers continue to learn and perform. The cycle leads to innovation that is conveyed through both learning and performance support to achieve continuous business performance improvement.

Within our firm, many training courses make use of performance support systems designed to assist in problem solving during learning activities. These performance support systems link to the knowledge management system for much of their material. Course participants are encouraged to make frequent use of the knowledge management system, either directly or through the performance support system. This knowledge management system use exposes participants to the procedures, scope, and benefits of knowledge management while they are still in the learning mode. Instructor-led and technology-based learning are also offered on how to use the knowledge management system, itself.

In turn, the knowledge management system supports training by providing course announcements, registration, and, in the case of many technology-based courses, actual training delivery. Recently, a number of new "virtual" instructor-led courses operated through the knowledge management system, allowing for online teaming and mentoring. Another new group of courses makes use of an intranet approach to delivering computer-based training that is directly linked to the knowledge management system. These courses allow for both the dissemination of knowledge and skills around specific topics and the focused capture of new knowledge capital around these topics. Participants are encouraged to add their comments and experiences about selected course topics. This input goes directly into the relevant sections of the knowledge management system. For example, one course links to the home page covering that topic and a section within the home page allows for course discussion to be available to others interested in the topic even if they are not taking the course. Course participants are required to comment on several submissions by prior participants to stimulate dialogue. The original participants are also notified whenever there is a response to their submission so they can reply in turn. New knowledge capital in the form of presentations and deliverables that have been generated by the course participants is directly fed into the relevant libraries for inclusion in the knowledge management system. The challenge for any organization that is implementing knowledge management is to determine how it fits into the total array of learning initiatives. Likewise, the challenge when implementing learning initiatives is to determine how knowledge management can be integrated to provide support and gain maximum leverage from the investment.

Motivation

While external rewards may help, knowledge sharing is best supported if it is also intrinsically rewarding to the participants.[14] These rewards could come from gaining essential information to complete a critical job task, saving work time, participating in a dialogue on useful and interesting issues, and the professional pride in being recognized as an expert and mentor to the organization. When additional rewards are offered they must be carefully balanced with existing reward structures. For example, an additional bonus for increased revenue by an entire team of sales agents may promote increased knowledge sharing of best practice sales techniques within the team. This would be particularly true if individual bonuses for top performers are not based on competitive measures (e.g., the top ten performers) but rather on a criterion basis (e.g., everyone who exceeds certain stretch sales targets).

Many of the issues that effect motivation to share knowledge have been covered under the previous factors; we add personal connection as another important motivator. Studies have shown that scientists and engineers exchange knowledge in direct proportion to the level of personal contact; Chrysler attributes a portion of its recent success in new car development to colocating everyone involved.[9] This colocation is not practical in many organizations, but supplementing electronic exchange with face-to-face meetings is more possible. In our firm, much effort is made in bringing different communities of similar practice together so that networking can occur and relationships can be established. These recurring face-to-face meetings help sustain communication and knowledge sharing through the knowledge management system once people are scattered back on their individual projects. Individuals are more likely to respond to a request for knowledge help from someone they know. They will also have a better understanding of what the others already know and what the others might need so that they can better target their response. Features to promote personal connection are also built into the system; for example, in some discussion databases, there is a button on discussion items that links to the personal profile of the individual making the contribution, so if someone has not met the contributor, they can learn their background. These profiles are not the same as the official resumes used for client work; they are more informal and not limited to business experience. Some personal context and interests are also provided, so readers have a better understanding of the individual.

Motivating people to become more knowledge competent does require an understanding of "care".[20] Effective knowledge creation puts demands on the way people relate to each other in a company. Untrustworthy behavior, constant competition, imbalances in giving and receiving information, and a "that's not my job" attitude endanger effective knowledge sharing. "Care" is something most human beings can relate to through their personal histories. These experiences might describe the way parents behaved toward their children, the way a teacher behaved toward a student, the way a manager behaves toward employees, etc. Regarding care in relationships, the philosopher, Milton Mayeroff suggested that "to care for another person, in the most significant sense, is to help him grow and actualize." To care for someone is to help them to learn, to increase an awareness of events, and consequences, and to help nurture personal knowledge creation, while sharing insights. This approach is also very consistent with the executive skills required for knowledge sharing that Glaxo Welcome identified as part of its knowledge management efforts and we discussed in the Ability section.

Significant research supports the critical need for trust to achieve consistent knowledge sharing within organizations, a continual focus on care also gives rise to trust.[15] Genuine care gives rise to empathy, making it possible to assess and understand people's needs. When care is low in organizations, individuals will try to hoard knowledge rather than share it voluntarily. An increased focus on social knowledge creation in organizations that allows genuine feelings to emerge will be an important core competency to develop in organizations serious about creating a knowledge creation and sharing culture.

Knowledge leaders must project a passion and excitement for the possibilities of what knowledge management can offer or the organization's will to change is not leveraged. One of the more impassioned perspectives on motivation and leadership that we have come across was in a letter that Jack Welch wrote in an annual report to his shareholders at General Electric[33] where he describes four types of leaders:

"Type 1—delivers on commitments—financial or otherwise and shares the values of the company. Employment prospects for this type of person is onward and upward. Type 2 is a leader who does not meet commitments and does not share the company values. Those are soon fired. Type 3 are leaders who miss commitments but share the values, and they usually get a second chance. Type 4 is the most difficult for many of us to deal with. That leader delivers on commitments, makes all the numbers, but does not share the values we must have. This is the individual who typically forces performance out of people rather than inspires it: the autocrat, the big shot—the tyrant. Too often all of us have looked the other way—tolerated these Type 4 managers because they always deliver—at least in the short term. Not anymore, Welch wrote "In an environment where we must have every good idea from every man and women in the organization, we cannot afford management styles that suppress and intimidate."

A knowledge competent organization will not tolerate the type 4 leadership behaviors that Jack Welch describes above. What is critical for leaders undertaking a cultural change to become a knowledge leader is that they must examine deeply the motivational and leadership styles of behavior in the current culture, examine the gaps and assess the depth of systemic change required to create a corporate culture that genuinely cares, enriches the human spirit, fosters and respects idea cultivation and sharing. In other words, knowledge management is also about having linkage to the "heart and soul"—an even more illusive intangible asset. We believe those companies that discover this and leap to apply it will move beyond a knowledge based culture to the next generation of organizational learning, and economic success. In summary, knowledge management and motivation is about respect for all people, and a genuine belief that every human being has good ideas to contribute to the success of an organization. Motivation is more complex because many people need to unlearn inappropriate behaviors, develop new mental models and realize that motivating leadership behaviors are now about: caring, diversity appreciation, listening, trust, respect, and "spirit." The desired motivation leadership commitment or desired outcome can simply be "to ensure that our people are supported to reach their full human potential." Ensuring organization's move beyond corporate rhetoric in their commitment to their employees needs to be architected into all human performance strategies and motivation is a critical requirement to unleash the best talents and capabilities of people in organizations.

Tara Jantzen, one of our Knowledge Managers, posted a question in a discussion database within our knowledge management system: "What would best motivate you to contribute to the knowledge management system?" The answers, recorded in 1997, varied, and reflected many of the factors already covered in this article. They included: make sure it can be done as a normal part of the job, know that promotion is dependent on it, receive thanks and recognition, notify supervisors of the value, be thanked by peers, receive news of how others used the contribution, and know that it is an expected part of the culture of the organization. There are individual and cultural differences in what drives any human performance. While being singled out as a "contributor of the month" may work in some U.S. organizations, in certain European countries it might result in ostracism by the worker's peers. At an individual level, for some, the key driver is recognition; for others, it may be reward, a fear of failure, or the acquisition of new knowledge essential to job success.

If all of the human performance factors are working in concert to support knowledge sharing, then each of these motivators will be addressed. Human performance is a key driver of organizational performance. This is particularly true in knowledge management.

References

1. C. Argyirs, "Good Communication that Blocks Learning," *Harvard Business Review*, July–August 1994, 45–53.
2. J. Bair, J. Fenn, R. Hunter, and D. Bosik, "Foundations for Enterprise Knowledge Management," *Gartner Group Strategic Analysis Report*, 1997.

3. O. Brie, "Knowledge Management Technologies," *Andersen Consulting White Paper*.

4. R. Chase, "The Knowledge-Based organization: An International Survey," *Journal of Knowledge Management* 1, no. 1 (1997a): 38–49.

5. R. Chase, "Knowledge management benchmarks," *Journal of Knowledge Management* 1, no. 1 (1997b): 83–90.

6. R. Chase, "Management Trends International," *The International Knowledge Management Newsletter*, November 1997c.

7. B. Cole, "Users Loathe to Share Their Know-How," *Computerworld* 6 (17 November 1998).

8. T. Davenport, "Components of Successful Knowledge Management," Babson College conference on Knowledge Management: The New Paradigm with a Focus on Technology, Wellesley, Mass., 1997.

9. T. Davenport, D. DeLong, and M. Beers, "Successful Knowledge Management Projects," *Sloan Management Review*, Winter 1998, 43–57.

10. T. Davenport and L. Prusak, *Working knowledge: How Organizations Manage What They Know* (Boston: Harvard Business School Press, 1998).

11. M. Earl, "Why Knowledge Management," Presentation at Andersen Consulting's Knowledge Management Workshop, London, March 9, 1998.

12. L. Edvinsson, "Knowledge Management: The Skandia Experience," Presentation at Andersen Consulting's Knowledge Management Workshop, London, March 10, 1998.

13. L. Edvinsson and M. Malone, Intellectual capital : Realizing Your Company's True Value by Finding its Hidden Roots (New York: Harper Business, 1997).

14. T. Finerty, "Knowledge—The Global Currency of the 21st Century," Knowledge Management 1 (1997): 20–26.

15. T. Gordon, "Trust and Integrity: The Heart of Knowledge Management," Knowledge, Inc., 1998.

16. G. Hidding and S. Catterall, "Anatomy of a Learning Organization," *Knowledge and Process Management* 5, no. 1 (1998): 3–13.

17. W. Ives, T. Gifford, and D. Hankins, "Integrating Knowledge and Skills Management," *ACM Groupware Bulletin* 19, no. 1 (1998): 51–55.

18. R. Kaplan, and D. Norton, *The Balanced Scorecard* (Boston: Harvard Business Review Press, 1996).

19. A. Kleiner and G.Roth, "How to Make Experience Your Company's Best Teacher," *Harvard Business Review*, 75, 172, 1997.

20. G. Von Krogh, "Care in Knowledge Creation," *California Management Review* 40, no. 3 (1998), Haas School of Business, Berkeley, California.

21. D. Morey and T. Frangioso, "Aligning an Organization for Learning: Six Principles of Effective Learning," *Journal of Knowledge Management* 1, no. 4 (1998): 308–314.

22. K. Nishida (trans. M. Abe and C. Ives), *An Inquiry in the Good* (New Haven: Yale University Press, 1990).

23. Nonaka, I. (Quote from: Cohen, *Don, Toward a Knowledge Context Report on the First Annual U.C. Berkeley Forum on Knowledge and the Firm*), Haas School of Business, Berkeley, California, 1998.

24. C. O'Dell and J. Grayson, "If Only We Know What We Know: Identification and Transfer of Internal Best Practices," *California Management Review* 40, no. 3 (1998): 154–174.

25. T. Ricks, "Army Devises System to Decide What Does, and What Does Not, Work," *Wall Street Journal*, May 23, 1997.

26. G. Rummler and A. Bache, *Improving Performance: How to Manage the White Space on the Organizational Chart* (San Francisco: Jossey Bass, 1996).

27. P. Senge, *The Fifth Discipline Handbook* (New York: Doubleday Dell Publishing, 1994).

28. T. Stewart, "Intellectual Capital vs. Knowledge Management," Presentation at the DCI Knowledge Management Conference, Boston, June 1998.

29. K. Sveiby, *The New Organizational Wealth: Managing and Measuring Knowledge-Based Assets* (San Francisco: Berrett-Koehler, 1997).

30. S. Shariq, "Knowledge management: An Emerging Discipline," *Journal of Knowledge Management* 1, no. 1 (1997): 75–82.

31. C. Von Hoffman, "Of Metrics and Moonbeams: Five Keys to Evaluating the Performance of Knowledge Workers," *Harvard Management Update* 3, nos. 1–3 (1998).

32. A. Wensley, "The Value of Story Telling," *Knowledge and Process Management* 5, nos. 1–2 (1998).

33. C. Wick, *The Learning Edge: How Smart Managers and Smart Companies Stay Ahead* (Boston: McGraw-Hill, 1993).

SECTION II

Introduction: Process

Sharing and Building Context

Bipin Junnarkar

Knowledge Management as a discipline has progressed considerably over the last few years. It is getting due academic recognition through academic programs that have been created in notable universities. Industry is also on the path of institutionalizing Knowledge Management by designating full-time staff as well as providing high-level sponsorship. Management consulting firms have established Knowledge Management practice to offer to their clients. Organizations still struggle in understanding how to extract value from this new and emerging discipline. Very few question the concept, but most flounder in putting the concept into practice. Methodologies, processes, roles of people, and supporting Information Technology–based tools all have to come together for Knowledge Management to sustain itself as value-enhancing and value-creating practice.

The difficulty that most practitioners face about implementing Knowledge Management emerges because of a simple dichotomy between Information Technology–based solutions that known to many for some time, and doing something radically different. Under the guise of Knowledge Management and also under the pretext of getting a handle over explicit or codified knowledge, known Information Technology–based solutions are suddenly being reclassified as Knowledge Management solutions. Software tools that helped organizations capture, organize, store, retrieve, search, browse, and navigate information are now being presented as Knowledge Management tools. In reality, this is only part of the solution set. The other part is conspicuously missing.

It is a well-known observation made by several experts that knowledge creation is essentially an individualistic phenomenon. However, learning is dominantly a social phenomenon. If this is the case, Knowledge Management should strive to foster the necessary processes for knowledge creation on an individual basis as well as those processes necessary for learning on a social basis. An essential prerequisite for knowledge creation (or leverage) is information. Hence, content management is a necessary evil and has to be well taken care of. From this perspective, players in the content management arena are indeed playing an important role. This is, as mathematicians would say, a necessary but not a sufficient condition. The other side of the coin has to do with learning as a social phenomenon. Although Information Technology can help immensely in creating and fostering social interactions, the ultimate act of learning from others and creating or leveraging knowledge is essentially an intimately personal act that is dependent on personal relationships, values, cultural orientation, and many other social factors.

Although the subject of social interactions is extremely complex, there are aspects of these interactions that are understandable. The reason hallway conversations are very lively is that this is when people get an opportunity to relate casually to each other. During these conversations, people are sharing their stories and anecdotes with each other. In other words, they are in fact sharing *context*. Interspersed during these conversations are bits and pieces of shared content or information. It is no secret that people remember vacations, weddings, parties, and other events in their life much more easily than they remember all the factual details of past events. What they remember is the *context* and they are able to recreate the *content* as they interact. It is relatively easy to remember the context and recreate the content as opposed to having the content nicely documented and then trying to recreate the context. Especially for someone who did not share the experience, recreating the context from a well-compiled content becomes an extremely arduous task. Simply put, content when presented in the right context is much more meaningful. Content without appropriate context is abstract and difficult to make sense of. Information Technology tools of today are inherently focused on *Content Management*. Context is essentially created by people and is very much experiential. It is not surprising that for that very reason, context is difficult to capture and share.

Knowledge Management has to foster the interplay between *content* and *context*. Although content lends itself nicely to being codified in books, computer databases, and other media, capturing context is an immensely difficult task and is best shared between people by people directly. Movies, for example, help recreate a context and help bring back vivid memories. Watching *Saving Private Ryan* was a very gripping experience to many who were not around during World War II but was too realistic to many who were fighting on the beaches of Normandy during World War II.

For Knowledge Management to advance into the next phase, it has to start focusing on *context management*. When we improve our ability to share context with a larger audience, transgressing the boundaries of time, physical proximity, and cultural boundaries, and couple that with relevant content, we better position ourselves to be able to leverage the collective intellect.

Effective Knowledge Management can take place when people are effortlessly able to share their individual mental models with multitudes of people. An individual's mental model is based on that person's expertise, education, past experiences, perceptions, biases, prejudices, and many other factors. Understanding of mental models is an essential prerequisite for meaningful dialogue between individuals. This understanding can lead to a shared point-of-view, that is, everybody understanding everybody else's mental models. A shared point-of-view can lead to collective understanding, and hence the creation of new knowledge or the leverage of existing knowledge.

Currently, with most of the emphasis being put on *content management*, very little progress is being made in the *context management* arena. First, a platform to capture and share context appropriately needs to be developed. Second, the platform has to be intuitively simple enough for anybody to understand and interact with it. Third, the platform should be able to mimic human behavior naturally. This need for context management opens up a tremendous opportunity to fill this void. The development of appropriate methodologies, processes, roles of people, and supporting Information Technology tools will help address some of the major needs in the industry. It would help more people within organizations to understand the complexity of their business; it would help capture institutional memory, facilitate organizational learning, sustain dynamic communities of practice or interest, and lastly the navigation to appropriate content.

Knowledge Management itself has come a long way and has a long way to go from where it is now. It started with integration of information where the focus has been on explicit or codified information. The next phase is for Knowledge Management to focus on interactivity between people, where the emphasis would be on capturing, sharing, and enhancing of context. Finally, Knowledge Management would then evolve into a multidisciplinary program that would foster collective thinking. The ability of any organization to effectively foster collective thinking would have a definite positive impact on its ability to create a valuable product faster and better than the competition.

Knowledge Management shall provide strategic advantage through organizational knowledge.

6

Classic Work: Theory of Organizational Knowledge Creation

Hirotaka Takeuchi and Ikujiro Nonaka

The distinctive approach of Western philosophy to knowledge has profoundly shaped the way organizational theorists treat knowledge. The Cartesian split between subject and object, the knower and the known, has given birth to a view of the organization as a mechanism for "information processing." According to this view, an organization processes information from the external environment in order to adapt to new circumstances. Although this view has proven to be effective in explaining how organizations function, it has a fundamental limitation. From our perspective, it does not really explain innovation. When organizations innovate, they do not simply process information, from the outside in, in order to solve existing problems and adapt to a changing environment. They actually create new knowledge and information, from the inside out, in order to redefine both problems and solutions and, in the process, to re-create their environment.

To explain innovation, we need a new theory of organizational knowledge creation. Like any approach to knowledge, it will have its own "epistemology" (the theory of knowledge), although one substantially different from the traditional Western approach. The cornerstone of our epistemology is the distinction between tacit and explicit knowledge. As we will see in this chapter, the key to knowledge creation lies in the mobilization and conversion of tacit knowledge. And because we are concerned with organizational knowledge creation, as opposed to individual knowledge creation, our theory will also have its own distinctive "ontology, which is concerned with the levels of knowledge creating entities

Reprinted from *The Knowledge Creating Company: How Japanese Companies Create the Dynamics of Innovation* (New York: Oxford University Press, 1995), pp. 56–94. ©1995 by Oxford University Press, Inc. Used by permission of Oxford University Press, Inc.

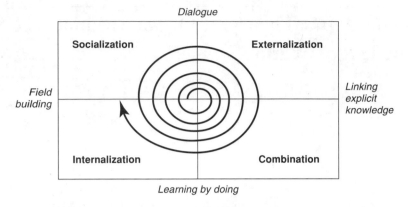

Figure 6.1
Knowledge spiral

(individual, group, organizational, and interorganizational). In this chapter we present our theory of knowledge creation, keeping in mind the two dimensions epistemological and ontological—of knowledge creation. Figure 6.1 presents the epistemological and ontological dimensions in which a knowledge creation "spiral" takes place. A spiral emerges when the interaction between tacit and explicit knowledge is elevated dynamically from a lower ontological level to higher levels.

The core of our theory lies in describing how such a spiral emerges We present the four modes of knowledge conversion that are created when tacit and explicit knowledge interact with each other. These four modes—which we refer to as socialization, externalization, combination, and internalization—constitute the "engine" of the entire knowledge-creation process. These modes are what the individual experiences. They are also the mechanisms by which individual knowledge gets articulated and "amplified" into and throughout the organization. After laying out these four modes and illustrating them with examples, we will describe five conditions that enable or promote this spiral model of organizational knowledge creation. We also present a five-phase process through which knowledge is created over time within the organization.

Knowledge and Information

Before delving into our theory, we first turn to describing how knowledge is similar to and different from information. Three observations become apparent in this section. First, knowledge, unlike information, is about *beliefs* and *commitment*. Knowledge is a function of a particular stance, perspective, or intention. Second, knowledge, unlike information, is about *action*. It is always knowledge "to some end." And third, knowledge, like information, is about *meaning*. It is context-specific and relational.

In our theory of organizational knowledge creation, we adopt the traditional definition of knowledge as "justified true belief." It should be noted, however, that while traditional Western epistemology has focused on "truthfulness" as the essential attribute of knowledge, we highlight the nature of knowledge as "justified belief." This difference in focus introduces another critical distinction between the view of knowledge of traditional Western epistemology and that of our theory of knowledge creation. While traditional epistemology emphasizes the absolute, static, and nonhuman nature of knowledge, typically expressed in propositions and formal logic, we consider knowledge as a *dynamic human process of justifying personal belief toward the "truth."*

Although the term's "information" and "knowledge" are often used interchangeably, there is a clear distinction between information and knowledge. As Bateson (1979) put it, "information consists of differences that make a difference" (p.5). Information provides a new point of view for interpreting events or objects, which makes visible previously invisible meanings or sheds light on unexpected connections. Thus information is a necessary medium or material for eliciting and constructing knowledge. It affects knowledge by adding something to it or restructuring it (Machlup 1983). Similarly, Dretske (1981) argued as follows: "Information is commodity capable of yielding knowledge, and what information a signal carries is what we can learn from it....Knowledge is identified with information-produced (or sustained) belief" (pp. 44, 86).

Information can be viewed from two perspectives: "syntactic" (or volume of) and "semantic" (or meaning of) information. An illustration of syntactic information is found in Shannon and Weaver's (1949) analysis of information flow measured without any regard to inherent meaning, although Shannon himself admitted that his way of viewing information is problematic.[1] The semantic aspect of information is more important for knowledge creation, as it focuses on conveyed meaning. If one limits the span of consideration to the syntactic aspect alone, one cannot capture the real importance of information in the knowledge-creation process. Any preoccupation with the formal definition of information will lead to a disproportionate emphasis on the role of information processing, which is insensitive to the creation of new meaning out of the chaotic, equivocal sea of information.

Thus information is a flow of messages, while knowledge is created by that very flow of information, anchored in the beliefs and commitment of its holder. This understanding emphasizes that *knowledge is essentially related to human action.*[2] Searle's (1969) discussion of the "speech act" also points out the close relationship between language and human action in terms of "intention" and the "commitment" of I speakers. As a fundamental basis for the theory of organizational knowledge creation, we focus attention on the active, subjective nature of knowledge represented by such terms as "commitment" and "belief" that are deeply rooted in individuals' value systems. Finally, both information and knowledge are context specific and relational in that they depend on the situation and are created dynamically in social interaction among people. Berger and Luckmann (1966) argue that people interacting in a certain historical and social context share information from which they construct social knowledge as a reality, which in turn influences their judgment, behavior, and attitude. Similarly, a corporate vision presented as an equivocal strategy by a leader is organizationally constructed into knowledge through interaction with the environment by the corporation's members, which in turn affects, its business behavior.

Two Dimensions of Knowledge Creation

Although much has been written about the importance of knowledge in management, little attention has been paid to how knowledge is created and how the knowledge-creation process is managed. In this section we will develop a framework in which traditional and nontraditional views of knowledge are integrated into the theory of organizational knowledge creation. As mentioned earlier, our basic framework contains two dimensions—epistemological and ontological (see figure 6.1).

Let us start with the ontological dimension. In a strict sense, knowledge is created only by individuals. An organization cannot create knowledge without individuals. The organization supports creative individuals or provides contexts for them to create knowledge. Organizational knowledge creation, therefore, should be understood as a process that "organizationally" amplifies the knowledge created by individuals and crystallizes it as a part of the knowledge network of the organization. This process takes place within an expanding "community of interaction," which crosses intra- and interorganizational levels and boundaries.[3]

As for the epistemological dimension, we draw on Michael Polanyi's (1966) distinction between *tacit knowledge* and *explicit knowledge*. Tacit knowledge is personal, context-specific, and therefore hard to formalize and communicate. Explicit or "codified" knowledge, on the other hand, refers to knowledge that is transmittable in formal, systematic language. Polanyi's argument on the importance of tacit knowledge in human cognition may correspond to the central argument of Gestalt psychology, which has asserted that perception is determined in terms of the way it is integrated into the overall pattern or *Gestalt*. However, while Gestalt psychology stresses that all images are intrinsically integrated, Polanyi contends that human beings acquire knowledge by actively creating and organizing their own experiences. Thus, knowledge that can be expressed in words and numbers represents only the tip of the iceberg of the entire body of knowledge. As Polanyi (1966) puts it, "We can know more than we can tell."[4]

In traditional epistemology, knowledge derives from the separation of the subject and the object of perception; human beings as the subject of perception acquire knowledge by analyzing external objects. In contrast, Polanyi contends that human beings create knowledge by involving themselves with objects, that is, through self-involvement and commitment, or what Polanyi called "indwelling." To know something is to create its image or pattern by-tacitly integrating particulars. In order to understand the pattern as a meaningful whole, it is necessary to integrate one's body with the particulars. Thus indwelling breaks the traditional dichotomies between mind and body, reason and emotion, subject and object, and knower and known. Therefore, scientific objectivity is not a sole source of knowledge. Much of our knowledge is the fruit of our own purposeful endeavors in dealing with the world.[5]

While Polanyi argues the contents of tacit knowledge further in a philosophical context, it is also possible to expand his idea in a more practical direction. Tacit knowledge includes cognitive and technical

Table 6.1
Two Types of Kowledge

Tacit knowledge (subjective)	Explicit knowledge (objective)
Knowledge of experience (body)	Knowledge of rationality (mind)
Simultaneous knowledge (here and now)	Sequential knowledge (there and then)
Analog knowledge (practice)	Digital knowledge (theory)

elements. The cognitive element's center on what Johnson-Laird (1983) calls "mental models," in which human beings create working models of the world by making and manipulating analogies in their minds. Mental models, such as schemata, paradigms, perspectives, beliefs, and viewpoints, help individuals to perceive and define their world. On the other hand, the technical element of tacit knowledge includes concrete know-how, crafts, and skills. It is important to note here that the cognitive elements of tacit knowledge refer to an individual's images of reality and visions for the future, that is, "what is" and "what ought to be." As will be discussed later, the articulation of tacit mental models, in a kind of "mobilization" process, is a key factor in creating new knowledge.

Some distinctions between tacit and explicit knowledge are shown in table 6.1. Features generally associated with the more tacit aspects of knowledge are listed on the left, while the corresponding qualities related to explicit knowledge are shown on the right. For example, knowledge of experience tends to be tacit, physical, and subjective, while knowledge of rationality tends to be explicit, metaphysical, and objective. Tacit knowledge is created "here and now" in a specific, practical context and entails what Bateson (1973) referred to as "analog" quality. Sharing tacit knowledge between individuals through communication is an analog process that requires a kind of "simultaneous processing" of the complexities of issues shared by the individuals. On the other hand, explicit knowledge is about past events or objects "there and then" and is oriented toward a context-free theory.[6] It is sequentially created by what Bateson calls "digital" activity.

Knowledge Conversion: Interaction Between Tacit and Explicit Knowledge

The history of Western epistemology can be seen as a continuous controversy about which type of knowledge is more truthful. While Westerners tend to emphasize explicit knowledge, the Japanese tend to stress tacit knowledge. In our view, however, tacit knowledge and explicit knowledge are not totally separate but mutually complementary entities. They interact with and interchange into each other in the creative activities of human beings. Our dynamic model of knowledge creation is anchored to a critical assumption that human knowledge is created and expanded. through social interaction between tacit knowledge and explicit knowledge. We call this interaction "knowledge conversion." It should be noted that this conversion is a "social" process *between* individuals and not confined *within* an individual.[7] According to the rationalist view, human cognition is a deductive process of individuals, but an individual is never isolated from social interaction when he or she perceives things. Thus, through this "social conversion" process, tacit and explicit knowledge expand in terms of both quality and quantity (Nonaka 1990b).

The idea of "knowledge conversion" may be partially consonant with the ACT model (Anderson 1983; Singley and Anderson 1989) developed in cognitive psychology. This model hypothesizes that for cognitive skills to develop, all declarative knowledge, which corresponds to explicit knowledge in our theory, has to be transformed into procedural knowledge, which corresponds to tacit knowledge, used in such activities as riding a bicycle or playing the piano.[8] But as Singley and Anderson admit, the ACT model has one limitation. It views the transformation as a special case, because this model's research interest is focused on the acquisition and transfer of procedural (tacit) knowledge, not declarative (explicit) knowledge. In other words, proponents of this model consider knowledge transformation as mainly unidirectional from declarative (explicit) to procedural (tacit), whereas we argue that the transformation is interactive and spiral.

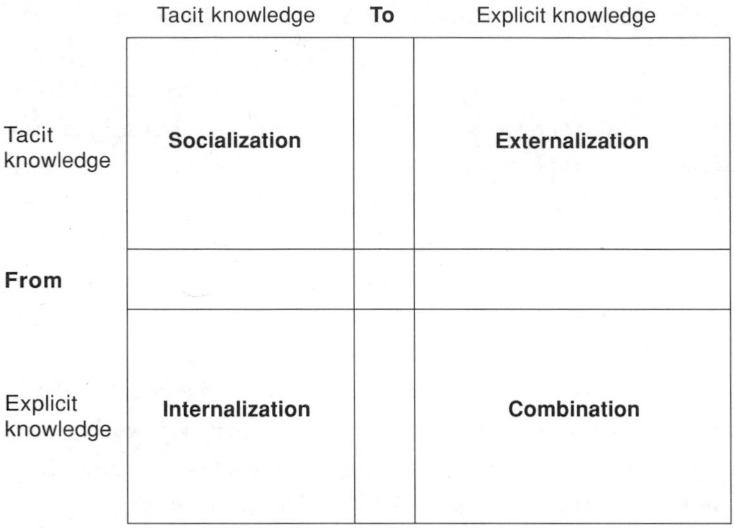

	Tacit knowledge	**To**	Explicit knowledge
Tacit knowledge	**Socialization**		**Externalization**
From			
Explicit knowledge	**Internalization**		**Combination**

Figure 6.2
Four modes of knowledge conversion

Four Modes of Knowledge Conversion

The assumption that knowledge is created through the interaction between tacit and explicit knowledge allows us to postulate four different modes of knowledge conversion. They are as follows: 1) from tacit knowledge to tacit knowledge, which we call socialization; 2) from tacit knowledge to explicit knowledge, or externalization; 3) from explicit knowledge to explicit knowledge, or combination; and 4) from explicit knowledge to tacit knowledge, or internalization.[9] Three of the four types of knowledge conversion—socialization, combination, and internalization—have been discussed from various perspectives in organizational theory. For example, socialization is connected with the theories of group processes and organizational culture; combination has its roots in information processing; and internalization is closely related to organizational learning. However, externalization has been somewhat neglected.[10] Figure 6.2 shows the four modes of knowledge conversion. Each of these four modes of knowledge conversion will be discussed in detail below, along with actual examples.

Socialization: From Tacit to Tacit

Socialization is a process of sharing experiences and thereby creating tacit knowledge such as shared mental models and technical skills.[11] An individual can acquire tacit knowledge directly from others without using language. Apprentices work with their masters and learn craftsmanship not through language but through observation, imitation, and practice. In the business setting, on-the-job training uses basically the same principle. The key to acquiring tacit knowledge is experience. Without some form of shared experience, it is extremely difficult for one person to project her or himself into another individual's thinking process. The mere transfer of information will often make little sense, if it is abstracted from associated emotions and specific contexts in which shared experiences are embedded. The following three examples illustrate how socialization is employed by Japanese companies within the product development context.

The first example of socialization comes from Honda, which set up "brainstorming camps" (*tama dashi kai*)—informal meetings for detailed discussions to solve difficult problems in development projects. The meetings are held outside the workplace, often at a resort inn where participants discuss difficult problems while drinking *sake*, sharing meals, and taking a bath together in a hot spring. The meetings are not limited to project team members but are open to any employees who are interested in the development project under way. In these discussions, the qualifications or status of the discussants are never questioned, but there is one taboo: criticism without constructive suggestions. Discussions are held with the understanding that "making criticism is ten-times easier than coming up with a constructive alternative." This kind of brainstorming camp is not unique to Honda but has been used by many other Japanese firms. It is also not unique to developing new products and services but is also used to develop managerial systems or corporate strategies. Such a camp is not only a forum for creative dialogue but also a medium for sharing experience and enhancing mutual trust among participants.[12] It is particularly effective in sharing tacit knowledge and creating a new perspective. It reorients the mental models of all individuals in the same direction, but not in a forceful way. Instead, brainstorming camps represent a mechanism through which individual's search for harmony by engaging themselves in bodily as well as mental experiences.

The second example, which shows how a tacit technical skill was socialized, comes from the Matsushita Electric Industrial Company. A major problem at the Osaka-based company in developing an automatic home bread-making machine in the late 1980s centered on how to mechanize the dough-kneading process, which is essentially tacit knowledge possessed by master bakers. Dough kneaded by a master baker and by a machine were x-rayed and compared, but no meaningful insights were obtained. Ikoko Tanaka, head of software development, knew that the area's best bread came from the Osaka International Hotel. To capture the tacit knowledge of kneading skill, she and several engineers volunteered to apprentice themselves to the hotel's head baker. Making the same delicious bread as the head baker's was not easy. No one could explain why. One day, however, she noticed that the baker was not only stretching but also "twisting" the dough, which turned out to be the secret for making tasty bread. Thus she socialized the head baker's tacit knowledge through observation, imitation, and practice.

Socialization also occurs between product developers and customers. Interactions with customers before product development and after market introduction are, in fact, a never-ending process of sharing tacit knowledge and creating ideas for improvement. The way NEC developed its first personal computer is a case in point. The new-product development process began when a group from the Semiconductor and IC Sales Division conceived of an idea to sell Japan's first microcomputer kit, the TK–80, to promote the sales of semiconductor devices. Selling the TK–80 to the public at large was a radical departure from NEC's history of responding to routine orders from Nippon Telegraph and Telephone (NTT). Unexpectedly, a wide variety of customers, ranging from high school students to professional computer enthusiasts, came to NEC's BIT-INN, a display service center in the Akihabara district of Tokyo, which is famous for its high concentration of electronic goods retailers. Sharing experiences and continuing dialogues with these customers at the BIT-INN resulted in the development of NEC's best-selling personal computer, the PC–8000, a few years later.

Externalization: From Tacit to Explicit
Externalization is a process of articulating tacit knowledge into explicit concepts. It is a quintessential knowledge-creation process in that tacit

knowledge becomes explicit, taking the shapes of metaphors, analogies, concepts, hypotheses, or models. When we attempt to conceptualize an image, we express its essence mostly in language—writing is an act of converting tacit knowledge into articulable knowledge (Emig 1983). Yet expressions are often inadequate, inconsistent, and insufficient. Such discrepancies and gaps between images and expressions, however, help promote "reflection" and interaction between individuals.

The externalization mode of knowledge conversion is typically seen in the process of concept creation and is triggered by dialogue or collective reflection.[13] A frequently used method to create a concept is to combine deduction and induction. Mazda, for example, combined these two reasoning methods when it developed the new RX–8 concept, which is described as "an authentic sports car that provides an exciting and comfortable drive." The concept was *deduced* from the car maker's corporate slogan: "create new values and present joyful driving pleasures" as well as the positioning of the new car as "a strategic car for the U.S. market and an image of innovation." At the same time, the new concept was *induced* from "concept" trips," which were driving experiences by development team members in the United States as well as from "concept clinics," which gathered opinions from customers and car experts. When we cannot find an adequate expression for an image through analytical methods of deduction or induction, we have to use a nonanalytical method. Externalization is, therefore, often driven by metaphor and/or analogy. Using an attractive metaphor and/or analogy is highly effective in fostering direct commitment to the creative process. Recall the Honda City example. In developing the car, Hiroo Watanabe and his team used a metaphor of "Automobile Evolution." His team viewed the automobile as an organism and sought its ultimate form. In essence, Watanabe was asking, "What will the automobile eventually evolve into?"

I insisted on allocating the minimum space for mechanics and the maximum space for passengers. This seemed to be the ideal car, into which

the automobile should evolve The first step toward this goal was to challenge the "reasoning of Detroit," which had sacrificed comfort for appearance. Our choice was a short but tall car... spherical, therefore lighter, less expensive, more comfortable, and solid.[14]

The concept of a tall and short car—"Tall Boy"—emerged through an analogy between the concept of "man-maximum, machine-minimum"

Table 6.2
Metaphor and/or Analogy for Concept Creation in Product Development

Product (company)	Metaphor/analogy	Influence on concept creation
City (Honda)	"Automobile evolution" (metaphor)	Hint of maximizing passenger space as ultimate auto development "Man-maximum, machine-minimum concept created"
	The sphere (analogy)	Hint of achieving maximum passenger space through minimizing surface area "Tall and short car (Tall Boy)"concept created
Mini-copier (Canon)	Aluminum beer can (analogy)	Hint of similarities between inexpensive aluminum beer can and photosensitive drum manufacture
Home bakery (Matsushita)	Hotel bread (metaphor)	"Low-cost manufacturing process" concept created
	Osaka International Hotel head baker (analogy)	Hint of more delicious bread "Twist dough" concept created

and an image of a sphere that contains the maximum volume within the minimum area of surface, which ultimately resulted in the Honda City.

The case of Canon's Mini-Copier is a good example of how an analogy was used effectively for product development. One of the most difficult problems faced by the development team was producing at low cost a disposable cartridge, which would eliminate the necessity for maintenance required in conventional machines. Without a disposable cartridge, maintenance staff would have to be stationed all over the country, since the copier was intended for family or personal use. If the usage frequency were high, maintenance costs could be negligible. But that was not the case with a personal copier. The fact that a large number of customers would be using the machine only occasionally meant that the new product had to have high reliability and no or minimum maintenance. A maintenance study showed that more than 90 percent of the problems came from the drum or its surrounding parts. Aimed at cutting maintenance costs while maintaining the highest reliability, the team developed the concept of a disposable cartridge system in which the drum or the heart of the copier is replaced after a certain amount of usage.

The next problem was whether the drum could be produced at a cost low enough to be consistent with the targeted low selling price of the copier. A task force assigned to solve this cost problem had many heated discussions about the production of conventional photosensitive drum cylinders with a base material of aluminum-drawn tube at a low cost. One day Hiroshi Tanaka, leader of the task force, sent out for some cans of beer. Once the beer was consumed, he asked, "How much does it cost to manufacture this can?" The team then explored the possibility of applying the process of manufacturing the beer can to manufacturing the drum cylinder, using the same material. By clarifying similarities and differences, they discovered a process technology to manufacture the aluminum drum at a low cost, thus giving rise to the disposable drum.

These examples within Japanese firms clearly show the effectiveness of the use of metaphor and analogy in creating and elaborating a concept (see table 6.2). As Honda's Watanabe commented, "We are more than halfway there, once a product concept has been created." In this sense, the leaders' wealth of figurative language and imagination is an essential factor in eliciting tacit knowledge from project members.

Among the four modes of knowledge conversion, externalization holds the key to knowledge creation, because it creates new, explicit concepts from tacit knowledge. How can we convert tacit knowledge into explicit knowledge effectively and efficiently? The answer lies in a sequential use of metaphor, analogy, and model. As Nisbet (1969) noted, "much of what Michael Polanyi has called 'tacit knowledge' is expressible—in so far as it is expressible at all—in metaphor" (p. 5). Metaphor is a way of perceiving or intuitively understanding one thing by imaging another thing symbolically. It is most often used in adductive reasoning or non-analytical methods for creating radical concepts (Bateson 1979). It is neither analysis nor synthesis of common attributes of associated things. Donnellon, Gray, and Bougon (1986) argue that "metaphors create novel interpretation of experience by asking the listener to see one thing in terms of something else" and "create new ways of experiencing reality" (pp. 48, 52). Thus, "metaphors are one communication mechanism that can function to reconcile discrepancies in meaning"[15] (p. 48).

Moreover, metaphor is an important tool for creating a network of new concepts. Because a metaphor is "two thoughts of different things supported by a single word, or phrase, whose meaning is a resultant of their interaction" (Richards 1936, p. 93), we can continuously relate concepts that are far apart in our mind, even relate abstract concepts to concrete ones. This creative, cognitive process continues as we think of the similarities among concepts and feel an imbalance, inconsistency, or contradiction in their associations, thus often leading to the discovery of new meaning or even to the formation of a new paradigm. Contradictions inherent in a metaphor are then harmonized by analogy, which reduces the unknown by highlighting the "commonness" of two different things. Metaphor and analogy are often confused. Association of two things through metaphor is driven mostly by intuition and holistic imagery and does not aim to find differences between them. On the other hand, association through analogy is carried out by rational thinking and focuses on structural/functional similarities between two things, and hence their differences. Thus analogy helps us understand the unknown through the known and bridges the gap between an image and a logical model.[16]

Once explicit concepts are created, they can then be modeled. In a logical model, no contradictions should exist and all concepts and propositions must be expressed in systematic language and coherent logic. But in business terms, models are often only rough descriptions or drawings, far from being fully specific. Models are usually generated from metaphors when new concepts are created in the business context.[17]

Combination: From Explicit to Explicit

Combination is a process of systemizing concepts into a knowledge system. This mode of knowledge conversion involves combining different bodies of explicit knowledge. Individual's exchange and combine knowledge through such media as documents, meetings, telephone conversations, or computerized communication networks. Reconfiguration of existing information through sorting, adding, combining, and categorizing of explicit knowledge (as conducted in computer databases) can lead to new knowledge. Knowledge creation carried out in formal education and training at schools usually takes this form. An MBA education is one of the best examples of this kind. In the business context, the combination mode of knowledge conversion is most often seen when middle managers break down and operationalize corporate visions, business concepts, or product concepts. Middle management plays a critical role in creating new concepts through networking of codified information and knowledge. Creative uses of computerized communication networks and large-scale databases facilitate this mode of knowledge conversion.[18]

At Kraft General Foods, a manufacturer of dairy and processed foods, data from the POS (point-of-sales) system of retailers is utilized not only to find out what does and does not sell well but also to create new "ways to sell," that is, new sales systems and methods. The company has developed an information-intensive marketing program called "micro-merchandizing," which provides supermarkets with timely and precise recommendations on the optimal merchandise mix and with sales pro-motions based on the analysis of data from its micro-merchandising system. Utilizing Kraft's individual method of data analysis, including its unique classification of stores and shoppers into six categories, the sys-tem is capable of pinpointing who shops where and how. Kraft success-fully manages its product sales through supermarkets by controlling four elements of the "category management" methodology—consumer and category dynamics, space management, merchandizing management, and pricing management.[19]

At the top management level of an organization, the combination mode is realized when mid-range concepts (such as product concepts) are com-bined with and integrated into grand concepts (such as a corporate vision) to generate a new meaning of the latter. Introducing a new cor-porate image in 1986, for example, Asahi Breweries adopted a grand concept dubbed "live Asahi for live people." The concept stood for the message that "Asahi will provide natural and authentic products and services for those who seek active minds and active lives." Along with this grand concept, Asahi inquired into the essence of what makes beer appealing, and developed Asahi Super Dry beer based on the new prod-uct concept of "richness and sharpness." The new-product concept is a mid-range concept that made the grand concept of Asahi more explicitly recognizable, which in turn altered the company's product development system. The taste of beer was hitherto decided by engineers in the pro-duction department without any participation by the sales department. The "richness and sharpness" concept was realized through cooperative product development by both departments.

Other examples of interaction between grand concepts and midrange concepts abound. For example, NEC's "C&C" (computers and commu-nications) concept induced the development of the epoch-making

PC–8000 personal computer, which was based on the midrange concept of "distributed processing." Canon's corporate policy, "Creation of an excellent company by transcending the camera business," led to the development of the Mini-Copier, which was developed with the mid-range product concept of "easy maintenance." Mazda's grand vision, "Create new values and present joyful driving," was realized in the new RX–8, "an authentic sports car that provides an exciting and comfortable drive."

Internalization: From Explicit to Tacit
Internalization is a process of embodying explicit knowledge into tacit knowledge. It is closely related to "learning by doing." When experiences through socialization, externalization, and combination are internalized into individuals' tacit knowledge bases in the form of shared mental models or technical know-how, they become valuable assets. All the members of the Honda City project team, for example, internalized their experiences of the late 1970s and are now making use of that know-how and leading R&D projects in the company. For organizational knowledge creation to take place, however, the tacit knowledge accumulated at the individual level needs to be socialized with other organizational members, thereby starting a new spiral of knowledge creation.

For explicit knowledge to become tacit, it helps if the knowledge is verbalized or diagrammed into documents, manuals, or oral stories. Documentation helps individuals internalize what they experienced, thus enriching their tacit knowledge. In addition, documents or manuals facilitate the transfer of explicit knowledge to other people, thereby helping them experience the experiences of others indirectly (i.e., "re-experience" them). GE, for example, documents all customer complaints and inquiries in a database at its Answer Center in Louisville, Kentucky, which can be used, for example, by members of a new product development team to "re-experience" what the telephone operators experienced. GE established the Answer Center in 1982 to process questions, requests for help, and complaints from customers on any product 24 hours a day, 365 days a year. Over 200 telephone operators respond to as many as 14,000 calls a day. GE has programmed 1.5 million potential problems and their solutions into its computerized database system. The system is equipped with an on-line diagnosis function utilizing the latest artificial intelligence technology for quick answers to inquiries; any problem-solution response can be retrieved by the telephone operator in two seconds. In case a solution is not available, 12 specialists with at least four years of repair experience think out solutions on site. Four full-time programers put the solutions into the database, so that the new information is usually installed into the system by the following day. This information is sent to the respective product divisions every month. Yet, the product divisions also frequently send their new-product development people to the Answer Center to chat with the telephone operators or the 12 specialists, thereby "re-experiencing" their experiences.

Internalization can also occur even without having actually to "re-experience" other people's experiences. For example, if reading or listening to a success story makes some members of the organization feel the realism and essence of the story, the experience that took place in the past may change into a tacit mental model. When such a mental model is shared by most members of the organization, tacit knowledge becomes part of the organizational culture. This practice is prevalent in Japan, where books and articles on companies or their leaders abound. Freelance writers or former employees publish them, sometimes at the request of the companies. One can find about two dozen books on Honda or Soichiro Honda in major bookstores today, all of which help instill a strong corporate culture for Honda.

An example of internalization through "learning by doing" can be seen at Matsushita when it launched a company wide policy in 1993 to reduce yearly working time to 1,800 hours. Called MIT'93 for "Mind and Management Innovation Toward 1993," the policy's objective was not to reduce costs but to innovate the mindset and management by reducing working hours and increasing individual creativity. Many departments were puzzled about how to implement the policy, which was clearly communicated as explicit knowledge. The MIT'93 promotion office advised each department to experiment with the policy for one month by working 150 hours. Through such a bodily experience, employees got to know what working 1,800 hours a year would be like. An explicit concept, reducing working time to 1,800 hours, was internalized through the one-month experience.

Expanding the scope of bodily experience is critical to internalization. For example, Honda City project leader Hiroo Watanabe kept saying "Let's give it a try" to encourage the team members' experimental spirit.

Tacit knowledge   **To**   Explicit knowledge

	Tacit knowledge	Explicit knowledge
Tacit knowledge	(Socialization) **Sympathetic knowledge**	(Externalization) **Conceptual knowledge**
Explicit knowledge	(Internalization) **Operational knowledge**	(Combination) **Sympathetic knowledge**

From

Figure 6.3
Contents of knowledge created by the four modes.

The fact that the development team was cross-functional enabled its members to learn and internalize a breadth of development experiences beyond their own functional specialization. Rapid prototyping also accelerated the accumulation of developmental experiences, which can lead to internalization.

Contents of Knowledge and the Knowledge Spiral
As already explained socialization aims at the sharing of tacit knowledge. On its own, however, it is a limited form of knowledge creation. Unless shared knowledge becomes explicit, it cannot be easily leveraged by the organization as a whole. Also, a mere combination of discrete pieces of explicit information into a new whole—for example, a comptroller of a company collects information from throughout the company and puts it together in a financial report—does not really extend the organization's existing knowledge base. But when tacit and explicit knowledge interact, as in the Matsushita example, an innovation emerges. Organizational knowledge creation is a continuous and dynamic interaction between tacit and explicit knowledge. This interaction is shaped by shifts between different modes of knowledge conversion, which are in turn induced by several triggers (see figure 6.3).

First, the socialization mode usually starts with building a "field" of interaction. This field facilitates the sharing of members' experiences and mental models. Second, the externalization mode is triggered by meaningful "dialogue or collective reflection," in which using appropriate metaphor or analogy helps team members to articulate hidden tacit knowledge that is otherwise hard to communicate. Third, the combination mode is triggered by "networking" newly created knowledge and existing knowledge from other sections of the organization, thereby crystallizing them into a new product, service, or managerial system. Finally, "learning by doing" triggers internalization.

The content of the knowledge created by each mode of knowledge conversion is naturally different (see figure 6.3). Socialization yields what can be called "sympathized knowledge," such as shared mental models and technical skills. The tacit skill of kneading dough in the Matsushita example is a sympathized knowledge. Externalization outputs "conceptual knowledge." The concept of "Tall Boy" in the Honda example is a conceptual knowledge created through the metaphor of "Automobile Evolution" and the analogy between a sphere and the concept of "man-maximum, machine-minimum." Combination gives rise to "systemic knowledge," such as a prototype and new component technologies. The micro-merchandizing program in the Kraft General Foods example is a systemic knowledge, which includes retail management methods as its components. Internalization produces "operational knowledge" about project management, production process, new-product usage, and policy implementation. The bodily experience of working 150 hours a month in the Matsushita case is an operational knowledge of policy implementation.

These contents of knowledge interact with each other in the spiral of knowledge creation. For example, sympathized knowledge about consumers' wants may become explicit conceptual knowledge about a new-product concept through socialization and externalization. Such conceptual knowledge becomes a guideline for creating systemic knowledge through combination. For example, a new-product concept steers the combination phase, in which newly developed and existing component technologies are combined to build a prototype. Systemic knowledge (e.g., a simulated production process for the new product) turns into operational knowledge for mass production of the product through internalization. In addition, experience-based operational knowledge often triggers a new cycle of knowledge creation. For example, the users' tacit operational knowledge about a product is often socialized, thereby initiating improvement of an existing product or development of an innovation.

Thus far, we have focused our discussion on the epistemological dimension of organizational knowledge creation. As noted before, however, an organization cannot create knowledge by itself. Tacit knowledge of individuals is the basis of organizational knowledge creation. The organization has to mobilize tacit knowledge created and accumulated at the individual level. The mobilized tacit knowledge is "organizationally" amplified through four modes of knowledge conversion and crystallized at higher ontological levels. We call this the "knowledge spiral," in which the interaction between tacit knowledge and explicit knowledge will become larger in scale as it moves up the ontological levels. Thus, organizational knowledge creation is a spiral process, starting at the individual level and moving up through expanding communities of interaction, that crosses sectional, departmental, divisional, and organizational boundaries (see figure 6.4).

This process is exemplified by product development. Creating a product concept involves a community of interacting individuals with different backgrounds and mental models. While the members from the R&D department focus on technological potential, those from the production and marketing departments are interested in other issues. Only some of those different experiences, mental models, motivations, and intentions can be expressed in explicit language. Thus, the socialization process of sharing tacit knowledge is required. Moreover, both socialization and externalization are necessary for linking individuals' tacit and explicit knowledge. Many Japanese companies have adopted brainstorming camps as a tool for that purpose.

The product created by this collective and cooperative process will then be reviewed for its coherence with mid-range and grand concepts. Even if the newly created product has superior quality, it may conflict with the divisional or organizational goals expressed by the mid-range and grand concepts. What is required is another process at a higher level to maintain the integrity of the whole, which will lead to another cycle of knowledge creation in a larger context.

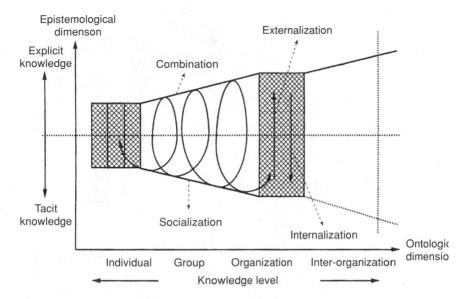

Figure 6.4
Spiral of organizational knowledge creation.

Enabling Conditions for Organizational Knowledge Creation

The role of the organization in the organizational knowledge-creation process is to provide the proper context for facilitating group activities as well as the creation and accumulation of knowledge at the individual level. In this section we will discuss five conditions required at the organizational level to promote the knowledge spiral.

Intention
The knowledge spiral is driven by organizational intention, which is defined as an organization's aspiration to its goals [20]. Efforts to achieve the intention usually take the form of strategy within a business setting. From the viewpoint of organizational knowledge creation, the essence of strategy lies in developing the organizational capability to acquire, create, accumulate, and exploit knowledge. The most critical element of corporate strategy is to conceptualize a vision about what kind of knowledge should be developed and to operationalize it into a management system for implementation.

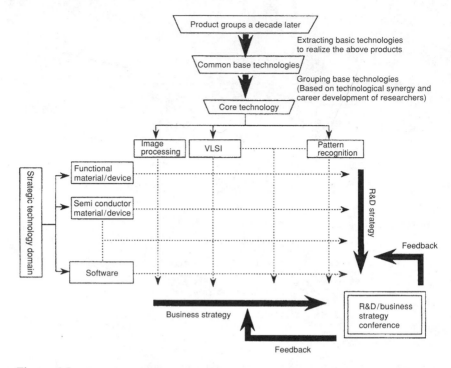

Figure 6.5
NEC's knowledge domain. Source: NEC

For example, NEC viewed technology as a knowledge system when it developed core technology programs at its Central Research Laboratories in 1975. At that time the company was engaged in three main businesses: communications, computers, and semiconductors. Because it was difficult to coordinate R&D of these different areas, it was necessary to grasp technologies at a higher and more abstract level—that is, knowledge. According to Michiyuki Uenohara, former executive vice president, "base technologies" were identified by forecasting product groups for a decade into the future, including the extraction of technologies common to and necessary for them. Synergistically related base technologies were then grouped into "core technologies," such as pattern recognition, image processing, and VLSI. Since 1975, NEC has expanded its core technology programs using autonomous teams; today it has 36 core technology programs in action.

In addition, NEC devised a concept called the "strategic technology domain" (STD) in order to match core technologies with business activities. An STD links several core technologies to create a concept for product development. Thus, an STD represents not only a product domain but also a knowledge domain. At present there are six STDs: (1) functional materials/devices; (2) semiconductors; (3) materials/devices functional machinery; (4) communications systems; (5) knowledge information systems; and (6) software. Those STDs interact with core technology programs in a matrix, as illustrated in figure 6.6. By combining core technology programs and the STDs, the knowledge bases at NEC are linked horizontally and vertically. Through this endeavor, NEC has attempted to develop a corporate strategic intention of knowledge creation at every organizational level.

Organizational intention provides the most important criterion for judging the truthfulness of a given piece of knowledge. If not for intention, it would be impossible to judge the value of information or knowledge perceived or created. At the organizational level, intention is often expressed by organizational standards or visions that can be used to evaluate and justify the created knowledge. It is necessarily value-laden.

To create knowledge, business organizations should foster their employees' commitment by formulating an organizational intention and proposing it to them. Top or middle managers can draw organizational attention to the importance of commitment to fundamental values by addressing such fundamental questions as "What is truth?" "What is a human being?" or "What is life?" This activity is more organizational than individual. Instead of relying solely on individuals' own thinking and behaviors, the organization can reorient and promote them through collective commitment. As Polanyi (1958) notes, commitment underlies the human knowledge-creating activity.

Autonomy
The second condition for promoting the knowledge spiral is autonomy. At the individual level, all members of an organization should be allowed to act autonomously as far as circumstances permit. By allowing them to act autonomously, the organization may increase the chance of introducing unexpected opportunities. Autonomy also increases the possibility that individuals will motivate themselves to create new knowledge. Moreover, autonomous individuals function as part of the holographic structure, in which the whole and each part share the same information. Original ideas emanate from autonomous individuals, diffuse within the

team, and then become organizational ideas. In this respect, the self-organizing individual assumes a position that may be seen as analogous to the core of a series of nested Russian dolls. From the viewpoint of knowledge creation, such an organization is more likely to maintain greater flexibility in acquiring, interpreting, and relating information. It is a system in which the "minimum critical specification" principle (Morgan 1986) is met as a prerequisite for self-organization, and therefore autonomy is assured as much as possible.[21]

A knowledge-creating organization that secures autonomy may also be depicted as an "autopoietic system" (Maturana and Varela 1980), which can be explained by the following analogy. Living organic systems are composed of various organs, which are again made up of numerous cells. Relationships between system and organs, and between organ and cells, are neither dominate-subordinate nor whole-part. Each unit, like an autonomous cell, controls all changes occurring continuously within itself. Moreover, each unit determines its boundary through self-reproduction. This self-referential nature is quintessential to the autopoietic system.

Similarly to an autopoietic system, autonomous individuals and groups in knowledge-creating organizations set their task boundaries by themselves to pursue the ultimate goal expressed in the higher intention of the organization. In the business organization, a powerful tool for creating circumstances in which individuals can act autonomously is provided by the self-organizing team.[22] Such a team should be cross-functional, involving members from a broad cross-section of different organizational activities. Project teams with cross-functional diversity are often used by Japanese firms at every phase of innovation. As illustrated in table 6.3, most innovation project teams consisted of 10 to 30 members with diverse functional backgrounds, such as R&D, planning, production, quality control, sales and marketing, and customer service. In most companies there are 4 to 5 core members, each of whom has had a multiple functional career. For example, the core members who developed Fuji Xerox's FX–3500 have had at least three functional shifts, even though they were only in their 30s at that time (see table 6.4).

The autonomous team can perform many functions, thereby amplifying and sublimating individual perspectives to higher levels. Honda, for example, organized a cross-functional project team to develop the City

Table 6.3

Functional Backgrounds of Product Development Team Members Functional Background

Company (Product)	R&D	Production	Sales Marketing	Planning	Service	Quality Control	Other	Total
Fuji Xerox (FX-3500)	5	4	1	4	1	1	1	17
Honda (City)	18	6	4	–	1	1	–	30
NEC (PC 8000)	5	–	2	2	2	–	–	11
Epson (EP101)	10	10	8	–	–	–	–	28
Canon (AE-1)	12	10	—	–	–	2	4	28
Canon [Mini-Copier)	8	3	2	1	–	–	1	15
Mazda (New RX-7)	13	6	7	1	1	1	–	29
Matsushita Electric (Automatic Home Bakery)	8	8	1	1	1	1	–	20

Source: Norzaka (1990a)

Table 6.4

Corporate Careers and Educational Backgrounds of Core Members of the FX-3500 Development Team

Name	Career Path within Fuii Xerox	University Specialization
Hiroshi Yoshida	Technical Service Staff → Personnel → Product Planning → Product Management	Education
Ken'ichiro Fujita	Marketing Staff → Product Planning → Product Management	Commerce
Masao Suzuki	Planning → Research → Planning	Mechanical Engineering
Mitsutoshi Kitajima	Technical Service Staff → Quality Guarantee → Production	Electrical Engineering

model that was composed of people from the sales, development, and production departments. This system was called the "SED system," reflecting the sales, engineering, and development functions. Its initial goal was to manage development activities more systematically by integrating the knowledge and wisdom of "ordinary people" instead of relying on a few heroes.

Its operation was very flexible. The three functional areas were nominally differentiated and there was a built-in learning process that encouraged invasion into other areas. The members jointly performed the following functions:

• procuring personnel, facilities, and budget for the production plant
• analyzing the automobile market and competition
• setting a market target
• determining a price and a production volume.

The actual work-flow required team members to collaborate with their colleagues. Hiroo Watanabe, the team leader, commented:

I am always telling the team members that our work is not a relay race in which my work starts here and yours there. Everyone should run all the way from start to finish. Like rugby, all of us should run together, pass the ball left and right, and reach the goal as a united body.[23]

Type C in figure 6.6 illustrates the rugby approach. Type A shows the relay approach in which each phase of the development process is clearly separated and the baton is passed from one group to another. Type B is called the "sashimi system" at Fuji Xerox, because it looks like sliced raw fish (sashimi) served on a plate with one piece overlapping another (Imai, Nonaka, and Takeuchi 1985, p. 351).

Fluctuation and Creative Chaos

The third organizational condition for promoting the knowledge spiral is fluctuation and creative chaos, which stimulate the interaction between the organization and the external environment.[24] Fluctuation is different from complete disorder and characterized by "order without recursiveness." It is an order whose pattern is hard to predict at the beginning (Gleick 1987). If organizations adopt an open attitude toward environmental signals, they can exploit those signals ambiguity, redundancy, or noise in order to improve their own knowledge system.

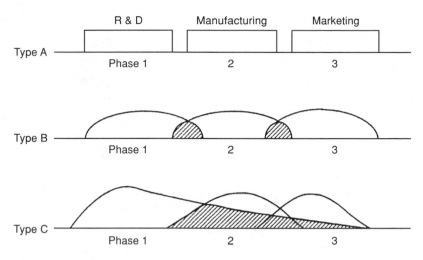

Figure 6.6
Sequential (A) vs. overlapped (B and C) phases of development. Source: Takeuchi and Nonaka, 1986

When fluctuation is introduced into an organization, its members face a "breakdown" of routines, habits, or cognitive frameworks. Winograd and Flores (1986) emphasize the importance of such periodic break-downs in the development of human perception. A breakdown refers to an interruption of our habitual, comfortable state of being. When we face such a breakdown, we have an opportunity to reconsider our fundamental thinking and perspective. In other words, we begin to question the validity of our basic attitudes toward the world. Such a process requires a deep personal commitment on the part of the individual. A breakdown demands that we turn our attention to dialogue as a means of social interaction, thus helping us to create new concepts.[25] This "continuous" process of questioning and reconsidering existing premises by individual members of the organization fosters organizational knowledge creation. An environmental fluctuation often triggers a breakdown within the organization, out of which new knowledge can be created. Some have called this phenomenon creating "order out of noise" or "order out of chaos."[26]

Chaos is generated naturally when the organization faces a real crisis, such as a rapid decline of performance due to changes in market needs

or significant growth of competitors. It can also be generated intentionally when the organization's leaders try to evoke a "sense of crisis"
among organizational members by proposing challenging goals. Ryuz-
aburo Kaku, chairman of Canon, often says, "The role of top management is to give employees a sense of crisis as well as a lofty ideal"
(Nonaka 1985, p. 142). This intentional chaos, which is referred to as
"creative chaos," increases tension within the organization and focuses
the attention of organizational members on defining the problem and
resolving the crisis situation.

This approach is in sharp contrast to the information-processing paradigm, in which a problem is simply given and a solution found through
a process of combining relevant information based upon a preset algo-
rithm. Such a process ignores the importance of defining the problem to
be solved. To attain such definition, problems must be constructed from
the knowledge available at a certain point in time and context.

Japanese companies often resort to the purposeful use of ambiguity
and "creative chaos." Top management often employs ambiguous visions
(or so-called "strategic equivocality") and intentionally creates a fluctuation within the organization. Nissan's CEO, Yutaka Kume, for example, coined the catch phrase "Let's change the flow," by which he tried
to promote creativity through an active investigation of alternatives to
established procedures. When the philosophy or vision of top management is ambiguous, that ambiguity leads to "interpretative equivocality"
at the level of the implementing staff.

It should be noted that the benefits of "creative chaos" can only be
realized when organizational members have the ability to reflect upon
their actions. Without reflection, fluctuation tends to lead to "destruc-
tive" chaos. Schön (1983) captures this key point as follows: "When someone reflects while in action, he becomes a researcher in the practice
context. He is not dependent on the categories of established theory
and technique, but constructs a new theory of the unique case" (p.68).
The knowledge-creating organization is required to institutionalize this
"reflection-in-action" in its process to make chaos truly "creative."

Top management's ambiguity with respect to philosophy or vision can
lead to a reflection or questioning of value premises as well as of factual
premises upon which corporate decision making is anchored. Value premises are subjective in nature and concern preferences; they make possible
a far broader range of choice. Factual premises, on the other hand, are

objective in nature and deal with how the real world operates; they provide a concrete but limited range of choice.

Chaos is sometimes created independently of top management's philosophy. An individual organizational member can set a high goal in order to elevate him or herself or the team to which he or she belongs. Hiroo Watanabe's pursuit of the "ideal" car, challenging the "reasoning of Detroit," is an example of a goal set high. High goals, whether set by top management or individual employees, enhance personal commitment. As Taiyu Kobayashi, the former chairman of Fujitsu, pointed out, high goals may intensify individual wisdom as well:

Relaxed in a comfortable place, one can hardly think sharply. Wisdom is squeezed out of someone who is standing on the cliff and is struggling to survive...without such struggles, we would have never been able to : catch up with IBM. (Kobayashi 1985, p. 171)

In sum, fluctuation in the organization can trigger creative chaos, which induces and strengthens the subjective commitment of individuals. In actual day-to-day operation, organizational members do not regularly face such a situation. But the example from Nissan has shown that top management may intentionally bring about fluctuation and allow "interpretative equivocality" to emerge at lower levels of the organization. This equivocality acts as a trigger for individual members to change their fundamental ways of thinking. It also helps to externalize their tacit knowledge.

Redundancy

Redundancy is the fourth condition that enables the knowledge spiral to take place organizationally. To Western managers who are preoccupied with the idea of efficient information processing or uncertainty reduction (Galbraith 1973), the term "redundancy" may sound pernicious because of its connotations of unnecessary duplication, waste, or information overload. What we mean here by redundancy is the existence of information that goes beyond the immediate operational requirements of organizational members. In business organizations, redundancy refers to intentional overlapping of information about business activities, management responsibilities, and the company as a whole.

For organizational knowledge creation to take place, a concept created by an individual or group needs to be shared by other individuals who may not need the concept immediately. Sharing redundant information

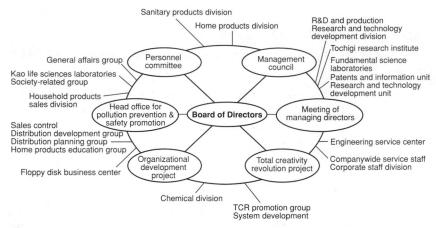

Figure 6.7
Kao's bio-function-type organizational structure. *Source:* Kao Corp.

promotes the sharing of tacit knowledge, because individuals can sense what others are trying to articulate. In this sense, redundancy of information speeds up the knowledge-creation process. Redundancy is especially important in the concept development stage, when it is critical to articulate images rooted in tacit knowledge. At this stage, redundant information enables individuals to invade each other's functional boundaries and offer advice or provide new information from different perspectives. In short, redundancy of information brings about "learning by intrusion" into each individual's sphere of perception.

Redundancy of information is also a prerequisite to realization of McCulloch's (1965) "principle of redundancy of potential command"—that is, each part of an entire system carrying the same degree of importance and having a potential of becoming its leader. Even within a strictly hierarchical organization, redundant information helps build unusual communication channels. Thus redundancy of information facilitates the interchange between hierarchy and nonhierarchy.[27] Sharing extra information also helps individuals understand where they stand in the organization, which in turn functions to control the direction of individual thinking and action. Individuals are not unconnected but loosely coupled with each other, and take meaningful positions in the whole organizational context. Thus redundancy of information provides the organization with a self-control mechanism to keep it heading in a certain direction.

There are several ways to build redundancy into the organization. One is to adopt an overlapping approach, as illustrated by Japanese companies' "rugby-style" product development in which different functional departments work together in a "fuzzy" division of labor (Takeuchi and Nonaka 1986). Some companies divide the product development team into competing groups that develop different approaches to the same project and then argue over advantages and disadvantages of their proposals. This internal competition encourages the team to look at a project from a variety of perspectives. Under the guidance of a team leader, the team eventually develops a common understanding of the "best" approach. Another way to build redundancy into the organization is through a "strategic rotation" of personnel, especially between vastly different areas of technology or functions such as R&D and marketing. Such rotation helps organizational members understand its business from multiple perspectives, thereby making organizational knowledge more "fluid" and easier to put into practice. It also enables each employee to diversify her or his skills and information sources. The extra information held by individuals across different functions helps the organization expand its knowledge-creation capacity.

One of the most notable characteristics of Japanese organizations compared with their Western counterparts is the value placed on redundant information. Leading Japanese firms have institutionalized redundancy within themselves in order to develop new products and services swiftly in response to fast-changing markets and technologies. Japanese firms have also developed many other organizational devices that increase and maintain redundancy. Among them are frequent meetings on both regular and irregular bases (e.g., Honda's brainstorming camp or tama dashi kai) and formal and informal communication networks (e.g., drinking sessions after working hours). These devices facilitate the sharing of both tacit and explicit knowledge.

Redundancy of information increases the amount of information to be processed and can lead to the problem of information overload. It also increases the cost of knowledge creation, at least in the short run (e.g., decreased operational efficiency). Therefore, balancing between creation and processing of information is another important issue. One way to deal with the possible downside of redundancy is to make clear where information can be located and where knowledge is stored within the organization.

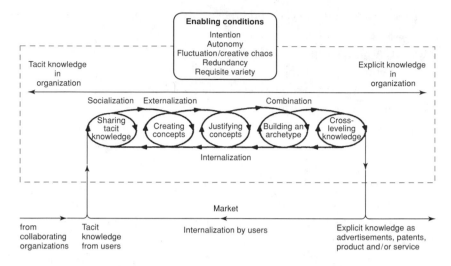

Figure 6.8
Five-phase model of the organizational knowledge-creation process

Requisite Variety

The fifth condition that helps to advance the knowledge spiral is requisite variety. According to Ashby (1956), an organization's internal diversity must match the variety and complexity of the environment in order to deal with challenges posed by the environment. Organizational members can cope with many contingencies if they possess requisite variety, which can be enhanced by combining information differently, flexibly, and quickly, and by providing equal access to information throughout the organization. To maximize variety, everyone in the organization should be assured of the fastest access to the broadest variety of necessary information, going through the fewest steps (Numagami, Ohta, and Nonaka 1989).

When information differentials exist within the organization, organizational members cannot interact on equal terms, which hinders the search for different interpretations of new information. Kao Corp., Japan's leading maker of household products such as detergents, believes that all employees should have equal access to corporate information. Kao has developed a computerized information network for this purpose. It has become the basis for opinion exchanges among various organizational units with different viewpoints.

Kao has also built an organizational structure, shown in figure 6.7, that allows the various organizational units and the computerized information network to be interwoven organically and flexibly. Kao named this structure a "bio-function-type" of organization. Under this structure, each organization unit works in unison with other units to cope with various environmental factors and events, just as a living Organism would. The human body, for example, reacts instinctively to itching by scratching the part of the body affected. The message relayed from the skin is received by the brain, which orders the hand movement. Lymph glands also go into action if necessary. Kao regards this kind of coordinated chain reaction an ideal way to cope with the external environment. Kao believes this "bio-function-type" structure helps to eliminate hierarchy and foster organizational knowledge creation.

Developing a flat and flexible organizational structure in which the different units are interlinked with an information network is one way to deal with the complexity of the environment. Another way to react quickly to unexpected fluctuations in the environment and maintain internal diversity is to change organizational structure frequently. Matsushita, for example, restructured its divisional system three times in the past decade. In addition, frequent rotation of personnel enables employees to acquire multifunctional knowledge, which helps them to cope with multifaceted problems and unexpected environmental fluctuations. Such a fast-cycle rotation of personnel can be seen at the Ministry of International Trade and Industry (MITI), where the bureaucrats rotate from one job to the next every two years.

Five-Phase Model of the Organizational Knowledge

Creation Process

Thus far we have looked at each of the four modes of knowledge conversion and the five enabling conditions that promote organizational knowledge creation. In this section we present an integrated, five-phase model of the organizational knowledge-creation process, using the basic constructs developed within the theoretical framework and incorporating the time dimension into our theory. The model, which should be interpreted as an ideal example of the process, consists of five phases: (1) sharing tacit knowledge; (2) creating concepts; (3) justifying concepts;

(4) building an archetype; and (5) cross-leveling knowledge (see figure 6.8).

The organizational knowledge-creation process starts with the sharing of tacit knowledge, which corresponds roughly to socialization, since the rich and untapped knowledge that resides in individuals must first be amplified within the organization. In the second phase, tacit knowledge shared by, for example, a self-organizing team is converted to explicit knowledge in the form of a new concept, a process similar to external-ization. The created concept has to be justified in the third phase, in which the organization determines if the new concept is truly worthy of pursuit. Receiving the go-ahead, the concepts are converted in the fourth phase into an archetype, which can take the form of a prototype in the case of "hard" product development or an operating mechanism in the case of "soft" innovations, such as a new corporate value, a novel man-agerial system, or an innovative organizational structure. The last phase extends the knowledge created in, for example, a division to others in the division, across to other divisions, or even to outside constituents in what we term cross-leveling of knowledge. These outside constituents include consumers, affiliated companies, universities, and distributors. A knowledge-creating company does not operate in a closed system but in an open system in which knowledge is constantly exchanged with the outside environment. We shall describe each of the five phases in more detail below.

The First Phase: Sharing Tacit Knowledge
As we have mentioned repeatedly, an organization cannot create knowl-edge by itself. Since tacit knowledge held by individuals is the basis of organizational knowledge creation, it seems natural to start the process by focusing on tacit knowledge, which is the rich, untapped source of new knowledge. But tacit knowledge cannot be communicated or passed onto others easily, since it is acquired primarily through experience and not easily expressible in words. Thus, the sharing of tacit knowledge among multiple individuals with different backgrounds, perspectives, and motivations becomes the critical step for organizational knowledge cre-ation to take place. The individuals' emotions, feelings, and mental mod-els have to be shared to build mutual trust.

To effect that sharing, we need a "field" in which individuals can interact with each other through face-to-face dialogues. It is here that they share experiences and synchronize their bodily and mental rhythms. The typical field of interaction is a self-organizing team, in which members from various functional departments' work together to achieve a common goal. Examples of a self-organizing team include Matsushita's Home Bakery team and the Honda City team. At Matsushita, team members apprenticed themselves to the head baker at the Osaka International Hotel to capture the essence of kneading skill through bodily experience. At Honda, team members shared their mental models and technical skills in discussing what an ideal car should evolve into, often over sake and away from the office. These examples show that the first phase of the organizational knowledge-creation process corresponds to socialization.

A self-organizing team facilitates organizational knowledge creation through the requisite variety of the team members, who experience redundancy of information and share their interpretations of organizational intention. Management injects creative chaos by setting challenging goals and endowing team members with a high degree of autonomy. An autonomous team starts to set its own task boundaries and, as a "boundary-spanning unit," begins to interact with the external environment, accumulating both tacit and explicit knowledge.

The Second Phase: Creating Concepts

The most intensive interaction between tacit and explicit knowledge occurs in the second phase. Once a shared mental model is formed in the field of interaction, the self-organizing team then articulates it through further continuous dialogue, in the form of collective reflection. The shared tacit mental model is verbalized into words and phrases, and finally crystallized into explicit concepts. In this sense, this phase corresponds to externalization.

This process of converting tacit knowledge into explicit knowledge is facilitated by the use of multiple reasoning methods such as deduction, induction, and abduction. Particularly useful for this phase is abduction, which employs figurative language such as metaphors and analogies. In developing City, for example, the Honda development team made ample use of figurative language such as "Automobile Evolution," "man-maximum, machine-minimum," and "Tall Boy." The quality of dialogue among team members can also be raised through the use of dialectics, which instills a creative way of thinking into the organization. It is an iterative and spiral process in which contradictions and paradoxes are utilized to synthesize new knowledge.

Concepts are created cooperatively in this phase through dialogue. Autonomy helps team members to diverge their thinking freely, with intention serving as a tool to converge their thinking in one direction. To create concepts, team members have to rethink their existing premises fundamentally. Requisite variety helps the team in this regard by providing different angles or perspectives for looking at a problem. Fluctuation and chaos, either from the outside or inside, also help members to change their way of thinking fundamentally. Redundancy of information enables team members to understand figurative language better and to crystallize their shared mental model.

The Third Phase: Justifying Concepts

In our theory of organizational knowledge creation, knowledge is defined as justified true belief. Therefore, new concepts created by individuals or the team need to be justified at some point in the procedure. Justification involves the process of determining if the newly created concepts are truly worthwhile for the organization and society. It is similar to a screening process. Individuals seem to be justifying or screening information, concepts, or knowledge continuously and unconsciously throughout the entire process. The organization, however, must conduct this justification in a more explicit way to check if the organizational intention is still intact and to ascertain if the concepts being generated meet the needs of society at large. The most appropriate time for the organization to conduct this screening process is right after the concepts have been created.[28]

For business organizations, the normal justification criteria include cost, profit margin, and the degree to which a product can contribute to the firm's growth. But justification criteria can be both quantitative and qualitative. For example, in the Honda City case, the "Tall Boy" concept had to be justified against the vision established by top management—to come up with a product concept fundamentally different from anything the company had done before and to make a car that was inexpensive but not cheap. It also had to be justified against the product-line concept articulated by middle management—to make the car "man-maximum, machine-minimum." More abstract criteria may include value premises such as adventure, romanticism, and aesthetics. Thus justification criteria need not be strictly objective and factual; they can also be judgmental and value-laden.

In a knowledge-creating company, it is primarily the role of top management to formulate the justification criteria in the form of organizational intention, which is expressed in terms of strategy or vision. Middle management can also formulate the justification criteria in the form of mid-range concepts. Although the key justification criteria are set by top management, and to some extent by middle management, this does not preclude other organizational units from having some autonomy in deciding their own subcriteria. For example, a committee comprised of 200 young employees within Matsushita determined that Matsushita employees in the twenty-first century should become "voluntary individuals" to adapt to expected social changes. To this extent, a company's justification criteria should be consistent with value systems or needs of the society at large, which should ideally be reflected in organizational intention. To avoid any misunderstanding about the company's intention, redundancy of information helps facilitate the justification process.

The Fourth Phase: Building an Archetype
In this fourth phase, the justified concept is converted into something tangible or concrete, namely, an archetype. An archetype can be thought of as a prototype in the case of a new-product development process. In the case of service or organizational innovation, an archetype could be thought of as a model operating mechanism. In either case, it is built by combining newly created explicit knowledge with existing explicit knowledge. In building a prototype, for example, the explicit knowledge to be combined could take the form of technologies or components. Because justified concepts, which are explicit, are converted into archetypes, which are also explicit, this phase is akin to combination.

Just as an architect builds a mock-up before starting the actual construction, organizational members engage in building a prototype of the real product or a model of the actual system. To build a prototype, they pull together people with differing expertise (e.g., R&D, production, marketing, quality control), develop specifications that meet everyone's approval, and actually manufacture the first full-scale form of a newly created product concept. To build a model, say, of a new organizational structure, people from the affected sections within the organization, as well as experts in different fields (e.g., human resources management, legal, strategic planning), are assembled to draw up a new organizational chart, job description, reporting system, or operating procedure. In a way, their role is similar to that of the architect—they are responsible for developing the blueprint as well as actually building the new form of an organizational concept. Attention to detail is the key to managing this complex process.

Because this phase is complex, dynamic cooperation of various departments within the organization is indispensable. Both requisite variety and redundancy of information facilitate this process. Organizational intention also serves as a useful tool for converging the various kinds of know-how and technologies that reside within the organization, as well as for promoting interpersonal and interdepartmental cooperation. On the other hand, autonomy and fluctuation are generally not that relevant at this stage of the organizational knowledge creation process.

The Fifth Phase: Cross-Leveling of Knowledge

Organizational knowledge creation is a never-ending process that upgrades itself continuously. It does not end once an archetype has been developed. The new concept, which has been created, justified, and modeled, moves on to a new cycle of knowledge creation at a different ontological level. This interactive and spiral process, which we call cross-leveling of knowledge, takes place both intraorganizationally and interorganizationally.

Intraorganizationally, knowledge that is made real or that takes form as an archetype can trigger a new cycle of knowledge creation, expanding horizontally and vertically across the organization. An example of horizontal cross-fertilization can be seen within Matsushita, where Home Bakery induced the creation of other "Easy & Rich" product concepts, such as a fully automatic coffee maker within the same division and a new generation of large-screen TV sets from another division. In these cases, cross-fertilization took place across different sections within a division as well as across different divisions. An example of vertical cross-fertilization also comes from Matsushita. The development of Home Bakery inspired Matsushita to adopt "Human Electronics" as the umbrella concept at the corporate level. This umbrella concept opened up a series of soul-searching activities within the company to address what kind of company Matsushita should be in the twenty-first century and how "human" Matsushita employees can be. These activities culminated in the development of MIT'93 (Mind and Management Innovation Toward '93), which was instrumental in reducing the number of annual working hours at the front line to 1,800 hours, thereby freeing up time for people at the front line. In this case, knowledge created in one division led to the adoption of an umbrella concept at the corporate level, which in turn affected the lives of employees at the front line.

Interorganizationally, knowledge created by the organization can mobilize knowledge of affiliated companies, customers, suppliers, competitors, and others outside the company through dynamic interaction. For example, an innovative new approach to budgetary control developed by one company could bring about changes in an affiliated company's financial control system, which in turn may trigger a new round of innovation. Or a customer's reaction or feedback to a new-product concept may initiate a new cycle of product development. At Apple Computer, for example, when product development engineers come up with ideas for new products, they build a prototype that embodies those ideas and bring it directly to customers to seek their reaction. Depending on the reaction or feedback, a new round of development may be initiated.

For this phase to function effectively, it is essential that each organizational unit have the autonomy to take the knowledge developed somewhere else and apply it freely across different levels and boundaries. Internal fluctuation, such as the frequent rotation of personnel, will facilitate knowledge transfer. So will redundancy of information and requisite variety. And in intraorganizational cross-leveling, organizational intention will act as a control mechanism on whether or not knowledge should be cross-fertilized within the company.

Summary

Recall that we started to develop our theoretical framework in this chapter by pointing out the two dimensions—epistemological and ontological—of organizational knowledge creation (see figure 6.1). The epistemological dimension, which is graphically represented on the vertical axis, is where knowledge conversion takes place between tacit knowledge and explicit knowledge. Four modes of this conversion—socialization, externalization, combination, and internalization—were discussed. These modes are not independent of each other, but their interactions produce a spiral when time is introduced as the third dimension. We introduced five organizational conditions—intention, fluctuation/chaos, autonomy, redundancy, and requisite variety—that enable (thus the term "enabling conditions") the four modes to be transformed into a knowledge spiral.

The ontological dimension, which is represented in the horizontal axis, is where knowledge created by individuals is transformed into knowledge at the group and organizational levels. These levels are not independent of each other, but interact with each other interactively and continuously. Again we introduced time as the third dimension to develop the five-phase process of organizational knowledge creation— sharing tacit knowledge, creating concepts, justifying concepts, building an archetype, and cross-leveling knowledge. Another spiral takes place at the ontological dimension, when knowledge developed at, for example, the project-team level is transformed into knowledge at the divisional level, and eventually at the corporate or interorganizational level. The five enabling conditions promote the entire process and facilitate the spiral.

The transformation process within these two knowledge spirals is the key to understanding our theory. If we had a three-dimensional chart, we could show that the knowledge spiral at the epistemological level rises upward, whereas the knowledge spiral at the ontological level moves from left to right and back again to the left in a cyclical motion. And, of course, the truly dynamic nature of our theory can be depicted as the interaction of the two knowledge spirals over time. Innovation emerges out of these spirals.

References

1. Shannon later commented: "I think perhaps the word *information* is causing more trouble...than it is worth, except that it is difficult to find another word that is anywhere near right. It should be kept solidly in mind that [information] is only a measure of the difficulty in transmitting the sequence produced by some information source" (quoted by Roszack 1986, p. 12). Boulding (1983) notes that Shannon's assessment was analogous to a telephone bill, which is calculated on the basis of time and distance but gives no insight into the content of information, and called it Bell Telephone (BT) information. Dretske (1981) argues that a genuine theory of information would be a theory about the content of our messages, not a theory about the form in which this content is embodied.

2. The importance of the knowledge-action relationship has been recognized in the area of artificial intelligence. For example, Gruber (1989) examined experts'

"strategic knowledge" that guides their actions and has attempted to develop tools for acquiring such knowledge.

3. Brown and Duguid's (1991) work on "evolving communities of practice" shows how individuals' actual ways of working and learning might be very different from relatively rigid, official practices specified by the organization. In reality, informal groups evolve among individuals seeking to solve a particular problem or pursuing other commonly held objectives. Membership in these groups is decided by individuals' abilities to trade practically valuable information. Orr (1990) argues that members exchange ideas and share narratives or "war stories," thereby building a shared understanding out of conflicting and confusing information. Thus knowledge creation includes not only innovation but also learning that can shape and develop approaches to daily work.

4. For example, we recognize our neighbor's face without being able to explain how to do so in words. Moreover, we sense others' feelings from their facial expressions, but explaining them in words is more difficult. Put another way, while it is virtually impossible to articulate the feelings we get from our neighbor's face, we are still aware of the overall impression. For further discussion on tacit knowledge, see Polanyi (1958) and Gelwick (1977).

5. We did not include Polanyi in chapter 2, because he is still considered minor in Western philosophy because of his view and background. Michael Polanyi was born in Hungary and was the brother of Karl Polanyi, an economist, who may be better known as the author of *The Great Transformation*. Michael Polanyi himself was a renowned chemist and rumored to be very close to the Nobel Prize until he turned to philosophy at the age of 50. Polanyi's philosophy has implicit or explicit agreements with those of "later" Wittgenstein and Merleau-Ponty in terms of their emphases on action, body, and tacit knowledge. For a discussion on an affinity between Polanyi and later Wittgenstein with regard to tacit knowledge, see Gill (1974).

6. Brown (1992) argues that "The organizations of the future will be 'knowledge refineries' in which employees will synthesize understanding and interpretations from the sea of information that threatens to flood them from all sides" (p. 3). In a knowledge refinery, he continues, workers need to collaborate with both the past and the present. While collaboration with the present is about sharing tacit knowledge, collaboration with the past draws on experiences gained from previous ways of doing things.

7. According to Maturana and Varela (1980), "The linguistic domain as a domain of orienting behavior requires at least two interacting organisms with comparable domains of interactions, so that a cooperative system of consensual interactions may be developed in which the emerging conduct of the two organisms is relevant for both... The central feature of human existence is its occurrence in a linguistic cognitive domain. This domain is constitutively social" (p. xxiv).

8. The ACT model is consonant with Ryle's (1949) categorization of knowledge into knowing that something "exists" and knowing "how" it operates. Also, Squire (1987) listed contending taxonomies with more than a dozen labels, such as "implicit" vs. "explicit" and "skill memory" vs. "fact memory." Most of these

distinctions separate properties to be grouped under "procedural" from those to be classified "declarative."

9. A survey of 105 Japanese middle managers was conducted to test the hypothesis that the knowledge creation construct is comprised of four knowledge conversion processes—socialization, externalization, combination, and internalization. Factor loadings from first-order and second-order factor analyses empirically validated the existence of these four conversion processes. For details, see Nonaka, Byosiere, Borucki, and Konno (1994).

10. For a limited analysis of externalization from a viewpoint of information creation, see Nonaka (1987).

11. Cannon-Bowers, Salas, and Converse (1993) define "shared mental models" as "knowledge structures held by members of a team that enable them to form accurate explanations and expectations for the task, and in turn, to coordinate their actions and adapt their behavior to demands of the task and other team members" (p. 228), based upon their extensive review of the literature on the shared mental model and their research on team decision making. To understand how a shared mental model is created, the German philosopher Hans-Georg Gadamer's concept of "fusion of horizons" is helpful. The concept was developed for philosophical hermeneutics or the study of methodology for interpreting historical texts. Gadamer (1989) argues that a true understanding of a text is a "fusion" of the interpreter's and the author's horizons. He defines the horizon as "the range of vision that includes everything that can be seen from a particular vantage point" (p. 302). Applying this concept to our context, we can argue that socialization is a "fusion" of participants' tacit knowledge into a shared mental model.

12. Proposing the concept of "field epistemology," Scheflen (1982) emphasizes the importance of "interaction rhythms" in forming a field for common understanding, and contends that communication is the simultaneous sharing of information existing in the situation. Similarly, Condon (1976) argues that communication is a simultaneous and contextual phenomenon in which people feel a change occurring, share the same sense of change, and are moved to take action. In other words, he says, communication is like a wave that passes through people's bodies and culminates when everyone synchronizes with the wave. From a social psychological perspective, Hogg and Abrams (1993) observe that "group behavior might be motivated by a search for meaning and a coherent self-concept" (p. 189).

13. Graumann (1990) views dialogue as multi-perspective cognition. As noted before, language is inherently related to action, as suggested by the term "speech act" (Austin 1962; Searle 1969). Dialogue, therefore, may be seen as a collective action. Moreover, according to Kant, the world is created by language, and creating concepts is creating the world.

14. Interviewed on January 25, 1984.

15. These authors emphasize the importance of creating shared meaning for organized action, arguing that "equifinal meanings" for joint experience need to be developed to create shared meaning in the organization. Metaphor is one of

four mechanisms to develop equifinal meanings that they found through their discourse analyses. For more discussion about metaphor and the other three mechanisms logical argument, affect modulation, and linguistic indirection—see Donnellon, Gray, and Bougon (1986).

16. The following famous episode illustrates the process. F. A. Kekule, a German chemist, discovered the chemical structure of benzene—a hexagonal ring of carbon atoms through a dream of a snake gripping its own tail. In this case, the snake pattern was a metaphor, and possible combinations of the pattern became analogies of other organic chemical compounds. Thus, Kekule developed the structural model of organic chemistry.

17. According to Lakoff and Johnson (1980), "metaphor is pervasive in everyday life, not just in language but in thought and action" (p. 3).

18. Information and communications technologies used for this purpose include VAN (Value-Added Network), LAN (Local Area Network), E-Mail (Electronic Mail), POS (Point-Of-Sales) system, "Groupware" for CSCW (Computer Supported Cooperative Work), and CAD/CAM (Computer-Aided Design/ Manufacturing).

19. In the triad database system, data from the Market Metrics' Supermarket Solutions system, which integrates POS data from supermarkets nationwide, is hooked to customized data on shopping behaviors provided by Information Resources, and lifestyle data from the Equifax Marketing Decision System's Microvision database. For more information, see "Micro-Merchandizing with KGF," *Food and Beverage Marketing*, 10, no. 6 (1991); "Dawn of Brand Analysis," *Food and Beverage Marketing*, 10, no. 10 (1991); and "Partnering," *Supermarket Business*, 46, no. 5 (1991).

20. Neisser (1976) argues that cognition as knowing and understanding occurs only in the context of purposeful activity. From an organization theory perspective, moreover, Weick (1979) contends that an organization's interpretation of environmental information has an element of self-fulfilling prophecy, because the organization has a strong will to self-actualize what it wants to become. He calls this phenomenon the "enactment" of environment.

21. Seen from the Simonian viewpoint of "bounded rationality" and the viewpoint that the goal of the organization is to process information efficiently, autonomy is merely a source of "noise" and therefore not desirable. The notion of cognitive limit is indeed a commonsensical one that is difficult to beat. If, however, we approach the same problem from the viewpoint that human beings have an unlimited capability to obtain and create knowledge, it appears that human beings know no boundary in experiencing and accumulating tacit knowledge. Underlying that accumulation of tacit knowledge is the sense of purpose and autonomy. Human beings often create noise intentionally, thereby overcoming themselves.

22. The team should be established with due consideration of the principles of self-organization such as learning to learn, requisite variety, minimum critical specification, and redundancy of functions (Morgan 1986). Requisite variety will be discussed later.

23. In our *Harvard Business Review* article entitled "The New New Product Development Game" (Takeuchi and Nonaka 1986), we argued that in today's fast-paced and fiercely competitive world, this overlapping, rugby-style approach has tremendous merit in terms of speed and flexibility.

24. Gibson (1979) hypothesizes that knowledge lies in the environment itself, contrary to the traditional epistemological view that it exists inside the human brain. Norman (1988) argues that knowledge exists not only inside the brain but also in the external world in the forms of things, others, and situations.

25. Piaget (1974) notes the importance of the role of contradiction in the interaction between subject and environment. The root of contradiction, he argues, lies in the coordination between the positive and negative sides of specific perception or behavior, which in turn is indispensable for creating new concepts.

26. According to the principle of "order out of noise" proposed by von Foerster (1984), the self-organizing system can increase its ability to survive by purposefully introducing such noise into itself. Order in the natural world includes not only the static and crystallized order in which entropy is zero but also the "unstable" order in which new structures are formed by the working of matter and energy. The latter is what Prigogine and Stengers (1984) call "order out of chaos" in their theory of dissipative structure. In an evolutionary planning perspective, moreover, Jantsch (1980) argues: "In contrast to widely held belief, planning in an evolutionary spirit therefore does not result in the reduction of uncertainty and complexity, but in their increases. Uncertainty increases because the spectrum of options is deliberately widened; imagination comes into play" (p. 267). Researchers who have developed the chaos theory have found the creative nature of chaos. See, for example, Gleick (1987) and Waldrop (1992). For applications of the chaos theory to management, see Nonaka (1988a) and Zimmerman (1993).

27. Using the term *heterarchy*, which means "nonhierarchy," Hedlund (1986) explains the role of redundant information as a vehicle for problem formulation and knowledge creation on the basis of procedures different from those officially specified by the organization.

28. The final justification of created concepts and their realized forms, i.e., products and/or services, occurs in the marketplace.

7

Reflection on Knowledge Management from Japan

Hirotaka Takeuchi and Ikujiro Nonaka

Emerging from the West is a wide consensus on the strategic importance of managing knowledge well. A recent poll of executives from 80 large companies in the US, such as Amoco, Chemical Bank, Hewlett-Packard, Kodak and Pillsbury, showed that four out of five believed managing knowledge of their organizations should be an essential or important part of business strategy.

The "knowledge management boom" has hit the West like lighting in recent years. The roots of knowledge go way back to Plato, in 400 BC, but knowledge management, which Business Week defines as the idea of capturing knowledge gained by individuals and spreading it to others in the organization, is heralded today as one of the newest ideas in business management. Signs of the boom are visible everywhere in the Western business world today. They include new books and journals on knowledge management, knowledge management conferences, knowledge management consulting services backed up by knowledge databases, and new corporate titles (chief knowledge officer), among other things.

Where does Japan stand with respect to knowledge management?

"Nowhere" is probably the most accurate answer. Visible signs of the boom we saw in the West are nowhere to be found in Japan...no onrush of new books and journals on knowledge management being published, no conferences being organized, no onrush of consulting engagements, no new databases being formed, and no new corporate titles being created. Neither are Japanese companies sending their managers in droves to Scandinavia to learn how knowledge is being measured, nor to the US to observe how knowledge initiatives are being managed at Hewlett-Packard, GE or 3M, as they have typically done with new management ideas.

Why are Japanese companies not jumping on the bandwagon with respect to knowledge management? It is not because they do not fully recognize the importance of knowledge as the resource and as the key source of innovation. They do, as we pointed out in The Knowledge-Creating Company: How Japanese Companies Create the Dynamics of Innovation. What they are not convinced about is the value of simply measuring and managing existing knowledge in a mechanical and systematic manner. Can you measure the tidbits of knowledge stored in the brains of managers? Can you really create new knowledge by trying to micro-manage it? We doubt if measuring and managing existing knowledge alone will enhance innovation.

The Japanese approach to knowledge differs from the West in a number of ways. We will highlight three fundamental differences here:

• how knowledge is viewed: knowledge is not viewed simply as data or information that can be stored in the computer in Japan; it also involves emotions, values, hunches;
• what companies do with knowledge: companies do not merely "manage" knowledge, but "create" it as well;
• who the key players are: everyone in the organization is involved in creating organizational knowledge, with middle managers serving as key knowledge engineers.

The distinction between explicit knowledge and tacit knowledge is the key to understanding the differences between the Western approach to knowledge (knowledge management) and the Japanese approach to knowledge (knowledge creation). The West has placed a strong emphasis on explicit knowledge and Japan on tacit knowledge.

An impression we have on the reason why Western managers tend to downplay the importance of organizational knowledge creation can be traced to the view of knowledge as necessarily explicit. They take for granted a view of the organization as a machine for "information processing." The view is deeply ingrained in the traditions of Western management, from Frederick Taylor to Herbert Simon.

The infatuation in the West with knowledge management reflects the bias toward "explicit" knowledge, which is the easier of the two kinds of knowledge to measure, control and process. Explicit knowledge can be much more easily put into a computer, stored into a database, and transmitted online than the highly subjective, personal and cognitive "tacit" knowledge. But in order to create new knowledge, we need the two kinds of knowledge to interact with each other through the actions of individuals within the organization.

Once the importance of tacit knowledge is realized, then one begins to think about innovation in a wholly new way. It is not just about putting together diverse bits of data and information. The personal commitment of the employees and their identifying with the company and its mission become crucial. Unlike information, knowledge is about commitment and beliefs; it is a function of a particular stance, perspective or intention. In this respect, the creation of new knowledge is as much about ideals as it is about ideas; and that fact fuels innovation. Similarly, unlike information, knowledge is about action; it is always knowledge "to some end." The unique information an individual possesses must be acted upon for new knowledge to be created. This voluntary action also fuels innovation.

Another impression we have is that the responsibility for knowledge management initiatives in the West rests with the selected few, not with everyone in the organization. Knowledge is managed by a few key players in staff positions, including information processing, internal consultancy or human resources management. In contrast in Japan, knowledge is created by the interaction of front-line employees, middle managers and top management, with middle managers in line positions playing the key synthesizing role.

With a few exceptions, notably GE and Hewlett-Packard, front-line employees are not an integral part of knowledge management. This situation is similar to the days of Frederick Taylor, which did not tap the experiences and judgments of front-line workers as a source of knowledge. Consequently, the creation of new work methods for scientific management became the responsibility of the selected few in managerial positions. These "elites" were charged with the chore of classifying, tabulating and reducing the knowledge into rules and formulae and applying them to daily work. The danger of knowledge management is in having the responsibility for capturing the knowledge gained by individuals and spreading it to others in the organization rest in the hands of the selected few.

This reflection serves as a warning to Western managers who have jumped on the "knowledge management" bandwagon. Although the growing recognition of knowledge as the critical resource is welcome news, the hoopla in the West associated with knowledge management could be a blessing in disguise. As we have seen, the focus in the West has been on (1) explicit knowledge, (2) measuring and managing existing knowledge, and (3) the selected few carrying out knowledge management initiatives. This bias reinforces the view of the organization simply as a machine for information processing.

What Western companies need to do is to "unlearn" their existing view of knowledge and pay more attention to (1) tacit knowledge, (2) creating new knowledge, and (3) having everyone in the organization be involved. Only then can the organization be viewed as a living organism capable of creating continuous innovation in a self-organizing manner.

There is no doubt in anyone's mind that knowledge holds the key to generating continuous innovation. An old concept dating back to 400 BC has emerged in the West as the newest management idea. It would be pitiful, however, if it ended up being just a buzzword or if "knowledge management" degenerated into little more than a fad, as many management concepts have done in the past. For example, reengineering started out as a perfectly sensible management concept when first written about in 1990. But the hype that subsequently developed meant that the human factor was too quickly ignored. It would be tragic if history repeated itself with knowledge management.

References

1. Thomas A. Stewart, *Intellectual Capital: The New Wealth of Organizations.* New York: Doubleday, 1997, p. 63.

2. Knowledge is defined as "justified, true belief," a concept first introduced by Plato.

8

Knowledge Management: Linking Theory with Practice

Rüdiger Reinhardt

Treating knowledge as the fourth essential resource of value adding processes has led to major changes in economic and management theory. Empirical proof of knowledge related hypotheses are scarce. There is a lack of coherence between the different concepts of knowledge management as well as a major gap between knowledge management theory and practice.

The first part of this chapter critically examines the similarities and differences of the leading perspectives of knowledge management and organizational learning. The result of this analysis is a new integrative approach of knowledge management that helps to link knowledge management theory with practice. The second part of this chapter applies this approach via a case study analysis of a large German automotive supplier. Results show how the know-how of 10,000 employees can be identified and transformed into shared action with regard to the strategic goals of the firm.

The Challenge of Managing Knowledge

On the national-economic level, a new structural shift can be observed. A number of studies show the increasing importance of knowledge and information for value creation, economic growth, and wealth [1][2][3][4]. For example, in countries such as Germany, Sweden, and the United Kingdom, the total intangible investment since mid 1980 has passed physical investment [5][6]. In 1991, the U.S. expenditures for information technology ($112 billion) for the first time surpassed expenditures for production technology ($107 billion) [7].

On the *managerial level*, the roots of competitive advantage seem to be discussed anew: "The chilling fact is: At this moment we have no idea which companies, large or small, young or old, have sustainable organizational capability"[8]. There seems to be a general understanding that knowledge is the central source of organizational success [9], regardless if it is referred to as an *invisible asset* [10], *absorptive capacity* [11], *core competence* [12], *strategic asset* [13], *core capability* [14], *intangible resource* [15], *organizational memory* [16], or *intellectual capital* [17] [18][19].

If knowledge is an essential resource to establish competitive advantage, management obviously should—especially concerning the resource-based view of the firm [20][21]—attempt to identify, generate, deploy, and develop knowledge. Hence, managers need more knowledge about knowledge [22]. This situation leads to the following two managerial core questions of knowledge management: (1) How can the impact of knowledge on business performance be measured? (2) How can the knowledge-related value-adding process be managed?

Even if the world is now increasingly trading more in ideas and knowledge than in finished goods, answers to these two core questions are still a major challenge. On one hand, it is much more difficult to see and count ideas and expertise than it is money or products. On the other hand, managers are not provided with a coherent and practical model of the knowledge management process. Since there have been several attempts to answer the first question from the perspective of intellectual capital, answers to the second question seem to be somehow difficult due to the following reasons:

An increasing number of studies indicate a high managerial demand for implementation policies and blueprints [23][24][25][26][27][28][29].

A high diversity of concepts and tools of knowledge management and organizational learning exist [30][31[32][33] and consequently this makes implementation decisions difficult.

The development of knowledge-based theories of the firm that would help to derive and prove hypotheses in this field is only a very recent subject of research [34][35[36][37][38].

Contrary to the input-based perspective of knowledge, a *process perspective* of knowledge management is needed to overcome the empirical weaknesses of knowledge management research and practice [39]. This

- How can relevant organizational knowledge be identified and new knowledge be created and utilized?

- How can a system of knowledge creation and utilization be designed and organized?

- What measures provide management with information about the quality of the knowledge-management process?

- What methods and tools support the implementation of knowledge management?

Figure 8.1
Key questions of knowledge management

chapter deals with answering the following key questions of knowledge management and provides some insight into the practical implications of the resulting conclusions (see figure 8.1).

In order to provide a framework for answering the key questions, this article will proceed as follows. The first section elaborates the key theoretical dimensions and elements of recent discussion of knowledge management and organizational learning in order to synthesize them with an integrative model of knowledge management. The second section, a case study analysis, provides insight into the integration of the conceptual framework and the practice of knowledge management. Finally, the results of the case study are discussed in the context of the proposed model of integrative knowledge management.

Theoretical Background
A careful examination of the history of management theory and practice shows that improvement of efficiency and effectiveness of production processes as well as of financial capital flows was based on an explicit understanding of the nature of the distinct production factors with regard to measures and standards. This resulted from a close connection between practice and theory. Managers experimented with various processes, while researchers analyzed business practices and provided suggestions to improve operations.

So far, the same has not been applied to the production factor "knowledge." Managers suffer from a large number of disconnected models that

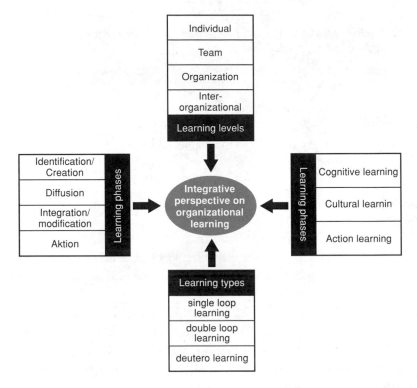

Figure 8.2
Integrative perspective on organizational learning concepts

fail to integrate overlapping components. Consequently, it is necessary to develop a process model of knowledge management that guides managers by implementing and monitoring knowledge related operations.

The literature on organizational learning and knowledge management seldom show integrative features [40]. Most authors add a new view on organizational learning without reference to the scope of existing literature.[1] Hence, the first step to put knowledge management into practice is to integrate the different perspectives of knowledge management with particular emphasis on the process perspective.

Theoretical Perspectives of Organizational Learning
Based on an extensive literature survey of organizational learning and knowledge management concepts, four analytical core perspectives on organizational learning and knowledge management can be identified: [44][45]

[46] *learning levels*, *learning modes*, *learning types*, and the *learning process* with its different phases (see figure 8.2).

The distinct characteristics of the model in figure 8.2 are briefly be described as follows:

Learning levels.   There has been extensive discussion on whether or not *organizational learning* can be treated distinctively from *individual learning* [47]. There is no doubt of the need to distinguish both classes of learning processes. An in-depth analysis of most organizational learning concepts makes it clear that team-learning processes are treated as key to organizational learning [48][49][50]. Most recently, the discussion of mergers and acquisitions are being reconstructed within the notion of *interorganizational learning* [51][52].

Learning modes.   There are three distinct perspectives to knowledge management and organizational learning: The cognitive perspective is based on theories of organizational decision making as well as on concepts of bounded rationality. The major attempt of this learning mode is to change the cognitive structures of the learning systems. The cultural perspective is based on interpretative human behavior concepts. It includes the assumption that reality is socially constructed by the sharing of meaning—especially as it relates to artifacts, symbols, metaphors, ceremonies, myths, etc., and how these factors are tied together on the basis of shared values and assumptions. Finally, the action perspective is rooted in experiential learning concepts as well as in the sociotechnical approach [53][54].

Learning types.   This analytical level was first outlined by Argyris & Schön as the distinction between single-loop, double-loop and deutero-learning.[2] *Single-loop learning* includes correction of deviations from actual performance concerning prescribed standard levels of performance. *Double-loop learning* is based on an analysis and the change of the actual organizational theory-in-use and includes the assumptions and rules that guide action—contrary to the espoused theory of the firm. Finally, *deutero learning* includes learning processes that result from reflection of learning processes and usually is a prerequisite of a sustainable change of norms, values and assumptions.

Learning Process: Finally distinct learning levels can be identified. Knowledge is *identified*—or, if not at hand—it has to be *created* [58]. This knowledge *diffuses* between several learning systems [59][60][61] and is at least *integrated* into existing knowledge systems on a collective and individual level or it is integrated into procedural rules of the organization whereby either integration or *modification* of the adopting system can take place [62][63]. Finally, this knowledge is *transformed into action* and applied in organizational routines in order to have an impact on behavior or on new products or services [64][65].

Implications for Knowledge Management Implementation

There are two major advantages of this integrative framework on organizational learning and knowledge management concepts:[3] As contemporary research shows that knowledge management can be understood as a goal-oriented process from a *theoretical perspective*. It can also be described based on:

- four different system levels of learning: the *individual*, the *team*, the *organizational* and the *interorganizational* levels of learning
- three different *learning modes*: the cognitive, the cultural and the action perspective
- three different *learning types*: single-loop, double-loop and deutero-learning
- four different *learning phases*: identification/creation, diffusion, integration/modification, and action.

This means that this integration helps to create a more in-depth understanding of the complexity of organizational learning and knowledge management processes.

Additionally, the *practical perspective* of the integrative framework provides an adequate analysis of the lack of empirical evidence of the implementation of organizational learning and knowledge management concepts. Alone, the implementation of knowledge management processes may take into account 144 distinct perspectives or models of organizational learning and knowledge management.[4]

Hence, it is clear that there is no single perspective that completely and thoroughly describes knowledge management and organizational learning. Consequently, with existing research, managers cannot expect *the* universal blueprint of implementing knowledge management with regards to improving the performance of a firm.

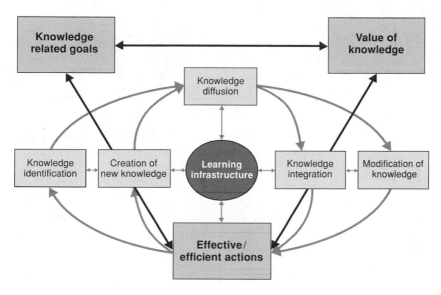

Figure 8.3
The practical perspective of knowledge management

Taking into account the major managerial tasks of designing, steering, and developing organizations, it additionally becomes clear that the analysis outlined above still lacks the core elements of management such as setting goals, measuring outcomes, and processes and organization of implementation processes (see figure 8.1).

From Organizational Learning Theory to *Practical* Knowledge Management

Since the analysis outlined above makes clear some of the general limitations in theory building and implementation of knowledge management, this article adds the managerial perspective of knowledge management to the process perspective of organizational learning, including goals and measures to knowledge, and the project perspective of the implementation perspective (see figure 8.3[5]).

Figure 8.3 contains the core elements of the integrative view of knowledge management regarding the consideration of synthesis of distinct theoretical perspectives as well as the integration of theory and practice[6]. The elements of the model of integrative knowledge management will be discussed below.

Table 8.1
Core Questions on the Phases of Knowledge Management

Identification/ creation	Where and how is knowledge, which is important to the organization outside the organization collected?
	How can internal knowledge systems be integrated in order to create new knowledge?
Diffusion	What exchange processes exist between the organization and its environment and within the organization?
	What kind of communication barriers can be identified— how can they removed?
Integration/ Modification	Which knowledge systems determine strategic decisions?
	How differentiated/integrated are the mental models of the dominant coalition?
Action	Do opportunities for testing new behaviors, without being punished, exist?
	What kind of structure, processes, and systems shape the transformation of knowledge into action?

The Process Perspective to Knowledge

Having already mentioned the learning phases in the previous section, the specific meaning of each of the learning phases can be defined and outlined by the following questions (see table 8.1).

On one hand, the questions in table 8.1 provide detailed insight into the process perspective of knowledge management. On the other hand, these questions also indicate the need for taking into account "classical" managerial perspectives to knowledge.

The Management Perspective of Knowledge

The above analysis has clearly identified the core features of knowledge management, but it also has shown an important weakness to practical knowledge management. Managers are not provided with the theoretical methods and tools that allow them to effectively formulate knowledge related goals, to organize a knowledge management process, and to monitor knowledge related operations. The following sections present how management can use this new integrative approach.

Knowledge Related Goals   Management activities are inseparable from goal setting. It is crucial to define knowledge-related goals in order to provide direction to knowledge management efforts. Regarding theories of strategic management, it is advantageous to distinguish between operational and strategic knowledge goals. The former deals with the direct impact of knowledge on daily work, while the latter includes long-term perspective of knowledge related benefits. Additionally, strategic knowledge goals provide a balance between operational duties and the time consumption of knowledge management activities [70].

Measuring and Valuing Knowledge   Behavior in business organizations is strongly shaped by measures [71]. Hence, managing knowledge resources in daily work implies to introduce knowledge related indicators. Below is a framework on enhancing traditional and process related business measures by reflective measures. Table 8.2 provides an overview on the core aspects of these indicators that are related to three evolutionary steps of management paradigms:

Table 8.2
Core Perspectives of Organizational Measures

Management Paradigm	Measuring/Monitoring criteria
Traditional management: Orientation to economic performance indicators	Which measures show that the organization has an economic survival capability, e.g., market share, sales, profit, ROI, cash flow, etc.?
Process management: *additional* attention to process measures	Which measures show that the value creation process leads to reliable, predictable, and customer satisfactory results, e.g., time to market, process reliability, cost of quality, etc.?
Knowledge management: *additional* attention to reflective measures	Which measures show that knowledge resources are explicitly taken into account in order to increase the organization's flexibility, e.g. explicit search for deviant information, explicit learning from other projects, implementing learning processes by systematic reflecting suboptimal outcomes and processes?

The implementation Perspective of Knowledge—the Learning infrastructure   Literature on strategy implementation includes many suggestions of the best way to implement change. Table 8.3 provides some major causes of mistakes in change processes [72][73][74].

Successful implementation efforts teach us that the existence of an informal infrastructure is supportive to the sustainability of change. This can be explained by the following three major reasons. If managers and employees are involved in project teams on several levels from the very beginning, the following often results: (1) commitment, responsibility, and ownership to the change process, (2) multiplication effects and (3) the adaptation of the process to the needs to all levels in an aligned way. These effects help to decrease the probability of the failures sketched in table 8.3.

Further Implications for the Implementation of Knowledge Management projects

The arguments developed above lead to the following two major consequences for practical knowledge management:

• Due to the amount of different knowledge management models, knowledge management in practice will be related to a specific combination of learning levels, learning modes, learning types, and learning phases. The implementation of knowledge management is strongly linked with the management of the different learning phases.

• Due to the management perspective of knowledge, additional elements of strategy implementation such as knowledge related goals and measures and an adequate project infrastructure have to be considered.

To understand the significance of this new model more clearly, a case study will shed light on the relevance of this integrative approach.

Implementing the Integrative Perspective of Knowledge Management—the Case Study

Before going into detail of the case study, some background information of the company and thereby of the restrictions of publishing results is provided.

The Company   The case study is based on experiences of a German automotive supplier (10,000 employees, 4 locations) from 1995 to 1998.

Table 8.3
Failures of Change Management

Barrier	Description
Internal focus	Organizations either fail to find or reject ideas and information from outside—the so-called "not invented here" syndrome.
Lack of credibility	Information sources, recommendations, and reports are perceived as political or biased and not taken seriously.
Secrecy	A need-to-know culture prevents people from developing a general perspective on important decisions and denies access to information required for specific situations.
Lack of proper skills	The people involved in the implementation of change are assigned with little regard to training or skill. There is little training or support from experienced people.
Lack of resources	Attempts to implement change are made without providing adequate resources. People are asked to do things "in their spare time."
Lack of discipline	Management will not kill projects; the process to choose among projects is inconsistently applied; there are many "special cases."
Lack of strategy	Corporate strategies are either vague vision statements or over-specified long-term plans. Neither provides much guidance. The result: conflicting priorities, and general confusion.
Metrics are misused	Predictions are turned in commitments. Uncertainties are represented by misleadingly precise forecasts. Historical measures are used for punishment rather than learning.
Tendency to oversimplify	Firms face increasingly new situations and systems and less time for really understanding them and developing perspective. Faced with too much data and not enough information, people tend to oversimplify to deal with overload.
People are reluctant to change	The new practices upset the status quo; people move to protect their positions and interests. Making a change leads those who built the current system to feel that they did a poor job.
Power and politics	Loud advocates, fear of accountability, resistance to relinquishing control, fear of being seen as disloyal, and lack of trust all conspire against the implementation of change.

Source: Matheson and Matheson, 1998, p. 89

Confidentiality and Costs   Since some crucial firm data may not be published under any circumstances, case studies may not include complete information on results and costs. Nevertheless, insight into project costs will be explored in order to provide an opportunity to get some insight into the commitment of the top managers to the change project.

Goals of the Knowledge Management Project   Based on prior experiences with a very technical Total Quality Management approach, top management has not been satisfied with its results. Due to increasing competition in the automotive supplier industry, a knowledge-based change management approach should lead to a positive impact on the short, medium, and long-term time frames. Hence, they decided to involve all employees in order to elicit and combine their knowledge and competencies for achieving (1) improvements in daily work, (2) creating product and process innovations, and (3) to improve organizational structure and culture.

Implementation Failures and Communication Barriers   The problems outlined in table 8.3 indicate that sensitivity to the organizational members should be provided in order to decrease resistance to change. Hence, top managers and consultants have decided not to talk about knowledge management but rather improving organizational performance by changing leadership style, organizational climate and culture.

How can the know-how of 10,000 employees be transformed into business actions so that:

• operational and strategy related benefits exceed at least the project costs

• operations do not suffer from change activities

• the company learns how to manage the knowledge management process

---

Figure 8.4
Practical key questions of knowledge management

Consequences for the Project   The questions in figure 8.4 have been critical for the company's top management to answer (see figure 8.4)

The Learning Infrastructure of the Knowledge Management Project

The primary goal of the learning infrastructure is to create and maintain momentum to the change process. From a practical perspective, this means on one hand that the barriers sketched in table 8.3 should be overcome. On the other hand, knowledge transfer from a consultant's know-how who provided support to the process, should take place.

The infrastructure included the following elements: (1) A project organization, with (2) different roles and responsibilities that fostered (3) a shared understanding of the implementation blueprint, (4) commitment of top management to change, and (5) transfer of the consultants' knowledge to the firm.

The project organization

The implementation of the knowledge management process effort was based on the following two core principles:

Principle 1 — "Buying in" of Power by Formal Decentralization   Along the formal organizational structure, the company has been subdivided into 13 units in order to take into account specific needs of each unit, as well to be able to formally involve second level managers into the knowledge management process. The activities between the units have been coordinated by a central project manager, and additionally have been supported by union representatives and a consultant responsible for the unit.

Principle 2 — "Total Involvement" by Informal Decentralization   Experiences of organizational development and strategy implementation efforts teaches that sustainable large scale change effects cannot only be triggered by formal or top down-structures, but also need to be heavily linked to a "total involvement" deployment process that are characterized by bottom up processes. Hence, the informal infrastructure consists of a project team per unit, the members of which are informal leaders per hierarchical level and one union representative. As the next section will

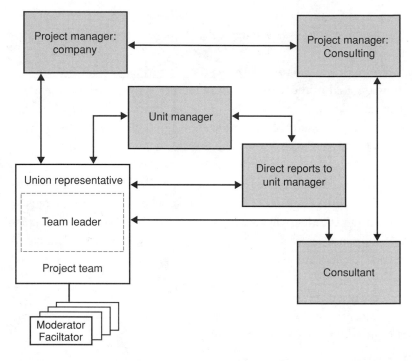

Figure 8.5
Learning infrastructure on unit level

make clear, the team leader and the facilitators have a primary role in the implementation process. Figure 8.5[7] shows the learning infrastructure on unit level and the relations between each element.

Diffusion of knowledge: Roles and Responsibilities

Since in organizations there are differences between operational and strategic knowledge, there is a need to share knowledge of operational experiences with decision-makers. Usually there are a number of barriers between top management and operational managers as well as with the staff. Hence, one of the core aims of the learning infrastructure is to support these diffusion processes of know-how and experiences. The following roles have a major impact on knowledge sharing activities.

Team Leader   The team leader is one of the protagonists of the diffusion of formal and informal knowledge, namely knowledge about the content, the process, and the results of the knowledge management activities. She is involved in the decision making process of the knowledge management activities as well as fosters the diffusion of knowledge within and between the project teams and units.

Facilitators   The facilitators have first been educated by the consultants in order to be able to facilitate the worksheet processes. Since every facilitator supports the unit he or she does not personally belong to, there is often knowledge diffusion between units and additionally *is* extended by self managed facilitator meetings.

Project Manager   Since strategy implementation efforts usually depends on consulting expertise, the top management of this company decided not to be become "addicted" to consultants. Explicitly this means that the formal role of a project manager has been established, with the primary tasks of supporting the complete knowledge management implementation process as well as an explicit learning of the consultant's know-how about the concepts and methods of knowledge management implementation. Formally, the second duty has been fostered by the outlook that the project manager will be completely responsible for the second or evaluative phase of knowledge management four years later.

The Knowledge Management Process
As noted above, top management refused to talk internally about knowledge management but only about improving organizational performance by changing leadership style, organizational climate, and culture. The major reason of this "hidden agenda" has been to avoid resistance to a new managerial fad. Two years ago the organizational members suffered from an ill-implemented Total Quality approach, which has been marketed as "the ultimate solution" to organizational performance problems. Hence, the content of the survey itself focused on leadership, climate and culture issues. As will be made clear in the subsequent sections, the survey's results have been used as the trigger to identification, creation, diffusion of knowledge, and its conversion into organizational action. Table 8.4 shows the ten major steps of the knowledge management project as well as the initialization and the follow-up steps of the project.

Table 8.4
Explicit steps (1–8) of the knowledge management project—completed by
additional implementation steps (italics)

Step	Goals
A. Initialization	*Top management: Developing need for change, making a decision about the advantage of a knowledge management perspective*
1. Overall planning	Defining goals of project (top management, consultants) Involvement of unions
2. Preparation per unit	Defining analysis units Identifying needs of units
3. Implementing formal project infrastructure	Involvement of line management (element of learning infrastructure)
4. Implementing informal project infrastructure	Involvement of project teams (1 per unit, 8 persons max.: consisting of 1 informal leader from each hierarchical level, including a team leader, and one union representative (element of learning infrastructure)
5. Questionnaire	Participation of all employees in the survey
6. Survey analysis	Total, and sub-unit analysis; results broken down to natural groups (one manager/supervisor with his or her direct reports)
7. Presentation of total and unit results	Top management, Unit management, unions Overall understanding of climate related areas of improvement
8. Training of internal facilitators	Providing skills for eliciting employee's knowledge for improvements (enhancing learning infrastructure)
9. Worksheet process	Each group identifies three areas of action on the basis of their own results: • Actions for each group to take immediately • Knowledge/Suggestions from each group for management actions • Knowledge/Suggestions for process improvements (action priorities that need co-ordination across functions or departments)

Table 8.4
(continued)

Step	Goals
10. Planning process	Feedback of suggestions to unit and top management
	Categorization of suggestions by project team leaders
	Analysis of suggestion categories, selection and planning for actions
B. Strategic action teams, Business Plan	*Defining and empowering strategic action teams to implement actions*
	Matching business plan with strategic relevant suggestions, adjustment of strategy
C. Learning infrastructure	*Introducing infrastructure that fosters implementation of actions, integrates formal and informal project infrastructure elements*
D. Next knowledge management approach	*Maintaining learning infrastructure*
	Systematic evaluation

The implementation of a change effort is an enormous challenge due to the complexity of the process. Hence, introducing elements that reduce complexity by standardizing elements can foster the implementation process.

The Questionnaire—Standardizing Initial Situation to all Organizational Members An organizational climate survey has been the starting-point for dealing with the goals of knowledge management. The questionnaire included 88 standard items (5 dimensions and 26 categories) that were supplemented by organization-specific items (4 categories with 17 items) and 15 unit specific items. Each participant first had to identify the supervisor/manager he or she directly reports to based on the formal organizational structure and then answer each of the items on the basis of a 7-point rating scale. This form of the identification process has been necessary due to confidentiality and due to the need to be able to provide specific results to each of the feedback sessions that are triggered by these results.

The Worksheet Process—Standardizing the Identification and Diffusion Phase The input for the worksheet process is the specific, group-related results of the survey. Since the realization of the total involvement principle is essential to the project goal, the worksheet process will be described more explicitly. The *worksheet process* was especially designed to increase the capability of an organization to share knowledge that is used on different learning levels. This means that the *worksheet process* leads to the transformation of the organizational knowledge base. Outcomes of organization-wide team learning processes are integrated into an organizational learning process. Hence, the *worksheet process* is a standardized structured approach that is the key to the identification and collection of individual knowledge on the team level. Each team identifies three areas of action on the basis of their own results:

• Actions for each group to take immediately
• Knowledge/Suggestions from each group for management actions
• Knowledge/Suggestions for process improvements (action priorities that need coordination across functions or departments)

Hence, the following aims are achieved by the support of the worksheet process:

• each organization member is part of a team learning process and is responsible for providing input for the improvement of processes.
• an explicit knowledge base of the organization on the team level is developed.
• input for the management's knowledge base is provided; this, in turn leads to team learning on management level.
• the integration of these different team learning processes lead to learning processes on the organizational level.

The Planning Process—Standardizing the Modification and the Action Phase After the completion of all worksheet process sessions, the top management and the unit managers have been provided with knowledge/suggestions from every (!) employee and manager. The suggestions are collected in a standardized way and categorized by the 13-team leaders in order to provide top management with an adequate sample of suggestions. Categories have been developed with regard to business goals, and expanded by the content of the suggestions. Additionally a shared learning process between top management and team leaders took place in order to get a shared understanding of categories to examined from a business perspective.

In relation to the scope of the suggestions, there are different planning sessions related either to top management or to unit management. Due to the different categories of plans (teams, top management, and unit management), the change processes are implemented and lead to synergetic effects between the different categories of actions. Consequently, this organizational change is supported heavily by these combinations of learning processes throughout the whole organization.

The Role of Top Management: Commitment and Resources

Top management heavily supported the implementation of the change process by behaving as a role model to change as well as by providing

Table 8.5
Overview on Costs for Implementing Knowledge Management*

		Costs (in DM)
Preparation/ infrastructure (step 1–4)	150 team members/5 days per person	720,000
Survey (step 6)	10.000 employees/1 hour per employee	1,200,000
Facilitator training (step 8)	250 employees/1 day per employee	240,000
Facilitating worksheet processes (step 9)	250 employees/3 days per employee	720,000
Worksheet process (step 9)	10,000 employees/4 hours per employee	4,800,000
Planning process (step 10)	10 team members/3 days	28,800
Implementation of action plans and maintaining learning infrastructure	160 organizational members in strategic action teams	(no data available)
Total costs		**6,988,800**
Costs per employee		**Ca.700**

*In this calculation consultant's budget and managerial time are not considered.

monetary and time related resources to the process. In the beginning of the project, any lack of managerial commitment has been punished by the managing director by showing opportunities to leave the company through dismissal. The involvement of the union representatives from the very beginning of the project also has been an important strategic success factor. Finally, the acceptance to invest time and money can be interpreted as high commitment to the process as well as an indicator of expecting acceptable results in terms of profit. Table 8.5 provides an overview of the costs of the complete process:

Results

Overview—survey results. The survey results[8] are described on the dimensional level depending on hierarchical status (managers vs. staff see

Table 8.6
Overview of Survey Results (Total Company)

1. Goals	M	E	2. Change	M	E	3. Flexibility	M	E
The Organization's ambitions	5.6	5.4	New ideas	4.7	4.1	Freedom of action	4.6	3.7
Attention to goals	5.5	5.2	Support for ideas	5.0	4.4	Co-operation within the department	4.9	4.4
Demand for performance	5.5	5.3	Attitudes	3.9	3.7	Co-operation between departments	3.5	3.6
Result-orientation	5.6	5.3	Encouragement	5.1	4.6	Decentralization	3.5	3.4
Consequences	4.1	4.5				Encouragement	4.7	4.3
Mutual self-confidence	5.3	5.1						
Encouragement	5.3	5.0						
Mean	5.3	5.1	*Mean*	4.7	4.2	*Mean*	4.2	3.9

table 8.6). Generally, participation in the survey has been about 95 percent, in some units it has reached 100 percent.

Table 8.6 shows that

- the organization is described by a high degree of goal orientation (Dim.1)
- motivation of managers and employees (Dim 4.) is high in relation to change (Dim. 2) and flexibility (Dim. 3)
- a great degree of distance and a low level of trust between employees and top management exists (Dim. 5)
- employees provide more critical feedback than managers

Since these results have minor relevance to the subsequent knowledge identification and diffusion processes, there is no need for an in-depth interpretation of these results.

Table 8.6
(Continued)

4. Motivation	M	E	5. Management	M	E	6. Focus areas	M	E
Possibilities for development	4.8	4.2	Trust: Top management	3.8	3.6	Customer orientation	5.9	5.4
Freedom in the job situation	4.9	4.0	Role model: top management	3.8	3.6	Employee orientation	4.6	4.3
Trust management	5.3	4.9	Trust: unit	4.3	3.8	Quality management	5.0	4.8
Liveliness	5.3	4.8	Role model: unit management	4.1	3.8	Change project	5.4	5.2
Group relations	4.9	4.4						
Encouragement	4.9	4.4						
Mean	*5.0*	*4.5*	*Mean*	*4.0*	*3.7*	*Mean*	*5.2*	*4.9*

Process of Knowledge Management

Identification and Creation   The worksheet processes have led to actions and suggestions on different levels—the results reached beyond the expectations of top management and unions:

• Knowledge for 5500 actions have been identified which each team has implemented immediately to improve the own area of responsibility
• About 6500 suggestions from each team for management actions and process improvement on the basis of about 750 feedback sessions have been identified
• Knowledge/Suggestions for process improvements (action priorities that need coordination across functions or departments)

Comparing these numbers with the average of the company's suggestion system, which reports 0.3 suggestions per employee per year, it becomes clear that the worksheet process shows an even better result on a quantitative perspective.

Diffusion   The 6500 suggestions have been collected and categorized by a project team consisting of the team leaders of each unit's project team. The results show that these suggestions could have been condensed into about 1582 suggestions and classified into 24 major categories (see table 8.7).

Table 8.7 shows that 62 per cent of all suggestions belong to five major areas—"leadership" (n = 138), "communication" (n = 141), "trust in top management" (n = 381), "wages" (n = 172) and "improvement for realization of the change project" (n = 147).

Integration and Modification   Unfortunately, integration and modification processes cannot be observed directly but can be reconstructed based on outcomes or communication processes. Top management felt very uncomfortable due to the minor results they have achieved by the survey and by the numbers of suggestions that directly belonged to this group. The consequences have been to formalize meetings between staff and top management by holding round table discussions[9] and by reinforcing the learning infrastructure.

Table 8.7
Categories of Suggestions for top Management

Category	Total number
1. Trust: top-management	381
2. Salary	172
3. Project realization	147
4. Communication	141
5. Leadership	138
6. Decision making	91
7. Reorganization	77
8. Strategic goals	52
9. Improvement system	47
10. Staff	46
11. Logistics	34
12. Working time	32
13. Image	32
14. Organizational structure	26
15. Location XXX	25
16. Flexibility	22
17. Bureaucracy	20
18. Innovation	18
19. Top-management as team	17
20. Status	17
21. Training	17
22. Involvement	14
23. Work environment	12
24. Transparency of costs	6

Action   Table 8.8 provides an overview on some strategically relevant projects based on employee suggestions. Strategic action teams are responsible for the implementation of these projects. Since the suggestions for top management had included concrete hints for improvements, the planning phase of action teams' work has consumed less time than traditional planning phases in strategy implementation efforts:

Table 8.8
Strategic Action Teams / Projects

Strategic Projects	Aim
1. Complaint management	Decreasing response time to customer complaints Increasing customer loyalty
2. Restructuring of administration	Leaning procedures and processes, improving quality of administrative functions
3. Personal function as service center	Increasing service orientation of personal function for internal customers
4. Process improvement	Process redesign in order to increase core processes' reliability and speed
5. Quality training	Improving customer relation oriented attitudes and skills for all organizational members
6. Logistics	Improving flow of material, implementing a monitoring system for material flow
7. Top management	Restructuring responsibilities of top management; exchanging top management positions
8. Culture	Improving relation between top management and staff by higher visibility
9. Leadership development	Training program for all managers

Implementation of the strategic projects started 10 months after the knowledge management project began.

Analyzing these projects, it becomes clear that most of these projects belong to the improvement of strategically relevant business processes and—maybe counter-intuitively—not to the leadership issue. That does not imply that the leadership issue is out of focus, since there also has been decisions on implementing leadership training for all managers.

Measures

On a *project basis* the following measures can be identified: financial and time related investment in the knowledge management project (financial measure), the participation rate in the survey, number of feedback sessions, number of implemented actions/projects, time frame of the project (process measures), and number of self organized meetings due to the intent to improve the implementation of the knowledge management effort (reflective measures).

Concerning the top management's initial questions (see figure 8.4) the following *business related measures* resulted:

• Improved market share and shareholder value
• Improvement in performance of key business processes
• Changing of organizational culture with respect to stronger relations and trust between levels and divisions/units.

Learning infrastructure

Based on the experiences of the project organization, a parallel structure of responsibilities has been implemented in the beginning (project infrastructure). Additionally, several aspects have been considered to provide support for maintaining the learning infrastructure.

Maintaining Momentum of Change / Commitment Employees should get an understanding that their suggestions have been taken seriously. This implies that they can realize what happened with their suggestions. All suggestions are collected and figured in the canteen and top management provides information about considered suggestions and the reasons for disregarding others.

Communicating Success Success stories are communicated through formal and informal communication channels.

Formal Aspects Senior management groups are responsible for the strategic action teams that work on the strategic relevant plans that have been derived from top management decisions on the basis of employee inputs.

Informal Aspects Project team leaders and facilitators are catalysts of knowledge management since they collected most of the knowledge on the project's process, goals and action plans.

Speed of Change Formal and informal elements of the project infrastructure have been key for providing information about the process and goals of the knowledge management process and thereby have fostered the speed of the change process. Within a period of three months, each of the 10,000 employees has been informed about the intent and process of the change effort. After four months, there has been nearly 95 percent participation within the survey; after ten months, most of the strategic action teams had started with their projects.

Expecting Evaluation — Planning the Next Knowledge Management Project   One of the most important features to gain momentum is the expectation that there will be a new process by which the quality of change can be evaluated.

Discussion

Two major attempts have been achieved by this study of knowledge management. On one hand, the conceptual framework of integrative knowledge management provides insight into the core elements of knowledge management and the complexity of different knowledge management approaches that have been identified. On the other hand, the case study shows the application of the proposed model of integrative management. Due to confidentiality reasons, there is no opportunity to report the all the results of the study. Nevertheless, some major lessons have been identified that refer to the tension between theoretical reasoning and practical implementation processes.

Linking theory with practice of knowledge management

Knowledge Management and Learning Phases   Since this chapter has made it clear that there is neither a universal approach to knowledge management nor a best way of implementation, some insights into the nature of the knowledge management process of the case study are provided. Table 8.9 shows the links between the key questions of knowledge management, the model of integrative knowledge management, and of the knowledge management process.

Table 8.9 provides insight into the close relationships between the conceptual framework and the practical implementation steps. The implementation process has considered all phases of knowledge management.

Table 8.9
Links between Knowledge Management Theory and Practice

Managerial needs to knowledge management *Knowledge management: key questions (see figure 1)*	Theoretical progress in the field of knowledge management *Integrative model of knowledge management (see figure 2)*	Linking theory with practice: The case study *Knowledge management implementation process (see table 4)*
How can organizational relevant knowledge be identified and new knowledge be created?	Identification/ Creation Diffusion Integration/Modification Learning Infrastructure	Linking survey with worksheet process (1, 2, 5, 6, 7, 9)
How can knowledge be utilized since it has been identified?	Diffusion Action Integration/Modification Learning Infrastructure	Planning process (10, B)
How can a system of knowledge creation and utilization be designed and organized?	Learning Infrastructure Measures	Implementing and maintaining learning infrastructure (3, 4, 8, C, D)

Linking Learning Phases with Learning Levels   A further analysis leads to insight into the relationship between the learning phases and learning levels (see table 8.10).

The analysis of table 8.10 shows that there is a majority of identification and diffusion activities that are triggered by different teams. This results should have been expected for the following two reasons: (1) One of the major aims of the project has been to identify and utilize the knowledge of the organizational members; (2) A "total involvement strategy" should usually rely on extensive communication processes.

Learning Modes   Concerning the project goals, two major modes are identifiable: On one hand the action perspective of learning plays a major role. On the other hand, there is evidence that the activities, which are implemented to improve the relations between top management and staff, initiate cultural changes.

Table 8.10
Analysis of Learning Phases x Learning Levels

	Identification Creation	Diffusion	Integration Modification	Action
Individual:				
• top management	5, D			
• unit management	5, D			
• staff	5, D			
• team leader	D			
• facilitators	8, D	8	8	
Team:				
• top management	A, 1, B	7, 10	7	
• unit management	2, 3, B	7, 10	7	
• project teams	4	4, 10		
• natural groups			9	9
• strategic action teams				B
Unit		4, 5, 10	9	B, C
Organization	8	4, 5, 10	9	B, C

Learning Types   Finally, the knowledge management process can be interpreted with regard to the three learning levels. The suggestions for top management, which have been identified during the feedback session, can be understood as double loop learning process, since team members identify major gaps between the theory-in-use and the espoused theory of the firm. Additionally deutero learning processes can be observed: Top management explicitly started to change their communication policies due the negative feedback of all organizational members. Additionally team leaders provided inputs for deutero learning to management, project manager and the consultants due to their experience with the firm and the change process. Finally, single loop learning processes can be identified on the basis of the implementation of the distinct plans.

The Impact of the Learning Infrastructure to Knowledge Management Activities   It has been made clear that the following two general features have been key to implementation success: (1) total involvement of *all* managers and *all* employees, (2) implementation of a system to organize the complex and dynamic process of organizational learning. If total involvement is one essential issue for implementing knowledge management processes, the question becomes "how can this process be managed"? The knowledge management approach outlined here shows that an integrated top-down bottom-up strategy implementation blueprint, such as Hoshin-planning [75] or goal deployment [76] is an adequate basis of a total involvement approach: Summarizing the project experiences, it can be stated that a learning infrastructure should have at least the following features:

• it acquires, communicates and interprets organizationally relevant knowledge for use in decision-making
• it attempts to objectify the subjective personal knowledge of individual members into an organizational knowledge base
• it is relevant to a broad range of organizational activities
• it simultaneously provides inputs to the decision-making process in multiple departments, divisions, and hierarchical levels of the organization
• it is not necessarily task specific or function specific
• it is rooted in organizational practices. Consequently it reflects the actual "theories-in-use" and not the "espoused theories" in organizational activities
• it is known, accepted, and used by the organizational members.

Knowledge Management and Learning from Implementation Failures
Another method of the advantage of the knowledge management approach discussed can be linked to the question, if—and how far—lessons from former change management projects have been adequately learned (see table 8.11):

Table 8.11 shows that many positive impacts of the knowledge management process on reducing implementation problems can be observed.

Further Implications
This case study shows that the theory driven framework of integrative knowledge management is able to provide a practical framework of implementing knowledge management principles. Since knowledge management research is a very recent subject, it is crucial to investigate the role of knowledge as a production factor more intensively and systematically based on empirical studies. A major problem here still lies in the deficits of adequate measuring and monitoring criteria to the resource knowledge.

Table 8.11
Decreasing Implementation Deficits by Integrative Knowledge Management

Barrier	Overcome by KM implementation
Internal focus	*(no relevance to KM project)*
Lack of credibility	Involvement of all stakeholders from the very beginning
	Open communication strategy
	Feedback of results: team- and organization-wide
	Feedback of suggestions
Secrecy	Feedback of suggestions
	Reasoning which suggestions have been followed and why
Lack of proper skills	Project team members: recruited by skills and image with their respective units.
	Facilitators: educated by consultants
Lack of resources	Investments of time and money.
Lack of discipline	High alignment and support of change process; no exceptions for senior managers; senior managers as role models.
Lack of strategy	Transparent strategy of the change project.
Metrics are misused	Survey results explicitly are not treated as source for career or punishment, but as learning opportunity.
Tendency to oversimplify	Change process has been sold as an enormous challenge to the system on one hand; on the other hand, standardizing methods supported alignment and implementation efforts.
People are reluctant to change	Values have been more important than results. Some senior managers were forced to quit their job due to the cultural impact of the knowledge management process.
Power and politics	Critics and resistance have been treated as a learning opportunity. For instance, the management and consultants followed critical inputs of team leaders or facilitators in order to improve the implementation process.

Notes

1. Exceptions are, for example, [41][42][43].

2. Cf. [55][56][57] with different notions for learning types.

3. For an in-depth discussion of this analytical framework see [66].

4. 144 perspectives = 4 phases x 4 levels x 3 modes x 4 types.

5. Small rectangles: process perspective of knowledge management; large rectangles: managerial perspective of knowledge management; ellipse: implementation perspective of knowledge management.

6. Cf. similar concepts such as "the core elements of knowledge management." [67]; "the knowledge creating company" [68]; "the knowledge market model" [69].

7. "Gray" = element of formal infrastructure; "white" = element of informal infrastructure.

8. M = managers; E = employees, scale from '1' to '7' with '7' being outstanding and '1' being weak.

9. One senior manager visits one location per month.

References

1. Drucker, P. (1993) *Post-Capitalist Society*. Oxford.

2. Drucker, P. (1997) *Management in einer turbulenten Zeit*. Düsseldorf: Econ.

3. Toffler, A. (1980) *The Third Wave*. New York.

4. OECD, eds. (1996) *Measuring What People Know: Human Capital Accounting for the Knowledge Economy*. Paris.

5. Deiaco, E., Hörnell, E., and Vickery, G., eds. (1990) *Technology and Investment: Crucial Issues for the 1990s*. Pinter Publishers: London, 1990.

6. BMFT (1996): *Zur technologischen Leistungsfähigkeit Deutschlands*. Zusammenfassender Endbericht an das Bundesministerium für Bildung, Wissenschaft, Forschung und Technologie. Niedersächsisches Institut für Wirtschaftförderung: Hannover, 1996.

7. Stewart, T. A. (1997) *Intellectual Capital: The New Wealth of Organizations*. London: Brealey, p. 21.

8. Edvinsson, L., and Malone, M.S. (1997): *Intellectual Capital*. New York: HarperCollins.

9. Roos, G., and Roos, J. (1996) *Intellectual Performance*. <http://www.imd.ch./fac/roos/paper–lr.html>.

10. Itami, H., and Roehl, T. (1987): *Mobilizing Invisible Assets*. Cambridge.

11. Cohen, W., and Levinthal, D. (1990): Absorptive Capacity: A New Perspective on Learning and Innovation. *Administrative Science Quarterly* 35: 128–152.

12. Hamel, G., and Prahalad, C. K. (1994) *Competing for the Future*. Boston.

13. Amit, R., and Shoemaker, P. (1993) Strategic Assets and Organizational Rent. *Strategic Management Journal* 14:33–46.

14. Zander, U., and Kogut, B. (1995): Knowledge and the Speed of the Transfer and Imitation of Organizational Capabilities: An Empirical Test. *Organization Science* 6, no. 1:76–92.

15. Hall, R. (1992) The Strategic Analysis of Intangible Resources. *Strategic Management Journal* 13:135–144.

16. Walsh, J. P., and Ungson, G.R. (1991) Organizational Memory. *Academy of Management Review* 16, no. 1:57–91.

17. Edvinsson, L., and Malone, M. S. (1997) *Intellectual Capital*. New York: HarperCollins.

18. Sveiby, K. E. (1997) *The New Organizational Wealth: Managing and Measuring Knowledge Based Assets*. San Francisco: Berret-Koehler.

19. Stewart, T. A. (1997) *Intellectual Capital: The New Wealth of Organizations*. London: Brealey.

20. Barney, J. B. (1986) *Strategic factor markets: Expectations, Luck and Business Strategy. Management Science* 32, no. 10:1231–1241.

21. Amit, R., and Shoemaker, P. (1993) Strategic Assets and Organizational Rent. *Strategic Management Journal* 14:33–46.

22. Drucker, P. (1993) *Post-Capitalist Society*. Oxford.

23. Bullinger, H. J., Wörner, K., and Prieto, J. (1997) *Wissensmanagement heute*. Stuttgart: Fraunhofer Institut für Arbeitswissenschaft und Organisation.

24. North, K. (1998) *Wissensorientierte Unternehmensführung (Knowledge Based Management)*. Wiesbaden: Gabler, 1998.

25. Wijg, K. M. (1993) *Knowledge Management Foundations: Thinking about Thinking*. Arlington: Schema Press.

26. Rock, S., ed. (1998) *Knowledge Management: A Real Business Guide*. London: Caspian Publishing.

27. The Delphi Group KM User Survey (1998) <http://www.knowledgebusi ness.com/delphiuser.htm>.

28. European KM Survey (1998) <http://www.knowledgebusiness.com/euro pean.htm>.

29. International Survey on Knowledge Management Drivers (1998) <http://www.knowledgebusiness.com/international.htm>.

30. Senge, P. M., et al. (1994) *The Fifth Discipline Fieldbook*. San Francisco.

31. Pedler, M., Burgoyne, J., and Boydell, T. (1994) *Das lernende Unternehmen*. Frankfurt.

32. Dixon, Nancy (1994) *The Organizational Learning Cycle—How We Can Learn Collectively*. London: McGraw-Hill Book Company.

33. Von Krogh, G., and Roos, J. (1996) *Managing Knowledge*. Sage: London.

34. Kogut, B., and Zander, U. (1996) What Do Firms Do? Coordination, Identity, and Learning. *Organization Science* 7 (1996):502–518.

35. Grant, R. M. (1996) Knowledge, Strategy and the Theory of the Firm. *Strategic Management Journal* 17, no. 12 (1996):109–122.

36. Spender, J.C. (1996) Making Knowledge the Basis of a Dynamic Theory of the Firm. *Strategic Management Journal* 17 (Winter Special Issue): 45–62.

37. Tsoukas, H. (1996) The firm as a Distributed Knowledge System: A Constructionist Approach. *Strategic Management Journal* 17 (Winter Special Issue): 11–25.

38. Boisot, M. H. (1998) *Knowledge Assets.* New York: Oxford University Press.

39. Reinhardt, R., Bornemann, M., Pawlowsky, P., and Schneider, U. (1999) Intellectual Capital and Knowledge Management. In H. Dierkes, J. Child, and I. Nonaka, eds., *Handbook of Organizational Learning* (in press).

40. Pawlowsky, P. (1999) Management Science and Organizational Learning. In H. Dierkes, J. Child, and I. Nonaka, eds., *Handbook of Organizational Learning.* (in press).

41. Shrivastava, P. (1983) A Typology of Organizational Learning Systems. *Journal of Management Studies* 20, no. 1:7–28.

42. Huber, G. P. (1991) Organizational Learning: The contributing processes and literatures. *Organization Science.*

43. Wiegand, M. (1996) *Prozesse organisationalen Lernens.* Wiesbaden.

44. Pawlowsky, P. (1994) *Wissensmanagement in der lernenden Organisation.* Unveröffentlichte Habilitationsschrift. Paderborn.

45. Pawlowsky, P. (1999) Management Science and Organizational Learning. In H. Dierkes, J. Child, and I. Nonaka, eds., *Handbook of Organizational Learning.* (in press).

46. Pawlowsky, P., Forslin, J., and Reinhardt, R. (1999) Theory and tools of organizational learning: An integrated view on knowledge management. In H. Dierkes, J. Child, and I. Nonaka, eds., *Handbook of Organizational Learning.* (in press).

47. Argyris, C., and Schön, D. A. (1978) *Organizational Learning. Reading.*

48. Duncan, R., and Weiss, A. (1979) *Organizational Learning: Implications for Organizational Design.* Research in Organizational Behavior.

49. Garratt, B. (1990) *Creating a Learning Organization.* Cambridge.

50. Senge, P. M., et al. (1994) *The Fifth Discipline Fieldbook.* San Francisco.

51. Sydow, J. and van Well, B. (1996) Wissensintensiv durch Netzwerkorganisation: Strukturationstheoretische Anaylse eines wissensintensiven Netzwerkes. In G. Schreyögg and P. Conrad (Hrsg.), *Wissensmanagement—Managementforschung Bd. 6.* Berlin/New York, S. 191–234.

52. Probst, G.J.B. and Knaese, B. (1998) *Risikofaktor Wissen.* Wiesbaden: Gabler, 1998.

53. Revans, R.W. (1982) The Enterprise as a Learning System. In Revans, R. W, (Hrsg.), *The Origins and Growth of Action Learning*. Chartwell Bratt.

54. Pedler, M., Burgoyne, J., and Boydell, T. (1994) *Das lernende Unternehmen*. Frankfurt.

55. Pawlowsky, P. (1992) Betriebliche Qualifikationsstrategien und organisationales Lernen. In Staehle, W.H. and Conrad, P. (Hrsg.) *Managementforschung* 2, S. 177–238. Berlin.

56. Reinhardt (1993) *Das Modell Organisationaler Lernfähigkeit und die Gestaltung Lernfähiger Organisationen*. Lang: Frankfurt.

57. Probst, G.J.B. and Büchel, B. (1994) *Organisationales Lernen: Wettbewerbsvorteil der Zukunft*. Wiesbaden: Gabler, 1994.

58. Nonaka, I. (1994) A Dynamic Theory of Organizational Knowledge Creation. In *Organizational Science*, 5/1, S. 14–37.

59. Duncan, R.; Weiss, A. (1979) *Organizational Learning: Implications for Organizational Design*. Research in Organizational Behavior.

60. Nonaka, I. (1994) A Dynamic Theory of Organizational Knowledge Creation. In *Organizational Science*, 5/1, S. 14–37.

61. Huber, G.P. (1991) Organizational Learning: The contributing processes and literatures. *Organization Science*.

62. Boulding, K. E. (1956) *The Image: Knowledge in Life and Society*. Ann Arbor: University of Michigan Press.

63. Shrivastava, P. (1983) A Typology of Organizational Learning Systems. *Journal of Management Studies*, Vol. 20, No.1 (1983), 7–28.

64. Peters, T. (1992) *Thriving on Chaos*. New York.

65. Drucker, P. (1996) *Umbruch im Management*. Econ: Düsseldorf, 1996.

66. Pawlowsky, P. (1999) Management Science and Organizational Learning. In H. Dierkes, J. Child, J. and I. Nonaka, eds., *Handbook of Organizational Learning*. (in press).

67. Probst, G., Raub, S., and Romhardt, K. (1997) *Wissen managen*. Wiesbaden: Gabler, 1997.

68. Nonaka, J., and Tageuchi, H. (1995) *The Knowledge Creating Company*. Oxford.

69. North, K. (1998) *Wissensorientierte Unternehmensführung (Knowledge Based Management)*. Wiesbaden: Gabler.

70. Probst, G., Raub, S., and Romhardt, K. (1997) *Wissen managen*. Wiesbaden: Gabler.

71. Stewart, T.A. (1997) *Intellectual Capital: The New Wealth of Organizations*. Brealey: London, 1997.

72. Matheson, D., and Matheson, J. (1998) *The Smart Organization*. Boston: Hravard Business School Press.

73. Pasmore, A. P., and Woodman, R. W. (1997) *Research in Organizational Change and Development*. Greenwich: Jai Press.

74. Clarke, T., and Clegg, S. (1998) *Changing Paradigms*. London: Harper Collins Business.

75. Soin, S. S. (1992) *Total Quality Control Essentials: Key Elements, Methodologies and Managing for Success*. New York.

76. Conti, T. (1993) *Building Total Quality*. London.

9

Tacit Knowledge, Unarticulated Needs, and Empathic Design in New Product Development[1]

Dorothy Leonard

Understanding market needs is one of the most critical knowledge management tasks for developers of new products and services. Yet potential customers often cannot articulate the tacit dimensions of their own knowledge and experience that drive preferences and needs. Moreover, developers may be unaware of how their existing knowledge assets can be shaped to accommodate market needs. Therefore, traditional market research tools, which rely heavily on explicit knowledge, are often inadequate to inform new product development—especially if the innovation is radical. This chapter introduces a set of techniques called *Empathic Design*, which are being explored by an increasing number of companies as an effective nontraditional channel for importing knowledge about the market.

How to Understand Market Needs—When the Customers Don't Know What They Know

New product and service development is one of the most knowledge-intensive of all business processes because successful commercialization requires the merger of knowledge from two very disparate sources: the provider organization (knowledge of what is possible) and the marketplace (knowledge of what is needed). Most of the time, the knowledge realms of product developers and customers overlap very little. Every year, thousands of new products fail in the market, demonstrating the difficulty of linking offerings in the market to needs and purchases. Therefore, the stakes are high for overcoming this inherent difficulty, and the key is to manage the flows not only of information, but, more importantly, of knowledge. Knowledge is information that is relevant, actionable, and at least partially based on experience;[2] for managers of innovation, the distinction (between information and knowledge) is far from theoretical. In fact, it is those managers' critical need to amass knowledge that makes new product and service development a useful venue within which to examine knowledge elicitation—especially its tacit dimensions. If would-be vendors cannot "get inside the heads" of their potential customers, how can they provide useful innovations? If, as suggested above, knowledge is experience-based, how can new product developers understand or share the critical aspects of their customers' experience? Market research, of course, attempts to provide that knowledge. However, when organizations attempt to identify new market opportunities or determine the market for a truly innovative product or service, market research often fails to provide accurate guidance.[3]

This failure is not because traditional market research techniques are crude in determining recognized needs and desires. Far from it. Market research has become so sophisticated that designers can elicit extremely detailed guidance. The more familiar the product category, the more specific are the customer demands—and the better equipped are new product developers to respond. For example, we all drive cars. Over the years, we have developed a keen sense of what we want in our vehicles, even in such relatively intangible attributes as smell and feel. Nissan Design International designed the smell of the leather in the Infiniti J-30 by trying out various leathers on prospective consumers, and selecting the top three preferred by U.S. noses. Consumers can talk knowledgeably about the relative stiffness of the car's steering, about feeling the road, or about smoothness of ride. They can even identify the relative desirability of various kinds of motor sounds. Harley Davidson sued Honda for imitating the distinctive and highly popular sound of the Harley motorcycle motor. In short, car buyers and car manufacturers have developed a large, shared body of explicit knowledge about what cars can and should be, for different market segments.

However, potential customers and clients also have needs that are buried in the tacit dimensions of their knowledge. That is, they have tacit knowledge about their work routines, their environments, their experience, about which they themselves may be unaware, but which could provide fruitful guidance for the design of new product experiences—if it could be made explicit and shared. Because knowledge is built through use, through interaction, some of this tacit knowledge comes to the surface to be made explicit as needs only when the clients are engaged in some task, attempting to use some product or process. Customers will not think of these needs in the abstract, or when offered a few lines of exposition on a questionnaire.[4] And some of these needs will never be articulated by clients because they are unaware of them as needs. The clients may experience difficulties or inconveniences that are so familiar they are not experienced as difficulties; they are just the way that task has to be done. Before the advent of the microwave oven, people reheated leftovers either by spooning them out into pans on top of the stove or popping them in the (conventional) oven. They did not know that leftovers could be heated any other way. In other cases, customers are highly aware of the problem, but can't think of a way to solve it. When canning food was first invented, contemporary consumers used everything from pick axes to revolvers for opening cans! In 1845, when Sir John Franklin hauled one of the new-fangled "tin cans" of veal to the Arctic, he had to be sure to have a hammer and chisel on hand to open it. The British Army and Navy Co-operative Society, whose catalog was the Walmart of the time, responded somewhat belatedly by offering its first can opener in 1885.[5]

The trick to innovation is to match need with solution. Some new products or services are born because both need and solution exist within one brain. Bill Hewlett challenged his engineers to come up with an "electronic sliderule" because he knew one could be invented—and he needed it! Robert Palmer, a retired pilot for Northwest Airlines, invented the now ubiquitous roll-on suitcase because he wanted an easier way to transport his belongings and thought of a way to do it. (He has a background in both engineering and marketing.) Oxo kitchen utensils (potato peelers, spatulas, spoons, etc.), were designed with fat, soft handles by Sam Farber because he and his wife both cooked, but she had arthritis and needed an easy grip on the equipment.[6] It turned out that a lot of us, whether we have arthritis or not, prefer the larger grip because it gives us a better purchase on utensils that are often wet and slippery.

But what if the need exists in one head and the potential solution in another? Even worse, what if neither need nor solution has ever been fully articulated? That is, the target user doesn't recognize the need and demand that it be satisfied and the target problem-solver doesn't realize that she has a solution buried in the capabilities of her organization that would enable her to meet that unarticulated need. In both cases, there is tacit knowledge that could be combined and made explicit for the benefit of all. Let us consider how managers approach this challenge.

The Limits of Inquiry

The way that we generally attempt to tap into those unarticulated user needs is inquiry: asking people what they want. As noted above, careful inquiry can lead to uncovering some highly complicated desires that may be difficult, but possible to articulate. However, inquiry falls short of providing the ultimate insight into a potential customer's mind for a host of reasons. First, most of the time, inquiry is conducted under less than ideal conditions. The interviewer must try to imagine all the different interpretations of his questions and the interviewee must squeeze his desired responses into the categories offered—a process that often entails considerable mental gymnastics. Questionnaires are often administered by telephone, at dinnertime, to impatient respondents trying to stir the spaghetti while the children turn up the television to glass-breaking levels. The inquirers know they have to make the questions very simple to answer, and that constraint often renders the answers ambiguous if not meaningless. To take a recent example from a political poll, if you were asked whether a scandal has changed your decision on whether or not to vote for candidate Mr. X, a "no" answer could be interpreted in one of at least two ways. You could say "no," because you never intended to vote for Mr. X to begin with, and so your decision is unaffected. Or you could say "no," because your support for Mr. X is unwavering, despite the scandal. Inquiry is also limited by a host of well-known response biases, including inhibition about taboo subjects, and the desire to impress or please the interviewers. Focus groups are subject to peer pressure and group dynamics that can skew results. And then there is the ultimate problem: people don't know what their opinion or attitude is, because (in contrast to the example of the automobile) they have never experienced what you are asking about. So inquiry is most useful when inquirer and respondent share a clear idea of the product, service, process about which the inquiry is being made. By definition, then, inquiry is less useful if we are trying to tap into the tacit dimensions in the potential user's head.

Usability Laboratories

To get somewhat closer to those tacit dimensions, we can set up usability laboratories, in which we scrutinize the behaviors of our customers as they interact with our products. Consumer product and computer companies are expert at soliciting some "typical" customers to come in and play with the latest prototypes of products to be released on the market. What do you learn in such laboratory situations that you cannot learn through inquiry? A great deal. Observation adds visual feedback channels through which information can flow. You watch the actual behavior of people interacting with your product. So, for example, when Intuit software engineers watch people trying out the latest version of the popular personal financial planning package, Quicken, they can notice how the customer uses the documentation and what mouse clicks the customer uses to get where she thinks she needs to go. More important, however, they see body language, which reflects tacit dimensions of knowledge—implicit reactions that the user may not be conscious of conveying. Observers note where the user hesitates or looks puzzled, where she back-tracks, where she immediately understands the operation of the program and where it takes her time. And researchers can intervene to make the tacit explicit through questions, such as "why did you...[engage in a particular behavior, or look a certain way]?" In this way, researchers obtain information about the product that no one is likely to remember if asked several hours or days apart from actual usage.

How much have we tapped into the tacit dimensions of customers' experience-based knowledge? Somewhat. More than we did with inquiry divorced from the context of usage. But even usability laboratories are limited. The laboratory situation, no matter how physically comfortable we make it, is still artificial. The users are time-constrained in conducting the task. And there is a zoo-like quality to the experience, whether the researchers watching the users are in the same room or peering at them through a one-way mirror.

Concept Engineering

We remove some of the artificiality and the constraints if we visit users where they live. At L.L. Bean, manufacturers of outdoor wear, product developers use a technique called "Concept Engineering" to dig deeper into the rich knowledge base held in people's heads.[7] For instance, when developers were designing a new hunting boot, they sent out 20 teams of two people each, to interview hunters in their homes. Then, instead of asking structured questions, they asked the hunters a few open-ended questions. Principally, they asked for stories about hunting, so that they could get closer to the actual experience of the people using their products. What did they learn through such customer visits? Details that arose during the telling of the experience-based stories. The boots that squeaked, alerting the birds being hunted to the presence of the hunter. Stitching on the boots that gave way under the repeated snagging of thorns and twigs in the underbrush. When people tell such stories about their use of a product or service, they draw upon a rich set of contextual details that they might not think to mention even in focus groups—and that interviewers would not know to ask about. In the story-telling, the users make explicit some of their tacit knowledge about the context in which a product is used. They frame that knowledge for the interviewers in their own words, with their own specialized vocabulary and using their own mental models, rather than those of the interviewers.

But the interviewers also learn some information that they would not get if they asked the informants to come to them. Sitting in their own living rooms or kitchens, the informants feel more relaxed than they would in a laboratory and are more likely to be candid. They also may use props from their surroundings to explain better what they mean—their own guns and outdoor wear in the case of L.L. Bean. Such props help to pull associated memories out of the informants' brains. (About 60% of the human brain is associated with vision; visual cues are very important to us.) The interviewers also see where their customers live, what other kinds of products they have in their home, what other activities are implied by the surroundings, etc. Thus, the researchers add to their own store of tacit knowledge about the users' world.

Empathic Design

Some of the most powerful techniques for uncovering the tacit dimensions of knowledge can be aggregated under the rubric of empathic design. The term Empathic Design was coined to describe various processes used by top engineering/design firms and a few forward-looking manufacturers.[8] More akin to anthropology than marketing science, these techniques embody several underlying similarities: 1) observation of potential or actual customers in their natural settings, 2) over time if possible, 3) by multi-functional teams of people, at least some of whose members are well-acquainted with the knowledge base of the organization providing the product or service. These teams go out to wherever potential users are engaged in routine behaviors—homes, factories, offices—and gather qualitative data, often in the form of photographs or videos. (If L.L. Bean were using empathic design to create the hunting boots, the product developers would go on the hunt rather than interview hunters, for example, and would carry a video camera to record the experience.) After the team has collected the on-the-spot data, they return to share the photographs, drawings and/or video with others from their organization who did not go on the anthropological expedition. Such individuals are included for the same reason that the team is made up of people from different backgrounds: to attempt to overcome the natural biases of any single individual in selecting and interpreting data from observation. Moreover, people viewing the photographs without the benefit and biasing effect of having personally experienced the people and the places, often make fresh observations. These sharing sessions create shared knowledge about the potential customers—and make explicit the collective tacit knowledge of the group. Second, in brainstorming sessions carefully structured to produce feasible options, the team members identify opportunities for products or services in response to perceived needs. Finally, they create and test prototypes of those solutions. Thus, empathic design techniques allow the people who have potential solutions in their heads to empathize so completely with the people who have the need, that need and solution can be brought together.

These tacit dimensions of knowledge, as noted above, are often untapped by direct inquiry, because people are unaware of their own behavior, or at least unaware of how their behavior offers opportunities for improvement and change. The highly astute observer can infer need or desire from overt but often routine and even unconscious behavior. Moreover, recognizing the users' needs may stimulate the observer's own tacit knowledge as she connects need to solution. Let us consider some of the opportunities afforded by observation.

Triggers of Use

What situations prompt customers to use a particular product or service? Do people actually use it when and as expected? The brand manager for a spray-on cooking oil was astounded to look out his window one Saturday morning and observe a neighbor, to whom he had given a sample can, spraying the oil on the bottom of his lawn mower. Pressed to explain, the neighbor pointed out that the oil prevented the cut grass from adhering to the mower blades and was nontoxic. The same principles applied to using the spray for snow blowers! Or how about the breakfast food Cheerios? The little rounds of oats are as likely to be carried around in bags by parents as a handy snack to mollify toddlers as they are to be heaped in the breakfast bowl with milk. And in the 1990s, Hewlett-Packard learned an interesting lesson when it allied with Lotus Development Corporation to produce the HP 95/100 LX series of personal digital assistants (PDAs). The original reason for working with Lotus was that product developers knew their "road warrior" customers valued the computing power of the 1–2–3 spreadsheet. However, in observing their customers, HP researchers discovered that the personal-organizer software licensed from Lotus was at least as important a trigger for using the PDA as was the spreadsheet. Users did not stop to reason about their usage patterns—their behaviors were largely unconscious. In surveys, therefore, they tended to emphasize the need for the computational software (perhaps also because they regarded it as more professional and prestigious), but their actual use was predicated on other, less well articulated needs.

Interactions with the User's Environment

New products and services never enter a vacuum. Rather, they will be deployed into a system that already exists—the users' own. Whether the innovation opportunity be an office, a factory, or a home, the people inhabiting that environment have created some sort of system for achieving their required tasks. Such a system is often highly developed—but aspects of it may be housed in the tacit dimensions of the users' minds; that is, parts of the routine may be unconscious. Moreover, some aspects of the system may be based on ignorance. The producers of household cleaning agents who took videos of people doing chores in their homes were intrigued (and sometimes appalled) by the ways that people organized and conducted those tasks. The homemakers made surprising assumptions about the way that products could interact (e.g., combine one cup of laundry detergent, one cup of baking soda, one-fourth cup of automatic dishwasher detergent, one cup of bleach—all to get the curtains white.) Some of the user systems had evolved according to implicit decision rules that are unlikely to emerge in surveys, focus groups or usability laboratories. One consumer used a liquid glass cleaner from one manufacturer, but always poured it into the spray bottle of another. She did not volunteer a reason why, because the act was enshrined in routine and hence unremarkable. (It turned out that there were multiple reasons for her routine, including a preference for the mechanics of one spray bottle but the cleaning characteristics of another.) Often people working in their habitual environment are totally unaware of their system. Watching the videos of people on their knees struggling to retrieve a particular bottle or box from under sinks, one quickly comes to the conclusion that storage of all the necessary household cleaning agents is a real problem in these homes—but no one mentioned it. In order to understand the users' systems, Intuit has a "Follow Me Home" program, in which researchers obtain permission from someone who has just purchased Quicken to follow him home and observe how he sets up and uses the software package for the first time. What researchers learn from this observation is not only where the computer resides and who the primary user is, but also what other software resides on the user's computer and what the consumer's system of filing information is. Such home visits also revealed to Intuit the importance of their product for home businesses. Understanding the user's system—especially its tacit dimensions —can stimulate ideas about how a particular product or service might better interact with that system, in ways that the user will not articulate.

User Customization

In evolving their own systems, users often come up with innovations— but again, the need that inspires such inventiveness may remain unarticulated. When the Sundberg-Ferar design firm was helping Rubbermaid develop a new walker for adults with limited mobility, they convened in nursing homes focus groups of people using walkers. "What could we do to improve your walkers?" they asked. "What don't you like about them?" The participants shook their heads. They liked their walkers as they were. No, they could not suggest any improvements if the walker could be redesigned from scratch. The researchers gave up and excused the group members. Only as the respondents got up and retrieved their walkers to exit the room did the researchers find that one woman had tied a bicycle basket to her walker with shoe strings; a man had fashioned a holder for his cordless phone out of duct tape; another had hung an aftermarket automotive cupholder on his walker! They had not thought to mention to the researchers these little homemade additions. These observations led Sundberg-Ferar to design a built in, flexible mesh pouch for walkers, providing what Rubbermaid called a CCA, a Compelling Competitive Advantage.[9] Yet because the elderly users had never articulated their desire, it remained unrecognized as a need. That is, the consumers had useful knowledge about their own needs, but it would have remained locked in their subconscious had their behavior not revealed it.

Intangible Attributes of the Product

Products and services have emotional, psychological and aesthetic attributes that may not be readily articulated by potential users. We are all familiar with the disparity of responses elicited by the form of a product: "It is pretty." Or "It's ugly." And people have difficulty tapping into the associations that stimulate such evaluations. They simply know that it appeals or not. Viewing a particular electric teapot for the first time, an international group was much divided on its aesthetic qualities. "Catchy." "Hideous." "I like it." "Wouldn't have it in my kitchen." Culture and background clearly have much influence on such evaluations. "It would sell well in Scandinavia," declared some observers of the teapot. "Too extreme for the U.S. market," said others. Pushed to explain, people found themselves at a loss for words. Because reactions to aesthetics are so difficult to explain, some researchers use a variety of stimuli and get people to cluster together physical objects that have similar, unarticulated appeal: clocks and paintings, pictures of nature and wine glasses. U.K.-based Angela Dumas finds that when people have a whole group of objects that convey to them the same aesthetic or otherwise evocative attributes, they begin to be able to articulate dimensions in terms such as energy, or rhythm or in abstract concepts such as "elegance".[10]

However, not just aesthetics draw upon the tacit dimensions of user knowledge. People also have strong associations—good and bad—with smell and taste. Recall the furor caused in the U.S. by the first ill-advised decision of the Coca-Cola Company to discontinue "old coke" in favor of a new, "improved" variety. Old coke's surprisingly strong nostalgic, even patriotic associations constituted some of its value to people. Working for diaper-maker Kimberly-Clark, designers at GVO were able to take advantage of some unarticulated but potent product attributes. After visiting the homes of customers, GVO observers recognized the emotional appeal of pull-on diapers to both parents and toddlers, who saw them as a step toward "grown-up" dress. Diapers were clothing, the researchers realized, and had highly symbolic as well as functional meaning. Their ability to tap into these tacit dimensions of the parental experience profited Kimberly-Clark immensely. Huggies Pull-Ups were rolled out nationally in 1991, and by the time competitors caught on, the company was selling $400 million worth of the product annually.

Unarticulated User Needs

Perhaps the most powerful use of empathic design techniques is in discovering needs buried in patterns of behavior observed over time. When activity unfolds in a dynamic fashion, tacit knowledge about that activity resides in longitudinal data. For example, nurses who work with a given patient in a hospital for hours, if not days and weeks, have a very different body of tacit knowledge than the doctors have. Doctors draw upon cross-sectional data: laboratory results of tests on blood, urine, etc., conducted at particular points in time. Nurses' "intuition" is based on dynamic, interactive data, patterns emerging over time (or at least, used to be, when nurses had longer term relationships with patients than today's medical care allows.) The literature on nursing is full of references to instances in which nurses acted upon their "intuition." For example, the medical team at Methodist Hospital in Indianapolis was able to revive a three-year old boy in respiratory distress because his nurse listened to her "insistent inner voice" and checked on the patient, although "logically" nothing should have been wrong.[11]

For its research on mobile communications, Doblin Group followed a lawyer for an entire day. From the moment she left her children at their day care center in the morning until after the children were in bed that night, the researchers observed her use of communications. Similarly, Intel researchers camped out in homes to observe the morning and afternoon rituals of families with children. Chicago-based eLab tracked the meal-making habits of each of more than a dozen families for more than a week. They videotaped from breakfast through lunch, shadowed people on shopping trips and traced snack foods and drinks throughout the home for the entire period. Product-developers in Hewlett-Packard's medical equipment division sit in operating rooms to watch surgeons at work. Such longitudinal observation reveals patterns of behavior rather than snapshots and places those patterns in context. It was through daylong studies such as following the lawyer that Doblin Group discovered that owners of cell phones and beepers combined their functions to screen and cluster calls. Intel researchers noted that communication in families in the morning takes place in a flurry of quick bursts in the kitchen and predicted that we may end up using an all-purpose communication device attached to the refrigerator. Such a device would contain voice, visual and text messages from parents to children and vice-versa, as well as the grocery list and other important household data. ELab researchers developed a way for their client to understand how and why certain foods were incorporated into family routines and how members decided whether to adopt a new item. One Hewlett-Packard product developer noted that when surgeons used a television screen to guide their movements within the patient's body, the physicians' vision of their work was momentarily blocked every time a nurse passed between the doctor and the television screen. From this observation came the notion of suspending a screen in front of the surgeon's eyes, so that his view could never be obscured. In none of these examples was the end user requesting a solution to a problem. Nor were these people self-consciously examining their own behavior so that they could report on it if asked. Rather, their behaviors revealed patterns of problem solving based on experience—on tacit dimensions of knowledge. In each case, trained observers could infer unarticulated needs and opportunities for unexpected solutions, often to unacknowledged problems.

Requirements

Clearly, the techniques of empathic design require very different skills than those that are taught in business school curriculum or that are offered in marketing departments as on-the-job-training. Moreover, individuals who are extremely competent and knowledgeable about the capabilities of their organization may be very inept observers. Therefore, the uncovering of latent needs buried in the tacit dimensions of a user's knowledge requires training—and the participation of multi-functional teams. That is, keen observers can identify and articulate some of the tacit dimensions of the users' knowledge and hence originate innovative ideas for new products and services. Since individuals screen their observations through the lens of their own life/work experiences, teams have to be balanced with a variety of professional backgrounds and interests. Some companies such as Intel, Hewlett-Packard and Xerox, have small but active departments devoted to anthropological expeditions. Most of the individuals who conduct this work are trained in anthropology or psychology. The work requires listening rather than asking, watching rather than drawing immediate conclusions and an ability to derive inherent patterns from apparently random behavior. However, empathic design supplements rather than substitutes for traditional market research. After potential solutions have been generated through empathic design techniques, the usual market research methodologies need to be applied to assess the appeal and probable value of the innovations to various market segments.

Conclusion

In many ways, the observational techniques described in this chapter take us back to the origins of marketing research, before we had the ability to analyze huge amounts of quantitative data. Why are they re-emerging now? There are many possible reasons, but among them are at least these: 1) the increased sophistication in our knowledge about the subtleties of the human mind and 2) an appreciation for how fragmented is the knowledge required to create the complex products and services needed today. Design is emerging as an ever more potent way to discriminate among competing products, and it is not just a matter of making something superficially attractive. Rather, design today involves delving back into the tradition of matching form to function and enhancing function through form. Yet much of people's responses to design remain buried in the tacit dimensions of their knowledge. We are only beginning to systematically explore the connections between experience, background, culture and personality with aesthetic, emotional, and psychological preferences. We are still at the stage of inferring connections through behavioral observation.[12]

Second, the knowledge available to solve complex problems often exists in the minds of specialists and is unavailable to the people who have need of the solutions. It is not possible (or desirable) for these specialists to convey all of their technical knowledge to potential customers, so that the customers could know what solutions are feasible. Yet it is commercially dangerous to produce products that no one has requested. When therefore needs are unarticulated or difficult to explain, inferring desire or requirements through keen observation is more likely to produce a happy marriage of need and solution. The more that we understand the tacit dimensions of knowledge, the greater will be our ability to explicate previously unarticulated user needs.

The arena of new product development is therefore a rich context in which to explore the tacit dimensions of knowledge—and in which to design techniques for managing knowledge elicitation, capture and use.

References

1. This chapter draws upon several previous publications on the topic: Dorothy Leonard and Jeffrey Rayport, "Spark Innovation Through Empathic Design," *Harvard Business Review*, November/December 1997, pp. 102–113. Reprint #97606 and Dorothy Leonard, Wellsprings of Knowledge (Boston: Harvard Business School Press, 1995, 1998).

2. Since there is no universally accepted definition of knowledge, I presume to use my own.

3. See Gerald Zaltman, "Rethinking market research: Putting people back in," *Journal of Marketing Research* 34 (November 1997): 424–437.

4. The activities of responding to abstract questions and making personal decisions are located in different parts of the brain, according to A. R. Domasio, *Descartes' Error* (New York: Putnam Books, 1994).

5. Henry Petroski "Form Follows Failure," *Invention and Technology* Fall 1992, pp. 54–61, passim. (Also see Petroski's book, *The Evolution of Useful Things* (New York: Alfred A. Knopf, 1992).

6. See H. Kent Bowen, Marilyn Matis, and Sylvie Ryckebusch, *Oxo International* (Boston, Mass.: Harvard Business School, Case #9-697-007, 1997).

7. For more details on this technique, see the video and workbook *Redesigning Product/Service Development* (Boston: Harvard Business School Publishing, 1997).

8. For a detailed description of some of these techniques, see Dorothy Leonard and Jeffrey Rayport, "Spark Innovation through Empathic Design," *Harvard Business Review*, November/December 1997, pp. 102–113. Reprint #97606.

9. Personal communication with Curt Bailey, President of Sundberg-Ferar, Walled Lake, Michigan, August 26, 1998.

10. See Angela Dumas, "Building Totems: Metaphor-Making in Product Development," *Design Management Journal* 5 (Winter 1996): 170–182.

11. Lynn Rew, "Nursing Intuition: Too Powerful and Too Valuable to Ignore," *Nursing*, July 1987, pp. 43–45.

12. Although I have emphasized behavioral observation in this chapter, readers should also be aware of work by researchers using the powerful techniques of metaphor to help individuals express the tacit dimensions of their cognition. See Daniel Pink, "Metaphor Marketing," an interview with Gerald Zaltman about his metaphor elicitation technique, Fast Company, April/May 1998.

10

Enabling Complex Adaptive Processes through Knowledge Management

Rudy Ruggles and Ross Little

Processes are supposed to take inputs, act on them, and produce output that is more valuable than the inputs. However, because of the speed of change, many processes need to adjust often if they are to maximize the value they add. This chapter describes how organizations can enable complex, knowledge-intensive processes to adapt to changes in their environment. We analyze processes through the lens of complexity science, a field that has focused on how groups of highly connected intelligent agents behave. We have established a taxonomy by which organizations can identify the types of processes upon which knowledge management efforts will have the highest payoff and how knowledge can be managed in the context of these processes in input, execution, and output terms. When linked to processes that create value for the organization, knowledge management is key to ensuring that complex adaptive processes are as effective as possible, providing the foundation for a true knowledge-based businesses.

Processes and Knowledge Management

There is a danger in the practice of knowledge management: that managing knowledge will be perceived as an end in itself, creating an internal bureaucracy focused on knowledge creation, acquisition, storage, and retrieval—a set of activities often grouped under the heading "the knowledge management process." Such a process set is important and useful only as it enables value to be created through the application of knowledge. This chapter does not limit the discussion of knowledge and processes to the knowledge management process, but looks at the application of knowledge in the context of all business processes.

Processes are the activities involved in turning a set of inputs into outputs. They are a basic unit of analysis for activity within organizations. As such, most organizations have focused a great deal of effort on making their processes more effective. From the time of Frederick Taylor through current business process reengineering efforts, effectiveness has often been measured in terms of efficiency. In turn, the drive toward efficiency has led to careful process codification, analysis, and streamlining activities. While there are many processes that benefit from such treatment, most knowledge-intensive processes—activities that require expertise, and ongoing judgment and sense-making—are not necessarily more effective as a result of such ministrations. The problem? Knowledge-intensive processes are extremely complex, integrating a large number of inputs, pursuing multiple (and sometimes conflicting) goals, and remaining sensitive to frequent and rapid changes in their context. And compounding this problem is the fact that their contexts do change; they change often and they change quickly, rewarding processes that can be adapted to these changes. This chapter argues that, while knowledge management can be valuable in many types of processes, it is absolutely key for the effectiveness of such knowledge-intensive, complex, adaptive processes.[1] In a world filled with resource allocation decisions, the framework outlined herein supports the appropriate choice of knowledge management tools and techniques to enhance each type of business process.

Understanding Processes as Systems

Our use of the words complex and adaptive to describe such processes is not incidental. In looking at the role of knowledge management in various types of processes, we have created a process typology based on the study of the behavior of complex adaptive systems (CAS), also called complexity theory. John Casti, editor of Complexity magazine and member of the Santa Fe Institute (the center where a great deal of complexity theory research takes place) provides an useful taxonomy for distinguishing complex adaptive systems (see figure 10.1).[2] We have, in turn, applied his terminology to processes to create the necessary distinctions.

We will walk through each of the categories from figure 10.1, describing the application of CAS ideas to processes and the role that knowledge management can play in supporting such processes.

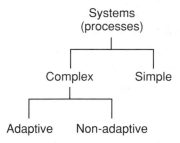

Figure 10.1
A categorization structure

The Simple

At the first level, systems fall into two camps. They are either simple or complex. Casti says that simple systems exist only in textbooks (the two-body problem in physics, for instance). They have few agents (elemental units) and exist in a relatively closed environment. Simple processes, meanwhile, do exist in real life. In fact, they exist everywhere. Examples include sharpening a pencil or making coffee. They are the lowest level operations we undertake, so low level that they are often done without much conscious effort once they are learned initially. These are not the processes on which to focus knowledge management efforts, since in general they do not warrant such attention.

The Complex, but Nonadaptive

Complex systems can be divided into two categories: nonadaptive (CnA) and adaptive (CA). Casti describes CnA systems as those that always use the same rules, systems such as those found in the fields of physics, chemistry, astronomy, engineering, and so on. While these rules may not be easy to understand, and the resulting dynamics extremely complicated (e.g., calculating the physics of three bodies in motion), there are basic immutable rules at play that do not adjust in the face of new information (a fourth body, say). By analogy, we can also classify processes as adaptive or nonadaptive. Intricate, intertwined procedures may be extremely complicated, but if their execution is predicated upon a set of unchanging rules, they are complex nonadaptive processes (CnAPs).[3] Microchip assembly would be one such process: extremely complicated, but nonadaptive, at least over the short run.

The effectiveness of CnA processes is determined by the rate of change in their environment. In a changing environment, CnAPs will become less and less useful as they become less attuned to their context. CnAPs in rapidly changing environments cannot effectively change inputs into valuable outputs, either because the process execution "costs" more than the value it adds, or because the resulting outputs are not as valuable in the new environment. However, if a CnA process exists in a "quiet" environment, one in which environmental shifts are few or do not effect the process, it can work quite well.

Complex nonadaptive processes are the type that benefit most from codification. Despite being complex, such processes are worth making explicit, capturing the knowledge entailed in their execution, and embedding that knowledge in the process support infrastructure. It is therefore worth automating certain complicated assembly lines that do not need to adapt to changing conditions, or codifying the subtleties of bread making, for example, into a machine to ease the task for the consumer.[4] The work of turning knowledge into code pays dividends in such an environment.

Processes that are complex but that do not need to change often, usually do not need an ongoing knowledge management effort to ensure that the associated knowledge is kept up-to-date. They can have relevant knowledge essentially "hard-wired" in from time to time, through computerization, automation, periodic training, or just detailed procedure manuals. These sorts of processes certainly draw upon knowledge, but do not benefit significantly from dynamic knowledge management techniques to support their execution, assuming that the processes actually work. This last provision is important, however. If the process does not work well, or if the tasks entailed often encounter problems, it can be extremely useful to access and bring to bear expertise to solve these problems through ongoing knowledge management. Interestingly, what this need often indicates is that what is being treated as a CnAP actually does need to be able to adapt either through overhaul (via process reengineering, for example) or dynamically, by being enabled as a complex adaptive process.

The Complex and Adaptive

While there is value in focusing on the types of processes described above, today's rapidly changing, knowledge-intensive work environment tends to entail complex processes that must change and adapt relatively quickly. Complexity theory focuses on the behaviors and implications of complex adaptive systems, so it is in this section that we can draw most from that field, applying what has been learned about systems to processes, and outlining the role of knowledge management in enabling their effectiveness.

According to Casti, complex adaptive systems have three characteristics.

• **They are composed of a medium number of individual components, or agents.** These components could be people, they could be vehicles, they could be bits of code, etc. Whatever their form, they are the actors in the system. The number is not so small that you can work out the interactions and behavior modes on the back of an envelope, but not so large that you can use statistical aggregation methods to understand how the system works.

• **Second, the agents are intelligent and adaptive.** Intelligent in that they use rules to decide what actions to take next, and adaptive in that they will change those rules, even to the extent of creating whole new ones, if they see that the old rules don't work well any more.

• **Lastly, the agents only have local information.** They do not know what all the other agents are doing at any given time, so they are only trying to complete their jobs armed with local information.[5]

Therefore, when we talk about complex adaptive processes, we mean those processes that have a medium sized number of knowledge-intensive adaptive components (people and process elements), interacting on the basis of local information. They are adaptive in that they can accommodate and adjust to incorporate changes in their local environment to maintain their effectiveness at producing valuable output. In rapidly changing environments, traditional process optimization activities will at best lead to short-term effectiveness, but usually create brittle processes that need to be reoptimized often, increasing the overall costs of the process. Therefore, the bottom-line value of complex adaptive processes is that they reduce the long-term total costs of achieving the greatest value output per input in rapidly changing environments.

Like the simple and complex nonadaptive processes described previously, CAPs can certainly benefit from a more active approach to understanding the knowledge needed to execute the processes and bringing that knowledge to bear on the effective execution of that process. However, the other types differ in that for them once the knowledge has been elicited and embedded, it can be drawn upon "as is" for quite some time without much decay in process effectiveness. But complex adaptive processes, by definition, tend to have a very short knowledge "half-life." What needs to be known for effective process execution is constantly changing. Active knowledge management can support these processes in such environments by giving the process executors ongoing access to the knowledge that keeps these processes effective, as well as enabling them to feed back what they have learned as they go.

So, how do you manage knowledge better to support the adaptivity of complex processes? There are opportunities in each of the three elements of any process: input, execution, and output. Complex adaptive processes benefit from consideration of how knowledge can be managed in each of these elements.

The Management of Knowledge as a Process Input

Adaptation requires interaction with, and feedback from, the environment. This information comes from many sources, ranging from data mining and customer feedback to scenario planning and visioning sessions. Knowledge is the result of integrating these input sources into a better understanding of the changing needs of the environment. If a process is to be truly adaptive and not just reactive, such inputs need to be put in context, made sense of, weighed against the value that would be created if the process stayed as is, and used in making a decision about whether or not to change current practice, and if so in what way. Therefore, it is knowledge, not just data, which must be used as an input to CAPs if they are to adapt appropriately.

The Management of Knowledge in Process Execution

Processes are essentially organized sets of tasks. Therefore, the knowledge related to their execution, which changes as complex processes adapt, falls into two categories: conduct knowledge and structural knowledge.[6] Conduct has to do with the tasks, the actions taken by the process executors. Structural knowledge deals with the parameters of the process itself, including the organization of the components.

Changes in conduct knowledge.   As process executors receive new inputs about the changes in their environment, they need to decide whether to adjust their actions in light of these developments. If some change is necessary to adapt to these changes, it may be enough merely to make changes at the task level of the process, without effecting the process structure. Process executors need to have access to knowledge that not only helps them decide what changes to make, but also how to best perform these new tasks. Picture the salesman who has been informed that the competition has started using real-time sales-support tools. His organization, in response, is rolling out cell phones with a CB-like open link to all other sales people, enabling him to respond immediately to customer inquiries that go beyond his own expertise by drawing upon the collective knowledge of the whole sales force. The structure of the sales process itself may not have changed dramatically, but the salesman needs to understand how to take advantage of this new capability at the task level. This knowledge can be made accessible in a variety of ways (e.g., JIT training, mentoring, etc.), but it must be made available effectively if the potential of this capability is to be realized.

Changes in structural knowledge.   The other way processes can adapt is to change their structure altogether. In the above example, the traditional sales process stayed intact. However, what if the competition suddenly switched to an Amazon.com-like approach, introducing a customer-pleasing internet-based sales strategy? Adapting a sales process to this shift in the environment entails a full rethinking of the nature of the sales process. The organization's knowledge about sales and customer relationships has just become insufficient, if not obsolete, in this new world. Changes of this magnitude require rapid adjustments in individual and organizational knowledge bases. Best practices and benchmarks need to be re-established to account for this new sales capability. While a great deal of the existing knowledge of sales may still be useful, in many cases the "experience clock" has been reset. Active knowledge management enables people to learn quickly what works and what doesn't by learning from experiences internally, accessing external information sources, and working from other knowledge inputs to upgrade their structural knowledge in order to create new approaches to sales that produce the greatest value in the new environment.

The Management of Knowledge as a Process Output
As CAPs adjust, they create new knowledge directly and as a by-product. As people learn from the changes in process structure and conduct, this

knowledge should be made accessible to others in the organization. What the salespeople learn about what an internet-enhanced sales process entails might be useful for marketers, planners, product designers, and operations folks as well. A strong knowledge management capability allows people to use knowledge from outside of their function or other focus area as input into their own processes. In addition, one knowledge by-product of process adaptation is simply a greater understanding of what it means to adapt.

Quick, effective adaptation comes with experience, and not all experiences will be good ones. Whatever the outcome, these experiences, their reasons, and their results are extremely valuable lessons for others dealing with CAPs.

Maximizing the Value of Knowledge Management

To read some of the widely-available literature (a.k.a. sales brochures), it sometimes seems like knowledge management is the answer to all organizational problems, that it will cure you of whatever ails you, be it staff turnover, culture clashes, or innovation stagnation. While the various knowledge management tools and techniques certainly have their usefulness, there is no such thing as a blanket solution. The framework laid out in this chapter is designed to help determine where certain types of knowledge management activities will have their greatest impact. Simple or complex nonadaptive processes lend themselves well to the solutions offered by codification tools, such as expert systems, decision support systems, and in some cases full process automation. Meanwhile, those processes that need to adjust will be enhanced by solutions that enable people to constantly interpret inputs and change their behavior accordingly. Studies of complex adaptive systems have shown repeatedly that this sort of flexibility allows much greater value realization than any hard-wired "optimization" approach.

The world of business is being shaped by the accelerating speed of change, the multiplying connections among its elements, and the increasing impact of knowledge as a primary driver of economic growth. While a greater proportion of the value being created in the world economy comes from minds than from muscles, the minds' work is made more difficult by the speed at which ideas change, by the decreasing "half-life" of information. Knowledge-based businesses are those that structure themselves to leverage the power of knowledge through their infrastructures, processes, product and service offerings, and strategies.

In this environment, complex, knowledge-intensive processes are the norm. We have used complexity theory as a lens through which to differentiate processes according to their structure and knowledge needs, and have described the role of knowledge management in each type. In the end, no matter what the lens or what the vocabulary, the intent remains the same: applying knowledge effectively to create the greatest value possible. This is the principle upon which knowledge-based businesses will succeed.

References

1. While generative learning and knowledge creation are also key for knowledge-based businesses, we focus in this chapter only on the usefulness of knowledge management in enhancing the ongoing effectiveness of processes, or as Peter Senge calls it, "coping." Coping is a difficult enough objective in and of itself these days (see P. Senge, "The Leader's New Work: Building Learning Organizations," *Sloan Management Review*, Fall 1990, p. 8).

2. As presented at Ernst and Young's Embracing Complexity 3 conference, August 1998.

3. We would like to officially apologize for using jargon like this, but we thought it less confusing than sorting through slight phrase variations containing the words "complex" and "adaptive" over and over again.

4. For more about this process see Ikujiro Nonaka and Hirotaka Takeuchi's account of Matsushita's creation of a home bread making machine in *The Knowledge-Creating Company* (Oxford University Press, New York, 1995), pp. 101–106.

5. Local here does not necessarily refer to geographic locality, it refers to information space locality. In this electronically connected world, I may know more about what someone on my project team half a continent away is doing than I know about what the person one office over is doing. I am therefore informationally closer to my teammate.

6. Game theory also uses these categories to describe realms of uncertainty, a discussion closely linked to knowledge. For more on the topic of uncertainty, see Brandenburger, Adam, "On the Existence of a Universal Belief Space," *Harvard Business School*, September 14, 1998.

11

Knowledge Sharing Shifts the Power Paradigm

Carol Willett

Most organizations pursue knowledge sharing in order to: innovate faster, speed up their response to marketplace demands, increase productivity and expand workforce competence. Installing the technical tools for knowledge sharing is also apt to bring about another affect—a wholesale shift in the power paradigm—an outcome that is not always anticipated or welcome. As Buckman Laboratories found, knowledge sharing is not merely a neutral exchange of information—it affects working relationships, distribution of power, patterns of influence, and alters how individual define their responsibilities. This article explores some of the dramatic shifts that took place at Buckman Laboratories, a winner of the Arthur Andersen Enterprise Award for Knowledge Sharing and describes the effects of knowledge sharing on power paradigms.

The Information to Act
In today's business environment, inability to respond quickly to the marketplace is a well-recognized form of corporate suicide. The organizational arthritis that results from bureaucratic, overly centralized decision making is a condition that few firms can afford. A decade ago, Bob Buckman of Buckman Laboratories, a Memphis-based manufacturer and distributor of chemicals, realized that something had to change. The centralized, hierarchical decision making structure that had guided the company since its founding in the 1940s could no longer provide the speed of response needed to support global operations in the 1980s.

Musing on the observation of Jan Carlson that "an individual without information cannot take responsibility but an individual who is given information cannot help but take responsibility,"[1] Bob framed the challenge of change at Buckman Laboratories in a novel way. "How" he wondered "can we effectively engage the intellectual and experiential horsepower of the entire organization despite the barriers of time, distance, language and different operational divisions?"[2] The principle of connecting these individuals led to technical innovations, but the purpose was firmly grounded in improving customer response.

Buckman reasoned, "If the greatest database in the company is housed in the individual minds or four associates, then that is where the power of the organization resides. These individual knowledge bases are continually changing and adapting to the real world. We have to connect these knowledge bases together so that they can do whatever they do best in the shortest possible time."[3] To enable people to act, they had to be given access to information distributed across more than 1,200 minds operating out of twenty-one different countries.

This was a tall order. While the technical challenge of setting up an Internet-based system using leased laptops seemed daunting enough in 1982, as it turned out, the harder issue to resolve was the question of "How do we move from a chain of command to a web of influence?"[4] Over the course of the next four years, Buckman discovered that the issues of power and information are inextricably intertwined and that a change in communication systems inevitably leads to a shift in power systems.

Forging the Chain of Command

Prior to Buckman's foray into knowledge sharing, the Laboratory had made its mark as a worldwide manufacturer and distributor of specialty chemicals used in industrial and agricultural processes. The Lab measured its product (and productivity) in barrels and pounds. Its primary value to customers derived from the quality and effectiveness of its products. Since its inception in the basement of a small house on McLean Boulevard in Memphis, the founder, Stanley Buckman, had run the lab in a hierarchical, centralized manner. Managers had evolved into gatekeepers of information, as control points for access to expertise, and as the routing mechanisms for directing any decisions of importance to the Chairman. Management was comfortable with these roles.

Within the Lab structure, there were clear line distinctions between divisions, operating companies and professional disciplines. Status derived from the amount and extent of information each individual controlled. Over the years, people had taught themselves to hoard knowledge to achieve power. Access to knowledge had become a basis of security within the organization.

Spinning the Web of Influence

Enter Bob Buckman with a determination to do things differently. Bob's vision was to create a different kind of value in the marketplace—selling knowledge about chemical processes, and not just the chemicals themselves. In order to effectively do this, he had to find a way to put the expertise of all his associates at the disposal of any one associate confronted with a customer problem.

His motivations were several. One, it was clear that the increasingly complex global operations of the lab could not effectively be run from Memphis without an unacceptably slow response time to customer needs. Two, he strongly doubted that the best information could only be found in the minds of managers in Memphis. Surely, he reasoned, the people with the most current, hands on experience would be those out there doing the work. Third, with the advent of Internet technology, he saw the possibility of near real time exchange despite differences in time zones and geographic distance. Finally, and most importantly, Bob envisioned a different sort of value added for customers if only his associates could access information that would enable them to act independently.

So, a knowledge sharing initiative via E-mail was launched in 1984–1985. The first attempt was to connect General Managers together so that best practices could be shared. A system was created, connections were put in place and what happened? Nothing happened. There was no sharing of best practices during the first six months—only a few polite "hello's." As it happened, managers felt that they had all the information they needed.

Buckman reassessed the situation. If the managers were content with their access to information, then the issue was how to extend the system to those that did not have access to information. How could the lab clue all associates into best practices? Seven years experience with E-mail led most people to interpret the move from point-to-point communication to a broader dialog as a purely a technical issue—a matter of adding a few phone lines and leasing new laptop computers. There was little sense of the major organizational shifts that would result.

First, Install the Technology

To implement the knowledge sharing initiative Buckman set up a Knowledge Transfer Department and appointed a 34 year old Ph.D. in organic chemistry to run it. Within thirty days, Buckman Labs put its entire worldwide network up on CompuServe, the public online service. CompuServe offered Email access to public networks as well as private bulletin boards for internal use. Every associate was issued a laptop and a phone number to call. For a total of $75,000 a month in access charges, Buckman created the potential for every associate to reach every other associate—directly.

Seven technical exchange Forums accessed through a local Internet dial-up began to spur discussions among far-flung sales people and researchers —a dialog that quickly crossed technical disciplines and organizational boundaries. Allison Tucker in Memphis was put in charge of making sure that whoever asked a question, got an answer. These seven Forums were collectively known as K'Netix.

Sales associates around the globe at last had a means to put out a company wide call for expertise. They had a venue for sharing information that crossed divisional and disciplinary lines. As the first tentative exchanges took place, it came as a surprise (mostly to managers) that the experts who responded most promptly to calls for help were not always in managerial positions. Some important paradigms were beginning to shift.

A Challenge to Command and Control

As the first Forums began to take shape, backlash from middle management started to make itself felt. This new plan for giving all associates equal access to information ran afoul of the hierarchical chain of command that had, up until that point, processed information vertically through organizational layers. People who had defined themselves as the protective filters guarding the core information of the organization suddenly felt irrelevant. From this insecure position they did little to "pass the word" on the new way of doing business or to support participation in the K'Netix Forums.

Managers at the lab had been schooled to be effective bosses, not mentors or coaches. They were comfortable leading from a position of command with authority. They had neither skills nor instruction in the art of managing by influence.[4]

Traditionally, people at the lab had gained influence by being promoted to managerial positions of increased responsibility. Now thanks to Internet technology, associates at all levels could experience a span of influence that was formerly the sole preserve of the Chairman. Associates were using the Forums to collaborate in ways that defied organizational boxes. In the process, they were learning a good bit about how to phrase their ideas so that they were accepted by more and more people. They were learning how to influence others. From the managerial perspective it looked and felt like chaos.

Most importantly, many in the managerial ranks saw K'Netix as a threat to their role as the designated providers of unimpeachable expertise. At a stroke, K'Netix had left many managers wondering, "So what am I supposed to do for a living? What is my role here?" While Bob Buckman exhorted his workforce to embrace the virtues of knowledge sharing, his middle managers were sending another message. What managers had originally viewed as a technical communications issue, very soon took on threatening cultural and personal overtones.

New Roles for Managers

Traditionally, we tend to think of those who have the most information as the ones who are (or who ought to be) in charge. There is a tacit assumption, fostered by cultural norms and practices that people with more information than ourselves are normally "above" us. Buckman Lab managers were comfortable with the notion that their role was to control information, to maintain boundaries and insure that decisions were made by those with the greatest seniority. They were happy with life at the top of the organizational pyramid.

By giving his work force both the technical capability (K'Netix) and explicit encouragement to connect with anyone in the company in order to resolve customer problems, Buckman effectively inverted that pyramid. The pointy end was now down and the flat base faced up. He created a structure in which associates could seek information from peers without regard to organizational boundaries or the niceties of seniority.

No longer did associates need permission to call on any other member of the company who might be able to assist them. In the new scheme of things, the customer occupied the uppermost base of this inverted pyramid. The most critical people in the company were those who were effectively engaged with that customer. That engagement was not limited to face to face encounters. Any associate who was able to provide value added to that customer was "effectively engaged" regardless of their geographic location, organizational affiliation or job title.

At a stroke, K'Netix created a new meritocracy where people gained influence based on how effectively they contributed to the success of others and how well they could share and apply what they knew. People from the far-flung reaches of the company began to gain visibility as proven "problem solvers" who were quick on the trigger to help others. They demonstrated that it was no longer a question of what you knew, but how well you were able to apply and share what you knew among your colleagues.

This exponential increase in lateral communication across the breadth of the organization left many managers at a loss. Knowledge sharing was not a skill they had been taught to prize nor to develop. Without the familiar element of control, taking part in Forum exchanges felt less like real work and more like free-form chatter. Management collectively balked. Not only did it seem that they were being asked to sell a concept (collaborative knowledge sharing) that seemed inherently chaotic, they were being asked to collude in putting themselves out of work. It appeared to many managers that they had been demoted to a function no more or less important than any other associate.

Champions for Change

While management mulled over how to put this genie back in the bottle, champions for change were stepping forward from all over the organization. People who were comfortable with sticking their neck out began to emerge.

Until the advent of K'Netix, it was as important "how" things got done as "what" was done. The emphasis on form took precedence over speed, responsiveness or innovation. It was the role of management to see that things got done in a certain way and along recognized channels of communication. Power lay not only in what you knew, but also in the ways in which you brought that knowledge to bear. Suddenly, here was a system, which broke all the previous molds for how power was shaped and applied.

Here's just one example from the K'Netix archives that illustrates the impact of this connectivity. Dennis Dalton, a managing director for Asian activities sent out the following call for assistance: "We will be proposing a pitch-control program to an Indonesian pulp mill," he wrote. "I would appreciate an update on successful recent pitch-control strategies in your parts of the world."

Phil Hoekstra was the first to respond from Memphis with a suggestion of the specific chemical to use and a reference to a master's thesis on pitch control of tropical hardwoods, written by an Indonesian studying at North Carolina University. Fifty minutes later Michael Sund logged on from Canada to share his experience in solving the pitch problem in British Columbia. Then Nils Hallberg chimed in with examples from Sweden. Wendy Biijker offered details from a New Zealand paper mill. Jose Vallcorba gave two examples from Spain and France. Chip Hill contributed scientific advice from the company's R&D team. Javier Del Rosal sent a detailed chemical formula and specific application directions from Mexico and Lionel Hughes weighed in with two types of pitch control programs used in South Africa. In all, Dalton's request for help generated eleven replies from six countries, and stimulated several sidebar conversations as participants followed up on the information that had surfaced. This on-line collaboration netted Buckman Labs a $6 million order from the Indonesian mill.[5]

As participation in K'Netix grew, those who were willing to use technology in new and aggressive ways to share their knowledge of the market and of chemical processes gained power. K'Netix allowed them to leverage what they knew across a far broader scope. Those who were willing to trust the input from colleagues they had never met found they could now bring the collective experience of all 1,200 colleagues to their customers.

Shifting Roles

While K'Netix put in the hands of every employee the power to influence, the power to inform, the power to make a difference in dealing with customers half a world away lay it also introduced a new responsibility—

knowledge reciprocity. In exchange for your help in solving my problem of today, I must stay active in the Forums to be able to help you with your problem tomorrow.

Individuals who demonstrated the most knowledge reciprocity in the various Forums gained visibility in the company as the thought leaders among the emerging communities of technical practice. A 1993 survey of those who had been most active in the Forums during the prior year identified 150 people who excelled at sharing their knowledge and using their expertise to accomplish something productive. This "4th Wave" of 150 people were rewarded with both visible incentives (advancement and new opportunities) and acknowledged influence among their colleagues. They became known corporately as "good people to ask for help."

Knowledge reciprocity also began to drive new norms for behavior—both for managers and for the rank and file. No longer was it sufficient to do your own job in isolation. As influence shifted to those who actively shared their expertise, it became commonplace to expect that "part of the job" was helping others to succeed—people who's earnings might not show up on your bottom line.

And what became of management? Some managers were able to adapt over time. They learned that helping their reports make the best use out of the newly available information flow was equally as important as their former function of managing the flow of information. In making that mental shift, they came to accept that their new job was to help steer company progress, although they might not always be the ones at the wheel. Some managers clung to their to the old paradigm of command and control and found themselves with increasingly less impact on developments that sustained business growth and success. Over time they were replaced by those who saw entrepreneurial opportunity in knowledge sharing that transcended the benefits of knowledge hoarding.

Reflections and Lessons Learned

Reflecting on the power shifts that K'Netix wrought, Bob Buckman has commented, "In hindsight, we should have sold the vision (what's in it for the organization) and the value (what's in it for the associate and the customer) much deeper in the organization. We depended on middle management to buy in to the process and communicate the vision for us.

That was a mistake. We did not realize just how much a perceived threat the new system of communicating was to the middle management group at the time."[6] The basic question of managers, "What's in it for me?" went unanswered.

As Buckman Labs discovered, where you stand on knowledge sharing and collaborative technology depends very much on where you sit. The equities, interests, concerns and rewards associated with knowledge sharing vary greatly depending on whether you are a sales associate, a first line supervisor, a middle manager or an executive. The ability to communicate in near real time with any member of the corporation might be viewed with either delight or horror depending on how you construe your job and how you believe you earn your pay.

When major change is proposed, most of us wonder whether this change will:

- Save me time? If so, how much?
- Make my work easier? In what ways?
- Help me succeed?
- Help me advance?
- Give me access to the information I need?
- Help me solve the problems I'm facing today?

No matter the organization, each of its members has a distinct and unique "bottom line" that must justify the time and effort to learn to work differently—whether that difference involves new technology or new patterns of collaboration. No one set of reasons or size of example "fits all." The process of answering "What's in it for me?" is a negotiation. Unless organizations step up to that question, the best state of the art communications will do no more than gather dust.

One way to think of this negotiation process is to draw a teeter-totter. Think of your own organization and on the left-hand side list all the disincentives or barriers to knowledge sharing be they personal ("I don't have the time to type everything"), organizational ("Managers are need line of sight control if they to are lead effectively") or technical ("It's too difficult and frustrating to get connectivity around here"). Once your list is complete, make a rough estimate of how large those barriers seem given the challenges you already face.

Next, look at the right hand side of the teeter-totter. List all the potential benefits and incentives for actively using knowledge sharing technology.

Think about what it would take to make this new way of working worth your while? What is your bottom line for investing the time and energy to change?

Now, which is larger—the organizational, personal and technical incentives, or the disincentives?

In retrospect, the question of what it would have taken for Buckman's managers to shift the balance from disincentives to incentives was an interesting one. While the lab found no magic silver bullet that promptly converted the opposition and inspired everyone to change over night, the evolutionary change that took place was perhaps more lasting. The introduction of knowledge sharing technology brought to a head the basic need to develop and maintain trust throughout the organization.

As is frequently the case with knowledge sharing initiatives, people began to embrace the process when they had personal experience that it worked. For every call for help that was promptly answered by a knowledgeable someone on the far side of the globe, K'Netix gained in credibility. As people discovered that they experienced greater success working collaboratively than as a singleton, the concept of knowledge sharing became realistic and practical. Each time an associate found that they could effectively influence others on the strength of their experience, their willingness to make the time for responding to others grew.

A Checklist for Shifting Paradigms

As Bob Buckman is quick to point out, it's important to look at knowledge sharing as a journey and not a project. Senior management must be actively involved and supportive for culture change of this magnitude to take place. Those organizations who would like to follow the Buckman model should begin by taking a hard look at the teeter-totter balance in their existing structure. The following questions form a basic checklist for focusing on what needs attention if knowledge sharing practices are to take hold.

Trust—To what extent:

• Are employees trusted to take independent action?
• Are people willing to stake their personal, professional reputation on the input of peers and colleagues?
• Do people assume "we are all in this together?"

Rewards—To what extent:

- Are people rewarded for independent achievement?
- Are people rewarded for interdependent or collaborative achievement?
- Are people rewarded for actively sharing their knowledge with others?
- Are people encouraged to network—to find out and apply what others know?
- Are managers rewarded for developing others?

Roles

- What are the key roles in the organization now?
- How will those roles change with knowledge sharing?
- What new roles are apt to emerge?
- How will you train people for those new roles?

As the Buckman experience made clear, new communication and collaboration tools invariably call into question long-terms roles and responsibilities. Supervisors may know how to supervise, but do they know how to coach? Managers may be adept at filtering the right information to the right person, but do they know how to make sure the right people are in the loop when it seems as if the whole world is talking to each other? The Buckman experience highlights the importance of looking at the power dynamic in attempting major communications change through technology.

References

1. Jan Carlson, former chairperson of Scandinavian Airlines.

2. Robert H. Buckman, "Knowledge Sharing at Buckman Labs," *Journal of Business Strategy*, January–February 1998.

3. Robert H. Buckman, "Arthur Andersen 1996 Enterprise Awards for Knowledge Sharing," *Fortune*, February 1997.

4. Kenneth Schatz and Linda Schatz, "Managing by Influence" (Englewood Cliffs, N.J.: Prentice-Hall, 1986).

5. Glenn Rifkin, "Buckman Labs is Nothing but Net," *Fast Company*, June–July 1996.

12

From Capitalizing on Company Knowledge to Knowledge Management

Michel Grundstein

This chapter emphasizes the problem of capitalizing on company knowledge. Capitalizing on company knowledge means considering certain knowledge used and produced by the company as a storehouse of riches and drawing from these riches interest that contributes to increasing the company's capital. Thus, capitalizing on company knowledge is not simply a technical activity, but also an essential management function. From this viewpoint, Knowledge Management, its future prospects, its role, and complementary and convergent approaches that are emerging worldwide are discussed. In addition, the guiding principle and the essential characteristics of a specific approach, GAMETH, are described. This approach is focused on the upstream aspect of the problem: how can we locate crucial knowledge for the company and identify the critical fields that require greater attention by managers to overtake worldwide competition? Finally, the results of two pilot studies performed in accordance with this approach are presented, and lessons learned from experience are pointed out.

Introduction

In 1993, Peter Drucker said,

More and more, the productivity of knowledge is going to become, for a country, an industry, or a company, the determining competitiveness factor. In the matter of knowledge, no one country, no one industry, no one company has a "natural" advantage or disadvantage. The only advantage that it can ensure to itself is to be able to draw more from the knowledge available to all than others are able to do.[4]

However, the need for greater competitiveness often requires cost reduction and leads to structural changes and personnel cutbacks that result in early retirement, transfers of employees, and outright layoffs. Such measures pose a risk of dispersion and loss of the knowledge, collective and individual, that is the lifeblood of the company. This can lead to a weakening of the forces and competitive advantages proper to each activity, and can detract from the other imperatives of competitiveness, which are quality, adherence to schedule, "reactivity" (flexibility and fast adjustment to changes), and creativity. At the same time, we have observed the weaknesses resulting from the little importance accorded to knowledge storage. Most often, pressed for time and subjected to the weight of economic constraints, the operational actors do not have available the human and material resources necessary to ensure the safeguarding of company knowledge. Consequently, more and more companies today are confronted with problems related to the need to conserve, control, and make the most out of their knowledge.

This chapter is focused on the upstream aspect of that problem: how can we locate this knowledge and identify the critical fields that require greater attention by managers. First, we attempt to clarify the concept of capitalizing on company knowledge. Then, we discuss a way for positioning knowledge management. Next, we introduce the guiding principle and the essential characteristics of an approach called *GAMETH*, that identifies the crucial knowledge for a company to overtake worldwide competition. Finally, we present the results of two pilot studies performed in accordance with this approach and point out lessons learned from the experience.

Capitalizing on Company's Knowledge

The knowledge-based system development operations that we have carried out since 1984 have highlighted the opportunities inherent in work performed in the knowledge domain, and the potential of artificial intelligence techniques:

• Development of knowledge-based systems enables, for each project, formalizing part of the know-how attached to a product, a process, or a working method, while at the same time leading to improvements in the usual activities of the persons involved.

• The modeling work, practiced by knowledge engineers on the knowledge held by the persons directly engaged in the company's production process, provokes a phenomena of clarification and deepening knowledge of problems, as well as reinforcement of people's proficiency. Above all, this work, by modifying our way of stating problems, opens new perspectives. It considerably improves our aptitude for comprehending the complexity of the situations and problems encountered, while at the same time enabling us to find better solutions and increasing our innovative capacities.

It is because of such observations that we have brought the concept of capitalizing on company knowledge to light: "Capitalizing on company knowledge means considering certain knowledge used and produced by the company as a storehouse of riches and drawing from these riches interest that contributes to increasing the company's capital"[3].

This definition calls for three observations, which respectively concern: the two main categories of company knowledge, the collective and private nature of an individual's knowledge, and the problem of capitalizing on company knowledge.

The Two Main Categories of Company Knowledge

A company's knowledge includes, on the one hand, the specific know-how that characterize a company's capability to design, produce, sell, and support its products and services. On the other hand, the individual and collective skills that characterize its capabilities to act, in accordance with circumstances, and to evolve.

Stored in archives, cabinets, and people's minds, it consists of tangible components (data, procedures, drawings, models, algorithms, documents of analysis, and synthesis) and intangible components (people's abilities, professional knack, private knowledge, "routines"—the unwritten logic of individual and collective action [5], knowledge of company history, and decisional contexts). This is summarized in figure 12.1, where company's knowledge is represented under two main categories: "Know-how" and "Skills" [6].

This knowledge is representative of the company's experience and culture. Diffuse, heterogeneous, incomplete, or redundant, it is often marked by the circumstances of its creation. However, it does not express the unspoken words of those who have formulated it, which are nonetheless necessary to its interpretation. In the absence of those who have formalized it, this knowledge is difficult to locate and to use in situations and for purposes other than those in which it was created. Additionally, one

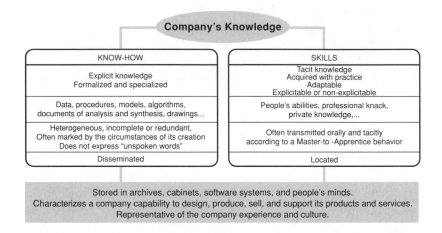

Figure 12.1
The two main categories of company's knowledge

notes that the collective knowledge of a company is often transmitted orally and implicitly. In other words, one can say that company knowledge strongly depends on the skills of a company's employees and on the continuity of their presence in the company. Therefore, a company's knowledge represents an extremely volatile intangible resource.

In a strict sense, When looking at the diagram shown in figure 12.1, one can imagine that a company's skills solely rest upon an individual's knowledge. Nevertheless, some of the individual's knowledge is characterized by a collective nature that has crystallized out of the regular and predictable behavioral patterns of the company. This remark leads to a reflection onto the collective and private nature of individual's knowledge.

The Collective and Private Nature of Individual's Knowledge
Here, we are referring to the knowledge classification of Michael Polanyi. He classifies the human knowledge into two categories:

Explicit knowledge refers to the knowledge that can be expressed through words, drawings, other articulate language like metaphors ; tacit knowledge is knowledge that is hard to express whatever the form of language is [7].

So, we will distinguish: on the one hand, the individual's explicit knowledge, articulated or formalized; on the other hand, the individual's tacit knowledge.

An individual's explicit knowledge can be expressed through speeches, metaphors, analogies, or diagrams; it is materialized through personal notes, wander sheets, notebooks, memorandum, sketches and the outline of various documents whether they are structured or not, and private computerized files.

An individual's tacit knowledge appears through talents, abilities, skills, professional knack, insight, wisdom, and shared behaviors (traditions, communities of practice, collusion).

During the action, the part of an individual's knowledge used and put to work every day, mixed with the company's knowledge, characterizes the competencies that allow a group of people to make complex tasks and that belong to the organization. This knowledge is as difficult to identify as it results from a collective learning and is produced by a group of people that are used to working together and accomplishing collective and specialized tasks. This part of knowledge is not visible with respect to the company. However, it is put to work for the company. Thus, it enters in the category of the company's knowledge, defined here as Skills.

However, if the part of the individual's knowledge acquired thanks to the interaction with a group of people inside the company has a collective nature and is not formalized or disseminated, it cannot be easily leveraged by the company as a whole.

This viewpoint on company knowledge is shared by Ikujiro Nonaka and Hirotaka Takeuchi [8], two Japanese authors that, referring to

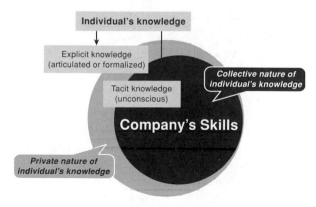

Figure 12.2
Collective and private nature of individual's knowledge

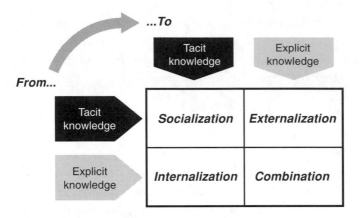

Source: *The Knowledge-Creating Company*, Oxford University Press, 1995.

Figure 12.3
Four modes of knowledge conversion

Michael Polanyi, discern two types of knowledge: tacit knowledge and explicit knowledge. "Tacit knowledge is personal, context- specific, and therefore hard to formalize and communicate. Explicit or 'codified' knowledge, on the other hand, refers to knowledge that is transmittable in formal, systematic language."

In their view, "tacit knowledge and explicit knowledge are not totally separated but mutually complementary entities." Thus, they propose a dynamic model of knowledge creation anchored to a critical assumption that "human knowledge is created and expanded through social interaction between tacit knowledge and explicit knowledge." They call this interaction "knowledge conversion." They insist on the fact that "this conversion is a 'social process' between individuals and not confined within an individual." From this assumption, they postulate four different modes of knowledge conversion (see figure 12.3).

• From tacit knowledge to tacit knowledge, which they call *socialization*, where an individual's tacit knowledge (in particular the one of a master) is directly shared to others (in particular apprentices) through observation, imitation, and practice. During this process, the master does not explain his skill in a way that makes it directly accessible to others. Thus, this knowledge is not accessible to the collective level of the company.

• From tacit knowledge to explicit knowledge, which they call *externalization*. During this process individuals attempt to articulate their tacit knowledge into explicit knowledge taking the shape of metaphors, analogies, concepts, hypotheses, or models.

• From explicit knowledge to explicit knowledge, which they call *combination*. During this process individuals exchange and combine explicit knowledge through such media as documents, meetings, telephone conversations, or computerized communication networks, so as to create new explicit knowledge.

• From explicit knowledge to tacit knowledge, which they call *internalization*, where gradually, experiences through socialization, externalization, and combination are internalized into an individual's tacit knowledge base in the form of shared mental models or technical skills.

In companies, we live with the assurance of having "Know-how," or at least of being able to master such "Know-how" via document management that is high-performance and intelligent. Only recently have we perceived the importance of "Skills." Under the influence of economic pressure, which has lead to workforce reductions, greater personnel mobility, and the acceleration of departures under early retirement, we have begun to realize that "Know-how," as detailed as it may be in procedures and documents, is not sufficient. Novices relying solely on these procedures and documents can not directly execute the tasks that we know how to perform under precise conditions of safety, quality, and profitability. Today, knowledge engineering and the technologies (methods, techniques, and tools) of artificial intelligence, Internet, and Groupware, give us the instruments that enable going farther by formalizing skills, and by permitting a wider distribution of the knowledge thus consolidated. However, skills are both difficult to pinpoint and can not always be formalized. An apprenticeship, although considerably accelerated by prior knowledge, remains necessary.

The Problem of Capitalizing on Company's Knowledge.

The problem of capitalizing on company knowledge can be seen as a cycle determined by four facets (see figure 12.4).

One of the first tasks is to *locate the crucial knowledge*: it must be identified, located, characterized and classified. Next, it must be *preserved*, in other words conceptualized, formalized and conserved. Furthermore, it must be *value-enhanced*, that is, put at the service of the development and expansion of the company. In other words, it must be accessed, disseminated, used more effectively, combined, and new

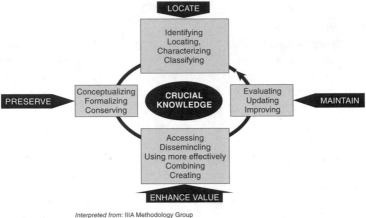

Interpreted from: IIIA Methodology Group

Figure 12.4
The facets of the problem

knowledge must be created. Finally, it must be *maintained*—evaluated, made updateable, and improved in accordance with rules governing its confidentiality and security.

Positioning Knowledge Management
Another facet of the problem deals with the capitalization's cycle itself. That is where Knowledge Management plays a role.

• What kind of processes have to be put to work in order to answer the four facets of the problem? How are those processes facilitated? What are the activities to develop and to promote them? How are they developed? Which approach? Which methods and which tools?

• How is the necessary investment justified? How is the value of the knowledge validated? How is the profit-earning capacity defined?

• How is a cultural change induced? What kind of organizational learning structures should be created? How are they developed?

• What kind of applications should be developed? How to choose the best technologies?

Future Prospects for Knowledge Management
Company's know-how, explicit knowledge, formalized and disseminated, represents the field of knowledge that may be managed through industrial ownership rules. Company's know-how constitutes, by itself,

tangible components that do not interfere with people, and appear as objects of knowledge's transfer that can be negotiated. This company's know-how is the result of knowledge conversion processes, highlighted by Ikujiro Nonaka and Hirotaka Takeuchi. This knowledge has to be revitalized all the time in order for it not to become fossilized.

Figure 12.5 shows the overall process that has to be reinforced, according to an axis of progress, for knowledge to be revitalized and fostered. This process fosters the production of individual knowledge and helps its conversion from the nonformalized and private status to a formalized and disseminated status.

The Knowledge Management Role

Through the previous perspective, we have to keep in mind that the organization has to develop by itself from its own diversity, creating new outlines of thinking and new ways of behaving. Thus, the Knowledge Management role should be to adjust efforts toward two directions.

On the one hand, it is important to set up the conditions that help "Skills" production, formalization, and dissemination. The goal is to show the importance of the active creation of knowledge in an organization: systematic organizational learning has to be encouraged. The organizational processes that help in the growth of an individual's knowledge are

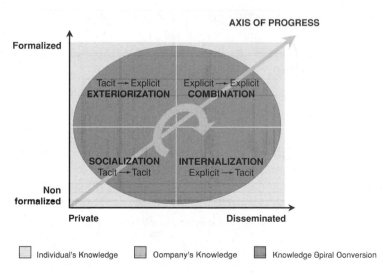

Figure 12.5
Future prospects for knowledge management

dialogue, talks, experience sharing, and observation. Interactions and networks has to be encouraged; crucial knowledge has to be located, preserved, value-enhanced, and maintained.

On the other hand, beyond looking at the knowledge put at work every day, it is necessary to promote and develop revitalization actions of fossilized knowledge. Fossilized knowledge is revitalized on knowledge stored in archives and data repositories through text mining, data-mining and knowledge discovery, information search and retrieval, intelligent agents, and visualization models.

In addition, the use of Intranet and Groupware technologies must be fostered. They allow the formalization of some parts of skills, and improve the ability to capitalize on knowledge. In this way, knowledge is incorporated into software able to restitute them, after a while, under a form directly understandable for people. Then, knowledge becomes accessible and can be manipulated.

Knowledge management is not a matter of human resources management. Ensuring that at all times the company has people available who, on the basis of their skills and through having the relevant know-how available, can adapt to situations and handle their respective jobs under optimum conditions is the domain of competencies management. It is also not a matter of reorganizing the company, optimizing its functional processes, and improving its means of communication, notably its information systems. That is the domain of the company's organization and business management. It is a matter of providing to each of these objectives an additional and decisive factor of value-added creation: mastery of "Know-how" and "Skills" of the company.

The Complementary and Convergent Approaches

The axis of progress points to a direction and puts the question of capitalizing on company knowledge in a dynamic perspective. Beyond actions launched to preserve some crucial knowledge, this axis leaves out any approach where capitalizing on company knowledge should be an end in itself. So, one must insist on the fact that capitalizing on company knowledge is a continuous necessity that is omnipresent in each person's activities and which must be notably impregnated more and more deeply into the management function. This can be expressed through three forms:

• The question can be dealt with on the strategic and decisional level and become the purpose of an executive responsibility. When we speak of the management of intellectual capital [10], we are speaking of a "Top-Down" Management approach advocated by some authors [11][12]. This approach is followed by some companies where the function of Intellectual Capital Manager, Chief Knowledge Officer, or Chief Learning Officer has been created (Skandia AFS, Dow chemical company, Monsanto company) [13][14].

• Intermediate managers solve the question. These actors serve as bridges between the "*What should be*" of top management, and the "*What is*" of the field. Thus they favor, even catalyze innovation and knowledge management processes. This is the "Middle-Up-Down" Management approach advocated by Ikujiro Nonaka and Hirotaka Takeuchi. Through their point of view, in the companies based on the knowledge, it is at the middle level that the tacit knowledge, kept by general managers and practitioners, is articulated, synthesized, and incorporated in technologies and new products. The intermediate managers would be in this way the real knowledge engineers [8].

• The question can be reduced on the operational level to a specific objective that is grafted onto the directly operational goals of industrial projects. This is the purpose of the approach of *GAMETH* that is described in the following sections.

GAMETH: An Approach to Locate and Identify Crucial Knowledge

The developments of industrial knowledge-based systems that were done within Framatome since 1984 and the many discussions that we had in IIIA Institute have clearly shown the necessity of starting from the field. They have given us a specific viewpoint that is at the origin of the approach described hereafter.

In general, capitalizing on company knowledge involves three main phases (see figure 12.6).

1. **An advisability analysis phase**, whose goal is to identify the places and situations for which capitalizing on knowledge is advisable, and to justify this action.

2. **A feasibility study phase**, whose goal is to identify and evaluate the possible alternative solutions: How can knowledge be capitalized? At what cost?

3. **An action phase**, whose goal is to implement the solutions adopted.

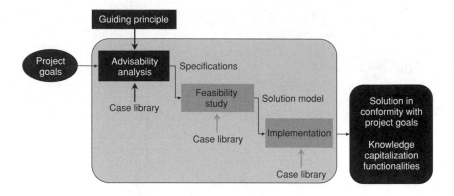

Figure 12.6
The three main phases

The Advisability Analysis Phase

The advisability analysis that we propose in this section is an accompanying approach aimed at integrating Knowledge Capitalization Functionality into the specifications of industrial projects. For example, in a quotation improvement project, this approach leads to highlighting a problem that we have decided to call "knowledge tracking." Knowledge tracking is a generic problem based on the following needs: the need to refer to earlier facts, the need to refer to analogous cases, the need to ask questions about earlier choices, and the need to rely on experience feedback. Beyond a system that helps in preparing quotations, the solution implements the functionality necessary for "knowledge tracking" (see figure 12.7). This functionality responds to the facets of the capitalizing on company knowledge problem defined above.

The advisability analysis phase is an indispensable step in any project aimed to take into consideration the problem of capitalizing on company knowledge independently of any anticipated solution.

Thus, the advisability analysis phase is designed to determine the nature and field of knowledge to be capitalized and to show the decisive nature of the operation. This is done by pointing out the risks that are run (from the economic, technical, and socio-organizational viewpoints) in case the operation is not finally initiated. Is the problem well stated? Are the objectives clearly defined? What knowledge must be capitalized? Who holds this knowledge? Where is it held? In what form? Who uses this knowledge? When? How? What are the associated challenges and risks?

The approach relies on a guiding principle, based on the modeling of the company envisaged from the viewpoint of the knowledge that it uses and produces. It presents essential characteristics that provide an innovative action framework.

The Guiding Principle

The company, perceived from the angle of the knowledge it uses and produces, can be represented as a set of activities that contribute to processes whose end purposes are to produce goods and services for a customer (internal or external to the company) under the most favorable conditions of cost, adherence to schedule, and quality.

Activities By the word *activities* we mean the individual and collective activities of the people in the company, thus accepting the term as defined by Philippe Lorino in his book [15], which we paraphrase as follows:

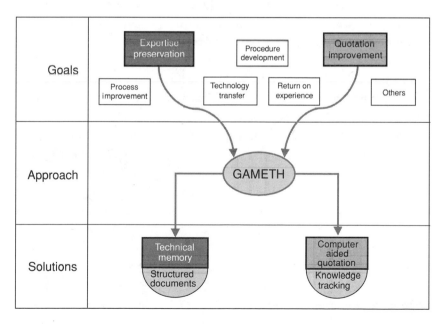

Figure 12.7
From goals . . . to technical solutions

Activities are everything that the men and women of the company do, hour after hour and day after day.…Everything that constitutes the substance of the company, all the work performed by the employees because they know how to do this work and because they feel that they must do this work; all of the "hows" that rely on specific "know-how," as simple as it may be.

These activities enable accomplishing the functions of the company that ensure its operation and the implementation of its organizational and production processes. They are carried out in the context of an organizational structure that encompasses the different organizational elements of the company (work sections, departments, divisions, etc.). They are strongly interrelated and connected to the processes to which they contribute and to the interactions that occur between these processes, which can be of a different nature (for example, production of products, production of orders, production of documents[1] [16]).

An activity is a set of elementary effective tasks, which are homogenous from the standpoint of their cost and performance behavior. These tasks correspond to the real work, performed by an individual or a group, oriented by an objective to be attained, that transforms materials into a product that consumes financial and technical resources. Activities use and produce specific knowledge (know-how and skills). They are subjected to constraints. Constraints can be external to the activities. These are the imposed conditions (obligatory safety rules, cost, schedule, and quality requirements, expressed in specifications; technical specifications to be respected; tolerance margins with respect to the expected results; available financial, material, and human resources) and the uncertainties of the delivery and quality of the flow of transformable materials. Constraints can be internal to the activities. These constraints are engendered by the limits of the maneuvering room left to the activity (autonomy zone). Activities may fall victim to malfunctions, directives, procedures, processes, and action logic specific to the activity. This leads to differences between the expected results and those actually achieved, going beyond the allowable tolerance margins. In general, an activity can be represented by the model presented in figure 12.8.

Organizational and Production Cycles   Depending on the goods or services produced by the process to which they contribute, these activities are accomplished sequentially or simultaneously. They are combined into homogenous packages, with common objectives, whose sequences are defined with respect to the production cycles.

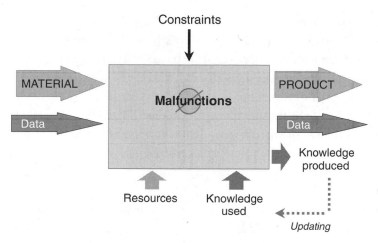

Figure 12.8
A knowledge-based model of a business activity

Organizational and production cycles represent the processes and are described by phases, which themselves consist of steps broken down into tasks that enable obtaining material or immaterial results.

Critical Activities, Determining Problems, and Crucial Knowledge
Constraints and malfunctions lead to problems that can make activities more fragile, and by that very fact endanger the organizational or production processes to which they contribute. Risk analysis, practiced for the "sensitive processes," i.e., those processes essential for the functioning of the company, enables determining the "critical activities." The problems related to these activities are called the "determining problems." Identification of these problems leads to locating the knowledge necessary to solve them. Depending on the value of this knowledge, measured in terms of vulnerability, cost, and acquisition time, and on the influence of these three factors on the life of the company, its markets, and its strategy, this knowledge may or may not be "crucial knowledge."

The Essential Characteristics of *GAMETH*
The *GAMETH* approach, proposed hereafter, provides an action framework to conduct the advisability analysis phase, independent of any anticipated solution. It relies on knowledge engineering and advanced technologies, notably artificial intelligence techniques that supply the indispensable modeling and implementation tools. It essentially leads to

identifying the problems and clarifying the knowledge needs. Which knowledge must be capitalized? Why? This analysis is not based on a strategic analysis of the company's objectives. It is based instead on the analysis of the knowledge useful to the activities that lead to the satisfactory functioning of the organizational processes and the production processes implemented to satisfy the company's missions. Thus, the *GAMETH* approach is a problem-oriented approach; it connects knowledge to action. It is characterized by the fact that it is centered on organizational and production processes. It improves project quality.

A Problem-Oriented Approach   The analysis is usually oriented by the solutions. The approach is based on the precise needs for knowledge expressed *a priori* and a response is provided as a function of the tools available. For example, the need to conserve the knowledge of an expert is expressed, and, having in mind a solution of the expert system type, the problem is posed in terms of choosing a tool capable of supporting the encoding of this knowledge without considering the question of the use of this knowledge.

In fact, the essential condition of the decision process is to attain a well-posed statement of the problem, or, as Gilbert de Terssac emphasizes: "a problem whose crucial character arises from collectively produced estimation and a formulation found to be acceptable by all the parties" [17].

The *GAMETH* approach is oriented by this principle. It is situated in the framework of the reflections set forth earlier in this communication, and characterized by the fact that it is "problem-oriented" and not "solution-oriented." The problems are located, the required needs for knowledge to allow their resolution as a function of the situations that they generate are clarified, the knowledge is characterized, and then the solutions most adapted to the problem-generating situations (procedures, training modules, knowledge-based systems, intelligent documentation systems, hypermedia, etc.) are determined.

An Approach that Connects Knowledge to Action   The *GAMETH* approach is built upon the assumption emphasized by Professor Shigehisa Tsuchiyaii concerning organizational knowledge creation [18]. From Professor Tsuchiya's viewpoint

Although terms *datum, information,* and *knowledge* are often used interchangeably, there exists a clear distinction among them. When datum is sense-given through interpretative framework, it becomes information, and when information is sense-read through interpretative framework, it becomes knowledge.

He emphases how organizational knowledge is created through dialogue and highlighted how "commensurability"[3] of the interpretative frameworks of the organization and its members is indispensable for an organization to create organizational knowledge for decision and action.

The original source of organizational knowledge is tacit knowledge of individual members. However, organizational knowledge is not a mere gathering of individual knowledge. Knowledge of individuals needs to be articulated, shared and legitimated before it becomes organizational knowledge. Knowledge of individual members is shared through dialogue. Since knowledge is mostly tacit, first of all, it has to be articulated and be expressed in language in a broad meaning. Then articulated individual knowledge, which is information for others members, needs to be communicated among members in the organization. It is important to clearly distinguish between sharing information and sharing knowledge. Information becomes knowledge only when it is sense-read through the interpretative framework of the receiver. Any information inconsistent with his interpretative framework is not perceived in most cases. Therefore, commensurability of interpretative frameworks of members is indispensable for individual knowledge to be shared.

The diagram presented in figure 12.9 shows our own interpretation. Tacit knowledge that resides in our mind results from the senses given,

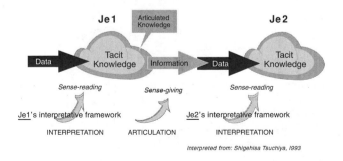

Figure 12.9 Creation of individual's tacit knowledge

passed through our interpretative frameworks, to data that we perceive from information that are transmitted to us.

In other words, we consider that knowledge does exist in the interaction between a person and data. This individual's knowledge is tacit knowledge. It can be articulated or not. It becomes collective knowledge when shared with others, if the interpretative frameworks of each of them are commensurable.

Our viewpoint is situated very much in the acceptance of the term "knowledge" that does not dissociate people, the actors placed in the heart of the company's processes, from the actions that they perform, the decisions that they make, and the relations that they have with their company environment (people and artifacts). Therefore, the information that they acquire and the data that they use are transformed by interaction with their own know-how and skills, their judgement, and the perspective in which they put themselves. This information is activated to form knowledge.

What is essential in this vision of things is the strongly creative relation between the person and his activity, taking into account his "intention," the end purpose of his action, and the orientation of knowledge toward an objective (see figure 12.10).

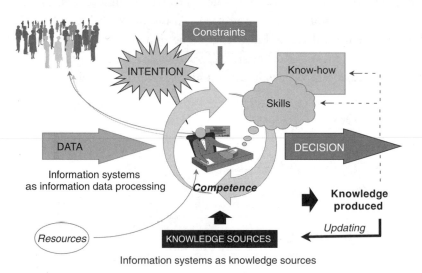

Figure 12.10 Connecting knowledge to action

In this way, the analysis is not based on a strategic analysis of the company's objectives, but instead on the analysis of the knowledge needed by the activities ensuring the proper functioning of organizational and production processes. Because knowledge is not separated from the activities that use this knowledge, the approach connects knowledge to action, and is somewhat comparable to that for constructing knowledge-based systems as "a collaborative effort to construct an unknown object" [19]. It consists in constructing the representation of the processes on the basis of the partial knowledge of the actors, derived from their actual activities. The approach is based on the observation that the processes described in numerous documents, defining rules of action and operating methods, frequently differ from the real processes as lived by the actors. Through the analysis, it is possible to identify the informal communication links between the actors, and to locate the corresponding knowledge. The analysis allows the mapping of the crucial knowledge associated with the sensitive processes.

An Approach Centered on Organizational and Production Cycles   The *GAMETH* approach consists in looking more directly at the organizational and production processes. It is finalized by the company's strategic orientations, and notably includes the three stages described below (see figure 12.11).

Stage 1: Identifying the Sensitive Processes   This stage enables identifying the field of action and determining the processes that will be the object of an in-depth analysis. It consists of:

• Taking a census of the goods and services for which a knowledge capitalization exercise is envisaged
• Delimiting the organizational and production processes and the organizational entities (business units, staff departments, partners, customers) concerned by the production of these goods and services
• Modeling the field of intervention (construction of functional and structural models of the organizational entities, construction of production cycles representing the processes)
• Determining the sensitive processes, i.e., those processes that are essential for management and production of the goods and services considered.

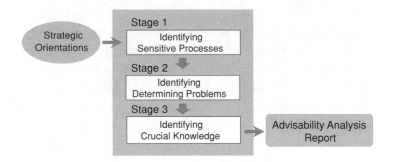

Figure 12.11
GAMETH three stages of analysis

Stage 2: Identifying the Determining Problems   This stage leads to distinguishing the problems that make certain of the activities contributing to these sensitive processes more fragile, which means that they can endanger these processes. It consists of:

• Analyzing the risks run by the sensitive processes and determining the critical activities for these processes
• Identifying the constraints and malfunctions that weigh on these activities
• Identifying the determining problems.

Stage 3: Identifying the Crucial Knowledge   This stage aims to define, locate, characterize, and classify the knowledge to be capitalized. It consists of:

• Clarifying the knowledge needed to solve the determining problems
• Locating and characterizing this knowledge
• Measuring the value of this knowledge and analyzing its impact on the life of the company, its markets, and its strategy
• Determining the crucial knowledge

The advisability analysis therefore makes it possible to draw up a "map" of the knowledge to be capitalized. Its locations, its characteristics, and its influences on the functioning of the company based upon its strategic orientations. At the end of the advisability analysis, the elements capitalizing on knowledge have been assembled, and make it possible to decide upon and undertake the feasibility study.[4]

An Approach that Improves Project Quality When practicing the *GAMETH* approach, we are led to consider capitalizing on company knowledge as a part of an industrial project specification. Thus, customer's requirements are studied in depth during the advisability phase. The study emphasizes the required needs for knowledge to allow the resolution of well-posed problems. People are involved in the construction of the solution. Furthermore, knowledge is accessible: it can be shared, used, and brought up to date easily. The domains of application are knowledge preservation, return on experience, knowledge tracking for decision-making, process improvement, procedure development, technology transfer, and core competencies management.

A Few Examples

The following examples were selected for their specific interest to the question of knowledge capitalization. They illustrate the type of problems encountered and give an idea of the solutions implemented. In these examples, the problem of knowledge capitalization has been reduced to the specific goal of each project (see figure 12.7).

Capitalizing on Expert's Knowledge

A pilot operation, being developed since 1991, has obtained the results indicated in figures 12.12 and 12.13. In this case, instead of creating a traditional expert system type solution for a soon to retire expert in chemistry and corrosion, the advisability analysis led to technical memory type solution instead.

The table shown in figure 12.12 correlates the functions (process design, structural design, equipment design, services, and contracting), units involved (Fuel Unit, Safety Unit, Reactor Block Unit, Systems Unit, Components Unit, etc.), the actors (A1, A2, A3, B1, C1, C2, D1, and E1), and the knowledge used throughout the production cycle (preliminary design phase, feasibility studies, basic design, detailed design, etc.) for a nuclear steam supply system. To simplify the representation, only the knowledge concerning the feasibility studies phase has been included in the table.

In the example considered here, the equipment design function is performed by two different departments, the Systems Unit and the

Activities		Knowledge used throughout the production cycle						
Process design	Fuel Operation A1 / A2 / Safety A3							
Structural design	Reactor block B1							
Equipment design	Systems C1 / Components C2	Design, Materials Thermal Hydraulic Chemical Corrosion						
Services	D1							
Contracting	E1							
		Preliminary Studies	Feasibility Studies	Basic Design	Detailed Design	Construction	Tests and Start-Up	Maintenance

Phases in the Production Cycle

Figure 12.12
Use of knowledge in the production cycle

Components Unit. C2 is an engineer working in the latter Unit. To perform his tasks during the feasibility study phase, he needs to use several knowledge fields: design, materials, thermal, hydraulic, chemical, and corrosion knowledge.

Figure 12.13 represents a blowup of the previous table, showing the partial results of the analysis.

Looking at engineer C2, who works in the Components Unit, we can see that 80% of his tasks in performing the equipment design function during the feasibility study phase of the production cycle depend on chemistry and corrosion knowledge. In addition, this knowledge can be broken down as follows: 15% fundamental knowledge, 23% biographical knowledge, 26% knowledge of experimental data, and 36% expert knowledge. So, nearly 30% of the tasks of engineer C2 depend on expert knowledge in chemistry and corrosion. What then would happen if this knowledge were to disappear? Depending on the context, the answer can make it possible to evaluate the risks, and, consequently, the advisability of capitalizing on this knowledge area.

ACREC (Archiving of Design and Manufacturing Choices)
The Context An evaluation mockup developed with CERCA, a Framatome subsidiary, concerned super-conducting cavities. This project

began in 1994, and was prolonged by the development of a generic platform called AREDA (System for Assistance in Preparing Quotations and Executing Contracts), destined to be deployed in different company business units.

The Needs

• To elaborate quotations with reference to previous contracts
• To be able to trace and especially to exploit previous experience, as well as the decision processes attached thereto

The Problem   CERCA's mechanical division manufactures products for research nuclear reactors and particle accelerators (particle detectors, accelerating cavities for particle beams, and control rods for nuclear reactors). This complex creates high-technology equipment with little recurrence that is destined for a clientele essentially consisting of research centers. Each contract brings its lot of new knowledge and experience, which must be available for reuse during future consultations and projects necessitating similar technology and techniques. The loss of know-how is often difficult to avoid, when several years separate two projects, or when a particular skill is lost.

The Solution   The CERCA system makes it possible to store all the acquired experience as it is built up, including the approach followed

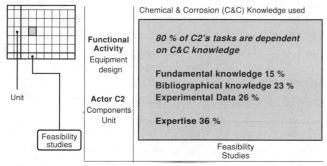

Figure 12.13
Who uses what knowledge at what phase

leading to a contract. It relies on advanced information technology solutions built around "case-based reasoning" (a case being defined by a context, a decision, a justification, and a choice). It enables loading and consultation of knowledge bases as a function of each person's habits. Thus, the user can choose among several entry points, such as the occupation (welding, ultra-vacuum, etc.), the product (cavities, detectors, etc.), the material (aluminum, alloy, ceramics, etc.), the customer, the standard, the procedure, etc.

Knowledge Capitalization   Beyond help in preparing quotations, the system makes it possible to minimize the development expenses in similar future cases, and to enhance the reliability of the choices made both from the quality and budgetary forecast standpoints. Additionally, the system allows storing all the acquired experience as the project goes along, including the approaches leading to completion. It therefore permits capitalizing previous experience, whether it led to success or failure. The results acquired during the work are used in the generic AREDA platform. This platform, destined for use by business units, makes it possible to capitalize on the knowledge resulting from past experience or from projects under way, for application to new quotations or contracts.

Lessons Learned

We can make several remarks drawn from our first experiences in implementing the *GAMETH* approach.

• When practicing the *GAMETH* approach, we are led to consider capitalizing on company knowledge as a part of an industrial project specification. Thus, customer requirements are studied in depth during the advisability analysis phase. The study emphasizes required needs for knowledge to allow the resolution of well-posed problems. People are involved in the construction of the solution. This leads to developing high quality and relevant systems, especially adapted to the users' working conditions.

• The *GAMETH* approach is not an auditing approach. The objective is not to draw up an inventory of the existing situation, which is only an instant picture seen through the available procedures and documents. Rather, the aim is to discover then to construct a representation of the real processes, via the partial knowledge that the different actors have, each for the part of the activities in which they themselves participate. In this sense, it must be implemented by engineers familiar with knowledge acquisition and modeling.

• Determination of the sensitive processes is done during a brainstorming session on the basis of the knowledge held by the managers of the field concerned.

• The process of knowledge acquisition and the construction of a representation of the real processes becomes rapidly fastidious in the absence of tools to assist in knowledge modeling and storage, so appropriate tools must be developed.

• The collective identification of critical activities is done rapidly by a working group, which achieves its coherence as soon as the representation of the process meets with the approval of all the actors who participate in this process.

Conclusions

Talking about complexity or incertitude when discussing organizations is becoming commonplace. The essential thing is no longer the product, with a very short life cycle, or even the service, but the company's capability of adapting to faster and faster changes, and therefore of mobilizing its expertise and skills as quickly as possible.

In this perspective, companies must act in three essential directions to evolve toward a learning organization. (1) They must move beyond the physical engineering and information engineering processes. While fostering a learning organization, companies must develop a knowledge engineering process. (2) Companies must strengthen their institutional "Top-Down" approaches, which involves identifying their distinctive core competence and the domains of strategic knowledge, exercising an active strategic and technological watch, implementing competence management, and managing a system of company experts. (3) Companies must promote a pragmatic approach matching the problems raised by knowledge capitalization. They must prepare their employees, promote the concepts, implement higher-performance communication habits, and set up working groups supported by information technology (electronic mail, groupware, local networks, intranet, etc.).

Notes

1. We thus return to the idea of "knowledge networks" elaborated at DEC in 1984 or to the notions of activities and processes defined by Philippe Lorino.

2. Professor, Ph.D., Department of Industrial Management, Chiba Institute of technology ; Hiromatsu lab, RCAST, The University of Tokyo

3. If the interpretative frameworks are incommensurable, sharing individual's knowledge to create organizational knowledge will not be possible because the same data or information can be interpreted differently in the organization.

4. Characterization of knowledge, study of its life cycle (birth, growth, updating, obsolescence), and its modeling are part of knowledge engineering. KADS methodology will be used if needed.

References

1. Michel Grundstein, Patrick de Bonnieres, and Serge Para, *Les Systèmes à Base de Connaissances, Systèmes Experts pour l'Entreprise* (Paris: AFNOR Gestion, 1988).

2. Michel Grundstein, "The Knowledge Engineering Profession in the 1990s, Towards Knowledge Assets Engineering Within the Company : A Prospective Point of View," *Heuristics* 4, no. 2 (Summer 1991).

3. Michel Grundstein, "CORPUS, An Approach to Capitalizing Company Knowledge," *AIEM4 Proceedings*, The Fourth International Workshop on Artificial Intelligence in Economics and Management (Tel-Aviv, Israel: Kluwer Academic Publishers, 1996).

4. Peter Drucker, *Post-capitalism Society* (Oxford, Great Britain: Butterworth-Heinemann, 1993).

5. R.R. Nelson, S.G. Winter, *An Evolutionary Theory of Economic Change* (Cambridge, Mass.: Harvard University Press, 1982).

6. Michel Grundstein: "From Developing Expert Systems to Capitalizing Company Knowledge, A Way to Transfer Artificial Intelligence Technologies," *VII International Symposium on Artificial Intelligence Proceedings*, Monterrey, México, 1994.

7. Michael Polanyi, *The Tacit Dimension* (London: Routledge & Kegan Paul, 1966).

8. Ikujiro Nonaka, and Hirotaka Takeuchi, *The Knowledge Creating Company. How Japanese Companies Create the Dynamics of Innovation* (New York: Oxford University Press, 1995).

9. P. Malvache and S. Tamisier, "ACCORE, a system to capitalize and restitute knowledge, after one year of use by 800 persons of CEA," *Fourth International ISMICK Symposium Proceedings* (Rotterdam: Ergon Verlag, 1996).

10. Leif Edvinsson, Michael S. Malone, *Intellectual capital* (New York: HarperBusiness, 1997).

11. Karl M. Wiig, "Knowledge Work in the Corporation," *IAKE'92 Tutorial*, Third Annual Symposium of the International Association of Knowledge Engineers, Washington, D.C., 1992.

12. Rob van der Spek: "Knowledge management: a multi-disciplinary approach of knowledge in organizations," *ISMICK'93 Proceedings*, International Symposium on the Management of Industrial and Corporate Knowledge, UTC, Compiègne, 1993.

13. International Communications for Management: "Creating Value Through Knowledge Management," *ICM Conference proceedings*, San Francisco, 1997.

14. Michel Grundstein, Yogesh Malhotra: "Companies and Executives in Knowledge Management," *@BRINT Virtual Library on Knowledge Management*, 1997–1998.

15. Philippe Lorino, *Le Contrôle de Gestion Stratégique*, la gestion par les activités (Paris: Dunod Entreprise, 1991).

16. F. Lynch, Charles Marshall, Denis O'Connor, Mike Kiskiel: "AI in Manufacturing at Digital," *AI Magazine* 7, no. 5 (Winter 1986).

17. Jean-Luc Soubie, Gilbert de Terssac: "VISE, Validation et Impact des Systèmes Experts," *Rapport de recherche PIRTTEM-CNRS* (contrat no. 89-D0076), Juillet 1991.

18. Shigehisa Tsuchiya: "Improving Knowledge Creation Ability through Organizational Learning," *ISMICK'93 Proceedings*, International Symposium on the Management of Industrial and Corporate Knowledge, UTC, Compiègne, 1993.

19. Michel Grundstein: "Développer un système à base de connaissances : un effort de coopération pour construire en commun un objet inconnu," *Actes de la journée "Innovation pour le travail en groupe*," Cercle pour les Projets Innovants en Informatique (CP2I), Paris, 1994.

13

Evolution through Knowledge Management: A Case Study

Barbara Lawton[1]

There are real and driving needs for Storage Technology Corporation to achieve substantial improvement in several core business areas, including marketing, new product development, and software development. Performance improvement on this scale requires knowledge management in its broad sense, in that improvement comes from harnessing individual and collective learning about new ways to do work and then taking action to change the way work is done. StorageTek's effort differs from the many popular approaches to knowledge management that focus on specific knowledge building and transfer mechanisms and/or knowledge asset definition and assessment. This effort is aimed at the development of an end-to-end system that supports learning, sharing, and deploying knowledge to meet the specific needs of the corporation based on recognized energy flow principles. This chapter describes one group's initial assumptions, knowledge management design, and lessons learned after one year of focused effort.

Introduction

Storage Technology Corporation (StorageTek®) was a phenomenal success story in the traditional mainframe and proprietary computer systems markets of the 1970s and 1980s. Today, there is tremendous growth in the storage industry, but the market has shifted. To remain a major player, StorageTek must leverage its traditional strengths of superior engineering and product performance to compete within the emerging market of nonproprietary, open systems.

StorageTek's CEO, David Weiss, has targeted a 20% annual growth rate for the company. The challenge of survival, growth and change

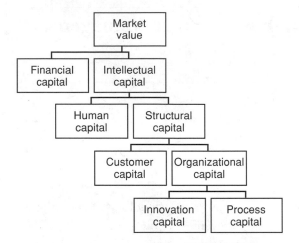

Figure 13.1
Skandia market value scheme

creates a perceived do or die situation. This in turn creates a powerful incentive inside the corporation. The challenge is to channel this motivational energy in a manner that enables the corporation to meet its goals and to adapt to its changing environment. One need is to develop the performance capabilities needed to compete in this new market space. The areas requiring improvement include marketing, new product development, software development, and the management of complex sales and distribution channels.

How do organizations achieve consistent, high-level performance? The mechanism that enables groups to provide consistent performance is organizational process—the system of procedures, habits, policies and guidelines that embody the cumulative knowledge of the organization to make it easy for employees to do "the right thing" and hard for them to do "the wrong thing." Process capital is thus considered one of the major stocks of an organization's intellectual capital [406] (see figure 13.1). It represents knowledge that belongs to the organization and supports the generation of revenue.

Organizations can close performance capability gaps by "buying" best-in-class processes from firms that offer such intellectual capital products and the services to implement those processes successfully. But a one-time improvement in performance would not be adequate since both

StorageTek's competitors and the environment itself are evolving. Storage-Tek needs the capacity to continually evolve—to change itself in response to its rapidly changing environment.

An organization's processes evolve through active learning, through work, by sharing the results and by capturing the knowledge that has been gained in repeatable processes. Process improvement is therefore a ratcheting mechanism of knowledge management: by capturing learning it enables everyone to perform at consistently higher levels. This was one of the major lessons of the 1980s Quality movement. To improve results, the processes that generate them must be improved. Today this insight should be a cornerstone of knowledge management.

The knowledge management effort needed for StorageTek to achieve its aggressive growth goal is a flow system as portrayed in figure 13.2. Building Human Capital (what employees know) is foundational to increasing Process Capital. Human Capital is deployed by process innovation to enhance core process capability. Our goal in the knowledge management effort is to increase the flow of knowledge and to focus its application. This requires changes in the following areas:

• Organizational processes must be visible so that a background for measurement exists.

• Innovations throughout the company must be measured against the improvement goals.

• Innovations that enhance the company's performance must be captured and incorporated into standard operating procedures.

• Organizational evolution (or learning) must be geared toward improving StorageTek's ability to innovate, to recognize and adopt innovations, and to "remember" good practice.

While this approach is portrayed logically and analytically, the changes required are transformational. The mechanics of evolution are antithetical to traditional, top-down, hierarchical management.

The Challenge

Business and Quality Processes (BQP) was created to help StorageTek improve business process performance. BQP builds upon StorageTek's dedication to learning for process improvement. We knew we needed to move beyond the traditional Corporate Quality modalities because StorageTek had been reorganized into business units. This group uses the

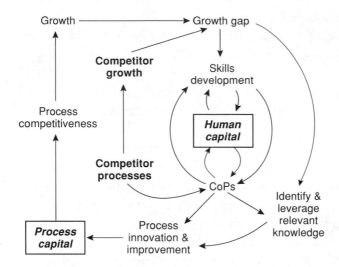

Figure 13.2
StorageTek's knowledge flow system for growth

traditional Quality skill sets, along with several new ones, to fulfill its charter within a very decentralized and heterogeneous business environment. Business Unit formation created new and significant challenges for the corporation, namely the coordination and creation of synergy across Business Units in core areas such as new product development, while maintaining local autonomy, diversity, and adaptation.

Our mission is to support autonomy, diversity, and adaptation in the Business Units, while sponsoring the exchange that will allow rapid learning and development of synergies. The ideas are reflected in the mission and core competencies of the new group (see figure 13.3).

The Approach

Two approaches to change were immediately ruled out because we believed they would not produce widespread, sustainable change within the necessary time frame. The first of these was the major top-down, corporate initiative approach, such as a traditional Total Quality Management program. StorageTek employees have had their fill of corporate initiatives that begin with lots of fanfare but do little to make lasting or fundamental change. StorageTek has developed powerful cultural antibodies to these kinds of top-down interventions.

The second approach that was ruled out was a "greenfield" approach, where innovation would be developed from the ground up, with new processes and technologies—but apart from the organization. This approach was rejected because of its slowness. By the time a greenfield became successful, it would be too late for the lessons to be transferred to the remainder of the business. While an individual battle would have been won, the war would have been lost because StorageTek would remain too far behind the curve in the new markets to recover. Furthermore, experience at StorageTek has taught us that lessons learned in a greenfield implementation are difficult to transfer to other parts of the corporation.

The only approach we considered viable was one that enables concurrent, local evolution, with both incremental and step-function changes occurring simultaneously throughout the organization. Our task was to find ways in which the organization as a whole and the business units could evolve in concert and to learn how best to support these evolutionary changes. We were particularly looking for ways to build momentum and reinforce mechanisms that speed evolution.

BQP began by articulating some of our own beliefs about organizational learning, change and evolution. We then tried to apply these principles in ways appropriate to the organization's current state. At the risk of omission or over-simplifying what we consider to be very important

Mission:

To support achievement of StorageTek's goals through focused innovation & improvement around StorageTek's core business processes. We do this by

- accelerating the learning and sharing of knowledge across the corporation around core processes, and

- actively assisting individual business units in applying this knowledge through process innovation and improvement.

Core Competencies

Specific core process knowledge, Business Process Consulting, Systems Thinking, Organizational Learning Organizational Change

Figure 13.3
Business and quality processes organization

work, the next section will summarize these principles. In the remainder of this chapter we describe the organizational situation and the actual work we have undertaken. We close with what we've learned to date and some proposals for the next steps.

Basic Principles

1. *Evolution is a form of learning which produces change. Evolutionary learning within an organization is a process of sensing and interpreting changes as they occur, and creating adaptive action in response.* Change is coevolutionary, in that it interdependently occurs within the organization, in the relationship between the organization and its environment, and within the environment itself.

2. *Evolution happens in response to, and is sustained by, energy gradients in the larger system.*[2] Energy build-ups can occur in the environment or within the organization, and become the drivers of change. Evolutionary management is the process of building paths to channel the flow of energy in ways that support organismic resilience and environmental service. The greater the rate of environmental change, the faster the pace of organismal change and vice versa. This is a continuous process of coevolution that produces incremental as well as step-function changes.

Typical, top-down organizational change efforts depend on massive amounts of energy being infused into the system by way of education programs, masses of consultants, and change agents. It is analogous to changing the course of a river by building a dam. Evolutionary change, on the other hand, uses the energy already in the system to make change. The analogy would be changing the course of a river by digging a small channel that enables the water to flow where it wants to (i.e., where the gradient would favor its flow) and then allowing the force of the water itself to change the course of the river by enlarging the channel through its own flow over time.

3. *Intelligence is distributed fractally throughout the organization.* Processing at lower levels in the organization increases the speed with which changes are detected and interpreted, and often the appropriateness of the response. For organizational learning to be practical, the principle of subsidiarity must be in effect. This means that sensing, perceiving, and interpreting information and the ability to use it all happens at the lowest possible level.

4. *Learning is thus both local and integrative.* The demands for change at lower levels are interpreted and integrated at higher levels of the organization, as necessary. The challenge of growth is to maintain smallness

(fine-grained connectivity) under an ever-growing umbrella of connectivity.

5. *New skill sets and ways of thinking are needed for transformational change.* Einstein said, "You will never solve a problem if you use the same thinking that created the problem in the first place." The same is true for behavior as well. For example, the skills of surfacing mental models are critical to dissolving the processes that guard the old and which block formation of the new.[3]

6. *Learning is a social process.* Emotions are critical to patterning—the ability to store and recall information[4]—and social interaction is a process of making meaning together.

7. *Individual learning happens best when motivated by intrinsic desire and when aided by a supportive environment.* Alfie Kohn and W. Edwards Deming[5] are perhaps the best-known advocates of this principle. Learning that is motivated by fear is narrow and reactive. Hostile environments make people downshift into more reactive and narrow modes of thought.[6] Learning motivated by intrinsic desire, on the other hand, is generative—it is the source of the creativity necessary for successful evolution.

8. *Change requires the confluence of three factors, namely the desire for change, an alternative model to which the state can be compared, and the means to change.*[7] The battered spouse is probably the most vivid illustration of this principle. The victim certainly has a desire to change and perhaps knows that alternatives to the present state do exist. What often keeps a battered spouse in an unfortunate situation is the lack of a means or pathway that they believe will lead to a better situation.

Design and Implementation

BQP was designed to support and nurture organizational learning and evolution based on the principles described above. Significant organizational transformation was needed to attain the company's goals.

We believe effective organizational evolution requires a fine-grained network of human relations and communication, both within the corporation and between the corporation and its environment. This network:

• Enables sensitive perception of the environment. Everyone in the organization is in contact with their external and internal environment and is making assessments, looking for solutions, adapting and changing [principles 1, 3, and 7].

• Facilitates interpretation of information and collective meaning-making, which in turn aids local action [principles 1 and 6].

• Aids sharing insights across business units without forcing global solutions, which may not be appropriate to specific locales [principles 3 and 4].

The energy (desire) for change already exists within the system and is sustained by the CEO and Business Unit General Managers through their shared determination to achieve 20% annual growth [principle 2 and 8]. Their desired business goals can only be met by developing core performance capabilities appropriate for the open systems market. BQP's strategy was first to support the selection of alternatives [principle 8]. We appointed subject matter resource people (called Practice Managers) to support business unit professionals in their efforts to identify alternative ways of working by benchmarking other companies. Practice Managers also aided the creation of a human learning and sharing network to circulate knowledge throughout the company. BQP's parallel strategy was to create new pathways for change [principle 8]. We created business unit consulting teams to support the individual unit efforts toward process innovation and improvement. These teams consisted of consultants whose specialty was business process reengineering.

Assessment of Current State

Our efforts started by assessing and evaluating the organization's current state. This included identifying what knowledge sharing and process improvement practices existed and could be leveraged. We also assessed the context for change, including the business circumstances, the internal and external forces driving change, and the state of the core processes as they operate today. Our findings and opportunities are listed below. We also include a brief description of the changes made within BQP as a result of our learning.

Assessment Area 1: Sensing Change and Collective Learning
We found several active communities of practice (CoPs) within Storage-Tek. The CoPs are informal gatherings of people working in similar professions who come together to share information, experiences, questions, and to help one another along the way. The most active community was part of the software development community. This group had identified relevant changes in software development practice and had gone as far as to develop curricula to support new levels of expertise within the community. StorageTek's Workforce Development department supports the

community by acting as a procurement agent for instruction rather than in the more traditional role of curriculum development.

This group was largely self-organized, with one person who took on the task of organizing meetings, communication vehicles, etc., in response to the group's needs. They used electronic tools such as e-mail lists and web sites to communicate with each other. They organized and ran their own seminar series to discuss topics of interest to the community. This same person, who is a faculty member at a local university, was also a primary source of formal instruction, new ideas, and information for the group.

This community has created its own, highly effective and efficient information flow channels. They are effective in that the individual members of the community have some information sources that they share, and many others that are unique. This broadens the information base accessible to the group. This information network is efficient in that individual members act as information filters and signal enhancers for the community, reducing the time it takes for any single individual to glean useful information. The interpretation that members add to information, based on their own experience also enhances the value of that information. The interaction between community members supports development of the common understanding necessary for process improvement.

There was also an active CoP in Service Engineering in one of the field offices, where members were sharing lessons learned amongst themselves through the company's old e-mail system. When the e-mail system was changed, the means used to create a common repository for information was lost. This group's complaint brought the repository to the attention of senior management, who then assigned to corporate marketing the task of creating a web-based repository known as the Knowledge Map. The Knowledge Map is available to all of StorageTek's sales and service people and is meant to enhance knowledge sharing around the world. After 18 months of operation, the Knowledge Map has become a good vehicle for the Business Units to broadcast product information to the field. What has been lost, however, is the direct knowledge sharing among people in the field.

There are two important lessons learned from these two examples that greatly influenced BQP's approach to cultivating and supporting active CoPs. First, merely creating a vehicle to facilitate communication does not assure effective knowledge sharing. Knowledge sharing is founded in relationships and culture. Second, management can inadvertently extinguish successful knowledge sharing efforts. Once the Knowledge Map was broadened beyond the boundaries of the social community that created it, many people no longer felt comfortable making their potential ignorance and concerns publicly visible. Some sales people were reluctant to share hard-won insights that help them maintain their competitive edge inside the company. Others were reluctant to discuss politically sensitive issues.

Assessment Area 2: Capturing Knowledge in Process

The StorageTek's Business Units, formed at the beginning of 1997, are dramatically different in their processes and culture. The two largest Business Units reflect the business culture and processes as they were during the mainframe market days. These groups value technical excellence and customer service, but this unfortunately makes them slow to market in the overheated open systems market. They also tend to have a love-hate relationship with formal process. Formal process enabled the company to successfully emerge from Chapter 11 bankruptcy in the 1980s, yet they feel process requirements have been used historically as a mechanism of creativity-stifling bureaucracy and control.

The Business Units trying to enter the open systems market have very different process performance requirements. The open systems market is said to operate in "dog years," meaning the equivalent of 7 years of change for every year of change in the mainframe environment. Their culture values speed and agility. These Business Units are very small and are still in a start-up mode, with few if any formal processes in place. They are hungry for explicit processes to reduce the chaos and ambiguity of a start-up operation and to bring greater efficiency to their operation.

Design and Implementation of BQP Strategy

Our initial plan within BQP was to nurture and support existing CoPs and to convene or reconvene communities in each area of strategic importance to the company. Practice Managers were hired to support the core areas of marketing, new product development, and quality management. In addition, BQP successfully recruited the individual who had been instrumental in building and supporting StorageTek's software engineering CoP.

Each Practice Manager sought to support the internal communication and knowledge sharing processes of CoPs in their area by providing whatever appeared to be lacking, ranging from facilitation, to note taking, to cookies, or technical support (including e-mail list maintenance and Web publication). Practice Managers are also well respected subject matter resources. They are expected to remain current with developments in their profession and the business community, and therefore to be ongoing sources of information about good practice.

A business process consulting group was established to support the evaluation and change of core business processes within the Business Units. The Business Unit Consultants have MBAs, business process reengineering backgrounds and significant consulting experience within other companies and other industries. They have a dotted line reporting relationship to their Business Unit's General Manager and are positioned to be knowledgeable business partners as well as process change experts. Their role is to use the Business Unit's strategic plans to prioritize core process capability development, and to use the energy or "pull" created by their general manager to power the necessary process innovation and improvement efforts.

It is at the local level that the three elements needed for successful change come together: First, the desire for change. Desire is the fuel that powers the engine. As such, it must be strong enough to overcome obstacles and power the long journey. Second is knowledge of some alternative way of being or working. Ongoing connectivity with one's profession (e.g., through CoPs) and other organizations helps in the development of these alternatives. And lastly, one needs the freedom and ability (pathway) to change. Without a method or pathway, the energy for change cannot be channeled effectively; there is no change, just increasing frustration.

Each member of BQP is expected to bring organizational learning skills and perspectives to the Business Units. All BQP staff members received training in systems thinking and organizational learning skills. An internal Organizational Learning Consultant, a System Dynamics Modeler, and an Organizational Development Consultant within BQP also support them in their work.

Given that this transformation effort is ambitious and the resources dedicated to the change are limited, we realized that we would have to find a way to build momentum so that BQP's efforts would begin to multiply themselves and propagate throughout the corporation.

Synergy has been gained in several ways. The Practice Managers and the CoPs identify and evaluate alternative ways to improve performance. This reduces the amount of time and resources a Business Unit needs to expend in researching on its own how to reengineer its core processes. It also improves the quality of the solutions. The CoP's content expertise also helps tailor the solution and solve emerging problems (see figure 13.2).

The Practice Managers and CoP involvement in the Business Unit reengineering efforts also enhances the transfer of knowledge from one Business Unit to another. When people are involved with process change in other Business Units, however peripherally, there is an element of constructing knowledge together. This builds tacit knowledge for all involved. It also builds appreciation for how the work might apply to one's own Business Unit. All of the above increases the potential rate of learning and adaptation in other Business Units facing similar challenges. It allows change to be modified as appropriate to each specific Business Unit's unique context.

Furthermore, sharing learning throughout a first implementation can enhance its probability of success. Teams involved in groundbreaking work often feel isolated and unsupported by the organization. Their CoP can provide support and aid a team in learning to mitigate risks.

What We've Learned so far about the CoPs

Nurturing and expanding existing communities of practice is easier than establishing new ones. Our assumption was that people had been separated by the company's reorganization into Business Units and had therefore lost touch with other community members, or that perhaps, they did not appreciate the importance of learning together as a community. What we found is that these people, as workers in those areas most important to StorageTek's future, were under tremendous pressure to produce. Immediate goal fulfillment overrode any desire for systematic learning unless they (or their managers) were convinced that learning would immediately and directly help them produce the desired result, for example, in the current quarter. Therefore, while it was relatively easy to gather practitioners from the different Business Units for one or two exploratory meetings, it was difficult to create a CoP that met regularly and thus would be able to have a deeper or more long-term impact on the fundamental processes of the corporation. This may be an area where top-down work may be needed to support the bottom-up work we have done in trying to build communities of practice.

Informal CoP meetings quickly became an accepted learning practice in the fast-paced environment of one open systems Business Unit. We found that people who managed similar processes within a Business Unit valued regular, informal communication with one another. The Program Managers in this Business Unit faced similar problems, had similar needs and saw immediate value to their exchange of information and knowledge. Once that group had coalesced, they began inviting people from other Business Units who shared common interests. At that point the learning agenda could grow to include an occasional presentation from an outside speaker who would introduce new ideas into the community. Starting small allowed the CoP to grow in a natural and sustainable fashion.

In our experience, communities have to find a common practice that acts as an organizing element or seed crystal around which to coalesce. Thus, the conversations and learning in which the community is engaged must meet the community's definition of relevance. In this, our experience follows closely with the theory for energy flow structure development,[8] more commonly known as self-organization. This theory also tells us that the community will form and hold together only as long as there is some important area of common concern that the group addresses in some way.

The software development community of practice continues to grow as existing communities spawn new ones. A Software Seminar Series led to the formation of a Design Patterns Study Group. A small software methodology conference led to the formation of a quarterly meeting of software managers. This is the fractal nature of the growing knowledge network at StorageTek.

The role of the Practice Manager as we have defined it within BQP is extremely important. The Practice Manager convenes some CoP meetings, taking on some of the coordination and communication tasks and thus reduces the cost to the community. In established communities, the Practice Manager can play the role of broker in the sense of connecting the community to other communities, including "management" and external communities.[9] For example, by conducting benchmarking studies, the practice manager can be a major source of external information for the community, whether it supports existing thought and practice or extends or even disconfirms it.

As a community develops a common conceptual framework, conversations become more rapid and productive. This can be, however, a mixed blessing. On the positive side, a shared conceptual framework allows the group to identify interesting and pertinent objects in the field for identification and discussion. It also makes conversations more efficient by minimizing the need for community members to reconcile conceptual and language differences.

A further consequence of a common framework, however, is that CoPs can thus be quite conservative. They may be especially good at evolving group action and standard operating procedures. This is yet another reason the connection between the CoPs and Business Unit change efforts are important. It is within the market context that there is the real drive for change. The balance between the need for coherence and the need to change must be handled as a timing and cost-benefit issue.

About the Process Consulting Work

BQP's greatest process change efforts to date have been in one of the new Business Units where there were virtually no formal, explicit processes in place. Here the business process consultants are moving quickly with the management team and their staff to put explicit processes in place that enable the Business Unit to function and to provide a starting point for continual learning and improvement.

We've had little success with process innovation and improvement efforts independent of immediate business needs. For example, reengineering of New Product Development process within a Business Unit in the mainframe market demanded far too much time from the management team. They were driven by more immediate business needs, such as the timely completion of product projects underway. This is a vicious cycle. Without improving their core processes they will always be late. If late, they will never have time to improve their processes.

Using the energy already in the system, we chose a third alternative, which was to drive process development and improvement through projects that focused on specific products. We identified the potential business failure modes for the Business Units' most important upcoming products. From there, we helped them identify the processes most critical to near-term product success. In one Business Unit, this analysis led to focused effort on the product launch process. In another, it drove improvement of the software test process.

We worried that these small-scale, short-term process development projects could be sub-optimizing Business Unit performance. We improve one piece in a larger, interdependent system of processes, but the impact on the larger system is unknown. Keeping this perspective in front of the clients has become one of the primary roles of the Business Unit Consultants. In this situation, process improvement becomes incremental and iterative rather than sweeping. It is a cycle of local improvement followed by global evaluation and then another round of targeted, local improvement. Causal loop diagrams and system dynamics modeling have proven to be invaluable tools in this context. They make various modes of interdependence explicit to people involved in process change initiatives, and this allows BQP staff to identify and exploit leverage points within the larger system.

As a case in point, the cycle time for software testing in one Business Unit was itself longer than the desired release cycle for software upgrades. The software test group believed that it needed more resources to get the work done in a more timely manner. Working with the system dynamics modeler from BQP, the group started with an analysis of the software test process. They quickly saw that the greatest leverage for improving test cycle time was in the requirements definition phase of a project, a change that did not require additional resources.

One final observation is that it is easier to get very busy people to give time to infrequent but intensive sessions than it is to get them to keep regular commitments, no matter how brief. This observation has changed our approach to coordinating process improvement efforts within the Business Units.

About the Whole System

Integrating CoPs with Business Unit improvement efforts appears to be a start toward improving the capacity for deliberate evolution at Storage-Tek. Much of the process knowledge needed to improve StorageTek's core performance capabilities already exists in the marketplace. The CoPs, supported by the Practice Managers, function very well in enabling local groups to rapidly acquire, share, and adapt existing tools, as locally needed. Several different improvement initiatives are also occurring through-out the community at any one time, such as learning to use risk assessment or error tracking tools to enhance software development practice.

After one group within the corporation adopts a new practice it becomes infinitely easier for other groups to adopt and adapt a similar practice. There is certainly a psychological aspect to this in that once one group evolves a new practice, others say, "We can too!" There is also a very practical and concrete aspect. The first group to implement a set of tools or change a particular practice usually experiences significant trial and error in implementation. This group then becomes an internal re-source to support adoption and adaptation of the change in other areas of the business. Furthermore, their learning is generally captured in process templates or specific tools that greatly advance the starting point for other groups. The effect of internal knowledge sharing is expected to yield a tremendous reduction in the time and effort needed to improve the process performance for the corporation as a whole.

Just as there are dangers associated with bringing communities of practice to the attention of management as evidenced by the Knowledge Map experience, there are equally significant dangers associated with not having these networks on the management radar screen. The primary dangers are a lack of support, both for the workers involved in these net-works and for the development and maintenance of infrastructure that they need. In the new, results-oriented culture at StorageTek, it seems easier to obtain a large resource allocation for a process-reengineering project with planned and explicit deliverables than it is to have a low but consistent level of resources dedicated to supporting a community of practice.

We have been able to use the reporting relationship of BQP to address the practices at higher levels in the organization opportunistically. The VP for Business and Quality Processes reports directly into StorageTek's CEO, along with the General Managers of the Business Units and the heads of several other corporate functional organizations. This is a perfect vantage point from which to identify system-wide business concerns which can be approached with an organizational learning perspective.

For example, two high-impact opportunities arose during BQP's first year. The first was the introduction of productive conversation skills and strategic story telling. At StorageTek's Leadership Forum, the top 250 people in the company used these skills to build a shared vision of StorageTek's future. The second opportunity arose from a business concern about potential changes in customer buying patterns in 1999 because of the year 2000 computer problem. Systems modeling and scenario planning were used to explore ways in which the company could mitigate any risks and take advantage of likely market opportunities.

At some point in time this approach to evolution will reach a limit to its ability to change the organization. This will likely occur when the changes to be made conflict with high-level management systems (or people) rooted in the old culture. We cannot know where or when the conflict will arise. It represents one of the "crisis points" that occurs in natural evolution. If worked through successfully, it can lead to a new and more powerful round of evolution for the organization.

Next Steps

BQP's initial approach was to try several different mechanisms to support evolution. We assessed what worked and built upon that foundation. Our continuing goal is to build pathways for evolution that build momentum through positive reinforcement.

Through this first year our focus has been primarily on supporting the development of process solutions for each Business Unit. As the chaos of Business Unit start-up begins to subside, the need for Business Unit interoperability becomes more obvious and pressing. Our next year will test the strength of the new culture we are trying to build and of our organizational learning skills as well. We will work with the Business Units' practitioners and management teams to determine the level of process commonality needed across the Business Units.

One of the more difficult challenges we face is to maintain CoP freedom and flexibility to evolve in the face of management's growing awareness of their power. It could be very tempting for management to direct and divert them from broader community service. In every case we've seen so far, even a very light management "touch" can have an adverse impact on the effectiveness of a CoP.

A further near-term goal is to increase the effectiveness of the human communication networks at StorageTek. We have two goals. The first is to find ways to integrate those individuals and groups who are not currently involved in the existing CoPs. The second is to increase the ease and timeliness with which the right information gets to the right people. A key point we must remember through all our planning is to "evolve with the need." If we get too far out in front of the communities we're trying to support, we risk creating a "push system" rather than a self-fueled one, which could easily kill our efforts to date. The evolution must remain self-fueled, with BQP anticipating what it is that might be useful and adapting our own practices based upon the feedback we receive from our environment.

As we develop our strategy for the next few years, BQP will conduct an external evaluation to better understand our role in the transformation underway at StorageTek. These learnings will guide our path forward. It is our ultimate hope that the efforts of this group will build the competence and confidence within StorageTek to envision and create its own future.

Thanks to John D. Smith for his help with the writing of this chapter, especially on the subject of communities of practice.

®*StorageTek is a registered trademark of Storage Technology Corporation.*

References

1. Lief Edvinsson and Michael S. Malone, *Intellectual Capital; Realizing Your Company's True Value by Finding its Hidden Roots* (New York: HarperBusiness, 1977).

2. Sally Goerner, *Chaos and the Evolving Ecological Universe* (Gordon and Breach, 1993).

3. Peter Senge, "A Leader's New Work: Building Learning Organizations," *Sloan Management Review*, 1990.

4. Renate Caine and Geoffrey Caine, *Making Connections: Teaching and the Human Brain* (Reading, Mass.: Addison-Wesley, 1991).

5. W. Edwards Deming, *The New Economics* (Cambridge, Mass.: MIT Press, 1993).

6. Renate Caine and Geoffrey Caine, *Making Connections: Teaching and the Human Brain* (Reading, Mass.: Addison-Wesley, 1991).

7. Daryl Conner, *Managing at the Speed of Change* (Villard Books, 1993).

8. Sally Goerner, *Chaos and the Evolving Ecological Universe* (Gordon and Breach, 1993).

9. Etienne Wenger, *Communities of Practice: Learning Meaning, and Identity* (New York: Cambridge University Press, 1998).

SECTION III

Introduction: Metrics

Metrics: Separating KM Fact from Fiction

Edward Swanstrom

Metrics

If the purpose of knowledge management is to help an individual or collective achieve goals faster and more effectively, the only way to tell that it is working is with the use of metrics. Metrics allow us to determine whether or not the KM initiative is working the way we intended. Without metrics, knowledge cannot be produced. Without metrics, knowledge about knowledge cannot be produced. With metrics, we can separate weak concepts from strong, folk KM from true KM.

If we let loose the wellsprings of knowledge and it flows freely throughout the organization, how do we decide which knowledge claims could most help the organization in accomplishing its goals and which ones could do serious damage? Or are we just going to be flooded with great ideas with no way of judging one claim over another? Without measurement criteria, we are clueless as to whether we are accomplishing anything or not. Without measures, we turn KM into a metaphysical exercise with little actionable value to anyone.

As a CEO, I would not allow a KM initiative to be implemented within my organization unless I was assured that I could monitor the impact on the organization's accomplishment of its goals such as increase in profitability, growth, market share, and customer satisfaction. If the KM initiative is not measurably tied to these goals, why should I invest?

Knowledge as a Natural Resource

Managing knowledge is like managing natural resources. For water, we filter it, check it for purity, create reservoirs for times when rain is scarce, implement conservation processes, and control the environment around water to keep it uncontaminated. In fact, knowledge is a natural resource that flows from humans and requires at least the same attention. We cannot use traditional business management practices to manage knowledge. Instead, like water, we must manage the environment around the knowledge and the knowledge producers—people—to improve knowledge processes and the quality of the knowledge itself.

To think of knowledge as a natural resource that flows from people requires a paradigm shift for most people, but it is a shift that makes it easier to conceptualize how to manage and measure knowledge. The four-minute mile was believed to be physically impossible. Then a doctor trying to commit suicide by trying to run himself to death discovered that the four-minute limitation was psychological. It is time to break the psychological barriers when thinking about knowledge.

John Holland's Measures
One of my favorite metrics was published by John Holland in 1976 in *Adaptation in Natural and Artificial Systems*. He developed a mathematical framework and a tool that helps us measure the effectiveness of knowledge against its effectiveness in helping an individual or collective respond successfully to the environment. Knowledge might be effective in one environment, but not in another. Knowledge might be valuable and effective one moment, but not the next.

Suppose a company has a successful strategy for responding to stock market declines, such as a freeze on hiring. I will call the stock market decline "Condition 1" and the strategy "Action 1." Now suppose that the company later learns that one of its competitors successfully used a strategy that was previously thought to be a weak strategy. I will call this strategy "Action 2." If the company tries Action 2 and validates that it works better than Action 1, Action 2 will gain greater weight for the company.

Having a wellspring of knowledge is not enough. Having a process for determining the effectiveness of each knowledge claim in the accomplishment of personal or collective goals is the key to applying knowledge to knowledge. This requires metrics.

Meta-Metrics
Even metrics needs metrics.

Good knowledge management requires that knowledge is continually measured against its effectiveness in helping a person or collective accomplish their strategic goals. This keeps knowledge fresh and alive. The metrics themselves need to be reevaluated for effectiveness. What we thought were powerful metrics one day might not be a valuable the next, based on new knowledge, new conditions, or new environment.

I am sure the authors of the following chapters will agree that the knowledge claims they assert are only that: knowledge claims. We are the testers of those claims and need our own meta-criteria to determine which model, framework, idea, and metric will best help us accomplish our goals faster and more effectively. For metrics, the Balanced Scorecard approach might be the most effective today, but a better one might be discovered tomorrow. By measuring the effectiveness of our metrics, we begin to manage our metrics as we do any other knowledge claim.

14

Classic Work: The Balanced Scorecard: Learning and Growth Perspective

Robert S. Kaplan and David P. Norton

The fourth and final perspective on the Balanced Scorecard develops objectives and measures to drive organizational learning and growth. The objectives established in the financial, customer, and internal-business-process perspectives identify where the organization must excel to achieve breakthrough performance. The objectives in the learning and growth perspective provide the infrastructure to enable ambitious objectives in the other three perspectives to be achieved. Objectives in the learning and growth perspective are the drivers for achieving excellent outcomes in the first three scorecard perspectives.

Managers in several organizations have noted that when they were evaluated solely on short-term financial performance, they often found it difficult to sustain investments to enhance the capability of their people, systems, and organizational processes. Expenditures on such investments are treated as period expenses by the financial accounting model so that cutbacks in these investments are an easy way to produce incremental short-term earnings. The adverse long-term consequences of consistent failure to enhance employee, systems, and organizational capabilities will not show up in the short run, and when they do, these managers reason, it may be on somebody else's "watch."

The Balanced Scorecard stresses the importance of investing for the future, and not just in traditional areas for investment, such as new equipment and new product research and development. Equipment and R&D investments are certainly important but they are unlikely to be sufficient by themselves. Organizations must also invest in their infrastructure—

people, systems, and procedures—if they are to achieve ambitious long-term financial growth objectives.

Our experience in building Balanced Scorecards across a wide variety of service and manufacturing organizations has revealed three principal categories for the learning and growth perspective:

- Employee capabilities
- Information systems capabilities
- Motivation, empowerment, and alignment

Employee Capabilities

One of the most dramatic changes in management thinking during the past 15 years has been the shift in the role of organizational employees. In fact, nothing better exemplifies the revolutionary transformation from industrial age thinking to information age thinking than the new management philosophy of how employees contribute to the organization. The emergence of giant industrial enterprises a century ago and the influence of the scientific management movement left a legacy where companies hired employees to perform well-specified and narrowly defined work. Organizational elites—the industrial engineers and managers—specified in detail the routine and repetitive tasks of individual workers, and established standards and monitoring systems to ensure that workers performed these tasks just as designed. Workers were hired to do physical work, not to think.

Today, almost all routine work has been automated: computer-controlled manufacturing operations have replaced workers for routine machining, processing, and assembly operations; and service companies are, increasingly, giving their customers direct access to transactions processing through advanced information systems and communications. In addition, doing the same job over and over, at the same level of efficiency and productivity, is no longer sufficient for organizational success. For an organization just to maintain its existing relative performance, it must continually improve. And, if it wants to grow beyond today's financial and customer performance, adhering to standard operating procedures established by organizational elites is not enough. Ideas for improving processes and performance for customers must increasingly come from front-line employees who are closest to internal processes and an organization's customers. Standards for how internal processes and customer responses were performed in the past provide a baseline from which improvements must continually be made. They cannot be a standard for current and future performance.

This shift requires major reskilling of employees so that their minds and creative abilities can be mobilized for achieving organizational objectives. Take an example from Metro Bank. In the past, the bank had emphasized efficient processing of customer transactions for their demand and time deposit accounts. The senior executives of Metro Bank had set, as a key financial objective, to market and sell effectively a much broader array of financial products and services. A customer walked into a Metro branch bank. She told the bank employee that she had changed jobs and wanted to know how to have payroll checks from her new employer deposited directly into her checking account. The employee duly and correctly informed the customer that she should go to her human resources department and sign a form authorizing the direct deposit of the payroll check. The customer left with her "need" satisfied.

The bank, however, had lost a major opportunity. This request could have provided the occasion for the bank employee to get a more complete personal financial profile of the customer, including:

- Own or rent a house/apartment?
- Automobiles: how many, how old?
- Credit and charge cards: how many, which?
- Annual income
- Household assets and liabilities
- Insurance
- Children: how many, how old?

Such a profile would have allowed the bank employee to suggest a much wider array of financial products and services—credit card, consolidating personal loan, home equity loan, investments, mutual funds, insurance policies, home mortgage, car loans, savings plans for college, and student loan programs, for example—in addition to the particular financial service that brought the customer into the bank: the direct deposit of a payroll check.

Before the financial profile could have been used effectively, however, the bank employee would have to have been trained in all the bank's product and service offerings, and would need the skills to match particular

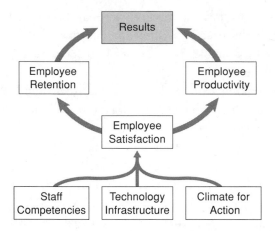

Figure 14.1
The learning and growth measurement framework

products and services to the needs of the individual customer. Metro Bank executives recognized that a multiyear program would be required for their front-line employees to obtain these capabilities to transform them from routine processors of customer requests into proactive, trusted, and valued financial counselors.

Core Employees Measurement Group

We have found most companies use employee objectives drawn from a common core of three outcome measurements (see figure 14.1). These core outcome measurements are then supplemented with situation-specific drivers of the outcomes. The three core employee measurements are
- Employee satisfaction
- Employee retention
- Employee productivity

Within this core, the employee satisfaction objective is generally considered the driver of the other two measures, employee retention and employee productivity.

Measuring Employee Satisfaction

The employee satisfaction objective recognizes that employee morale and overall job satisfaction are now considered highly important by most organizations. Satisfied employees are a precondition for increasing productivity, responsiveness, quality, and customer service. Rockwater noticed early in its scorecard implementation process that employees who scored highest in the satisfaction surveys tended to have the most satisfied customers. So, for companies to achieve a high level of customer satisfaction, they may need to have the customers served by satisfied employees.

Employee morale is especially important for many service businesses where, frequently, the lowest-paid and lowest-skilled employees interact directly with customers. Companies typically measure employee satisfaction with an annual survey, or a rolling survey in which a specified percentage of randomly chosen employees is surveyed each month. Elements in an employee satisfaction survey could include:

- Involvement with decisions
- Recognition for doing a good job
- Access to sufficient information to do the job well
- Active encouragement to be creative and use initiative
- Support level from staff functions
- Overall satisfaction with company

Employees would be asked to score their feelings on a 1 to 3 or 1 to 5 scale, anchored at the low end with "Discontented" and at the high end with "Very (or Extremely) Satisfied." An aggregate index of employee satisfaction could then be posted on the Balanced Scorecard, with executives having a drill-down capability to determine satisfaction by division, department, location and supervisor.

Measuring Employee Retention

Employee retention captures an objective to retain those employees in whom the organization has a long-term interest. The theory underlying this measure is that the organization is making long-term investments in its employees so that any unwanted departures represents a loss in the intellectual capital of the business. Long-term, loyal employees carry the values of the organization, knowledge of organizational processes, and, we hope, sensitivity to the needs of customers. Employee retention is generally measured by percentage of key staff turnover.

Measuring Employee Productivity

Employee productivity is an outcome measure of the aggregate impact from enhancing employee skills and morale, innovation, improving internal processes, and satisfying customers. The goal is to relate the output produced by employees to the number of employees used to produce that output. There are many ways in which employee productivity has been measured.

The simplest productivity measure is revenue per employee. This measure represents how much output can be generated per employee. As employees and the organization become more effective in selling a higher volume and a higher value-added set of products and services, revenue per employee should increase.

Revenue per employee, while a simple and easy-to-understand productivity measure, has some limitations, particularly if there is too much pressure to achieve an ambitious target. For example, one problem is that the costs associated with the revenue are not included. So revenue per employee can increase while profits decrease when additional business is accepted at below the incremental costs of providing the goods or services associated with this business. Also, any time a ratio is used to measure an objective, managers have two ways of achieving targets. The first, and usually preferred, way is to increase the numerator—in this case, increasing output (revenues) without increasing the denominator (the number of employees). The second, and usually less preferred, method is to decrease the denominator—in this case, downsizing the organization, which might yield short-term benefits but risks sacrificing long-term capabilities. Another way of increasing the revenue per employee ratio through denominator decreases is to outsource functions. This enables the organization to support the same level of output (revenue) but with fewer internal employees. Whether outsourcing is a sensible element in the organization's long-term strategy must be determined by a comparison of the capabilities of the internally supplied service (cost, quality, and responsiveness) versus those of the external supplier. But the revenue per employee is not likely to be relevant to this decision.

One way to avoid the incentive to outsource to achieve a higher revenue per employee statistic is to measure value-added per employee, subtracting externally purchased materials, supplied, and services from revenues in the numerator of this ratio. Another modification, to control for the substitution of more productive but higher paid employees, is to measure the denominator by employee compensation rather than number of employees. The ratio of output produced to employee compensa-

Staff Competencies	Technology Infrastructure	Climate for Action
Strategic skills	Strategic technologies	Key decision cycle
Training levels	Strategic databases	Strategic focus
Skill leverage	Experience capture	Staff empowerment
	Proprietary software	Personal alignment
	Parents, copyrights	Morale
		Teaming

Figure 14.2
Situation-specific drivers of learning and growth

tion measures the return on compensation, rather than return to number of employees.

So, like many other measures, revenue per employee is a useful diagnostic indicator as long as the internal structure of the business does not change too radically, as it would if the organization substitutes capital or external suppliers for internal labor. If a revenue-per-employee measure is used to motivate higher productivity of individual employees, it must be balanced with other measures of economic success so that the targets for the measure are not achieved in dysfunctional ways.

Situation-Specific Drivers of Learning and Growth

Once companies have chosen measures for the core employee measurement group—satisfaction, retention, and productivity—they should then identify the situation-specific, unique drivers in the learning and growth perspective. We have found that the drivers tend to be drawn from three critical enablers (see figure 14.2); reskilling the work force, information systems capabilities, and motivation, empowerment, and alignment.

Reskilling the Work Force
Many organizations building Balanced Scorecards are undergoing radical change. Their employees must take on dramatically new responsibilities if the business is to achieve its customer and internal-business-process objectives. The example, earlier in this chapter, illustrates how front-line employees in Metro Bank must be retained. They must shift

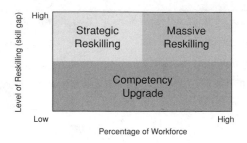

The Reskilling Scenarios	The key strategic theme is the need to reskill or upgrade the skills of the work force in order to achieve the vision.
Strategic Reskilling	A focused portion of the work force requires a high level of new, strategic skills.
Massive Reskilling	A large proportion of the work force requires massive skill renovation.
Competency Upgrade	Some portion of the work force, small or large, requires an upgrade of core skills.

Figure 14.3
Learning and growth measurement-reskilling

from merely reacting to customer requests to proactively anticipating customers' needs and marketing an expanded set of products and services to them. This transformation is representative of the change in roles and responsibilities that many organizations now need from their employees.

We can view the demand for reskilling employees along two dimensions: level of reskilling required and percentage of work force requiring reskilling (see figure 14.3). When the degree of employees reskilling is low (the lower half of figure 14.3), normal training and education will be sufficient to maintain employee capabilities. In this case, employee reskilling will not be of sufficient priority to merit a place on the organizational Balanced Scorecard.

Companies in the upper half of figure 14.3, however, need to significantly reskill their employees if they are to achieve their internal-business-process customer, and long-run financial objectives. We have seen several organizations, in different industries, develop a new measure, the strategic job coverage ratio, for its reskilling objective. This ratio track the number of employees qualified for specific strategic jobs relative to anticipated organizational needs. The qualifications for a given position are defined so that employees in this position can deliver key capabilities for achieving particular customer and internal-business-process objectives. Figure 14.4 illustrates the sequence of steps followed by one company in developing its strategic job coverage ratio.

Usually, the ratio reveals a significant gap between future needs and present competencies, as measured along dimensions of skills, knowl-

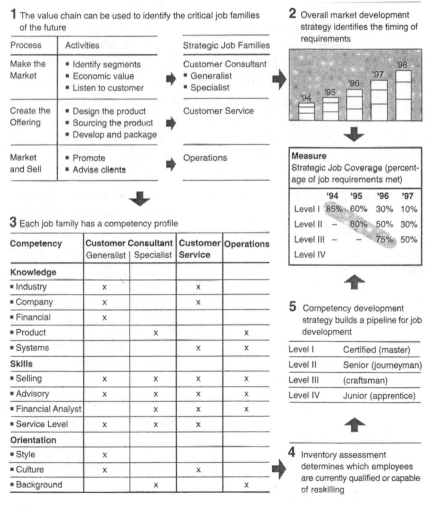

Figure 14.4
The strategic job coverage ratio-measurement concept

edge, and attitudes. This gap provides the motivation for strategic initiatives designed to close this human resource staffing gap.

For the organizations needing massive reskilling (the upper righthand
quadrant of figure 14.3), another measure could be the length of time
required to take existing employees to the new, required levels of competency. If the massive reskilling objective is to be met, the organization
itself must be skillful in reducing the cycle time required per employee to
achieve the reskilling.

Information Systems Capabilities
Employee motivation and skills may be necessary to achieve stretch targets for customer and internal-business-process objectives. But they are
unlikely to be sufficient. If employees are to be effective in today's competitive environment, they need excellent information—on customers, on
internal processes, and of the financial consequences of their decisions.

Front-line employees need accurate and timely information about each
customer's total relationship with the organization. This could likely
include, as Metro Bank has done, an estimate, derived from an activity-
based cost analysis, of the profitability of each customer. Front-line
employees should also be informed about which segment an individual
customer occupies so that they can judge how much effort should be
expended not only to satisfy the customer on the existing relationship or
transaction, but also on learning about and attempting to satisfy emerging needs from that customer.

Employees in the operations side of the business need rapid, timely,
and accurate feedback on the product just produced or the service just
delivered. Only by having such feedback can employees be expected to
sustain improvement programs where they systematically eliminate
defects and drive excess cost, time, and waste out of the production system. Excellent information systems are a requirement for employees to
improve processes, either continuously, via TQM efforts, or discontinu-
ously, through process redesign and reengineering projects. Several companies have defined a strategic information coverage ration. This ratio,
analogous to the strategic job coverage ratio introduced the preceding
section, assesses the current availability of information relative to anticipated needs. Measures of strategic information availability could be percentage of processes with real-time quality, cycle time, and cost feedback

available and percentage of customer-facing employees having on-line access to information about customers.

Motivation, Empowerment, and Alignment
Even skilled employees, provided with superb access to information, will not contribute to organizational success if they are not motivated to act in the best interest of an organization or if they are not given freedom to make decisions and take actions. Thus the third of the enablers for the learning and growth objectives focuses on the organizational climate for employee motivation and initiative.

Measures of Suggestions Made and Implemented
One can measure the outcome of having motivated, empowered employees in several ways. One simple, and widely used, measure is the number of suggestions per employee. This measure captures the ongoing participation of employees in improving the organization's performance. Such a measure can be reinforced by a complementary measure, number of suggestions implemented, which tracks the quality of the suggestions being made, as well as communicating to the work force that its suggestions are valued and taken seriously.

For example, senior management in one company was disappointed in the level and quality of employee participation in suggesting improvement opportunities. They deployed an initiative that:

• Published successful suggestions to increase the visibility and credibility of the process
• Illustrated the benefits and improvements that had been achieved through employee suggestions, and
• Communicated a new reward structure for implemented suggestions

This initiative led to dramatic increases in both the number of suggestions submitted and the number implemented.

Rockwater used numbers of suggestions as one of its early scorecard measures but was disappointed in the measured results. An investigation revealed that employees felt that their suggestions were not being acted upon. Senior executives then directed project managers to follow up and provide feedback to employees on every submitted suggestion. This feedback and implementation of many of the submitted suggestions led to an increased number of suggestions. The sum total of implementing these

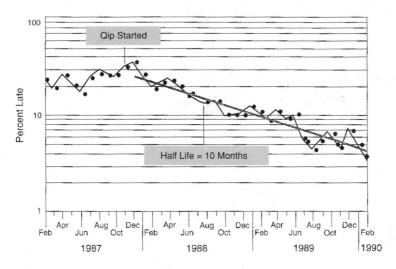

Figure 14.5
The half-life metric

suggestions led to savings that Rockwater executives estimated at several hundred thousand dollars per year.

Measures of Improvement

The tangible outcome from successfully implemented employee suggestions does not have to be restricted to expense savings. Organizations can also look for improvements, say in quality, time, or performance, for specific internal and customer processes. The half-life metric (see figure 14.5), developed by Art Schneiderman when he was vice president of quality improvement and productivity at Analog Devices, measures the length of time required for process performance to improve by 50%.[1] The half-life metric can be applied to any process metric (such as cost, quality, or time) that the organization wants to reduce to zero. Examples of such metrics are late deliveries, number of defects, scrap, and absenteeism. The metric can even be applied to the "waste" time in process cycle times and new product-development times.

The half-life metric assumes that when TQM teams are successfully applying formal quality improvement processes, they should be able to reduce defects at a constant rate (see table below). For example, suppose the organization has identified on-time delivery as a critical customer objective. Currently, the business unit may be missing promised delivery dates on 30% of orders. If its goal is to reduce the missed delivery percentage to 1% over a four-year (48 month) period, a 30-fold improvement, it can reach (actually exceed) this target by a continuous improvement process that reduces missed deliveries by 50% every nine months, as shown below:

Month	Missed Delivery %
0	30
9	15
18	7.5
27	3.8
36	1.9
45	1.0

By establishing the rate at which defects are expected to be eliminated from the system, managers can validate whether they are on a trajectory that will yield the desired performance over the specified time period. While the Chinese proverb tells us that a voyage of 1,000 miles starts with a single step, a continuous improvement metric, like the half-life, tells us whether we are stepping in the correct direction, and at a rate that will enable us to reach our ambitious target in the requisite time period.

To use the half-life metric as an outcome measure for employee suggestions and involvement in process improvement, a company should:

• Identify the process metrics where it wants process improvements
• Estimate the half-lives expected for these processes, and
• Construct an index that will report the percentage of processes that are improving at the rate specified by the estimated half-lives

Measuring the number of suggestions successfully implemented and the rate of improvements actually occurring in critical processes are good outcome measures for the organizational and individual alignment objective. These measures indicate that employees are actively participating in organizational improvement activities.

Measures of Individual and Organizational Alignment
The performance drivers for individual and organizational alignment focus on whether departments and individuals have their goals aligned

with the company objectives articulated in the Balanced Scorecard. One organization described an evolving process by which senior management implemented a process for introducing the scorecard to lower levels of the organization (see figure 14.6). The rollout process had two principal objectives:

1. Individual and organizational sub unit goals, and reward, and recognition systems aligned with achieving business objectives

2. Team-based measures of performance

The measurements for the rollout procedure evolved over the course of the implementation process. In the first phase, senior management established the context and framework for the Balanced Scorecard. It

1. Top-Down Management Rollout
- Establish context for BSC as a means to communicate shared objects
- Build understanding and acceptance of the BSC
- Engage managers to adapt the measures to fit their area of responsibility
- Engage managers to track performance to establish a baseline of information for establishing targets
- Engage managers to develop and execute an implementation plan for cascading the BSC down within their organizations

2. Employee Rollout
- Communicate context, organizational strategies, and initiatives
- Introduce the BSC—What is it; How is it being used; What's the implementation plan; What's been accomplished; What are the next steps?

3. Profit Plan/Target Setting
- Implement top-down process for defining financial targets
- Implement bottom-up process for establishing targets for nonfinancial measures

4. Personal Goals Alignment
- Each employee establishes a strategy-aligned goal by identifying an activity which they perform (and/or a measure) which will impact a measurement on the scorecard
- Personal goals established through negotiation process with management

Measurement Approach
Measure Evolves through Implementation
1. Percent of top managers exposed to BSC
2. Percent of staff exposed to BSC
3. Percent of top managers with personal goals aligned to BSC
4. Percent of staff with personal goals aligned to BSC and percent of employees who achieved personal goals

Figure 14.6
Personal goals alignment-measurement concept

engaged managers to develop measures for their areas of responsibility and develop an implementation plan for cascading the scorecard approach downward within their organizations. The initial measure for accomplishing this implementation phase was percentage of top managers exposed to BSC. After the introductory phase had been completed, the Balanced Scorecard was communicated throughout the organization, along with specific implementation plans. The organizational alignment measure shifted to percentage of staff employees exposed to BSC. In the third phase, senior management and executives were to define specific targets for the financial and nonfinancial measures on the scorecard, and to link their incentive pay to achieving these targets. They introduced a new measure, percentage of top managers with personal goals aligned to BSC, to reflect the outcome from this process.

And, in the final implementation phase, all individuals were to have their activities and goals linked to scorecard objectives and measures. The alignment outcome measures for this phase became percentage of employees with personal goals aligned to BSC and percentage of employees who achieved personal goals.

Another organization tracked how many of the 20 business units that reported directly to the senior executives had been aligned with BSC objectives. The executives established a schedule of in-depth meetings with the 20 business units to gain agreement on the following:

• How the major activities of the business unit align to the scorecard
• Development of measures for these activities to indicate success
• Communication of the BSC alignment of business unit managers to their staffs
• Alignment of individual performance goals to the scorecard

The organizational alignment measure was the percentage of business units that had successfully completed this alignment process.

Organizations can measure not only outcomes but also short-term, intermediate indicators about their attempts to communicate and align individuals with organizational objectives. One company conducted a periodic climate survey to assess employees' motivation and drive to achieve the BSC objectives. A step before assessing motivation is determining awareness. Some organizations, especially in the early stages of the scorecard implementation process, measured percentage of employees who recognized and understood the company vision.

One organization, a consumer goods company that used extensive market research to gain feedback on its advertising, promotion, and merchandising programs, used its expertise to gauge the reactions and buy-in of employees to its new strategy. The company treated the introduction of the Balanced Scorecard as a new product launch and surveyed employees every six months to estimate the market penetration of the program in different parts of the organization. The survey classified employee responses into one of four levels of awareness:

Awareness Level	Typical Response
I. Brand Awareness	"I have heard about the new strategy and the Balanced Scorecard, but it hasn't affected me yet."
II. Customer	"I have started to do things differently based on what I learned from the Balanced Scorecard."
III. Brand Preference	"The new things I am trying are working. I can see them helping me, our customers, and the company."
IV. Brand Loyalty	"I'm a believer. I'm convinced that the new strategy is the right way to go. I'm an active missionary, trying to get others on the bandwagon."

This survey (see figure 14.7) helped managers measure progress in gaining awareness and commitment to the objectives and measures for the Balanced Scorecard, and identify areas that needed additional effort and attention.

Measures of Team Performance

Many organizations today recognize that meeting ambitious targets for customers and shareholders require superb internal business processes. Managers in these organizations often believe that their stretch targets for internal-business-process performance cannot be achieved just by individuals working harder, smarter, and more informed, by themselves. Increasingly, organizations are turning to teams to accomplish important business processes—product development, customer service, and internal operations. These organizations want objectives and measures to motivate and monitor the success of team building and team performance. National Insurance, as part of its turnaround strategy to become a specialist property and casualty insurer, organized all its work processes

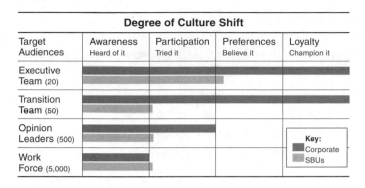

Figure 14.7
"Mindshare campaign" measurements for understanding the new vision/strategy

around teams. In its learning and growth perspective, National developed six measures of team building and team performance:

1. Internal Survey on Teaming: Survey of employees to determine if business units are supporting and creating opportunities for one another.
2. Gain-Sharing Level: Tracks the degree to which the organization is entering team-based relationships with other business units, organizations, or customers.
3. Number of Integrated Engagements: The number of projects on which more than one business unit participated.
4. Loss Control Utilization: The percentage of new policies written in which the loss control unit was consulted.
5. Percentage of Business Plans Developed by Teams: The proportion of business units that develop their plan with the assistance of headquarters-support resources.
6. Percentage of Teams with Shared Incentives: The number of teams where team members share common objectives and incentives.

These measures communicated clearly the corporate objective for individuals to work effectively in teams, and for teams in different parts of the organization to provide mutual assistance and support.

The teaming concept can be extended even further by coupling it to gain-sharing plans. Gain sharing distributes rewards to all team members when the team achieves a common goal. One organization proposed three measures of gain-sharing activity:

- Percentage of all project with customer gain sharing
- Percentage of projects in which potential gains were achieved
- Percentage of projects with individual team incentives linked to project success

Missing Measurements

Unlike some of the specific measures developed for individual companies that we have described previously for the financial, customer, and internal-business-process perspectives, we can supply many fewer examples of company-specific measures for the learning and growth perspective. We have found that many companies already have excellent starts on specific measures for their financial, customer, innovation, and operating process objectives. But when it comes to specific measures concerning employee skills, strategic information availability, and organizational alignment, companies have devoted virtually no effort for measuring either the outcomes or the drivers of these capabilities. This gap is disappointing since one of the most important goals for adopting the scorecard measurement and management framework is to promote the growth of individual organizational capabilities.

Note that the absence of specific measures is an unusually reliable indication that the company is not linking its strategic objectives to activities for reskilling employees supplying information, and aligning individuals, teams, and organizational units to the company's strategy and long-run objectives. Frequently, the advocates for employee training and reskilling, for employees empowerment, for information systems, and for motivating the work force take these programs as ends in themselves. The programs are justified as being inherently virtuous, but not as means to help the organization accomplish specific long-run economic and customer objectives. Resources and initiatives are committed to these programs, but the programs have not been held specifically and measurably accountable to achieving strategic objectives. This gap leads to frustration: senior executives wonder how long they are expected to continue to make heavy investments in employees and systems without measurable outcomes, while human resource and information system advocates wonder why their efforts are not considered more central and more strategic to the organization.

We believe that the absence, at this time, of more explicit, company-specific measures for learning and growth objectives is not an inherent limitation or weakness of incorporating this perspective in the Balanced Scorecard. Rather, it reflects the limited progress that most organizations have made in linking employees, information systems, and organizational alignment with their strategic objectives. We expect that as companies implement management processes based on the measurement framework of the Balanced Scorecard that we will soon see many more examples of creative, customized measures for the learning and growth perspective.

Rather than ignore the learning and growth perspective until companies develop these customized measures, we prefer to use the generic measures identified in this chapter—strategic job coverage, strategic information availability, percentage of processes achieving targeted rates of improvement, and percentage of key employees aligned to strategic BSC objectives. These generic measures do identify gaps in organizational capabilities, and also serve as markers until managers and employees can develop more customized and specific measures.

Measurement as Markers

An additional approach, suggested by Michael Beer, based on his strategic human-resource-management research, is to substitute text when measurements are undeveloped or unavailable.[2] Suppose an organization has set an objective to upgrade the skills of employees so that they can better implement and improve the strategy. Currently, exactly what this objective means is too uncertain to be measured with any accuracy or credibility, or at a reasonable cost. But each time, perhaps quarterly, that mangers conduct a strategic review of this human-resource-development process, key managers write a one- to two-page memorandum describing, as best they can, the actions taken during the most recent period, the outcomes achieved, and the current state of the organization's human resource capabilities. This memorandum substitutes text for measurements as the basis for active dialogue and debate about the initiatives being performed and the outcomes being achieved. While not the same as measurements, and not a long-term substitute for measurement, the text is a marker that serves many of the same objectives as a formal measurement system. It motivates action in intended directions since key managers know that each strategic review period, they must report on programs and outcomes. It provides a tangible basis for periodic accountability, review, feedback, and learning. And the report serves as a signal that a gap in measurement exists. The signal reminds executives of the need to continue to quantify strategic objectives, and to develop a system of measurement that provides a more tangible basis for communicating and evaluating objectives for developing capabilities of employees, information systems, and organizational units.

Summary

Ultimately, the ability to meet ambitious targets for financial, customer, and internal-business-process objectives depends on the organizational capabilities for learning and growth. The enablers for learning and growth come primarily from three sources: employees, systems, and organizational alignment. Strategies for superior performance will generally require significant investments in people, systems, and processes that build organizational capabilities. Consequently, objectives and measures for these enablers of superior performance in the future should be an integral part of any organization's Balanced Scorecard.

A core group of three employee-based measures—satisfaction, productivity, and retention—provide outcome measures from investments in employees, systems, and organizational alignment. The drivers of these outcomes are, to date, somewhat generic and less developed than those of the other three balanced scorecard perspectives. These drivers include summary indices of strategic job coverage, strategic information availability, and degree of personal, team, and departmental alignment with strategic objectives. The absence of company-specific measures indicate the opportunity for future development of customized employee, systems, and organizational metrics that can be more closely linked to a business unit's strategy.

References

1. A. Schneiderman, "Setting Quality Goals," *Quality Progress* (April 1988): 51–57; see also R. Kaplan, "Analog Devices, Inc.: The Half-Life System," 9-190-061 (Boston: Harvard Business School, 1990).

2. M. Beer, R. Eisenstat, and R. Biggadike, "Developing an Organization Capable of Strategy Implementation and Reformulation," in *Organizational Learning and Competitive Advantage*, ed. B. Moingon and A. Edmonson (London: Sage, 1996).

15

Measuring Intangibles and Intellectual Capital

Karl-Erik Sveiby

The high stock market premiums on today's stock markets can be one of the indications of an emerging new Knowledge Economy. The parallel development of two approaches using score card formats for presenting indicators in Sweden and in the United States have now laid the ground for a first standard for measuring intangible assets, featuring three categories of Intangible assets plus a fourth category, financial assets. The Swedish concepts have been tested in practice in some cases by up to ten years. The practical results suggest that it is useful to measure Intangible assets and that it is possible for managers to create shareholder value, without relying primarily on the traditional financial indicators. We should measure as close to the source as possible, and money is only one of possible proxies. When trying to assess the commercial value of knowledge, the only reliable method is to establish values arising from transactions, such as the stock market.

The Wellspring

In the spruce forest behind my parents home in northern Sweden springs a natural well. It is so small that you don't notice it until you almost stumble upon it. What you see is a pond of water no more than half a meter in diameter. The surface looks calm, but then you see that water is slowly emerging on to the surface from a source hidden beneath. The water is slowly flowing over the edge of the pond and spreading into the ground below it.

When I was little my brother and I sometimes used to play there. It was great fun, we could build dams in the small streams that the water formed and we sent our bark ships to each other on the water surface along it. I could see the clear water surface, but I did not think much about where the water came from.

We were forbidden to even dip our hands into the pond; in fact, we were forbidden to play there, because our family depended on the well for drinking water. The water tasted so good that my parents had refused the communal serviced water pipe when it was drawn through the village in the fifties.

The surface was clear, yet the pond so dark. If I had dared to look under the surface of the pond, lighting it with a torch, I would probably have seen a bubbling, streaming, surging movement of water, blended with sand and a few dangling sprouts of water lilies. But I would still not have seen the actual source from where the water was coming.

The wellspring seems an endless resource, my brother who now owns the farm, still taps it for drinking water. When I visited it a couple of years ago the surface of the pond looks the same today as it always has. But the water is not the same, of course. It changes every second. Still, the pond looks the same, from the surface. The real value of a wellspring is its *renewal rate*, not its reservoir.

Dorothy Leonard-Barton, in her book Wellsprings of Knowledge[1] inspired me to this wellspring metaphor for an organization's unlimited resource of knowledge. The visible surface is the explicit knowledge, the deep dark dynamic constantly renewing pool beneath is the tacit. The visible surface of the water, explicit knowledge, is a very small proportion of he total, maybe 1% of the pond and we use it for visible communication, our ships of messages.

All our knowledge starts with a tacit process, which is unlimited scope and unknown. The explicit is only the surface of it. We know the source of the tacit knowledge, it comes from the individuals, and they are constantly renewing it. Indeed, as Michael Polanyi[2] expresses it: "Knowledge is an activity which would be better described as a process of knowing."

Measure the Flow of Knowledge

Let me stretch the metaphor a bit. Suppose we get the task to measure the water. The solution of the task will depend on the purpose of measurement, and on the values of the measurer.

The water engineer probably wants to know how much water there is in the pond, and how it develops over the year. Measuring the volume in the wellspring itself adds to our understanding, but only the first time. Next time the volume is roughly the same, although comprised of different atoms. To measure the atoms one by one would be desirable, but would be very costly because they change all the time. How about measuring the diameter of the surface? Yes, but it measures only the visible part, and again it remains the same. The water engineer might suggest that we try to put a gauge that measures the input or the output stream, into the water source, as an indicator of how much one might tap.

The accountant would probably suggest that we measure the commercial value of the wellspring using dollars as our metric. There is a market for water, so it is fairly easy to find out the commercial value of water, but do we learn more about the true state(s) of the wellspring? Will we know more about where the water comes from? The quality of it? Where it ends up? The renewal rate? What we can do to improve the quality? The risks of drought? The efficiency of the actions we take for improving the wellspring?

Trying to measure the hidden source seems a better approach, but it is a risky enterprise. If the engineer helps us to drill a hole into the ground and insert an instrument, we might accidentally dry out the pond.

Measure Closer to the Source and Measure Flows
The accountant's approach seems outright silly; money indicators give at best indirect indications on a very aggregate level, but no accurate guidelines for where the companies or processes are going. And what if there is no market for the water in the area? Does that mean that, in an economic sense, the water has no value? Does that mean the water does not exist?

Water, just as knowledge, has little to do with money, so why measure in money terms? Would not we be better off with proxies that come closer to the source? The engineer's approach is therefore slightly better, because it uses proxies closer to the natural processes, but it can also be quite risky since we might accidentally kill the source.

How about using a more indirect way, for instance a seismographic instrument to send sound waves down and then try to learn indirectly from the reflection?

This indirect way is what I prefer, because it is nonintrusive. The indirect approach is to design indicators that *correlate* to some extent with the processes we wish to monitor. And we need to come as close as possible to the source. Therefore *nonfinancial indicators*, such as volumes, speed of flows, change, risk, growth would be better. The best are the ones that can capture the dynamics, the flows. The problem with indirect metrics is of course that they are, well, indirect.

We must therefore try to find correlations rather than causal relationships. But correlations change over time. Therefore the art of measuring knowledge is too imprecise to be used for control purposes—we must see the measuring process as an invitation to dialogue in our endless quest to understand the world around us. As platform for dialogue, numbers are good, because they crystallize a wealth of information and can be analyzed using mathematical methods.

The Commercial value of Knowledge

That knowledge has a commercial value is not contested.

The commercial value is more visible in companies that lack traditional tangible values, so let us have a look at the "full" balance sheet of the Australian management consulting and recruitment firm Morgan & Banks, listed on the Sydney stock exchange. M&B's balance sheet is typical for knowledge organizations.

With some 1000 people employed and sales of A$221M in 1997, M&B is one of the largest consulting firms in Australia. The market value of M&B in April 1998 was A$ 200 Mill

The material or "visible" component is the familiar balance sheet in annual reports. It itemizes material assets, and shows how they are financed. As per June 30, 1997, M&B had A$11M in cash, A$32M in other Current Assets and A$23M in property, plant and other "tangible" investments.

Visible financing in a knowledge organization is usually very simple, and M&B is no exception: short-term debt (A$51M), no long-term loans (hard to arrange, because the characteristic lack of tangible "collateral" makes banks uneasy), and A$15.4M in equity (shareholders' capital).

This equity "earns" a very high return, an after tax profit of 9.9 million in 1996–97 equates to 64% ROE. Such high ROEs are not uncommon in knowledge companies, and that tells us that there must be something missing in the equation, namely the Equity is understated.

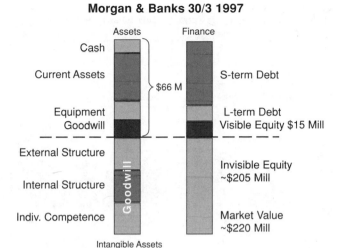

Figure 15.1
7/97 Invisible balance sheet of Morgan & Banks

So where is the missing equity? Let us look "under the surface." No less than A$185M in "invisible equity" and intangible assets. From where did I derive that figure? It is the difference between the market value A$200M and the net book value A$15.4M. Note that the division of the 185M into 3 equal parts is arbitrary. We lack data to make a more accurate estimate and Morgan&Banks own annual report does not give us any clues. The market value can be seen as the market's perception of the value of all the intangible assets, as a whole. The profit 9.9 Mill divided by A$200 Mill is a mere 5%.

Actually, in an international perspective, Morgan & Banks employees are not particularly productive. Its profit is only around A$15,000 per employee.

The important issue from a management information perspective is that the present standards grossly understate the value of the assets, and therefore gives a skewed picture for companies where there are no traditional assets. This is quite dangerous for all stakeholders in the new high-tech industries and where people are pivotal for business success, such as knowledge companies and service companies.

The high value put on the intangible assets of Morgan & Banks is by no means unique. "Market premiums" are common features on all mar-

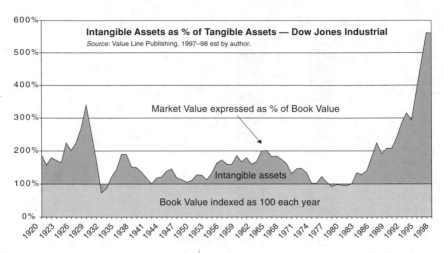

Figure 15.2
Intangible assets 1920-1995. Value Line Publishing

kets and has been so on the stock markets ever since they became more organized and institutionalized.

Have we entered a new economy with invisible values?

The stock market premium has never been higher than in the mid1990s. The companies making up the Dow Jones Index are at the highest ever level since the depression in the 1920s. The data in the chart below are Intangible assets as % of Book Value each year for all companies making up the Dow Jones Industrial Index (Data Source Value Line Inc.). Based on the data I have computed an "Intangible Assets Index" for each year. The Book Value for each year was set to 100%. The index value 87% in 1920 means that in year 1920 the Intangible assets were 87% of the Book Value, so the total Market Value in 1920 was 187%.

So does this mean that we have a "new economy" that is somehow ruled by other laws, like the law of increasing returns?[3] We do not know yet, but if the market does *not* fall substantially, and if the United States does not experience a depression in 1999–2000, I believe we have a serious indication that something has in fact happened in the U.S. economy, something that will have worldwide implications.

Why Nonfinancial Indicators?

It is tempting to try to design a measuring system equivalent of double entry bookkeeping with money as the common denominator. It is an established framework with definitions and standards and therefore "common sense." *This is precisely the reason we should break with it.* If we measure the new with the tools of the old, we will not "see" the new. There is no difference between financial indicators and nonfinancial indicators. *Both are uncertain* and all interpretations are dependent on the observer. There exist no "objective" measures. *Money is merely a proxy for human effort*, and the 500-year-old system of accounting sheds little light on the vital processes in organizations whose assets are largely non-monetary, and intangible. The main reasons why the financial measures seem more "objective" and "real" are that they are founded on implicit concepts of what a company is and that the measures have been around for so long that definitions and standards guide their interpretations.

As of today, there exists no comprehensive system that takes both intangible assets and financial and uses money as the common denominator. Depending on the purpose for measuring, I do not think it is necessary either. Knowledge flows and intangible assets are essentially nonmonetary. We need new proxies.

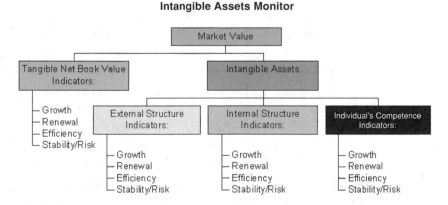

Intangible Assets Monitor

Figure 15.3
The intangible assets monitor framework

This lack of a coherent theoretical framework that fits the emerging knowledge economy is characteristic [4] of the present development: It is not the academic world that has been defining the turf so far. Instead, it seems that an emerging practice is currently driving the concept makers.

Most companies measure at least some of their intangible assets and they use nonmonetary indicators particularly for measuring operational efficiency. Manufacturing companies have for instance measured their output in "tons per hour." Hospitals and hotels measure bed utilization. Schools measure average marks. Universities measure number of Ph.D. dissertations per year, etc.

The Intangible Assets Monitor Framework

Existing management information systems tend to focus on Operational efficiency—the efficiency of the *Internal Structure* as called in the Intangible Assets Monitor and some Human Resource related metrics, such as staff turnover.[5] But there exists no comprehensive well-established system for measuring intangible assets.

The problem is not that "intangible indicators" are difficult to design. The problems are more what to measure and that the indicators seem difficult to interpret. Most managers tend to believe that the money measures are more "real" than other data and they are rewarded based on financial grounds and they are not encouraged by their superiors to question the established financial framework.

The "invisible" intangible part of the balance sheet can be classified as a family of three:

Individual competence is people's capacity to act in various situations. It includes skill, education, experience, values and social skills. People are the only true agents in business; all assets and structures, whether tangible physical products or intangible relations, are the result of human action and depend ultimately on people for their continued existence.

Competence cannot be owned by anyone or anything but the person who possesses them, because when all is said and done employees are voluntary members of the organization. A case can, however, be made for including competence in the balance sheet, because it is impossible to conceive of an organization without people. People tend to be loyal, if they are treated fairly and feel a sense of shared responsibility. That is why companies are generally willing to pay some kind of compensation to those who retire, or have to be laid off.

This kind of compensation varies from country to country, but often takes the form of redundancy pay, umbrella agreements ("golden parachutes") and pensions. Although such commitments are not recorded as liabilities in the balance sheet, they can be seen as pledges or commitments, like leasing or rental contracts, and thus a form of invisible financing of employee competence.

Internal structure consists of a wide range of patents, concepts, models, and computer and administrative systems. These are created by the employees and are thus generally "owned" by the organization, and adhere to it. Sometimes they can be acquired from elsewhere. Decisions to develop or invest in such assets can be made with some degree of confidence, because the work is done in-house, or bought from outside. In addition, the informal organization, the internal networks, the "culture" or the "spirit" belongs to the internal structure. The internal structure and the people together constitute what we generally call the "organization."

External structure consists of relationships with customers and suppliers, brand names, trademarks and reputation, or "image." Some of these can be considered legal property, but the bond is not as strong as in the case of internal assets because investments in them cannot be made with the same degree of confidence. The value of such assets is primarily influenced by how well the company solves its customer's problems, and there is always an element of uncertainty here. Reputations and relationships can be good or bad, and can change over time. The external structure is not particularly liquid, and unlike the material assets, they may or may not be legally owned by the company.

The economic value of a customer relation is no more "invisible" than the market value of a house. The reasons why the value of a relation seems invisible today is because it does not have a generally accepted definition and that it is not measured according to a standard. But these drawbacks do not mean that it is impossible or unnecessary to measure it, only that comparison between companies and over time are difficult to make.

Because of the reluctance of banks to lend for investment in intangible assets, the development of intangible assets is mostly self-financed. In other words, the invisible assets are matched, on the financing side of the balance sheet, by equally invisible finance, most of which in the form of invisible equity.

Knowledge organizations like Morgan & Banks or WM-data have little machinery, other than their employees and because only people can act, they are both the minders of the machines and the "machines," the revenue creators, themselves. For the most part, their competence is directed outwards, to the task of generating revenue, by solving customer's problems. This outward-directed energy creates the relationships, networks, and images that comprise the organizations external structure.

Similarly, it is the smaller amount of human competence that is directed inward that creates, maintains, develops or erodes the organization's internal structure.

Monitoring Intangible Assets for Financial Success

But can a nonmonetary management information system guarantee financial success and shareholder value? An example is Swedish WM-data, which uses nonfinancial indicators to monitor its knowledge-based strategy.

WM-data is today the biggest of the Swedish listed independent computer software and consulting companies, after more than a decade of unprecedented growth. The main reason for the success is a very deliberate strategic policy of focusing on corporate knowledge build up, customer relations and competence development. In the terminology of this book, WM-data has pursued a *knowledge-focused strategy*[6] ever since its foundation more than 25 years ago.

WM-data attributes its rapid growth to the fact that it lacks a central headquarters function, like marketing and HR. It consists of a "web" of quite independent subsidiaries and a very small top management team. The aim of the corporate structure is to support creativity and enable close customer relations; the ideal size should not exceed 50 employees per work environment.

Top management keeps a tight control supported by a management information system. WM-data considers financial measures useless for management control and has designed a *system of nonmonetary indicators*, which top management uses to follow up their operation on a weekly, monthly and annual basis.

Table 15.1
WM-data's Financial Performance 1987–1997.

	1987	1997	Average increase 1987-1997
# of employees	560	5150	25%
Turnover MSEK	275	7951	40%
Net profit MSEK	48	570	28%
Market value MSEK Dec 31	212	10325	47%
Intangible assets MSEK	90	8838	
	1993	1997	
Return on capital employed	37.0%	37.8%	
Return on equity	26.4%	30.7%	
Profit per employee '000 SEK	80	131	

Source: WM-data Annual Report 1997

WM-data uses traditional indicators like return on equity and return on investment only at group level. In their Annual Report 1997 (p.25) they state that "traditional financial controls are of limited use in managing, understanding and assessing a knowledge-based company. This requires more in-depth analysis of the knowledge-based company's critical business targets and concepts."

Can one create shareholder value without focusing on the return on equity? WM-data's record speaks for itself. "A knowledge-based company also requires a certain level of financial capital, but it is rarely crucial for solving the customers' problems." (WM-data Annual Report 1997). As WM-data's track record shows, their approach does create shareholder value.

And it makes sense: If the financial capital is not essential for the customers and if it is not the bottleneck for the service, why use money as the common denominator?

As can be seen above, it is the intangible assets that make up the lion part of the value growth, not the financial capital. If the Intangible Assets make up most of the capital, one should try to measure those.

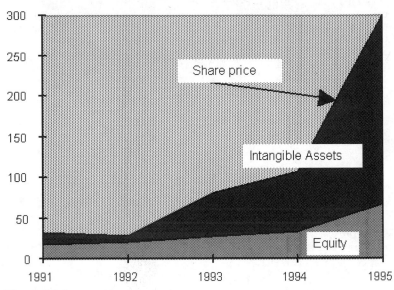

Figure 15.4
WM-data intangible assets per share. Annual Report 1995

Emerging Standard

This "Family-of-three" categorization and corresponding theory about measuring intangible assets was developed by a Swedish working group in 1987 and published in a report in Swedish language,[7] and later in a book.[8] The "Konrad theory" has since become widely used in Scandinavia. More than 40 Swedish companies measured and reported their intangible assets according to these principles in 1995.[9] WM-data adopted the original Konrad-theory for measuring and presenting in their Annual Reports already in 1988, so WM-data now has a unique 10-year track record.

The theory was further developed for management information purposes, which is called the "Intangible Assets Monitor".[10]

An internationally well known approach is the "Balanced Scorecard,"[11] which was developed in the United States around 1990, independently from the Swedish efforts at the time. BSC is not designed specifically to measure and publish intangible assets, only to take a more "balanced view" on internal performance measurement.

There are some similarities between the two theories. Both theories suggest that nonfinancial measures must complement the financial indicators. Both concepts categorize the nonfinancial, the "intangible" areas into three. Both also argue that the nonfinancial ratios and indicators must be lifted from the operational to the strategic level of the firm. Both also agree that this approach to measuring is not a new control instrument; it should be used for improving learning and dialogue.

But there are also some important theoretical differences.

1. The Intangible Assets Monitor is based on the notion of people as an organization's only profit generators. The profits generated from people's actions are signs of that success, but not the originator of it. Human actions are converted into both tangible and intangible knowledge "structures." These structures are directed outwards (external structures) or inwards (internal structures). These structures are assets, because they affect the revenue streams. BSC does not make this assumption.

2. The Intangible Assets Monitor assumes a set of three Intangible Assets, and that we should try and find metrics indicating the growth, renewal, efficiency and stability of these assets. The idea should be to get a "peek" into how the intangible asset(s) are developing, by designing indicators that correlate with the growth of the asset in question, its renewal rate, how efficiently we are at utilizing it, and the risk of losing it. BSC achieves its purpose to balance the traditional perspective by adding the three other perspectives, there could in principle be many more perspectives.

3. BSC does not question the foundation of "what constitutes a firm." While the Intangible Assets Monitor is based on the notion of a "knowledge perspective" of a firm, Kaplan and Norton regard the notion of the firm as given by its strategy. They just want managers to take a more "balanced view." They argue in their book,[11] "The Balanced Scorecard complements financial measures of past performance with measures of the drivers of future performance. The objectives and the measures of the Scorecard are derived from an organization's vision and strategy."

The authors of both concepts thus agree that money is only one of many possible proxies for measuring human action, but the conceptual standing point is different.

I argue that in a knowledge economy people should not be regarded as costs but rather revenue creators and that knowledge or people's competence are sources of wealth creation. If the notion of people as revenue creators is accepted, we have to come closer to "the source" of their knowledge if we wish to measure it more accurately.

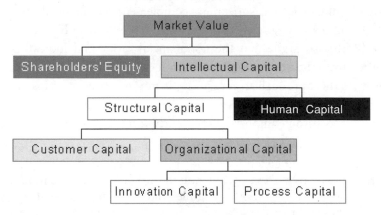

Figure 15.5
The Skandia framework

So even if the BSC on the surface of it may look similar as the Intangible Assets Monitor, the origins and the concepts beneath are very different. Therefore BSC users will probably develop nonfinancial indicators that are different from those using the Intangible Assets Monitor.

In 1993, Leif Edvinsson combined the two theories, the Konrad conceptual framework and the Balanced Scorecard. He applied a Balanced Scorecard presentation format to the Konrad—theory and published it in a supplement to Skandia's Annual Report, using for the first time the word, "Intellectual Capital," instead of the accounting term "Intangible Assets."[12]

The emergence of two similar categorizations independently of each other, one in Sweden and one in the USA is encouraging because it suggests a certain robustness. The categorization of intangibles into a "family of three": assets, capitals, focuses, structures, perspectives or what other labels one prefers, is now widespread. We also have a number of organizations testing it in practice so it has the potential of becoming a first global standard.

A Standard Approach to Measuring Intangible Assets

A possible standard for measuring and presenting Intangible Assets could be:

1. The organization monitors and presents itself using a Score Card approach with Indicators.

2. The intangible assets are categorized into three:

- External to the organization
- Internal to the organization (but outside the individual employees)
- Individual (internal to the individual employees)

3. Indicators for Financial or tangible assets are presented as the fourth category.

4. Indicators are a combination of financial and nonfinancial.

5. The indicators are presented in a coherent fashion together in a separate section or supplement.

6. The traditional accounting system and the rest of the Annual Report remains unchanged.

Wanted: New Dialogue for a New Economy

Measurement systems can be used for control or for dialogue. As language for dialogue, metrics are excellent, because they force us to define relationships mathematically and to be stringent. Well-designed indicators based in a coherent theoretical framework are like the words and

Table 15.1
WM-data's Financial Performance 1987–1997.

	1987	1997	Average increase 1987-1997
# of employees	560	5150	25%
Turnover MSEK	275	7951	40%
Net profit MSEK	48	570	28%
Market value MSEK Dec 31	212	10325	47%
Intangible assets MSEK	90	8838	
	1993	1997	
Return on capital employed	37.0%	37.8%	
Return on equity	26.4%	30.7%	
Profit per employee '000 SEK	80	131	

Source: WM-data Annual Report 1997

the grammatical syntax of a language. It can help managers understand how the relationships between people and profit look like in their own company.

Unfortunately, the requests I have received from executives in Australia and the USA tend to focus on the control aspect. Managers that install new measurement systems for controlling the performance of their people are missing the plot and they risk alienating their staff and destroy the source of revenue creation capacity: their people.

Our organizations do not need more control, they need liberalization from the straitjackets of an irrelevant financial control system; the legacy of a long passed industrial era. Individuals need more creative space and they need systems that support a more open dialogue so they can contribute more to the strategy of their companies.

The Scorecard approaches, with processes that emphases intangible assets as consisting of mainly human relationships and knowledge creation, are designed for dialogue. The underlying principle of measuring intangible assets, intellectual capital or what we prefer to call it, must be that it complements the accounting system with a new language for the dialogue of peers, not another system for controlling subordinates.

The choice of assets to measure and the design of indicators depend on the company, its strategy and the most important value creating processes.

Measuring intangible assets is an art form very much in its early stages and Australia needs people who have both the qualifications to develop measurement systems in their companies, and who understand the problems involved in measuring intangibles and reporting and interpreting this fuzzy stuff. They have to be pioneers, willing to accept the hardships involved in arguing their case to bean counting accountants and doubting financial markets.

Then we will not destroy the wellspring—only help each other to expand it and utilize it better.

References

1. Dorothy Leonard-Barton, *Wellsprings of Knowledge* (Boston: Harvard Business School Press, 1995).
2. Missing Reference {AU: Please supply]

3. B. Arthur, "Increasing returns and the new world of Business," *Harvard Business Review*, July-August 1996.

4. Debra Amidon, "Knowledge Management gains Momentum in Industry," *Research-Technology Management*, May/June 1996.

5. Ulf Johanson, "Increasing the Transparency of Investments in Intangibles," Personnel Economics Institute, Stockholm University 1996.

6. Karl-Erik Sveiby, *The New Organisational Wealth: Managing and Measuring Knowledge-Based Assets* (San Francisco: Berrett-Koehler, 1997).

7. Karl-Erik Sveiby and T. Lloyd, "Managing Knowhow," 1987.

8. Karl-Erik Sveiby, *Den osynliga* (Stockholm: Ledarskap, 1989).

9. Per Öhman, "Kunskap i årsredovisningen," Examensarbete, 1996:05, C. Högskolan i Luleå.

10. Karl-Erik Sveiby, "The Intangible Assets Monitor," *Journal of Human Resource Costing and Accounting* 2, no. 1 (Spring 1997).

11. R.S. Kaplan and D.P. Norton, *The Balanced Scorecard* (Boston: Harvard Business School Press, 1996).

12. L. Edvinsson and Michael S. Malone, *Intellectual Capital: Realizing your company's true value by finding its hidden brainpower* (New York: Harper Collins, 1997).

16

New Measures for a New Era

Laurie J. Bassi and Mark E. Van Buren

In the dawning knowledge era, the future performance of firms will be determined in large part by their intellectual capital. Firms that create and leverage this unique source of competitive advantage most effectively will be tomorrow's winners. The measurement of the value of investments in intellectual capital is a critical obstacle to turning those investments into true assets. Most organizations have only a vague understanding of how much they spend on intellectual capital, let alone what they receive from those investments. Without methods of measuring intellectual capital and its management, the many firms will not realize the value of their intellectual capital. Without standards, firms' stakeholders have no means of judging the value and effectiveness of investments in intellectual capital across firms. The assessment framework developed by the Effective Knowledge Management Working Group represents a major step toward providing precisely such methods and standards for seeing into the future.

The New Era

According to some observers the industrial era's successor—the information age, wherein white-collar jobs exceeded blue-collar jobs and entire industries arose just to help companies manage and process information—is already at or past the midpoint of its life cycle. The ever-declining cost of processing information has made it ubiquitous. Indeed, information has become a commodity that is readily bought and sold. As a result, it is no longer sufficient to define competitive advantage. Gone are the days, for example, when banks could compete exclusively on the basis of who had the fastest information technology or who could slice and dice their account information in more ways than anyone else.

Hence the rapidly growing interest in intellectual capital as the "new" source of competitive advantage and the realization that we have now entered a new era—the knowledge era. In many ways, this is nothing new at all. A firm's intellectual capital—the brains of its employees, their know-how, the processes and customer knowledge that they create—has always been a source of competitive advantage. And by extension, so too has been intellectual capital or knowledge management—the processes by which a firm creates and leverages intellectual capital. What is unique about the era that we are entering is that intellectual capital is becoming the primary source of competitive advantage within a growing number of industries. Organizations from industrial era industries, such as automobile manufacturing, to information age industries, such as banking, are recognizing that they each have a unique storehouse of intellectual capital, and that the future belongs to those who can grow their intellectual capital and then apply and use it best.

With the benefit of hindsight, it is apparent that in the knowledge era, creating and leveraging intellectual capital is the business of business. By all available measures, the stock market is already providing handsome rewards to companies that successfully leverage their intellectual capital—a phenomenon that will almost surely grow in significance as knowledge-based organizations increase in size and numbers. A few firms are anticipating this and looking to enhance, measure and manage their employees' skills and knowledge more effectively, thereby attracting the capital needed for growth. However, these efforts are, for the most part, idiosyncratic and only beginning to be formalized.

What Isn't Measured Isn't (Well) Managed

One of the largest impediments to managing intellectual capital lies in the area of measurement. Initiatives to manage intellectual capital, on the whole, are hampered by a lack of sound methods for measuring stocks of intellectual capital, their value, and the impacts of investing in intellectual capital. Most firms have, at best, only a dim notion of their intellectual capital assets and investments. Standard accounting systems do not allow for easy estimation of intellectual capital investments, even after they have been clearly identified. Sound measurement requires formalized information sharing, common definitions and metrics, and shared measurement methodologies, none of which can be overcome by market forces or the work of isolated organizations.

Measuring the value of an organization's intellectual capital stocks is, of course, but the first step in beginning to manage it effectively. Much more important—but impossible if basic measurement systems have not been put in place—is evaluating the effectiveness of alternative intellectual capital management activities. Yet, most economic decision-makers know very little about the effectiveness of those activities. Two results are almost inevitable: 1) firms will under-invest in their intellectual capital, and 2) many of the investments that they do make will be ineffective.

The importance of measurement is difficult to overstate. A report from The Conference Board and the American Society for Training and Development entitled Leveraging Human Capital[1] observes: "Measurement is a critical issue for executives. They realize that even if they are not expected to present measurable deliverables today, they probably will be tomorrow." The significance and lack of progress on the issue are also clear from a survey called "Twenty Questions on Knowledge in the Organization" by Ernst and Young's Center for Business Innovation.[2] Measuring the value and performance of knowledge assets ranked as the second most important challenge companies face today, surpassed only by changing people's behavior (54 versus 43 percent respectively). On the other hand, only 4 percent claimed to be good or excellent at "measuring the value of knowledge assets and/or impact of knowledge management."

Although identifying the impacts attributable to intellectual capital management is a difficult task, we do not believe it is impossible. Only by doing so will firms be able to develop sound methods for determining which efforts have a high payoff and should be nurtured, and which have a low payoff and should either be revised or eliminated. The standard of evidence for evaluating the effectiveness of intellectual capital management may, of course, vary with the nature of the activity; an insistence on extremely rigorous evidence could, in some cases, rule out the possibility of making long-term, strategic investments.

The important point, however, is that the ultimate purpose of developing sound methods for evaluating the impacts of intellectual capital is to generate the information needed for continuously improving its value to an organization. While such information may not be needed in an environment where spending on intellectual capital is typically viewed as a cost, it is essential when it becomes a strategic investment.

Moving Forward on Intellectual Capital Measurement

There have been a number of well-documented cases of companies that have made clear inroads into the task of measuring and leveraging their intellectual capital assets, including Skandia AFS, Dow Chemical, and Buckman Laboratories, among others. To their credit, many of these organizations have made their measurement systems publicly available in one form or another. However, idiosyncratic or company-specific measurement systems developed in isolation of one another will do little to create widely accepted measurement methods that are robust enough to be adopted across the diverse set of organizations moving forward into the knowledge-era.

Greater strides can only be made by collective endeavors on intellectual capital assessment. To further the sound management of intellectual capital through better measurement, seven large U.S. corporations that have made significant investments in intellectual capital management initiatives began a collaborative cross-industry effort with the American Society for Training and Development in December, 1997. Entitled the Effective Knowledge Management Working Group, its members include Charles Schwab, Chevron, Dow Chemical, EDS, Motorola, Polaroid, and PriceWaterhouseCoopers. Together these firms have created the foundation for a widely applicable and accessible framework for the measurement of intellectual capital. By bringing together companies from different industries with a diversity of intellectual capital management initiatives, the work of these firms has laid the groundwork for developing a standard set of measures that can be used to undertake assessments of intellectual capital management activities across a wide variety of firms.

After describing what we mean by the phrase "intellectual capital management," we provide an overview of what others have done to measure intellectual capital and its value. Next, we introduce the measurement framework we have developed with the Effective Knowledge

Management Working Group. We provide a general conceptual model of intellectual capital management, then identify a core set of indicators that we believe can be used by most firms to measure their intellectual capital stocks. Finally, we discuss our ongoing research to validate this model and indicators.

What Is Intellectual Capital Management?

As the economic significance, and interest in, intellectual capital has grown in recent years, a variety of definitions and conceptualizations of intellectual capital have appeared. What often distinguishes one definition of intellectual capital from another is the types of assets that they place under the rubric. One of the most widely cited comes from Leif Edvinsson of Skandia AFS, who along with Michael Malone[3] defines intellectual capital as "the possession of the knowledge, applied experience, organizational technology, customer relationships and professional skills that provide [an organization] with a competitive edge in the market." Also frequently quoted is Thomas Stewart's[4] definition: "intellectual material—knowledge, information, intellectual property, experience —that can be put to use to create wealth." The items labeled as intellectual capital are so varied that the authors of each definition usually rely upon taxonomies to classify and differentiate them. In general, taxonomies of intellectual capital contain three primary types of capital: human capital, structural capital, and customer capital.

Despite their differences, intellectual capital conceptualizations have in common a focus on the intangible assets of an organization. As intangible, these assets are distinct from the tangible assets that make up the forms of capital, physical and financial, upon which organizations have traditionally competed. As assets, they are viewed not as costs to an organization, but as sources of future economic value.

Another way of distinguishing perspectives on intellectual capital involves the degree to which they explicitly equate intellectual capital with knowledge. Some use the concepts interchangeably—the management of intellectual capital is synonymous with knowledge management. Karl-Erik Sveiby, author of *The New Organizational Wealth*,[5] for instance, views knowledge management as "the art of creating value from an organization's intangible assets." For others, knowledge management is confined to the management of the codified, formalized, explicit forms of knowledge such as repositories of lessons learned, documents, databases, and company yellow pages, rather than all types of intangible assets. Thus, David Skyrme and Debra Amidon[6] define knowledge management as "the explicit and systematic management of vital knowledge and its associated processes of creating, gathering, organizing, diffusion, use, and exploitation." Adding further confusion to these distinctions is the fact that what some call knowledge management is in reality "information" management, by failing to realize that knowledge without some context is merely information.

Adapting Skyrme and Amidon's definition, we define "intellectual capital management" as the explicit and systematic management of intellectual capital and the associated processes of creating, gathering, organizing, disseminating, leveraging and using intellectual capital. This definition allows us to consider a plethora of activities under the domain of intellectual capital management, including training, decision making, marketing, electronic discussion groups, organizational learning (including best practice sharing), total quality management, and succession planning.

Measuring Intellectual Capital

Efforts to address the measurement challenges surrounding intellectual capital fall into two basic, but overlapping types. The first basic type is focused on measuring stocks of intellectual capital. The simplest form of this type of measurement is a straightforward enumeration of the intellectual capital of an organization—the number of patents, Ph.D. professionals, or Fortune 500 contracts. Enumeration results in an inventory of intangible assets, but tells an organization relatively little other than the types and amounts of assets it "possesses."

Usually, organizations are more interested in measuring the value of their intellectual capital stocks. These efforts attempt to assign monetary values to intangible assets. However, the intangible qualities of these assets make such valuations exceedingly difficult. Thus, most attempts at valuation provide an approximation of the aggregate value of an organization's entire intellectual capital stock without enumerating every intangible asset. One such formula for measuring the value of intellectual capital is Paul Strassman's[7] method for valuing "Knowledge Capital."

Under his formula, the value of knowledge capital can be estimated as the ratio of "management value-added" to the price of capital, where management value-added is essentially profits after tax minus shareholder equity.

One especially popular approximate measure of intellectual capital that explicitly compares the value of an organization's intellectual capital to its financial and physical capital is the Market-to-Book Value (based upon, and often referred, to Tobin's q). Market value is a company's stock price multiplied by the number of outstanding shares, while its book value is the replacement value of its physical assets. The assumption is that the portion of a company's market value in excess of its book value is the value that the market places on its intangible assets. According to Charles Handy,[8] the intellectual capital values of most organizations assessed in this manner are worth three to four times their book values. This measure constantly changes as a company's stock prices fluctuates, may reflect other factors such as takeover rumors or global volatility, and can only be constructed for publicly-traded firms. A major drawback to such aggregate measures of intellectual capital is the inability to see how certain actions or changes affect specific types of intangible assets.

A second basic type of measurement goes beyond the value of the stocks of intellectual capital themselves to the value they produce or create. The emphasis shifts from intellectual capital to the processes by which it is managed (i.e., intellectual capital management)—from stocks to flow. Likening these processes to production functions, this form of measurement looks at the output side of the equation as well as the input side. The purpose of measurement becomes one of ascertaining the effectiveness of these activities. Recently, there have been a number of calls for greater progress on the measurement of effectiveness. Carla O'Dell of the American Productivity and Quality Center,[9] for instance, commenting on the current state of knowledge management practice, has argued that "We should focus on what works and what doesn't." The Conference Board's report entitled Managing Knowledge for Business Success[10] likewise states that "Measuring the economic value of knowledge and knowledge management initiatives is a critical challenge for organizations."

Effectiveness measures fall into two different categories. On the one hand, effectiveness can be measured as changes in an organization's stock (quantity or quality) of intangible assets themselves. This class of effectiveness measures leads one, by necessity, to undertake the first type of measurement discussed above as well. It is relatively easy to see how some intellectual capital management activities, such as selection and recruitment or marketing are aimed at creating more intellectual capital and lend themselves to this class of measures.

The second class of effectiveness measures assesses how knowledge management affects performance, that is, how well intellectual capital assets are leveraged or the returns they achieve. Performance can be assessed at various levels (e.g., individual, team, and organizational), units/functions (e.g., HR or finance), product lines, markets, and so on. Those who use performance measures are particularly interested in the economic value produced by a firm's intellectual capital. Inevitably, discussions on economic value turn to the "Holy Grail" of measures— Return on Investment (ROI). However, financial assessments of effectiveness, such as ROI, are particularly difficult to make. A recent study by the American Productivity and Quality Center[11] found that 80 percent of companies do not calculate ROI on their knowledge management activities.

One example of this form of measurement comes from Ante Pulic of the Institute for International Management in Austria.[12] He proposes the "value added intellectual capital coefficient" (VAIC), defined simply as value added divided by intellectual capital. Like Strassman's, his formula relies upon proxies for both parts of the ratio. Value added is loosely defined as the difference between sales and all inputs, except labor expenses. Total labor expenses, likewise, approximate intellectual capital. The higher the ratio, the more efficient the use of intellectual capital.

As with the first type of measurement, the intangible nature of intellectual capital makes the measurement of effectiveness very challenging. The Managing Knowledge for Business Success report[13] observes that, because knowledge is continually evolving and so deeply woven into the fabric of organizations, "the effects of using it better can never really be measured as a simple one-to-one correspondence (so much knowledge in, so much product out). That kind of measure belongs to an older, industrial business model. Clinging to it in today's world may prove to be a liability." Moreover, an excessive emphasis on quantitative financial measures of success can undermine activities that promise much larger returns in the long term. The report concludes that "measuring the impact of knowledge on business performance is both essential and difficult, and that gauging the success even of individual knowledge projects can be a baffling problem." A few who have tackled this conundrum have simply tossed up their hands, concluding "We can exhaust ourselves in attempting to measure the unmeasurable" (Verna Allee, author of *The Knowledge Evolution*).[14]

Some have chosen approaches to measuring the effectiveness of intellectual capital management that do not focus exclusively on financial measures—Skandia's Navigator and Sveiby's Intangible Asset Monitor, for example. Charles Lucier (Booz-Allen and Hamilton's first chief knowledge officer) and Janet Torsilieri[15] suggest two tiers of nonfinancial outcome measures: operating performance outcomes and direct measures of learning. Examples of operating performance measures include lead times, customer satisfaction, employee productivity. Learning measures include items such as the number of participants in communities of practice, people trained, and customers impacted by the use of knowledge.

A General Model of Intellectual Capital Management

The Effective Knowledge Management Working Group has tackled the issue of measuring intellectual capital in both ways, believing that both are necessary and important. After a year of work, the leading firms that comprise the group have produced a measurement framework containing a small set of indicators of intellectual capital stocks that are common to most organizations. In addition, the framework identifies several key measures of the economic value these stocks bring to organizations. The framework also goes one step further to help organizations understand the flow from these stocks into something of value by introducing a matrix of intellectual capital management processes and enablers.

The framework developed by the Effective Knowledge Management Working Group is situated within a model of Intellectual Capital Management developed by the group from the collective experience of the members and the best thinking on intellectual capital measurement

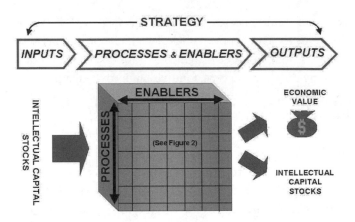

Figure 16.1
Intellectual capital management model

today. As shown in figure 16.1, the model has three primary parts. Working from left to right, a firm begins with its existing stocks of intellectual capital. These stocks become inputs into the second part of the model, the firm's intellectual capital management processes. The processes and their enablers produce two primary types of outputs: 1) changes in the stocks of intellectual capital themselves, and 2) economic value.

With the Intellectual Capital Management Model in hand, it is possible to address the measurement of intellectual capital stocks as well as outputs. On the front end and back end of the model, a firm must measure its existing stocks of intellectual capital and then the changes in those stocks. On the back end, the firm must also measure the economic value produced by the intellectual capital management processes and enablers.

Building upon the measures of intellectual capital stocks, others have proposed or used previously, we identify two sets of intellectual capital indicators: a core set and an "elective" set. The lists of core and elective indicators were created through a conceptual exercise of ranking the universe of possible intellectual capital indicators. All indicators were ranked first based on their relevance to the firms' intellectual capital management objectives. Indicators that ranked roughly in the top quartile were considered eligible to be core indicators. Indicators falling in the second quartiles were labeled "elective" indicators. They are considered elective because, for organizations in certain industries or lines of business, several of the indicators in this group may actually be highly relevant for their intellectual capital management efforts. However, they were not seen as relevant indicators for all firms.

To trim the list of core indicators further and move closer to developing a parsimonious set of key intellectual capital measures, the core indicators were subjected to a second ranking process. In this step each core indicator was ranked according to the following criteria:

- Strategic importance to top executives and external stakeholders
- Availability of information/data
- Applicability to a wide variety of firms

The second ranking process resulted in the set of core indicators found in table 16.1A, with those failing to meet these three criteria falling into the set of elective indicators (see table 16.1B). A similar two-staged process was also undertaken to identify sets of core and elective financial performance outcomes (i.e., measures of economic value). The resulting sets of financial performance measures appear in table 16.2.

The heart of this model, however, is the middle section of processes and enablers. Heretofore, much of the work on intellectual capital has treated this area as a black box. Yet, the processes and enablers are the critical leverage points for enhancing a firm's intellectual capital management capability.

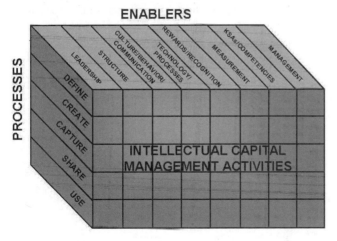

Figure 16.2
Intellectual capital management matrix

Table 16.1a
Core Intellectual Capital Indicators

Human Capital	
Indicator	Measure
Retention of key personnel	The percentage of employees most essential to the organization retained during the previous year.
Ability to attract talented people	Percentage of openings requiring advanced degrees or substantial experience filled in the previous year.
IT literacy	Percentage of employees with a basic level of proficiency in standard office computer applications.
Training expenditures as a percent of payroll	Total expenditures on training in the previous year as a percent of the organization's annual payroll.
Replacement costs of key personnel	Average cost to recruit, hire, and train a someone to fill an essential job in the organization.
Employee satisfaction	Percentage of employees' highly satisfied with the organization and their jobs.
Employee commitment	Percentage of employees' highly dedicated and committed to the organization.
Innovation capital	
R&D expenditures	Total expenditures on conceiving and designing new products and/or services in the previous year.
% of workforce involved in innovation	Percentage of employees with responsibility for conception and design of new products and/or services.
Product freshness	Percentage of all current products and/or services introduced in the last three years.
Process Capital	
Processes documented and mapped	Percentage of business-critical processes documented and analyzed.
Use of documented processes	Percentage of document processes being fully utilized.

Table 16.1a
(continued)

Customer Capital	
Customer satisfaction	Percentage of customers completely satisfied with products and/or services.
Customer retention	Percentage of top customers ending sales contract in the previous year.
Product/service quality	Percentage of customers reporting complaints about products and/or services.
Average duration of customer relationship	Average number of years existing customers have been purchasing products and/or services.
Repeat orders	Percentage current customers that previously purchased products and/or services.

The Intellectual Capital Management Matrix in figure 16.2 begins to unpack the block box of processes.

• Down the left-hand side of the matrix, we identify five general categories of processes:

• Define: Identifying IC Types, Needs, and Requirements

• Create: Creating New IC and Uncovering Existing IC

• Capture: Compiling, Gathering, Representing, Codifying, and Re/Organizing IC

• Share: Disseminating, Distributing, and Transferring IC

• Use: Applying, Incorporating, Reusing, Exploiting, and Leveraging IC

Although the process categories are listed sequentially, in reality, the activities within these processes overlap and reinforce one another (i.e., nonlinear).

Across the top of the matrix, we list the categories of intellectual capital management enablers.

• Leadership: The actions and statements of a company's leaders that demonstrate a strong belief in, understanding of, and commitment to the values and business objectives of the company.

• Structure: The organization of individuals, work groups, teams, and business units within and across a company.

• Culture (Behavior/Communications): Widely shared beliefs, norms, and values about appropriate ways of behaving and conducting work within a company.

Table 16.1b
Elective Intellectual Capital Indicators

Human Capital	Process Capital
Organizational learning measure	Strategy execution
Effectiveness of learning transfer in key areas	Quality of decisions
	Percent of revenues invested in knowledge management
Management credibility	
Employee wages and salaries	Percent of company effectively engaged with customer
Educational levels — % college graduates	
Employee empowerment	IT access (/ employee)
Management experience	Strategy innovativeness
Time in training	Cycle time
% of employees 1 with X + years of service	IT investment/employee
Empowered teams	Process quality (e.g., defects, error rates)
	Time to market
	Collaboration levels
	IT capacity (CPU/DASD/MB)
	IT capacity/employee
	Operating expense ratio
	Administrative expense/total revenues

Innovation Capital	Customer Capital
Number of copyrights/trademarks	Market growth
Number of patents used effectively	Customer needs met
Planned obsolescence	Marketing effectiveness
New opportunities exploited	Annual sales/customer
New markets development investment	Market share
R&D productivity	Average customer size ($)
Sales from products in released last 5 years	Five largest customers as % of revenues
Research leadership	
Net present value (NPV) of patents	Days spent visiting customers
Effectiveness of feedback mechanisms	Support expense/customer
Average age of patents	Image enhancing customers as % of revenues
R&D invested in product design (%)	
Number of patents pending	
Number of new ideas in KM database	
Direct communications to customer/year	

Table 16.2
Core and Elective Financial Performance Measures

Core Measures

Return on equity
Earnings per share
Growth rank in industry
Total shareholder return

Elective Measures

Market capitalization
Return-on-assets
Revenue growth
Market share
Revenue per employee
New product sales
Value added per employee
Market value

• Technology/Processes: The formal tools and methods employed by a company in carrying out its core business activities.
• Rewards and Recognition Systems: The methods of positive reinforcement used by a company to encourage desired behaviors.
• Measurement: The tools and methods used to record, monitor, and track the performance of individuals, units, and the company as a whole.
• Knowledge, Skills, and Abilities / Competencies: The existing capabilities of employees to carry out the work of the company.
• Management: The tasks associated with ensuring that the activities of the company are performed as planned.

While the enablers and the process categories are not in any way new, the matrix represents a novel way of thinking about their interaction and intellectual capital management process as a whole. Each cell of the matrix can be used to identify particular activities that firms undertake as part of a given process with a given enabler. For example, in the Share-Leadership cell, one activity that a firm may undertake is to have their CEO or President model knowledge sharing behaviors through widely visible participation in popular communities of practice within the firm.

Table 16.3
Intellectual Capital Management Activities

Defining IC	Creating IC	Capturing IC	Sharing IC	Using IC
Defining core competencies	Training	Building best practice databases	Sharing best practices	Decision making
Establishing staffing requirements	Succession planning	Building yellow pages	Forming knowledge networks	Strategic planning
Setting competency requirements	Market research	Building expert directories	Forming on-line discussion groups	Product development
Writing job descriptions	Competitive intelligence	Creating knowledge repositories	Deploying decision support systems	Marketing
Defining core processes	Selection and recruitment	Total quality management	Deploying intranets	Forecasting
Defining market segments	Identifying core competencies	Data warehousing	Deploying extranets	
Identifying potential partners or alliances	Best practice searches	Process documentation and reengineering	Internal communication tools	

In table 16.3, we use a sample list of some of the intellectual capital management activities that can be construed as falling within each of these categories of processes in a typical firm. A close look at these examples will reveal activities that most companies already perform but have not previously considered part of their intellectual capital management.

One Step of Many

What the Effective Knowledge Management Working Group has accomplished by creating this intellectual capital measurement framework is but a first step in a process that is likely to take years to unfold. Before the core intellectual capital indicators and financial performance measures can be finalized, for instance, they must be subjected to a wider empirical validation process. Therefore, the next stage of our work is to build a large set of data on the core intellectual capital and financial measures from sizeable number of firms. In 1999, these measures became a standard part of the ASTD Measurement Kit, a data collection tool made available to all types of organizations around the world through the ASTD Benchmarking Service.

The ASTD Benchmarking Service is a free service that collects data from thousands of firms and will allow us to conduct rigorous statistical analyses of the intellectual capital indicators and their value. The statistical analyses of association between the indicators of intellectual capital and financial performance will pinpoint which stocks of intellectual capital are most highly related to positive economic returns.

The outcome of this stage, scheduled to be completed in late 1999, is intended to be a final set of key intellectual capital indicators and a sense of the economic value they produce across a variety of firms. The power of this set of indicators is easy to underestimate for it will provide a standard that allows firms to compare investments in intellectual capital not only across intellectual capital management endeavors, but also with other firms. Systematic comparisons using these standard measures will facilitate the attempts of external stakeholders, particularly investors, to assess the potential future performance of firms using more than just today's backward-looking balance sheets.

The set of key intellectual capital measures, however, is only half of the measurement toolkit that firms and their stakeholders will need to evaluate their intellectual capital management. These indicators and their relationships to financial performance only illustrate what intellectual capital firms have and its contribution to financial performance. That is, they answer the question of what, but not how—in particular, how do firms create economic value from their stocks of intellectual capital?

This is the question that will be addressed in the third stage of our work with the help of the Intellectual Capital Management Matrix of processes and enablers. Once the core intellectual capital indicators are finalized, the firms participating in the ASTD Benchmarking service will provide information using this matrix on the intellectual capital management activities they undertake internally. Further analyses will permit the identification of the intellectual capital management activities associated with positive economic returns. These activities in essence will constitute a set of points at which firms can better leverage their intellectual capital management process. The result of this stage will be a widely applicable tool by which firms can diagnose the strengths and weaknesses of their intellectual capital management efforts.

Seeing the Future

The future belongs to intellectual capital in many ways. In the dawning Knowledge Era, the future performance of firms will be determined in large part by its intellectual capital. Firms that create and leverage this unique source of competitive advantage most effectively will be the winners in tomorrow's business climate. In addition, because intellectual capital is at the bottom of every firm's value chain, it is the best predictor of a firm's potential future performance. Without methods of measuring the value of firms' intellectual capital stocks and efforts to manage those stocks, however, this potential will be not be realized by many firms, even some with tremendous potential. Without standard measures, firms and their stakeholders will have no means of judging the value and effectiveness of firms' investments in intellectual capital. The Intellectual Capital Management assessment framework represents a major step toward providing precisely the kinds of methods that firms and their stakeholders need to see into the future.

References

1. Laurie Bassi and Brian Hackett, "Leveraging Intellectual Capital," *HR Executive Review* 5, no. 3 (1997).

2. Ernst & Young, LLP. *Executive Perspectives on Knowledge in the Organization* (Cambridge, Mass.: Ernst & Young, 1997).

3. Leif Edvinsson and Michael Malone, *Intellectual Capital: Realizing Your Company's True Value by Finding Its Hidden Brainpower* (New York: Harper Business, 1997).

4. Thomas Stewart, *Intellectual Capital: The New Wealth of Organizations (New York: Currency/Doubleday, 1997).*

5. Karl-Erik Sveiby, *The New Organizational Wealth: Managing and Measuring Knowledge-Based Assets* (San Francisco: Berrett-Koehler, 1997).

6. David Skyrme and Debra Amidon, *Creating the Knowledge-Based Business* (London: Business Intelligence, 1997).

7. Paul Strassmann, *The Value of Computers, Information, and Knowledge,* (Unpublished manuscript, 1996).

8. Charles Handy, *The Age of Unreason*, (London: Arrow Books, 1989).

9. S. Lankler, "Through Knowledge Management Initiatives, Employers Turn Intellectual Resources into Capital," *Bulletin to Management* 47, no. 45 (1996).

10. D. Cohen, D. E. Smith, L. Prusak, and R. Azzarello, *Managing Knowledge for Business Success*. Report No. 1194-97-CH. (New York: The Conference Board, 1997).

11. American Productivity and Quality Center, *Knowledge Management*, (Houston, Texas, 1996).

12. Ante Pulic, "The Physical and Intellectual Capital of Austrian Banks," (Unpublished manuscript, University Graz, Austria: Institute for International Management, 1996).

13. Cohen, Smith, and Azzarello, *Managing Knowledge for Business Success*.

14. Verna Allee, *The Knowledge Evolution: Expanding Organizational Intelligence*, (Boston: Butterworth-Heinemann, 1997).

15. Charles Lucier and Janet Torsilieri, "Why Knowledge Programs Fail: A C.E.O.'S Guide to Managing Learning," *Strategy and Business* 9 (4th Quarter 1997).

17

Managing Organizational Knowledge by Diagnosing Intellectual Capital

Nick Bontis

Managers and researchers alike recognize the importance of managing a firm's most critical resource: organizational knowledge. The advent of the knowledge era drives the importance of recognizing intellectual capital even further. Interest in the field of intellectual capital is accelerating. This chapter conceptualizes intellectual capital using extant theories of strategic management. The purpose is to take stock and advance the state of the field by reviewing past and current studies. The field is cross-disciplinary and this offers a variety of functional perspectives. Accountants are interested in how to measure it on the balance sheet, information technologists want to codify it on systems, sociologists want to balance power with it, psychologists want to develop minds because of it, human resource managers want to calculate an ROI on it, and training and development officers want to make sure that they can build it. A conceptualization of intellectual capital yielding three subconstructs is presented which include human capital, structural capital, and relational capital. Finally, suggestions are made to managers on how they can leverage the knowledge in their organizations.

Introduction

As the third millennium approaches, managers and researchers alike require new conceptualizations that deal with the management of knowledge. For this reason, intellectual capital is a critically important area of research that warrants further study. The field of intellectual capital initially started appearing in the popular press in the early 1990s when Stewart described it as a "brand new tennis ball—fuzzy, but with a lot of bounce" in FORTUNE [1][2]. However, this statement acts as a detriment for the survival of this field in academia. Most "bouncy" topics that are researched extensively (e.g., reengineering, quality circles, management by objectives) are sometimes frowned upon in academic circles because they are considered nothing more than popular fads. Due to their temporal shortcomings, they are deemed not worthy of serious study. On the other hand, the "fuzzy" aspect of intellectual capital captures the curious interest of practitioners who are always on the prowl for finding solutions to difficult challenges. Hence, the popularity of this topic during its genesis has been sponsored by business practitioners. It is for this audience that the conceptualization of intellectual capital resonates most.

The study of the field of intellectual capital is akin to the pursuit of the "elusive intangible." Academics and practitioners alike recognize and appreciate the tacit nature of organizational knowledge. Furthermore, intellectual capital is typically conceptualized as a set of sub-phenomena. The real problem with intellectual capital lies in its measurement. Unfortunately, an invisible conceptualization—regardless of its underlying simplicity—becomes an abyss for the academic researcher. To make matters worse, intellectual capital is conceptualized from numerous disciplines making the field a mosaic of perspectives. Accountants are interested in how to measure it on the balance sheet, information technologists want to codify it on systems, sociologists want to balance power with it, psychologists want to develop minds because of it, human resource managers want to calculate an ROI on it, and training and development officers want to make sure that they can build it. This field may be growing at a fantastic rate, but does anyone know where it is heading? Academics may want to ask their customers.

Business students have spent decades learning how to manage scarce resources. The traditional economic model rests on the tenets of the scarcity assumption that states that supply and demand determine market price. As all introductory economic students have learned, if supply goes down, then price goes up (assuming demand is constant). However, knowledge as a resource does not comply with the scarcity assumption. The more knowledge is supplied (or shared) the more highly it is valued. Furthermore, when was the last time the demand for knowledge went down? In fact, scientific folklore in the early 1900s stated that all the information in the world doubled every 30 years. As the 1970s approached, that number was reduced to 7 years. Prognosticators have pushed this notion further and state that by the year 2010 all the information in the world will double every 11 hours. Do we need a better reason to appreciate the importance of educating our management students within the intellectual capital framework?

Intellectual Capital is an Organizational Resource

In our present economy, more and more businesses are evolving whose value is not based on their tangible resources but on what Itami calls their *intangible resources* [3]. Tangible resources are those typically found on the balance sheet of a company such as cash, buildings, and machinery. The other category comprises intangible resources: people and their expertise, business processes and market assets such as customer loyalty, repeat business, reputation, and so forth. The annual reports of companies like Skandia are working toward a new balance sheet that makes more sense in today's marketplace [4][5][6][7][8][9]. This new balance sheet highlights the difference between visible (explicit) accounting and invisible (implicit) accounting. Traditional annual reports have concentrated on reporting what can be explicitly calculated such as receivables, fixed assets and so forth. Skandia has made an effort to report on their invisible assets such as intellectual capital, which provides the company with much of its market value added. Bontis cites other organizations that are following Skandia's lead that can be found in the service sector and any enterprise where businesses, such as software development start-ups, management consultants, high-technology ventures, life sciences and health care, media and entertainment and law firms, rely primarily on people [10].

Although intangible assets may represent competitive advantage, Collis reports that organizations do not understand their nature and value [11]. Managers do not know the value of their own intellectual capital. They do not know if they have the people, resources or business processes in place to make a success of a new strategy. They do not understand what know-how, management potential or creativity they have access to with their employees. Because they are devoid of such information, they are rightsizing, downsizing and reengineering in a vacuum.

That organizations are operating in a vacuum is not surprising, as they do not have any methods or tools to use which would enable them to analyze their intellectual capital stocks and organizational learning flows. To that end, a methodology and valuation system is required that will enable managers to identify, document and value their knowledge management. This will enable them to make information-rich decisions when they are planning to invest in the protection of their various intellectual properties.

As mentioned earlier, intellectual capital research has primarily evolved from the desires of practitioners [10][12][13][14][15]. Consequently, recent developments have come largely in the form of popular press articles in business magazines and national newspapers. The challenge for academics is to frame the phenomenon using extant theories in order to develop a more rigorous conceptualization. This chapter coalesces many perspectives from numerous fields of study in an attempt to raise the understanding and importance of this phenomenon. The objective here is to conceptualize and frame the existing literature on intellectual capital as a foundation for further study.

Knowledge creation by business organizations has been virtually neglected in management studies even though Nonaka and Takeuchi are convinced that this process has been the most important source of international competitiveness for some time [16]. Even management guru Peter Drucker heralds the arrival of a new economy, referred to as the "knowledge society" [17]. He claims that in this society, knowledge is not just another resource alongside the traditional factors of production—labor, capital, and land—but the only meaningful resource today.

Until recently there has been little attempt to identify, and give structure to, the nature and role of intangible resources in the strategic management of a business. This is partly due to the fact that it is often very difficult for accountants and economists to allocate an orthodox valuation to intangibles as they rarely have an exchange value. In consequence, Hall writes that they usually lie outside the province of the commodity-based models of economics and accountancy [18]. Johnson and Kaplan state that:

A company's economic value is not merely the sum of the values of its tangible assets, whether measurable at historic cost, replacement cost, or current market value prices. It also includes the value of intangible assets: the stock of innovative products, the knowledge of flexible and high-quality production processes, employee talent, and morals, customer loyalty and product awareness, reliable suppliers, efficient distribution networks and the like. Reported earnings cannot show the company's decline in value when it depletes its stock of intangible resources. Recent overemphasis on achieving superior long-term earnings performance is occurring just at the time when such performance has become a far less valid indicator of changes in the company's long-term competitive position. [19: 202]

Having discussed the importance of the intellectual capital field, we now turn to a review of the literature in order to understand the genesis of its conceptualization.

Review of the Literature

Today, the nature and performance consequences of the strategies used by organizations to develop, maintain and exploit knowledge for innovation, constitutes an important topic in the field of business strategy, but one that has received inadequate treatment in the extant literature [20]. Orthodox economics side-steps the topic completely by assuming that all firms may choose from a set of universally accessible "production functions" that completely determine production cost structures and therefore do not lead to any knowledge-based performance differences [21] [22].

Partly in response to this shortcoming, a number of theories have developed during the past several decades in the field of strategy. Organizational economics and organization theory hold that firm-level differences in knowledge do exist and, moreover, that these differences play a large role in determining economic performance. These approaches include mainstream strategy [23][24], the resource-based view of the firm [18] [22][25][26][27][28][29][30], evolutionary theory [31][32], and core competencies [33].

Economic analysis of competitive advantage focuses on how industry structure determines the profitability of firms in an industry. However, firm differences, not industry differences, are thought by many to be at the heart of strategic analysis [21][34]. Furthermore, while most formal economic tools are used to determine optimal product-market activities, the traditional concept of strategy is phrased in terms of the resource position of the firm [27][35]. Generally speaking, the indifferent treatment of knowledge in the neoclassical economics tradition endures. Firms are assumed to have the same fixed knowledge as the invisible hand of the market jockeys them around. This theoretical lens is deficient in describing the phenomenon of knowledge because of two important assumptions. Neoclassical economics assumes that all parties have perfect and complete information and that resources are completely mobile. These two assumptions are in conflict with the notion that individuals have limits to their cognitive abilities [36] and that some forms of tacit knowledge are impossible to articulate [37]. This form of tacit knowledge that is embedded in the organization can be better explained by the evolutionary theory of the firm.

Polanyi's tacit-explicit distinction was introduced into the literature by Nelson and Winter in their evolutionary theory of the firm [31][37]. At the crux of Nelson and Winter's evolutionary theory are *organizational routines* that allow firms the special context in which tacit and explicit knowledge interact:

Organizational routines are the organization's genetic material, some explicit in bureaucratic rules, some implicit in the organization's culture. The interaction between the explicit and the tacit is evolutionary in that the choices made by individuals are selected in or out according to their utility in a specific historical and economic reality, and eventually embedded in organizational routines that then shape and constrain further individual choices. [31: 134]

Although the evolutionary theory of the firm improves on the deficiencies of the neoclassical economic tradition, it still lacks the contextual implications of a changing business environment. It may be true that organizational knowledge is embedded in routines, but evolutionary theory does not describe persistence or change of routines over time. For example, if explicit rules have been codified at one point in time, one can argue that these routines may not be appropriate at some later point in time when environmental conditions have forced an alternative strategic orientation. Pushing this notion forward, it is argued that organizational routines represent a collection of embedded rules from different times representing different environmental contexts. This internal focus on the firm's rules and resources is the basis for the resource-based view of the firm.

The resource-based view of the firm suggests that a business enterprise is best viewed as a collection of sticky and difficult-to-imitate resources and capabilities [25][27][28]. Firm-specific resources can be physical, such as production techniques protected by patents or trade secrets, or intangible, such as brand equity or operating routines.

A confusing issue with the resource-based view begins with definitions [38]. There is an embarrassing profusion of riches in phrases such as *distinctive competence* [39], *strategic firm resources* [40], *invisible assets* [3], *strategic firm-specific assets* [30], *core competencies* [33], *corporate capabilities* [41], *dynamic capabilities* [42], *combinative capabilities* [43] and others. Although some researchers claim differences in meanings, a few have simply found an opportunity to add their own two cents worth to a growing market of definitions. An alternate route to the nomenclature regurgitation would be to start with a general definition of resources as inputs and then to analyze the circumstances under which they are useful [38].

The resource-based view has other limitations. Given the emphasis on firm resources, it is argued that the only feasible unit of analysis for the resource-based view paradigm is the organization. However, past research has shown that this is somewhat limiting. Empirically, Schmalensee discovered that profit differences are attributable mostly to industry effects, and firm effects are insignificant [44]. Hansen and Wernerfelt found that both industry and firm effects were significant and independent [45]. Later, Kessides discovered significant firm effects but these were dominated by industry effects [46]. In sum, the resource-based view may have too much of an internal focus on the firm. Other researchers have taken the resource-based view further by emphasizing knowledge and learning as the critical resource. Thus, the knowledge-based view of the firm was created as an extension of the resource-based view.

Knowledge management theorists argue that knowledge is the preeminent resource of the firm [47][48][49][50][51][52]. The knowledge-based view of the firm identifies the primary rationale for the firm as the creation and application of knowledge [16][43][47][48][49][53][54]. Spender states that the knowledge-based view of the firm "can yield insights beyond the production-function and resource-based theories by creating a new view of the firm as a dynamic, evolving, quasi-autonomous system of knowledge production and application" [50: 59]. Viewing the firm as a knowledge system focuses the attention not on the allegedly given resources that the firm must use but, to use Penrose's [25: 25] language, on the services rendered by a firm's resources.

Much of the literature on intellectual capital stems from an accounting and financial perspective. Many of these researchers are interested in answering the following two questions: i) what is causing firms to be worth so much more than their book value? and ii) what specifically is in this intangible asset? Stewart defines intellectual capital as the intellectual material that has been formalized, captured, and leveraged to create wealth by producing a higher-valued asset [1][2][55]. Following the work of Bontis [10][56], Roos, Roos, Dragonetti and Edvinsson [57], Stewart [1][2][55], Sveiby [58], Edvinsson and Malone [59], Saint-Onge [15], Sullivan and Edvinsson [60], as well as Edvinsson and Sullivan [14], among others, intellectual capital is defined as encompassing: i) human capital; ii) structural capital; and iii) relational capital. These sub-phenomena encompass the intelligence found in human beings, organizational routines and network relationships respectively. This field typically looks at organizational knowledge as a static asset in an organization—a so-called stock. This concerns many theorists who are also interested in the flow of knowledge. Furthermore, intellectual capital research does not cater to changes in cognition or behavior of individuals, which is necessary for learning and improvement.

Proposed Conceptualization

Adopting Kogut and Zander's [43] perspective on higher-order organizing principles, a proposed conceptualization of intellectual capital is put forth (see figure 17.1). Intellectual capital is a second order multi-dimensional construct. Its three sub-domains include: i) Human Capital—the tacit knowledge embedded in the minds of the employees; ii) Structural Capital—the organizational routines of the business, and iii) Relational Capital—the knowledge embedded in the relationships established with the outside environment [10][14].

Organizational learning, as described by Chris Argyris at Harvard, among others, has been thought of as the flow of knowledge in a firm [61]; it follows then that intellectual capital is the stock of knowledge in the firm. To marry the two, it may be useful to consider intellectual capital as the stock unit of organizational learning. However, intellectual capital cannot necessarily be taught through education. The most precious knowledge in an organization often cannot be passed on [62].

Prior to continuing the conceptualization of intellectual capital stocks, it may be helpful to define *what it is not*. Intellectual capital does not

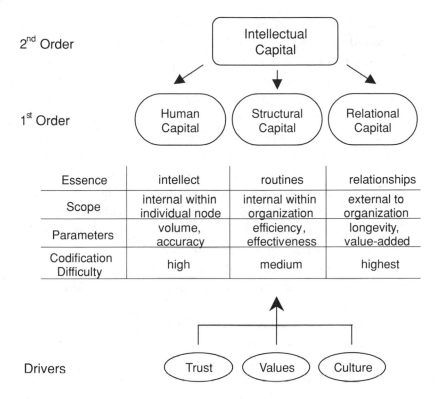

Figure 17.1
2nd-order conceptualization of intellectual capital.

include intellectual property. Intellectual property are assets that include copyrights, patents, semiconductor topography rights, and various design rights. They also include trade and service marks. Undertaking an intellectual property audit is not a new idea. However many organizations find that the results of an intellectual property audit are not particularly useful. After all, knowing that you own a patent is not a lot of use if that fact is not accompanied with information concerning its potential. This is evaluated from the various aspects that the patent can be viewed from including: return on investment; commercial potential; competitive advantage, and so on. It is important to note that intellectual property assets are usually considered from their legal perspective, which should mirror that "raison d'être." A patent for its own sake has no point or value. Therefore, intellectual property and intellectual capital are considered mutually exclusive but the former can be considered an output of the latter.

The conceptualization of intellectual capital shall continue with an examination of the "organizational knowledge" literature. Although theories differ in their terminology and the degree to which they explicitly discuss the attributes of organizational knowledge, they all concur that superior performance, including the procurement of economic profits, results at least in part from the exploitation of distinctive process knowledge that is not articulable and that can be acquired only through experience—in short, knowledge that is "tacit" in nature [32][37]. Yet, in emphasizing the positive effects of tacit knowledge on economic performance, these theories suffer from a serious shortcoming as well. While they concede that tacit knowledge limits the ability of the organization to compete in a new industrial environment in which a substantially different knowledge base is required for competitive success, they fail to recognize that tacit knowledge also limits the ability of the organization to adapt to the changing competitive requirements of the existing industry within which it already operates.

The phenomenon of intellectual capital can be dissected into three sub-domains. Each will be described in the context of its essence, scope, parameter and codification difficulty. Subsequent to that description, three drivers—*trust*, *values*, and *culture*—will be evaluated for their impact on intellectual capital development.

Human Capital

First, the organization's members possess individual tacit knowledge (i.e., inarticulable skills and intellect necessary to perform their functions) [31]. In order to illustrate the degree to which tacit knowledge characterizes the human capital of an organization, it is useful to conceive of the organization as a productive process that receives tangible and informational inputs from the environment, produces tangible and informational outputs that enter the environment, and is characterized internally by a series of flows among a network of nodes and ties or links (see figure 17.2).

A node represents the work performed—either pure decision-making, innovative creativity, improvisation [63] or some combination of the three —by a single member of the organization or by parallel, functionally equivalent members who do not interact with one another as part of the productive process (see figure 17.2). Thus, individual tacit knowledge, when present, exists at the nodes themselves. A tie or link is directional in nature and represents a flow of intermediate product or information from a given node. Every node has at least one tie or link originating from it, while multiple ties originating from a single node imply that the task performed at the node includes a decision about where to direct the subsequent flow. Structural tacit knowledge, when present, implies that no member of the organization has an explicit overview of these ties and consequently of the corresponding arrangement of nodes (see subsequent discussion on *Structural Capital*). Accordingly, a productive process characterized by a substantial degree of tacit knowledge is arranged as a hodgepodge of nodes lacking any discernible organizational logic.

Point A in figure 17.2 represents the core of human capital. Multiple nodes (human capital units) attempt to align themselves in some form of recognizable pattern so that intellectual capital becomes more readily interpretable. This point represents the lowest level of difficulty for development as well as the lowest level of externality from the core of the organization. Human capital has also been defined on an individual level by Hudson as the combination of these four factors: i) your genetic inheritance; ii) your education; iii) your experience; and iv) your attitudes about life and business [64]. Human capital is important because it is a source of innovation and strategic renewal, whether it is from brainstorming in a research lab, daydreaming at the office, throwing out old files, re-engineering new processes, improving personal skills or developing new leads in a sales rep's little black book. The essence of human capital is the sheer intelligence of the organizational member. The scope of human capital is limited to the knowledge node (i.e., internal to the mind of the employee). It can be measured (although it is difficult) as a function of volume (i.e., a third degree measure encompassing size, location and time). Unfortunately, human capital is also very difficult to codify.

Wright, McMahan, and McWilliams working from a resource-based perspective argue that in certain circumstances sustained competitive advantage can accrue from "a pool of human capital" that is larger than those groups, such as senior managers and other elites, who are traditionally identified as determining organizational success or failure [65].

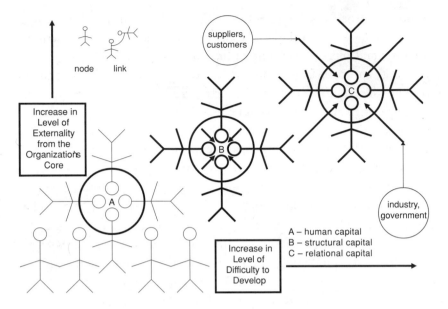

Figure 17.2
Discriminating intellectual capital sub-domains

This is achieved through the human capital adding value, being unique or rare, imperfectly imitable and not substitutable with another resource by competing firms. Storey supports this focus:

This type of resource [human capital] can embody intangible assets such as unique configurations of complementary skills, and tacit knowledge, painstakingly accumulated, of customer wants and internal processes. [66: 4]

Structural Capital

The organization itself embodies structural tacit knowledge, which exists, as Winter points out, in "the myriad of relationships that enable the organization to function in a coordinated way [but] are reasonably understood by [at most] the participants in the relationship and a few others..." This means that "the organization is...accomplishing its aims by following rules that are not known as such to most of the participants in the organization" [32: 171].

This construct deals with the mechanisms and structures of the organization that can help support employees in their quest for optimum intellectual performance and therefore overall business performance. An individual can have a high level of intellect, but if the organization has poor systems and procedures by which to track his or her actions, the overall intellectual capital will not reach its fullest potential.

An organization with strong structural capital will have a supportive culture that allows individuals to try things, to fail, to learn, and to try again. If the culture unduly penalizes failure, its success will be minimal. Structuring intellectual assets with information systems can turn individual know-how into group property [67]. It is the concept of structural capital that allows intellectual capital to be measured and developed in an organization. In effect, without structural capital, intellectual capital would just be human capital. This construct therefore contains elements of efficiency, transaction times, procedural innovativeness and access to information for codification into knowledge. It also supports elements of cost minimization and profit maximization per employee. Structural capital is the critical link that allows intellectual capital to be measured at an organizational level.

Point B in figure 17.2 illustrates the structural ties or links of human capital nodes that are required to transform human capital into structural capital. The arrows within structural capital represent the focus of intellectual capital development from the nodes into the organization's core. The essence of structural capital is the knowledge embedded within the routines of an organization. Its scope lies internal to the firm but external to the human capital nodes. It can be measured (although it is difficult) as a function of efficiency (i.e., an output function per some temporal unit). Organizational processes (such as those found in structural capital) can eventually be codified.

Infrastructure assets are those technologies, methodologies and processes that enable the organization to function. Examples include methodologies for assessing risk, methods of managing a sales force, databases of information on the market or customers, communication systems such as e-mail and teleconferencing systems. Basically, the elements that make up the way the organization works. Such elements are peculiar to each business, and their value to the organization can only be attained by survey within the target organization. Sadly the acquisition of infrastructure assets is frequently as a result of some crisis, positioning them as a necessary evil rather than the structure which makes the organization strong. Marketing the value of infrastructure assets to the individual within the organization is also important, in order to share with them the aspects where infrastructure protects, enhances and coordinates organizational resources.

Relational Capital

Knowledge of market channels, customer and supplier relationships, as well as a sound understanding of governmental or industry association impacts, is the main theme of relational capital. Frustrated managers often do not recognize that they can tap into a wealth of knowledge from their own clients and suppliers. After all, understanding what customers want in a product or a service better than anyone else is what makes someone a business leader as opposed to a follower.

Relational capital represents the potential an organization has due to ex-firm intangibles. These intangibles include the knowledge embedded in customers, suppliers, the government or related industry associations. Point C in figure 17.2 illustrates that relational capital is the most difficult of the three sub-domains to develop since it is the most external to the organization's core. The arrows represent the knowledge that must flow from external to the organization (i.e., its environment) into the organization's core by way of linked nodes. The essence of relational capital is knowledge embedded in relationships external to the firm. Its scope lies external to the firm and external to the human capital nodes. It can be measured (although it is difficult) as a function of longevity (i.e., relational capital becomes more valuable as time goes on). Due to its external nature, knowledge embedded in relational capital is the most difficult to codify.

One manifestation of relational capital that is often referred to is "market orientation." There is no consensus on a definition of market orientation, but two recent definitions have become widely accepted. The first is from Kohli and Jaworski , who define market orientation as the organization-wide generation of market intelligence pertaining to current and future needs of customers, dissemination of intelligence horizontally and vertically within the organization, and organization-wide action or responsiveness to market intelligence [68]. The second is from Narver and Slater, who define market orientation as a one-dimension construct consisting of three behavioral components and two decision criteria—customer orientation, competitor orientation, interfunctional coordination, a long-term focus, and a profit objective [69]. With close parallels to Kohli and Jaworski, Narver and Slater include the generation and dissemination of market intelligence as well as managerial action. Hulland posits that there exist two dimensions of organizational learning in the marketing context: market orientation (as discussed above) and market learning systems (which, in the context of this particular conceptualization of intellectual capital, will be considered as a function of structural capital) [70].

Teece discussed the importance of interorganizational and intraorganizational relationships and linkages to the development and profitable commercialization of new technology [71]. He argued that as firms have moved from a serial product-delivery process (i.e., a sequential, lock step process through the value chain) to a parallel product-delivery process (i.e., simultaneous development throughout the various functions), the need for cooperative and coordinating capabilities have increased. Pennings and Harianto also presented a theory of innovation which presumes that new technologies emerge from a firm's accumulated stock of skills (i.e., internal innovative capabilities) and their history of technological networking (i.e., external innovative capabilities) [72]. Relational capital builds on the intraorganizational relationships and technological networking that is available in the environment.

The organizing principles established in an innovative firm include rules by which work is coordinated and by which information is gathered and communicated. This social knowledge is not easily disseminated because it is embedded in the idiosyncratic firm-specific history and routines of the organizations entire system [73][74]. Companies need intelligence-gathering capabilities to keep up with technology development both inside and outside the industry. This includes not only formal processes and information systems but informal systems based on tacit understanding by employees and senior managers that they have a responsibility to the company to gather and disseminate technological information [75][76]. Effective communication between partners is essential in technology collaboration and can prove difficult to build [77]. However, once established this communication channel serves as an important source of information about the other interdependent organization.

Trust, Values and Culture as Intellectual Capital Drivers

As depicted in figure 17.1, the conceptualization of intellectual capital includes three supporting drivers for sub-domain development. Trust is a very important element of both inter- and intraorganizational cooperation [78]. Although the importance of trust has always been evident and is widely articulated in the nonacademic literature, it has only recently become a topic of major academic concern. Organizational group members need to have mutual confidence that tasks can be delegated (i.e., that others know what to do, are motivated to do it, and are competent to do it) and that monitoring can be fairly casual. The literature on external cooperative relationships suggests that choosing an external partner with complementary technologies and strategies and building a cooperative relationship based on trust and mutual respect can be problematic [77]. Trust, mutual respect, and compatible modes of behavior cannot be decreed or even adequately specified as an abstract entity. That is why many firms typically begin a relationship by cooperating in less strategically central areas and build up a body of experience in working with a partner over a period of years [79]. Generally, all participants are seen to have an affect on the trust in a relationship [80].

As organizations become flatter, more geographically dispersed, and more prone to reorganization, traditional notions of control are being updated to reflect an increased need to trust individuals and groups to carry out critical organizational tasks without close and frequent supervision [81]. Trust is a belief related to likely outcomes, a belief that reflects an actor's cognitive representations of situational contingencies. Since researchers have tended to have difficulty separating antecedents and outcomes of trust, this dual role may also be salient in the context of intellectual capital.

Organizations that have a culture that supports and encourages cooperative innovation should attempt to understand what it is about their culture that gives them a competitive advantage and develop and nurture those cultural attributes [28]. Culture constitutes the beliefs, values, and attitudes pervasive in the organization and results in a language, symbols, and habits of behavior and thought. Increasingly it is recognized as the conscious or unconscious product of the senior management's belief [18]. Barney discussed the potential for organizational culture to serve as a source of sustained competitive advantage. He concluded that "firms that do not have the required cultures cannot engage in activities that will modify their cultures and generate sustained superior performance because their modified cultures typically will be neither rare nor imperfectly imitable" [28: 656].

The core of culture is formed by values [83]. In most organizations that have pursued formalized intellectual capital management initiatives, the common component that drives the program is value alignment. Brian Hall's work on value alignment in organizations is fascinating [82]. In much of his research and consulting work, organizations whose employees possess higher value alignment tend to realize above average performance. Value alignment seems to be critical in tempering the fine line between "knowledge hoarding" and "knowledge sharing" in organizations. If employees' goals and values are synchronized together as group, there is higher possibility of creating greater human capital for the organization since most individuals would be willing to share what they know for the greater good. Hall claims that values are the key to any successful organizational transformation because "values are basically a quality information system that when understood tell about what drives human beings and organizations and causes them to be exceptional" [82:viii].

Past and Future Research

Intellectual capital research thus far has been primarily of the anecdotal variety. Most researchers have conducted case-based reviews of organizations that have established intellectual capital initiatives. Other researchers have documented the metrics that have been developed by Skandia and others. What the field needs at this point is a more concentrated focus on rigorous, metric development and quantitative evaluation.

Using survey data, Bontis has already shown a very strong and positive relationship between Likert-type measures of intellectual capital and business performance in a pilot study (see figure 17.3) [56]. Likert-type scales tap into the perceptions of individuals by agreeing or disagreeing to certain statements. The explanatory power of the final specified model was highly significant and substantive (R2 = 56.0%, p-value < 0.001).

The model in figure 17.3 confirms that human capital is the critical antecedent that leads to structural and customer capital in boosting business performance [56]. Several other researchers have also supplied

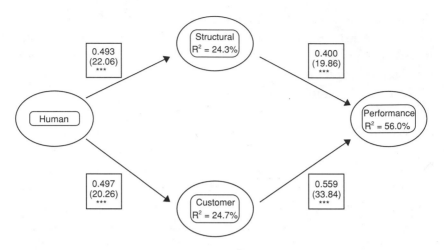

Figure 17.3
Diamond specification model. Source: Bontis [56]

evidence of a positive relationship between an organization's financial, as
well as organizational performance, and its level of one of the sub-domains
of intellectual capital: relational capital. As discussed previously, contained
within the conceptualization of relational capital is market orientation.
Narver and Slater find that market orientation and business performance
(ROA) are strongly related [69]. Jaworski and Kohli report on a study of
222 US business units suggesting that market orientation is an important
determinant of performance, regardless of market turbulence, competitive intensity, and technological turbulence [84]. Also Ruekert reports a
positive relationship between degree of market orientation and long run
financial performance [85]. In the UK, Greenley observed that a group of
companies with higher market orientation performed better (ROI) than
a group with lower market orientation [86]. Back in 1987, Lusch and
Laczniak investigated how a company's increased emphasis on an extended
marketing concept, similar to market orientation, is positively associated
with financial performance [87]. Not directly related to business performance, but yet in line with intellectual capital, Atuahene-Gima infers
from an Australian sample that market orientation is an important contributor to new product success [88]. Biemans and Harmsen have also
concluded on the basis of several other studies that having a market orientation in product development has proven to be a highly critical factor
for new product success [89].

Covin and Stivers surveyed companies in the US and Canada and found that the importance of intellectual capital varied with the amount of knowledge management focus that each firmed possessed [90]. Recent trends in organizational structure have seen a move toward "de-layering," "lean production," making decisions "closer to the customer," establishing "semi-autonomous work-groups" and an emphasis on employee involvement and empowerment [91][92][93][94]. Again it seems reasonable to hypothesize that, other things being equal, the increased intellectual capital development and thus "nodal" power generated by environmental turbulence should be more evenly distributed throughout the organization in these "leaner," "flatter" structures.

There has also been research that contrasts different knowledge-based tools. Bontis, Dragonetti, Roos, and Jacobsen contrast intellectual capital frameworks with the balanced score card, economic value added and human resource accounting [95]. Metric development has also moved forward in the related field of organizational learning where Mary Crossan and her colleagues have developed frameworks and instruments that examine knowledge stocks and flows using an organizational learning framework [96][97][98].

Conclusion

Some critics have argued that intellectual capital is just another organizational fad that will last for three to five more years, and then managers will move on to the next attempt at finding the philosophical silver bullet. In a recent ASAP feature article Rutledge blasts the intellectual capital field and emphatically claims that you are a fool if you buy into this [99]. He warns managers that if by chance they meet people with the word "knowledge" or "intellectual capital" on their business cards, they should walk quickly and quietly away. His argument centers around the fact that the driving force behind this field are stakeholders and not shareholders of companies and therefore social agendas, not performance, will drive business decisions. Although he is correct in touting the importance of the "softer stuff" related to intellectual capital, he cannot argue against its mass appeal. Dozens upon dozens of conferences, workshops and seminars are being offered all over the world on how to measure and value intellectual capital each year. Practitioners are voting with their feet.

Although its popularity is not disputed, it is important to be skeptical when anyone claims that they have found the magical formula or calculation for intellectual capital. It will never be measured in the traditional dollar terms we know. At best, we will see a slow proliferation of customized metrics that will be disclosed in traditional financial statements as addendums. Metrics such as those used by Skandia and others in the financial services industry as reported by Bontis will continue to be developed and analyzed longitudinally [100]. Bassi and Van Buren note that even though the stock market is already providing handsome rewards to companies that successfully leverage their intellectual capital, few firms have formalized a measurement process [12]. The significance and lack of progress on the issue are also clear from a recent survey of 431 organizations in the U.S. and Europe by Skyrme and Amidon who ranked "measuring the value and performance of knowledge assets" highest in importance more than any other management issue except "changing people's behavior" 43 versus 54 percent respectively [101].

If it is a fad, when will it end? The immense proliferation of the "Internet" as an information-sharing vehicle supports the argument that knowledge management and the development of intellectual capital is most sustainable as an organizational goal [102]. As long as the economic forces embrace new knowledge-intensive industries, the field of intellectual capital will have an important place in the minds of academics and practitioners. As with the human body's muscles, intellectual capital management may suffer from, "if you don't use it, you lose it." There is an increasing emphasis on survival of the fittest in international competitiveness. In order to stay alive, organizations must win the race [103]. Future research in this area may want to tap into comparisons of intellectual capital characteristics by personality type with the use of the Myers-Briggs Type Indicator [104]. Also, researchers could correlate intellectual capital metrics with cultural diversity and values.

The emphasis on knowledge management and intellectual capital has grown tremendously during the past decade, but these concepts suffer from certain limitations. Researchers have done a fair job identifying where intellectual capital resides in an organization. But most managers are more interested in learning how to measure and leverage this knowledge. Accountants and financial analysts have tried to develop metrics to measure these intangible assets, but these metrics typically are company-specific, do not easily conform to Generally Accepted Accounting Principles (GAAP), and are not general enough for the Canadian Institute of Chartered Accountants (CICA), the Financial Accounting Standards Board (FASB) or the Securities and Exchange Commission (SEC) to adopt.

Despite the challenges, senior managers can begin to strategically manage their intellectual capital by following these steps as suggested by Bontis [10]:

1. Conduct an initial intellectual capital audit. Such an examination may include designing and administering a survey using Likert-type scales to get a snapshot of the benchmark level of intellectual capital in existence. Firms such as Skandia use their own metrics for measuring intellectual capital. Each firm is different and must thrive in the context of its own industry. Each organization should design metrics for its own strategic purposes.

2. Make knowledge management a requirement for evaluation purposes for each employee and assign personal targets for intellectual capital development. For example, you might have each employee aim to learn something the organization currently does not know.

3. Formally define the role of knowledge in your business and in your industry. Find and secure the greatest resources for intellectual capital inside and outside your firm from sources such as industry associations, academia, customers, suppliers, and the government.

4. Recruit a leader responsible for the development of intellectual capital. This person must have an integrated background in human resources, strategy, and information technology.

5. Classify your intellectual portfolio by producing a knowledge map of your organization—that is, determine in which people and systems knowledge resides. For example, you could create a central database in which all competitive intelligence information can be accumulated and accessed.

6. Use information systems and information-sharing tools that aid in knowledge exchange and codifying. Such tools include e-mail, intranets, groupware such as Lotus Notes, Dataware, video tele-conferencing, corporate universities, and storytelling among employees.

7. Send employees to conferences and trade shows and have them spy. Do not pay for their travel unless they share what they learned with the rest of the organization when they return.

8. Consistently conduct intellectual capital audits to re-evaluate the organization's knowledge accumulation. Use monetary values if possible,

but do not be afraid to develop customized indexes and metrics.

9. Identify gaps that must be filled based on weaknesses relative to competitors, customers, suppliers, and best practices.

10. Assemble the organization's new knowledge portfolio in an intellectual capital addendum to the annual report.

Finally, the field of intellectual capital provides researchers with a wealth of perspectives to study. More importantly, there is a true hunger from practitioners who desire methods that can acquire, capture, distribute and ultimately value intellectual capital. This is good news for the field's research trajectory in the short-term. The ANSI/ISO (International Standards Organization) who inaugurated such standards as ISO 9000, etc., are also getting into the game by launching a new program to examine the development of knowledge management standards. Furthermore, strategic initiatives devoted to intellectual capital research such as the one at McMaster University in Canada continue to thrive. This is good news for the field in the long-term.

References

1. Thomas A. Stewart, "Brainpower: How Intellectual Capital is Becoming America's Most Valuable Asset," *Fortune*, June 3, 1991.

2. Thomas A. Stewart, "Your Company's Most Valuable Asset: Intellectual Capital," *Fortune*, October 3, 1994.

3. H. Itami, *Mobilizing Invisible Assets*, (Boston: Harvard University Press, 1987).

4. Skandia, "Visualizing Intellectual Capital in Skandia," *A supplement to Skandia's 1994 Annual Report*, Sweden, 1994.

5. Skandia, "Renewal and Development: Intellectual Capital," *A supplement to Skandia's 1995 Interim Annual Report*, Sweden, 1995.

6. Skandia, "Value-Creating Processes: Intellectual Capital," *A supplement to Skandia's 1995 Annual Report*, Sweden, 1995.

7. Skandia, "Power of Innovation: Intellectual Capital," *A supplement to Skandia's 1996 Interim Annual Report*, Sweden, 1996.

8. Skandia, "Customer Value," *A supplement to Skandia's 1996 Annual Report*, Sweden, 1996.

9. Skandia, "Intelligent Enterprising," *A Supplement to Skandia's 6-Month Interim Report*, Sweden, 1997.

10. Nick Bontis, "There's a price on your head: Managing intellectual capital strategically," *Business Quarterly*, Summer, 1996.

11. D.J. Collis, "Organizational Capability as a Source of Profit," In B. Moingeon and A. Edmondson (Eds.) *Organizational Learning and Competitive Advantage* (London: Sage, 1996).

12. L.J. Bassi, and Mark E. Van Buren, "Investments in Intellectual capital: Creating methods for measuring impact and value," *ASTD working paper*, American Society of Training and Development, 1998.

13. M. Darling, "Building the Knowledge Organization," *Business Quarterly*, Winter, 1996.

14. L. Edvinsson and P. Sullivan, "Developing a Model for Managing Intellectual Capital," *European Management Journal* 14, no. 4 (1996).

15. H. Saint-Onge, "Tacit Knowledge: The key to the strategic alignment of intellectual capital," *Strategy & Leadership*, April 1996.

16. B. Nonaka and H. Takeuchi, *The Knowledge-Creating Company* (New York: Oxford University Press, 1995).

17. Peter F. Drucker, *Post-Capitalist Society* (Oxford: Butterworth Heinemann, 1993).

18. Richard Hall, "The Strategic Analysis of Intangible Resources," *Strategic Management Journal* 13 (1993).

19. H. T. Johnson and Kaplan, R.S, *Relevance Lost* (Boston: Harvard Business School Press, 1987).

20. R. McGrath, M. Tsai, S. Venkatraman and I. MacMillan, "Innovation, competitive advantage and rent: A model and test," *Management Science* 42, no. 3 (1996)

21. Richard R. Nelson, "Why Do Firms Differ, and How Does It Matter?" *Strategic Management Journal* 12 (1991).

22. David J. Teece, "Towards an Economic Theory of the Multiproduct Firm," *Journal of Economic Behavior and Organization* 3:39–63.

23. H. I. Ansoff, *Corporate Strategy: An Analytical Approach to Business Policy for Growth and Expansion* (New York: McGraw-Hill, 1965).

24. Kenneth R. Andrews, *The Concept of Corporate Strategy* (Homewood, Illinois: Dow Jones-Irwin, 1971).

25. Edith Tilton Penrose, *The Theory of the Growth of the Firm* (Oxford: Basil Blackwell, 1959).

26. P. H. Rubin, "The Expansion of Firms," *Journal of Political Economy* 81:936–949,1973.

27. Birger Wernerfelt, "A Resource-Based View of the Firm," *Strategic Management Journal* 5 (1984): 171–180.

28. Jay B. Barney, "Organizational culture: Can it be a source of sustained competitive advantage?," *Academy of Management Review* 11, no. 3 (1986).

29. Jay B. Barney, "Firm Resources and Sustained Competitive Advantage," *Journal of Management* 17 (1991): 99–120.

30. Ingemar Dierickx and Karel Cool, "Asset Stock Accumulation and the Sustainability of Competitive Advantage," *Management Science* 35 (1989): 1504–1513.

31. Richard R. Nelson, and Sidney G. Winter, *An Evolutionary Theory of Economic Change* (Cambridge, Mass.: Belknap Press, 1982)

32. Sidney G. Winter, "Knowledge and Competence as Strategic Assets," *The Competitive Challenge: Strategies of Industrial Innovation and Renewal*, ed. David J. Teece (Cambridge, Mass.: Ballinger Publishing Company, 1987).

33. C. K. Prahalad and Gary Hamel,"The Core Competence of the Corporation," *Harvard Business Review*, May-June 1990.

34. R. P. Rumelt, "How much does industry matter?" *Strategic Management Journal* 12 (1991): 167–185.

35. E. Learned, Christensen, C., Andrews, K., and Guth, W., *Business policy: Text and cases* (Homewood, Ill.: Irwin, 1965).

36. Herbert A. Simon, "Bounded rationality and organizational learning," *Organization Science* 2, no. 1 (1991).

37. Michael Polanyi, *The Tacit Dimension* (New York: Anchor Day Books, 1967).

38. Nanda, "Resources, Capabilities and Competencies," In B. Moingeon and A. Edmondson, eds., *Organizational Learning and Competitive Advantage* (London: Sage, 1996).

39. P. Selznick, *Leadership in Administration* (New York: Harper and Row, 1957).

40. Jay B. Barney, "Strategic factor markets: Expectations, luck, and business strategy," *Management Science* 32, no. 10 (1986): 1231–1241.

41. N. Nohria and R. Eccles."Corporate Capability," *Working Paper* No. 92–038, Harvard Business School, 1991.

42. David J. Teece, G. Pisano, and A. Shuen, "Dynamic Capabilities and Strategic Management," *Working Paper*, Center for Research in Management, University of California at Berkeley, 1994.

43. Bruce Kogut and Udo Zander, "Knowledge of the Firm, Combinative capabilities, and the Replication of Technology," *Organization Science* 3 (1992).

44. R. Schmalensee, "Do markets differ much?," *American Economic Review* 75 (1985).

45. G. Hansen and B. Wernerfelt, "Determinants of firm performance: The relative importance of economic and organizational factors," *Strategic Management Journal* 10 (1989).

46. Kessides, "Internal vs. external market conditions and firm profitability: An exploratory model," *Economic Journal* 100 (1990).

47. R. M. Grant, "Prospering in dynamically-competitive environments: Organizational capability as knowledge integration," *Organization Science* 7, no. 4 (1996).

48. R. M. Grant, "Toward a knowledge-based theory of the firm," *Strategic Management Journal* 17 (Winter Special Issue, 1996).

49. J. C. Spender, "Organizational knowledge, collective practice and Penrose rents," *International Business Review* 3, no. 4 (1994).

50. J. C. Spender, "Making knowledge the basis of a dynamic theory of the firm," *Strategic Management Journal* 17 (Winter Special Issue, 1996).

51. Baden-Fuller and M. Pitt, "The nature of innovating strategic management," In C. Baden-Fuller and M. Pitt, eds., *Strategic Innovation* (London: Routledge, 1996).

52. T. Davenport and L. Prusak, *Information Ecology: Mastering the information and knowledge environment* (New York: Oxford University Press, 1997).

53. H. Demsetz, "The theory of the firm revisited," In O. Williamson and S. Winter, eds., *The Nature of the Firm* (New York: Oxford University Press, 1991).

54. K. Conner and C. Prahalad, "A resource-based theory of the firm: Knowledge versus opportunism," *Organization Science* 7, no. 5 (1996).

55. Thomas A. Stewart, *Intellectual Capital: The New Wealth of Organizations* (New York: Doubleday/Currency, 1997).

56. Nick Bontis, "Intellectual Capital: An Exploratory Study that Develops Measures and Models," *Management Decision* 36, no. 2 (1998).

57. J. Roos, G. Roos, N. Dragonetti, and L. Edvinsson, *Intellectual Capital: Navigating in the New Business Landscape* (New York: New York University Press , 1998).

58. K. E. Sveiby, *The New Organizational Wealth: Managing and Measuring Knowledge-Based Assets* (Berrett-Koehler: New York, 1997).

59. L. Edvinsson, and M. Malone, *Intellectual Capital* (New York: Harper Business, 1997).

60. P. Sullivan and L. Edvinsson, "A model for managing intellectual capital," In R. Parr and P. Sullivan, eds., *Technology Licensing* (New York: John Wiley & Sons, 1996).

61. Chris Argyris, *On Organizational Learning* (Cambridge Mass.: Blackwell, 1992).

62. T. Levitt, *Marketing Imagination* (New York: The Free Press, 1991).

63. Mary Crossan, R. E. White, H. W. Lane, and Leo Klus, "The Improvising Organization: Where Planning Meets Opportunity," *Organization Dynamics* 24, no. 4 (1996).

64. W. Hudson, *Intellectual Capital: How to build it, enhance it, use it* (New York: John Wiley & Sons, 1993).

65. P. M. Wright, G. C. McMahan, and A. McWilliams, "Human Resources and sustained competitive advantage: a resource-based perspective," *International Journal of Human Resource Management* 5, no. 2 (1994).

66. J. Storey, "HRM: still marching on, or marching out?" In Storey, J., ed., *Human Resource Management: A Critical Text* (London: Routledge, 1995).

67. Nicolini, "Apprendimento Organizzativo e Pubblica Amministrazione Locale," *Autonomie Locali e Servizi Sociali* 16, no. 2 (1993).

68. A. K. Kohli and B. J. Jaworski, "Market orientation: The construct, research propositions, and managerial implications," *Journal of Marketing* 54 (April 1990).

69. J. C. Narver and S. F. Slater, "The effect of a market orientation on business profitability," *Journal of Marketing*, October 1990.

70. J. Hulland, "Market Orientation and Market Learning Systems: An Environment—Strategy—Performance Perspective," *Working Paper*, University of Western Ontario, 1995.

71. David J. Teece, "Technological Change and the Nature of the Firm," In G. Dosi, C. Freeman, R. Nelson, G. Silverberg, and L. Soete, eds., *Technical Change and Economic Theory* (London: Frances Pinter, 1988).

72. J. M. Pennings and F. Harianto, "Technological networking and innovation implementation," *Organization Science* 3, no. 3 (1992).

73. U. Zander and B. Kogut, "Knowledge and the speed of the transfer and imitation of organizational capabilities: An empirical test," *Organization Science* 6, no. 1 (1995).

74. Jay B. Barney, "Integrating organizational behavior and strategy formulation research: A resource based analysis," In P. Shrivastava, A. Huff, and J. Dutton, eds., *Advances in Strategic Management* 8: 39–62 (Greenwich, Conn.: JAI Press, 1992).

75. G. Hamel, "Competition for competence and inter-partner learning within international strategic alliances," *Strategic Management Journal* 12 (1991).

76. F. Kodama, "Technology fusion and the new R&D," *Harvard Business Review* 70, no. 4 (1992).

77. M. Dodgson, "The future for technological collaboration," *Futures*, June 1992.

78. Jay Barney and M. H. Hansen. "Trustworthiness as a source of competitive advantage," *Strategic Management Journal* 15 (1994).

79 R. Gulati, "Does familiarity breed trust? The implications of repeated ties for contractual choice in alliances," *Academy of Management Journal* 38, no. 1 (1995).

80. R. Mayer, J. Davis, and F. Schoorman, "An integrative model of organizational trust," *Academy of Management Review* 20, no. 3 (1995).

81. B. Moingeon and A. Edmondson, "Trust and organizational learning," *Proceedings of Organizational Learning and Learning Organization Symposium '96*, Lancaster, UK, 1996.

82. Brian Hall, *Values Shift: A guide to personal and organizational transformation*, (Rockport, Mass.: Twin Lights, 1995).

83. G. Hofstede, *Cultures and Organizations: Intercultural Cooperation and Its Importance to Survival* (Glasgow: HarperCollins, 1991).

84. B. J. Jaworski and A. K. Kohli,"Market orientation: Antecedents and consequences," *Journal of Marketing* 57 (July 1993).

85. R. W. Ruekert, "Developing a market orientation: An organizational strategy perspective," *International Journal of Research in Marketing* 9 (1992).

86. G. E. Greenly, "Forms of market orientation in UK companies," *Journal of Management Studies* 32, no. 1 (1995).

87. R. F. Lusch and G. R. Laczniak, "The evolving marketing concept, competitive intensity and organizational performance," *Journal of the Academy of Marketing Science* 15, no. 3 (1987).

88. K. Atuahene-Gima, "An exploratory analysis of the impact of market orientation on new product performance. A contingency approach," *Journal of Product Innovation Management* 12 (1995).

89. W. G. Biemans and H. Harmsen, "Overcoming the barriers to market-oriented product development," *Journal of Marketing Practice: Applied Marketing Science* 1, no. 2 (1995).

90. T. J. Covin and B. P. Stivers, "Knowledge Management Focus in US and Canadian Firms," *Creativity and Innovation Management* 6, no. 3 (1997).

91. R. S. Wellins, W. C. Byham, J. M. Wilson, *Empowered teams: creating self-directed groups that improve quality, productivity and participation*, (San Francisco: Jossey Bass, 1991).

92. Docherty, "Getting the Best out of Knowledge-Workers," *Involvement and Participation* 619 (1993).

93. Papahristodoulou, "Is Lean Production the Solution?," *Economic and Industrial Democracy* 15 (1994).

94. E. Yeatts, M. Hipskind, and D. Barnes. "Lessons Learned from Self-Managed Work Teams," *Business Horizons*, July–August 1994.

95. Nick Bontis, N. Dragonetti, K. Jacobsen, and G. Roos,. "The Knowledge Toolbox: A review of the tools available to measure and manage intangible resources," *European Management Journal* 17, no. 4 (1999).

96. Mary Crossan and Nick Bontis, The strategic management of organization learning," *Presentation at the Academy of Management 1998*, San Diego, Calif., 1998.

97. Mary Crossan, H. W. Lane, Roderick E. White. "An Organizational Learning Framework: From intuition to institution," *Academy of Management Review* 24, no. 3 (1999).

98. Nick Bontis, "Managing an Organizational Learning System by Aligning Stocks and Flows of Knowledge: An empirical examination of intellectual capital, knowledge management and business performance," PhD dissertation, London, Canada: Ivey School of Business, University of Western Ontario, 1999.

99. J. Rutledge, "You're a fool if you buy into this," ASAP, April 7, 1997.

100. Nick Bontis, "Royal Bank Invests in Knowledge-Based Industries," *Knowledge Inc.* 2, no. 8 (1997).

101. D. J. Skyrme and D. M. Amidon, *Creating the knowledge-based business*, (London: Business Intelligence, 1997).

102. L. Prusak, "The Knowledge Advantage," *Strategy & Leadership*, March/April 1996.

103. Hampden-Turner, *Creating corporate culture: From discord to harmony*, (Reading, Mass.: Addison-Wesley, 1992).

104. B. Wiele, "Competing from the neck up," *Performance & Instruction*, March, 1993.

18

Knowledge Sharing Metrics for Large Organizations

Laurence Lock Lee

Knowledge sharing is a fundamental knowledge management process. For large organizations, the ability to effectively share knowledge across the organization can lead to new competitive intelligence being created and best practices being achieved, organization wide. This chapter introduces the concept of "in process" metrics for tacit to tacit knowledge sharing. Drawing from TQM concepts, "in process" knowledge sharing metrics can provide a means for continuously improving knowledge sharing performance, reducing the reliance on outcome based measures typically found in balanced scorecards. BHP's global maintenance engineering practice network is used as a case study to illustrate the practical application of these knowledge sharing metrics. The maintenance-engineering network is charged with the responsibility for achieving best maintenance practice performance, through knowledge sharing, worldwide. Measures for tacit to tacit knowledge sharing are derived from social network analyses. Quantitative measures are derived for knowledge sharing intensity and density as well as characteristics like inter- and intrabusiness unit sharing.

Introduction

While the field of knowledge management is currently enjoying "latest fad" status, its long-term endurance in the business world will only come with demonstrable results. This means an ability to measure knowledge management performance and demonstrate a clear cause and effect relationship between excellent knowledge management practices and superior business results. To date the cause and effect relationships are mostly represented by anecdotal evidence.[1] This is unlikely to be sufficient to sustain knowledge management at the forefront of best management practices. More detailed metrics will be required.

Proof of a strong correlation between knowledge management practices and business performance using a comprehensive suite of knowledge management and business metrics cannot happen overnight. Intellectual asset measures pioneered by the Swedes[2,3,4] and further progressed to the "Balanced Scorecard" concept by Kaplan and Norton[5] have been in the making for more than 10 years. They are only now making inroads into the mainstream of corporate reporting as knowledge based service companies displace physical asset based industrial and resource stocks at the top of the world's stock markets.

The balanced scorecard concepts have been successful in highlighting the importance of nonfinancial measures in assessing the long-term health of an organization. The measures encompassed within balanced scorecards are however largely "outcomes." Measures like customer loyalty, staff satisfaction level, R&D expenditure, and revenue per employee all indicate results without providing any insight into the processes that have led to the result being achieved or the cause and effect relationships. This chapter addresses some "in process" metrics for knowledge sharing as a key knowledge management process. In particular, the focus is on how we might measure levels of knowledge sharing within large organizations. BHP's Global Maintenance Improvement Practice network is used as a case study to illustrate its use. The importance of "in process" metrics has been demonstrated by the Total Quality Management (TQM) movement in industrial domains. TQM practitioners have demonstrated

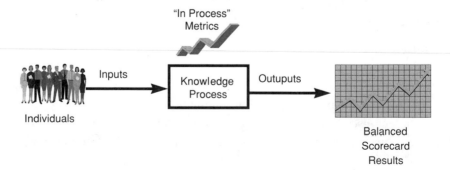

Figure 18.1
A knowledge management process

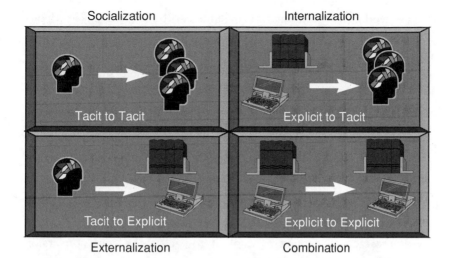

Figure 18.2
Knowledge conversion (Nonaka and Takeuchi)

that superior quality can be achieved without the need for extensive inspection checks, by keeping processes "in control." If Knowledge Management processes could likewise be kept "in control" excellent performance could be "designed in" rather than relying on "inspections" using extensive balanced scorecard metrics.

Knowledge Processes

Knowledge Management could be viewed as a suite of sub-processes that together make up the field of knowledge management. Some examples of knowledge management sub-processes are knowledge publishing, knowledge acquisition (for expert systems), and knowledge discovery (through data mining). Figure 18.1 provides a generic representation of a Knowledge Management process. Individuals provide input into a knowledge process, which in turn provides a given result that can be reported on. Example outputs could be published documents, staff education levels, patents, etc. Without the benefit of "in process" metrics, the effectiveness of the knowledge process will be compromised by an over reliance on output measures and long process improvement cycles.

Nonaka and Takeuchi[6] have provided an elegant characterization of knowledge conversion processes connecting tacit and explicit knowledge sources (see figure 18.2). Tacit knowledge can be defined as knowledge that is personal, experiential, and context specific. Explicit knowledge is knowledge that has been codified, articulated, or published in some way. Arguably, the most critical of Knowledge Management processes is the process of knowledge sharing amongst individuals. Knowledge sharing is fundamental to the sharing of best practices, creating new knowledge, and achieving shared learning. Knowledge sharing is mostly achieved through tacit to tacit communication, though clearly knowledge sharing can also be achieved through the tacit to explicit to tacit conversion loop.

The Knowledge Sharing Process
Virtually all suggested knowledge sharing metrics focus on the effectiveness of the tacit to explicit or explicit to tacit knowledge conversion processes. Table 18.1 provides some examples.

The tacit to explicit to tacit cycle is however by far the least effective means of knowledge sharing. If we were to rely on this cycle alone, leaving out socialization, the knowledge sharing effectiveness could be less than 10%.* It is generally accepted that we know far more than we can make explicit.[7] Experience over the past 10 to 15 years with knowledge based expert systems reinforces this view. Even with the most advanced knowledge acquisition tools and techniques available to us from this field, there would be few knowledge engineers who would claim to have captured, in computational form, more than a shallow layer of knowl-

Table 18.1
Explicit-Tacit Conversion Metrics

Tacit to Explicit Knowledge Conversion Process	Explicit to Tacit Knowledge Conversion Process
Number of shared documents published	Number of hits on document repository
Number of improvement suggestions made	Subscriptions to journals
Corporate directory coverage	Attendance at group presentations
Number of patents published	Size of discussion data bases
Number of presentations made	

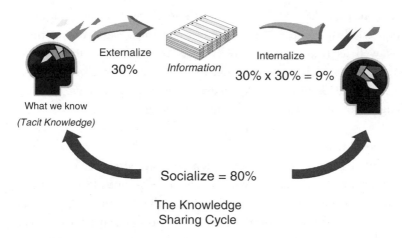

Externalize
30%

Information

Internalize
30% x 30% = 9%

What we know
(*Tacit Knowledge*)

Socialize = 80%

The Knowledge
Sharing Cycle

Figure 18.3
Knowledge sharing effectiveness

edge from their human expert subjects. Likewise, one is unlikely to internalize explicit information identically to others given the different values, beliefs and experiences that we might have. If we enable socialization (tacit to tacit conversion) the percentage could be as high as 80% (see figure 18.3).

Ultimately we cannot progress without some measure for the tacit to tacit knowledge transfer process, given the impact it has on effective knowledge sharing. Nearly by definition, tacit knowledge cannot be measured directly. But the tacit to tacit knowledge transfer process is a social process and therefore it is in the area of social science that one should be looking for assistance. Good examples of tacit to tacit knowledge sharing can be seen when observing good teams or partnerships at work. A basketball player knowing where his teammate is going to run, before passing him the ball. Long term coworkers, able to speak comfortably for each other in business meetings. Often the knowledge transfer may not be explicitly by word of mouth, but by actions or even body language. Lipnack & Stamps[8] talk about the concept of "social capital" and the density of social networks, how the number of social interactions is directly correlated with the degree of trust and commitment to the network, and ultimately, the performance of that network. Likewise, the author is claiming that the density of social interactions will be directly correlated with the degree of tacit to tacit knowledge sharing. In a business context, this would include business meetings, seminars, conferences as well as traditional social events. As such, measuring social interactions (for which there are a number of available techniques) can provide a workable proxy for measuring the degree of tacit to tacit knowledge sharing occurring within an organization.

Social Network Analysis

Social Network Analysis has become a well-accepted technique for understanding the informal networks which exist outside the formal structure of an organization, or for diagnosing the dysfunctional aspects of formal structures.[9,10] Typically, questionnaires are used to collect information on "who communicates with whom." The interactions can then be plotted using specialized graphical software for analysis. Dysfunctional behavior can easily be identified, for example, are R&D and marketing communicating sufficiently? Are the human resource people being used or bypassed? How well is the new finance manager being accepted across the organization? With only some modest changes this technique has been used to create a knowledge sharing metric for tacit to tacit knowledge transfer, based on the number, and perceived quality, of relationships within the organization.

BHP Case Study

The Business Driver

BHP is a large global resources company. Headquartered in Australia, BHP has interests in Minerals, Oil and Gas, Steel, Transport, Engineering and Information Technology that span the globe. The Company has grown substantially over the past 10 years, now operating through 8 major business divisions in over 50 countries. In 1997, BHP created a Global Maintenance Network (GMN) from a number of site and business unit networks. The network now spans all eight business divisions. This initiative was triggered by the realization that substantial economies from the over $2 billion annual maintenance expense could not be achieved without gaining best maintenance practices, through knowledge sharing worldwide. The network members determined that the value of sharing best maintenance practices across the Company could be between $0.5 billion and $1billion per year in sustainable benefit to the bottom line, within three years of GMN establishment. As a cross-divisional network, it is critically important for the GMN to demonstrate the value it adds. The network is now working to an agreed set of key performance measures akin to those found in a balanced scorecard. To complement these measures a set of "in process" knowledge-sharing metrics have now been designed and implemented to monitor tacit to tacit knowledge sharing.

The Network Structure and Operation

The GMN is a mixture of formal and informal structures. The network is facilitated by a "full-time" secretariat and has a steering committee and leadership group drawn from the major business units. Less formal sub-networks exist at regional sites. Informal structures have emerged around particular maintenance topics like condition monitoring, maintenance management systems, etc. Unlike a community of practice, which is largely unstructured, the GMN is an example of a facilitated network. Some structure exists but the principles of operation are closer to a community of practice than a traditional business unit. The rationale for a facilitated network over a pure community of practice is the business need to meet performance targets and deadlines, which are less of a driver for communities of practice. The interplay between the structured (both in the network and in the member's business unit) and unstructured roles generates some quite unique dynamics in the network. The full-time secretariat team of facilitators has had a considerable influence over network activities. The secretariat formally organizes "events" like practice meetings, maintenance reviews, best practice studies, all of which generate enhanced activity in the network, while at the same time sharing best practices. The secretariat also facilitates a number of electronic discussion groups. With the assistance of the secretariat, over 2,000 discussion transactions have occurred in the first year of operation. Anecdotal evidence indicates that many of these interactions have generated real value to the company from time saved on developing a practice through to brokering unused equipment around the Company.

Figure 18.4 maps the participation rate in one of the divisional maintenance networks up to and including the formation of the Global Maintenance Network. Of interest is the impact the formal "events" have on re-energizing the network over time.

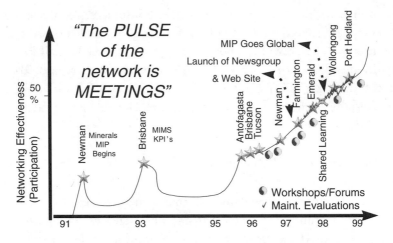

Figure 18.4
Network participation over time. Source: BHP Global Maintenance Network

Social Network Analysis

The GMN has processes in place to measure the benefits that its activities achieve. They also have a suite of KPI's to monitor their improvement in maintenance capability. The metrics derived from social network analysis are aimed at providing a leading indicator of the "health" of the network. The inference is that if the network is active in both number and breadth of contact, more knowledge sharing will occur, which will result in superior maintenance practices being more broadly adopted, and clearly a better financial result for the Company. The conduct of the social network analysis exercise at the creation of the Global Network from prior business divisional networks was important in developing a base line to assess improvement in the Global Network as it evolves.

Social network analysis techniques, a software package and accompanying methodology from NetMap Solutions[†] were used to generate the knowledge sharing metrics based on the strength of relationships that exist in the network. Questionnaires were used to collect the base data. Unlike traditional social network analyses, respondents were not asked whom they communicate with, but *who they seek advice from in an area they had already nominated themselves as a specialist in.* While only a subtle change, this enabled a separation between communications that support day to day operations and communications that are quality knowledge sharing contacts. This change is important in that within a network there will be many contacts that do not result in a sharing of tacit knowledge. However, where there exists a respectful relationship we could reasonably expect tacit to tacit knowledge sharing is occurring. Where two individuals nominate each other, we would infer a relationship of strong mutual respect exists. Questions on frequency of advice seeking were also collected as an additional attribute for tacit to tacit knowledge transfer. Business unit membership and geographic location were also collected, enabling social network maps to be drawn from a business unit or a geographic perspective.

Figure 18.5 illustrates the knowledge sharing connections between and within business units. The satellites represent different business units and

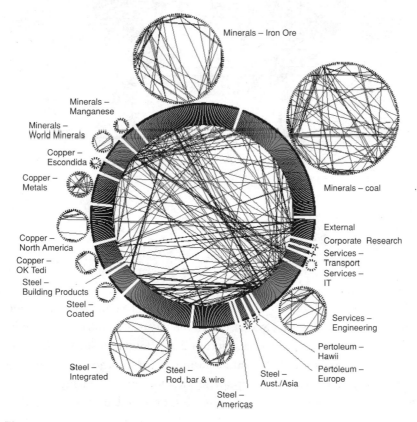

Figure 18.5
Knowledge sharing Netmap(tm) by Business Unit

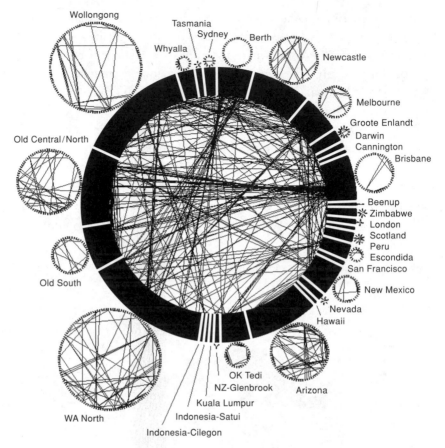

Wollongong
Tasmania
Sydney
Berth
Whyalla
Newcastle
Melbourne
Groote Enlandt
Darwin
Cannington
Brisbane
Old Central / North
Beenup
Zimbabwe
London
Scotland
Peru
Escondida
San Francisco
Old South
New Mexico
Nevada
Hawaii
OK Tedi
NZ-Glenbrook
Arizona
Kuala Lumpur
WA North
Indonesia-Satui
Indonesia-Cilegon

Figure 18.6
Knowledge sharing Netmap(tm) by Geographic Site

connections within those units. The links between the arcs in front of the satellites indicate interbusiness unit connections. Each line indicates a link between two individuals. The links are directional, indicating who nominates whom. Figure 18.5 describes the nature of interpersonal links between some 1,000 individuals across 20 different business units. As well as providing a means for understanding current knowledge sharing relationships and identifying opportunities for improvement, the data underlying the maps are a rich source for knowledge sharing metrics. The Netmap™ software incorporates a data warehouse for capturing relationship data. As with most databases, once the data is established there is nearly an unlimited number of questions that can be posed and results analyzed. The base data collected (see Appendix) was somewhat limited but did enable assessment of the impacts of business unit membership (formal structure) and geographic location on network activity patterns. The data could be grouped and sub-divided to enable different analyses to be conducted. Some of the more interesting findings were:

• Business Unit membership appeared to have a large influence over knowledge sharing patterns. Some business units were quite insular with many internal contacts compared to external contacts. Some of this is explained by the newness of the network. But not all, as some business units belonging to the same division showed relatively poor networking.

• Geographic location, surprisingly, was not as big a barrier to knowledge sharing as business unit membership. The denseness of the links within the inner circle in figure 18.6 compared to that in figure 18.5 clearly illustrates this.

• A newly acquired business in the USA that spanned two sites had very strong internal interactions but few links to the rest of the Company. One could interpret that because this unit networked within itself very well it probably had developed some good maintenance practices, indicating that integration with the rest of the Company should be accelerated.

• The Engineering Services business unit predictably had links to most areas of the Company, but very few to one particular division. Are there issues with the relationship between Engineering and this division?

Further analyses were conducted around identified special interest areas of Maintenance Management, Resource Management, Equipment, Work Control and Enabling Functions (areas that were nominated in the survey). Using the relationship data around each interest topic, emerging "centers of excellence" were identified by looking at where there was a concentration of links across business units colocated in a single geographic site. These emerging centers could be used to concentrate best practice development initiatives. Also, a league table of "good contacts" in each of the special interest areas was identified.

Knowledge Sharing Metrics
Social Network Analysis is a diagnostic tool. It identifies potential problem areas or new opportunities. The GMN, through their facilitation and management of maintenance "events," are able to orchestrate the

Table 18.2
Tacit to Tacit Knowledge Sharing Metrics

Knowledge Sharing Metric	Interpretation
Number of links per respondents	Knowledge sharing density
Frequency of advice seeking	Intensity of knowledge sharing contacts
Individuals with highest number of nominations	Identifies the true experts. Frequency chart indicates how expertise is spread (concentrated or thinly spread)
Ratio of internal to external links	How inward looking, or otherwise a business unit is
Proportion of total contacts that are inward	How sought after the knowledge of that business unit is
Proportion of total contacts that are outward	Which business units seek help the most

Table 18.3
Business Units Seeking Advice Internally

Business Unit	External/Internal Link Ratio
Coal	0.14
Copper	0.17
Steel	0.23

membership of maintenance reviews or best practice studies teams to encourage working relationships to develop across poor networking areas identified by the social network analysis. Once areas of concern are identified, the role of the knowledge sharing metrics is to monitor overall improvement in the network, especially in areas where corrective action has been performed. Some of the knowledge sharing metrics derived from the data for the GMN base case are seen in table 18.2.

The first three metrics characterize the intensity of knowledge sharing occurring. The remaining measures describe the nature of knowledge sharing occurring. With the help of the data warehouse, the number of metrics that can be easily derived is only limited by one's imagination. Some example metrics reported are given in table 18.3 (names have been changed).

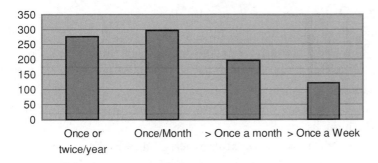

Figure 18.7
Frequency of advice

Table 18.3 indicates that 14% of engineers in the coal business have relationships outside that business, with 86% of the relationships directed inside the business unit. For copper, the percentage is 17% and Steel 23%.

The measure seen in table 18.4 indicates that Information Technology has an average of 1.28 links pointing to each nominated engineer, with external suppliers having an average 0.96 links and so on. The businesses that are at the top of the table are service groups with a charter to offer advice, and therefore the result is not unexpected. The Minerals group has the highest score when comparing "operational" business units.

Figure 18.7 provides some measure of knowledge sharing intensity. A movement toward higher frequency advice seeking would indicate a higher intensity of knowledge sharing.

Table 18.4
Business Units Most Sought after for Advice

Business Unit	Inward Links / #Contacts
Services—Information Technology	1.28
External Suppliers	0.96
Services—Engineering	0.85
Minerals	0.53
Copper	0.43
Steel	0.36

Figure 18.8 identifies those individuals who have the most identified relationships. One could infer that these people are the network gate-keepers or knowledge brokers. For the major part, members of the league table are assisted by roles they play in the "formal structure," for example, maintenance consultants, maintenance coordinators, and members of the network secretariat. However, there were also several "pure networkers" on the list.

By identifying "the most sought after experts," the absolute number of nominations, and the overall spread, this technique provides an indicator of the breadth and depth of expertise within an organization.

All of the above measures constitute "in knowledge process" metrics to complement the traditional Balanced Scorecard metrics that the MIP network reports to management. This case study provided anecdotal evidence that the connections were virtually all person to person (tacit to tacit). The above metrics therefore provide some measure of tacit to tacit knowledge sharing which can be achieved across large organizations in a relatively cost effective manner. The metrics at this stage only provide relative assessments of groups within the network. Assessing improvement in the knowledge sharing process will be conducted during a repeat of the initial survey, to provide a comparative view over time. Comparisons can also be made with other networks or organizational units, for benchmarking purposes.

Future work

A cost effective means for measuring tacit to tacit knowledge sharing performance has been achieved but a clear limitation is that data collection through surveys can only be replicated at relatively infrequent periods (annually at best). At this rate, it could take a number of years to achieve some confidence in the derived measures. It is also vitally important to be able to correlate knowledge sharing performance with business performance. The more data points the better if such a correlation is to be demonstrated.

For a more frequent and less intrusive means of generating data to describe social interactions, a current study is being undertaken to map discussions within the GMN facilitated electronic discussion group. Being a discussion group, the majority of interactions could be described

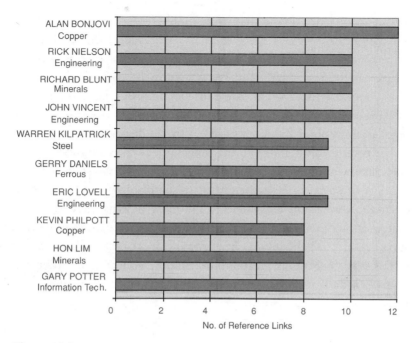

Figure 18.8
League table of "best knowledge sharers"

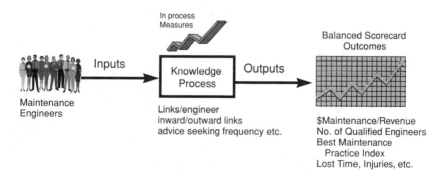

Figure 18.9
Knowledge sharing process for global MIP network

as true knowledge sharing contacts (unlike e-mail). Unlike the survey, one could not infer that these contacts constituted tacit to tacit knowledge transfer, but they could act as triggers to follow up personal contacts, which could then result in tacit knowledge sharing. Preliminary results indicate that the electronic discussion group is becoming a powerful means for enhancing the number of contacts between business units or geographic sites. Participants in electronic discussions are not identified by their position in the formal structure, or which business unit they come from, so knowledge sharing can largely progress untethered by political or social biases. In contrast to the results from the survey, the electronic discussion logs indicate far more activity between business units than within business units. The intention is to use the more reliable survey results to help qualify the electronically collected data and results. In this way continuous information could be collected and reported on virtually a daily or weekly basis, with "reality checks" achieved via the survey process.

Summary

This chapter introduces the concept of "in process" metrics for knowledge management processes. Building on lessons learned from the TQM movement, "in knowledge process" metrics have the potential to more rapidly improve the quality of knowledge management processes and usurp the need for extensive outcome based measures. Knowledge processes were then described in terms of the interaction between explicit and tacit knowledge. The argument was made that the tacit to tacit knowledge transfer process is responsible for over 90% of true knowledge sharing while 90% of the currently promoted knowledge management metrics focus on the tacit to explicit to tacit knowledge transfer cycle. Given that tacit to tacit knowledge sharing is a social process, the field of social science and social network analysis was introduced as a means for achieving workable metrics for the tacit to tacit knowledge sharing process.

BHP's newly formed Global Maintenance Improvement Practice network was used as a case study to illustrate how metrics derived from social network analysis could be practically used to provide in-process measures for knowledge sharing within the network.

Finally, current work on incorporating electronically collected electronic discussion group logs to augment the survey-derived measures was described. This should enable more regular monitoring of knowledge sharing performance and provide more data points for assessing the correlation between knowledge sharing performance and business performance.

Notes

*Author's estimate based on many years as a knowledge engineer building expert systems

†Netmap™ software and the OrgMap methodology from NetMap Solutions Pty Ltd. (Sydney, Australia: telephone +61 (2) 9438 5900; fax +61 (2) 9438 5911; email info@netmap.com.au)

References

1. Arthur Andersen Best Practices Handbook.

2. L. Edvinsson and M. Malone, *Intellectual Capital: Realising Your Company's True Value by Finding Its Roots,* Harperbusiness, 1997.

3. Michael S Malone, "New Metrics for a New Age," *Forbes*, April 7, 1997.

4. Karl Erik Sveiby, *The New Organisational Wealth: Managing & Measuring Knowledge Based Assets*, Berrett-Koehler Publishers, 1997.

5. Robert S Kaplan and David P Norton, *The Balanced Scorecard*, Harvard Business School Press, 1996.

6. Ikujiro Nonaka, and Hirotaka Takeuchi, *The Knowledge Creating Company*, Oxford University Press, 1995.

7. M. Polanyi, *The Tacit Dimension*, London: Routledge & Kegan Paul, 1966.

8. Jessica Lipnack and Jeffrey Stamps, *Virtual Teams: Reaching across space, time, and organisations with technology*, John Wiley & Sons, 1997.

9. Carol Hilderbrand, "Mapping the Invisible Workplace," *CIO Magazine*, July 15, 1998.

10. D. Krackhardt and J. Hanson, "Informal Networks: The Company," *Harvard Business Review*, July–August 1993.

Appendix

Extract from Maintenance Engineer's Survey

Maintenance Engineers Knowledge Sharing Survey

To complete this form, left button click in the highlighted fields and enter text or select the appropriate option.

Section One—Your Details:

Q1.1 Name (optional):

Q1.2 BHP Business Unit:

Q1.3 Site or City: Other:

The following questions will ask you to identify firstly your primary and then secondary areas of specialty and the people that you might consult for advice or assistance in those areas.

Section Two—Primary Area of Work
Firstly, please indicate which is your primary area of maintenance engineering expertise—what you spend the majority of you time doing. Select from the list provided:

Q2.1 Primary Area of Work:

Equipment, e.g.:   **Resource Management,** e.g.:

Equipment Strategies   Contractor Management

Failure Analysis   Materials Management

Plant Acquisition and Modification

Enabling Functions, e.g.:	**Work Control,** e.g.:
Safety	Planning
Environment	Scheduling
Drawing and Documents	Shutdown Management
Maintenance Information	Work Completion and Recording
Systems Management	Work Allocation and Execution
Facilities, Equipment and Tools	Work Originating and Recording

Maintenance Management, e.g.:

Budgeting and Cost Control

Maintenance Policy

Employee Capability

Performance Measurement

Organization

Continuous Improvement Management

Q2.2 Have you had to seek advice or opinions from colleagues in this area of work over the last 12 months?

Section Three—Colleagues for Primary Area of Work

If you answered Q2.2 with a "Yes," please nominate up to three colleagues from whom you most often receive assistance:

Name:

BHP Business Unit (or external):

Site or City:

Other:

How often in the last 12 months would you have consulted this expert?

Contact the Authors

Bassi, Laurie J.
Vice President, Research
The American Society for Training &
Development
1640 King Street, Alexandria, VA
22313–2043
lbassi@astd.org
703–683–9582
FAX: 703–548–2383
http:// www.astd.org/

Bontis, Nick
Assistant Professor of Strategic
Management
McMaster University
DeGroote School of Business
1280 Main Street West, MGD#207
Hamilton, Ontario Canada L8S 4M4
nbontis@mcmaster.ca
905–525–9140 x23918
FAX 905–521–8995
*http://www.business.mcmaster.ca/mkt
g/nbontis*

De Long, David
Principal
David De Long & Associates
339 Heath's Bridge Rd., Concord, MA
ddelong@bu.edu
978–369–5083
FAX: 978–369–0833

Gordon, Cindy
Associate Partner
Andersen Consulting
185 The West Mall, Suite 500
Etobicoke, Ontario M9C–5L5
cindy.m.gordon@ac.com
416–641–5597
FAX: 416–695–5050

Grundstein, Michel
Consultant, MG Conseil
4, rue Anquetil, 94130 Nogent-sur-
Marne, France
mgrundstein@mgconseil.fr
33 1 48 76 26 63
FAX: 33 1 48 76 26 63
http://www.mgconseil.fr/

Guthrie, Edward
President, Values International, Inc.
324 Eagleton Golf Drive,
Palm Beach Gardens, FL 33418
ERGuthrie@aol.com
FAX: 561–627–8291

Ives, Dr. William
Global Director
Knowledge Management Practice
Andersen Consulting
s.william.ives@ac.com
617–454–4447
FAX: 617–454–4224

Junnarkar, Bipin
Chief Knowledge Officer
Gateway
4545 Towne Centre Court
San Diego, CA 92121
bipin.junnarkar@gateway.com
619–899–2526

Lawton, Barbara
V.P. Business and Quality Processes
Storage Technology Corporation
2270 South 88th Street, Louisville,
CO 80028–5255
barbara_lawton@stortek.com
303–661–5444
FAX: 303–673–5847
http://intwww.stortek.com/

Leonard, Dorothy
William J. Abernathy Professor
Harvard University Graduate School
of Business Morgan Hall T93,
Soldiers Field Road
Boston, MA 02163
dleonard@hbs.edu
617–495–6637
FAX: 617–496–5265
*http://www.people.hbs.edu/dleonard/
bio.html*

Little, Ross
Consultant
Ernst & Young Center for Business
Innovation
One Cambridge Center, Cambridge,
MA 02142
ross.little@ey.com
617–861–4012
FAX: 617–861–4040
http://www.businessinnovation.ey.com

Lock Lee, Laurence
BHP Information Technology
Vale St., Shortland NSW 2307
AUSTRALIA
lock_lee.laurie.lg@bhp.com.au
+61–2–49792068
FAX: +61–2–49792099

Maybury, Mark
Executive Director
Information Technology Division
The MITRE Corporation
202 Burlington Road, Bedford, MA
01730
maybury@mitre.org
781–271–7230
FAX: 781–271–2780
*http://www.mitre.org/resources/centers/
it/maybury/mark.html*

Morey, Daryl
Senior Knowledge Management
Engineer
The MITRE Corporation
202 Burlington Road, Bedford, MA
01730
dmorey@morey.org
781–209–1535
http://www.morey.org/

Petrash, Gordon
Partner Intellectual Asset Managment
Practice
200 East Randolph Drive, Chicago,
IL, 60601
gordon.petrash@us.pwcglobal.com
312–540–2293
FAX: 312–540–1916

Reinhardt, Rüdiger
Chemnitz University of Technology
Reichenhainer Strasse 39, D 09126
Chemnitz, Germany
r.reinhardt@wirtschaft.tu-chemnitz.de
+49–371–531–4938
FAX: + 49 371 531 4342
http://bwl6.wirtschaft.tu-chemnitz.de

Ruggles, Rudy
Ernst & Young Center for Business
Innovation
One Cambridge Center
Cambridge, MA 02142–1406
rudy.ruggles@ey.com
617–861–4024
FAX: 617–861–4040

Seemann, Patricia
Managing Partner
Group 21
9490 Vaduz
Fuerstentum Liechtenstein
patricia.seemann@zurich.com
+41 75 230 1888
FAX: +41 75 230 1889

Skyrme, David J.
David Skyrme Associates Limited
Highclere, England
david@skyrme.com
http://www.skyrme.com

Stucky, Susan
Associate Director
Institute for Research on Learning
66 Willow Place, Menlo Park, CA
94025
Susan_Stucky@irl.org
650–687–8920
FAX: 650–687–8957
http://www.irl.org/

Swanstrom, Edward
President/CEO
Knowledge Management Consortium
International
312 Fairgrove Terrace
Gaithersburg, MD 20877
swanstrom.e@km.org
301–590–0102
FAX: 301–519–9197
http://km.org/

Thuraisingham, Bhavani
Department Head
Data and Object Management
The MITRE Corporation
202 Burlington Road, Bedford, MA
01730
thura@mitre.org
781–271–8873
FAX: 781–271–2780

Torrey, Reuben G. "Ben"
Manager
Andersen Consulting
reuben.g.torrey@ac.com

Van Buren, Mark E.
Senior Research Officer
The American Society for Training &
Development
1640 King Street, Alexandria, VA
22313–2043
mvanburen@astd.org
703–683–8257
FAX: 7030–548–2383
http://www.astd.org/

Willett, Carol
Director of Training
The Applied Knowledge Group
11921 Freedom Drive Suite 550,
Reston, VA 20190
cwillett@akgroup.com
703–904–0304
FAX: 703–834–6991
http:// www.akgroup.com

Index